TATES CREEK CHRISTIAN CHURCH
3150 TATES CREEK RD.
LEXINGTON, KY. 40502

D1544603

# The Ministers Manual for 1977

FIFTY-SECOND ANNUAL ISSUE

*The*

# MINISTERS MANUAL

*(Doran's)*

## 1977 EDITION

*Edited by*
CHARLES L. WALLIS

HARPER & ROW, PUBLISHERS
*New York, Hagerstown, San Francisco, London*

*Editors of* THE MINISTERS MANUAL

G. B. F. HALLOCK, D.D., 1926–1958
M. K. W. HEICHER, PH.D., 1943–1968
CHARLES L. WALLIS, M.A., M.DIV., 1969–

THE MINISTERS MANUAL FOR 1977

Copyright © 1976 by Charles L. Wallis. Printed in the
United States of America. All rights reserved. For in-
formation address Harper & Row, Publishers, Inc., 10
East 53rd Street, New York, N.Y. 10022.

FIRST EDITION

ISBN: 0-06-069022-4

LIBRARY OF CONGRESS CATALOG CARD NUMBER: 25-21658

# PREFACE

Editing a volume like *The Ministers Manual* year after year, a friend said, must represent drudgery and a monotonous routine. I'd never thought of it as either, although the routines one follows tend in time to lighten the work. And always there is the checking and double checking in the hope that all biblical citations will be accurate and all names spelled correctly.

"Well," I asked my friend, "don't you find preaching twice on Sundays and funerals and weddings and all kinds of occasional speaking engagements between Sundays to be a treadmill?"

"Oh, no, but my work is different." He added with emphasis: "I work with people. That makes a big difference."

And I thought of many writers and editors I've known and of the ministry through the written word to which they've been called and of the complete emptiness of their calling apart from the people with whom they communicate.

And I remembered a wise and talented editor who many years ago said: "Don't write books. That gets too abstract and impersonal. Rather converse with people and not with too many at a time. Keep always in your mind one or two individuals, and if what you write interests them or helps them or inspires them, you will have done a good job."

Although I'm gratified that the circulation of *The Ministers Manual* has, as it were, a worldwide circulation, the greatest satisfaction comes from a letter in the mail or an unexpected telephone call or a stranger in another community who corners me long enough to say he likes this or that or offers a helpful suggestion or makes a generous comment.

People are very much a part of the editing of *The Ministers Manual*. There are people, hundreds of them in a year's time, who send in manuscripts or whose manuscripts I solicit or whose permissions I must receive. I am grateful for their assistance and encouragement, for without their talents and insights *The Ministers Manual* would soon wither away.

And there are the people at Harper & Row whose varied skills in editing, production, and marketing turn a twelve-inch pile of typed pages into an attractive book.

And there are the readers who make our labors meaningful and purposeful.

And all of us, I trust, have in common one commitment, and that is to glorify God and especially as we know him in the redemptive life, ministry, death, and resurrection of the Lord Jesus.

*Rev. Charles L. Wallis*

*Keuka College*
*Keuka Park, N. Y. 14478*

v

# CONTENTS

# SECTION I. *General Aids and Resources*

## Civil Year Calendars

# 1977

| JANUARY | FEBRUARY | MARCH | APRIL |
|---|---|---|---|
| S M T W T F S | S M T W T F S | S M T W T F S | S M T W T F S |
| 1 | 1 2 3 4 5 | 1 2 3 4 5 | 1 2 |
| 2 3 4 5 6 7 8 | 6 7 8 9 10 11 12 | 6 7 8 9 10 11 12 | 3 4 5 6 7 8 9 |
| 9 10 11 12 13 14 15 | 13 14 15 16 17 18 19 | 13 14 15 16 17 18 19 | 10 11 12 13 14 15 16 |
| 16 17 18 19 20 21 22 | 20 21 22 23 24 25 26 | 20 21 22 23 24 25 26 | 17 18 19 20 21 22 23 |
| 23 24 25 26 27 28 29 | 27 28 | 27 28 29 30 31 | 24 25 26 27 28 29 30 |
| 30 31 | | | |

| MAY | JUNE | JULY | AUGUST |
|---|---|---|---|
| S M T W T F S | S M T W T F S | S M T W T F S | S M T W T F S |
| 1 2 3 4 5 6 7 | 1 2 3 4 | 1 2 | 1 2 3 4 5 6 |
| 8 9 10 11 12 13 14 | 5 6 7 8 9 10 11 | 3 4 5 6 7 8 9 | 7 8 9 10 11 12 13 |
| 15 16 17 18 19 20 21 | 12 13 14 15 16 17 18 | 10 11 12 13 14 15 16 | 14 15 16 17 18 19 20 |
| 22 23 24 25 26 27 28 | 19 20 21 22 23 24 25 | 17 18 19 20 21 22 23 | 21 22 23 24 25 26 27 |
| 29 30 31 | 26 27 28 29 30 | 24 25 26 27 28 29 30 | 28 29 30 31 |
| | | 31 | |

| SEPTEMBER | OCTOBER | NOVEMBER | DECEMBER |
|---|---|---|---|
| S M T W T F S | S M T W T F S | S M T W T F S | S M T W T F S |
| 1 2 3 | 1 | 1 2 3 4 5 | 1 2 3 |
| 4 5 6 7 8 9 10 | 2 3 4 5 6 7 8 | 6 7 8 9 10 11 12 | 4 5 6 7 8 9 10 |
| 11 12 13 14 15 16 17 | 9 10 11 12 13 14 15 | 13 14 15 16 17 18 19 | 11 12 13 14 15 16 17 |
| 18 19 20 21 22 23 24 | 16 17 18 19 20 21 22 | 20 21 22 23 24 25 26 | 18 19 20 21 22 23 24 |
| 25 26 27 28 29 30 | 23 24 25 26 27 28 29 | 27 28 29 30 | 25 26 27 28 29 30 31 |
| | 30 31 | | |

# 1978

| JANUARY | FEBRUARY | MARCH | APRIL |
|---|---|---|---|
| S M T W T F S | S M T W T F S | S M T W T F S | S M T W T F S |
| 1 2 3 4 5 6 7 | 1 2 3 4 | 1 2 3 4 | 1 |
| 8 9 10 11 12 13 14 | 5 6 7 8 9 10 11 | 5 6 7 8 9 10 11 | 2 3 4 5 6 7 8 |
| 15 16 17 18 19 20 21 | 12 13 14 15 16 17 18 | 12 13 14 15 16 17 18 | 9 10 11 12 13 14 15 |
| 22 23 24 25 26 27 28 | 19 20 21 22 23 24 25 | 19 20 21 22 23 24 25 | 16 17 18 19 20 21 22 |
| 29 30 31 | 26 27 28 | 26 27 28 29 30 31 | 23 24 25 26 27 28 29 |
| | | | 30 |

| MAY | JUNE | JULY | AUGUST |
|---|---|---|---|
| S M T W T F S | S M T W T F S | S M T W T F S | S M T W T F S |
| 1 2 3 4 5 6 | 1 2 3 | 1 | 1 2 3 4 5 |
| 7 8 9 10 11 12 13 | 4 5 6 7 8 9 10 | 2 3 4 5 6 7 8 | 6 7 8 9 10 11 12 |
| 14 15 16 17 18 19 20 | 11 12 13 14 15 16 17 | 9 10 11 12 13 14 15 | 13 14 15 16 17 18 19 |
| 21 22 23 24 25 26 27 | 18 19 20 21 22 23 24 | 16 17 18 19 20 21 22 | 20 21 22 23 24 25 26 |
| 28 29 30 31 | 25 26 27 28 29 30 | 23 24 25 26 27 28 29 | 27 28 29 30 31 |
| | | 30 31 | |

| SEPTEMBER | OCTOBER | NOVEMBER | DECEMBER |
|---|---|---|---|
| S M T W T F S | S M T W T F S | S M T W T F S | S M T W T F S |
| 1 2 | 1 2 3 4 5 6 7 | 1 2 3 4 | 1 2 |
| 3 4 5 6 7 8 9 | 8 9 10 11 12 13 14 | 5 6 7 8 9 10 11 | 3 4 5 6 7 8 9 |
| 10 11 12 13 14 15 16 | 15 16 17 18 19 20 21 | 12 13 14 15 16 17 18 | 10 11 12 13 14 15 16 |
| 17 18 19 20 21 22 23 | 22 23 24 25 26 27 28 | 19 20 21 22 23 24 25 | 17 18 19 20 21 22 23 |
| 24 25 26 27 28 29 30 | 29 30 31 | 26 27 28 29 30 | 24 25 26 27 28 29 30 |
| | | | 31 |

## Christian Calendar for 1977

### JANUARY

1  New Year's Day
   Festival of the Christening
   The Name of Jesus (*EC, Lu*)
2  Covenant Sunday (*UMC*)
2–8  Universal Week of Prayer
3–7  Bible Study Week (*SBC*)
5  Twelfth Night
6  Epiphany
9  Soul-Winning Commitment Day
   (*SBC*)
15  Martin Luther King, Jr. Birthday
16  Missionary Day
   Seminary Sunday (*UPC*)
18  Confession of St. Peter
18–25  Week of Prayer for Christian
   Unity
19  Robert E. Lee Birthday
20  Inauguration Day
23  Men's Day (*SBC*)
   Boys and Girls Missionary
   Crusade (*AG*)
23–29  Week of Laity (*CC*)
25  Conversion of St. Paul
30  Human Relations Day (UMC)

### FEBRUARY

2  Presentation of Jesus in the
   Temple
6  Septuagesima Sunday
   Baptist World Alliance Sunday
   (*ABC, SBC*)
   Race Relations Sunday (*UPC*)
12  Lincoln's Birthday
13  Boy Scout Sunday
   Race Relations Sunday
   Outreach Day (*AG*)
   World Mission Sunday (*UPC*)
14  St. Valentine's Day
20  The Transfiguration
   Seminaries, Colleges, and Schools
   Day (*SBC*)
   Witness Season Offering (*PCUS*)
20–27  Brotherhood Week
   Week of Compassion (*CC*)
21  Washington's Birthday
22  Shrove Tuesday
23  Ash Wednesday
24  St. Matthias, Apostle

27  First Sunday in Lent
   Women's Ministries Day (*AG*)

### MARCH

4  World Day of Prayer
6  Second Sunday in Lent
   Girl Scout Sunday
6–13  Week of Prayer for Home
   Missions (*SBC*)
13  Third Sunday in Lent
13–20  Youth Week (*SBC*)
17  St. Patrick's Day
20  Fourth Sunday in Lent
   Camp Fire Girl Sunday
   One Great Hour of Sharing
25  The Annunciation
27  Passion Sunday
   Good News Crusade Day (*AG*)
30  National Shut-In Day (*AG*)

### APRIL

3  Palm Sunday
   Sunday of the Passion (*EC, Lu*)
3–9  Holy Week
3–10  Easter Week of Prayer (*CC*)
7  Maundy Thursday
8  Good Friday
10  Easter
   One Great Hour of Sharing
   (alternate)
11–17  Jewish Fellowship Week (*SBC*)
17  National Christian College Day
   Youth Week (*AG*)
18–22  Doctrinal Emphasis Week (*SBC*)
24  Life Commitment Sunday (*SBC*)
   National Christian College Day
   (*PCUS*)
25  St. Mark, Evangelist
29  Arbor Day

### MAY

1  St. Philip and St. James, Apostles
   Golden Cross Sunday (*UMC*)
   Light for the Lost Day (*AG*)
1–8  National Family Week
6  May Fellowship Day
8  Mother's Day
   Festival of the Christian Home

15 Rogation Sunday
Rural Life Sunday
High School Day (*AG*)
Radio and Television Sunday
(*SBC*)
19 Ascension Day
21 Armed Forces Day
22 Sunday after Ascension Day
Heritage Sunday (*UMC*)
23 Victoria Day (Canada)
24 Aldersgate Day (*UMC*)
29 Pentecost (Whitsunday)
Aged Ministers Assistance Day
(*AG*)
30 Memorial Day

## JUNE

5 Trinity Sunday
9 Corpus Christi Day
St. Columba's Day (*UPC*)
12 Children's Day
Religious Liberty Sunday (*SBC*)
Student Day (*UMC*)
14 Flag Day
19 Father's Day
Men's Day (*AG*)
24 Nativity of St. John the Baptist
25 Presentation of the Augsburg
Confession (*Lu*)
26 Achievement Day (*CC*)
29 St. Peter and St. Paul, Apostles

## JULY

1 Dominion Day (Canada)
2 The Visitation
3 Independence Sunday
Christian Citizenship Sunday
(*SBC*)
Freedom and Democracy Sunday
(*CC*)
Servicemen's Day (*AG*)
4 Independence Day
10 Christian Literature Day (*SBC*)
25 St. James the Elder, Apostle

## AUGUST

1 Civic Holiday (Canada)
6 The Transfiguration (alternate)
14 Language Missions Day (*SBC*)

15 Mary, Mother of Our Lord
24 St. Bartholomew, Apostle
28 Festival of Christ the King

## SEPTEMBER

4 Labor Sunday
5 Labor Day
11 Lord's Day Observance (*PCUS*)
Special Ministries Day (*AG*)
17 Citizenship Day
18 Christian Education Sunday
(*PCUS*)
Ministry Day (*UMC*)
21 St. Matthew, Evangelist and
Apostle
23 American Indian Day
25 Christian Education Sunday
(*UMC*)
25–1 Christian Education Week
25–2 Sunday School Preparation Week
(*SBC*)
25–3 Reconciliation Emphasis Week
(*CC*)
29 St. Michael and All Angels

## OCTOBER

2 World Communion Sunday
3 Child Health Day
9 Laity Sunday
9–15 Week of the Ministry (*CC*)
10 Columbus Day
Thanksgiving Day (Canada)
16 World Order and Peace Sunday
A Great Day of Singing (*UMC*)
Laity Sunday (*PCUS*)
Speed-the-Light Day (*AG*)
18 St. Luke Evangelist
24 United Nations Day
Veterans Day
28 St. Simon and St. Jude, Apostles
30 Reformation Sunday
31 Reformation Day
UNICEF Day

## NOVEMBER

1 All Saints Day
2 All Soul's Day
4 World Community Day

6 World Temperance Day
First Stewardship Sunday (*UPC*)
8 Election Day
11 Remembrance Day (Canada)
Veterans Day (alternate)
13 Stewardship Day
American Bible Society Day
(*SBC*)
Drug and Alcohol Concerns
Sunday (*UMC*)
Second Stewardship Sunday
(*UPC*)
Stewardship Dedication Sunday
(*PCUS*)
20 Universal Bible Sunday
Thanksgiving Sunday
Child Care Day (*SBC*)
World Prayer Meeting (*AG*)
24 Thanksgiving Day
27 First Sunday in Advent
30 St. Andrew, Apostle

4 Second Sunday in Advent
4–11 Week of Prayer for Foreign
Missions (*SBC*)
9 Human Rights Day
11 Third Sunday in Advent
Bible Sunday (*AG*)
15 Bill of Rights Day
18 Fourth Sunday in Advent
Joy Gift Sunday (*PCUS*)
21 Forefathers' Day
St. Thomas, Apostle
25 Christmas
Christian Student Sunday
(*PCUS*)
Student Recognition Day (*UMC*)
26 St. Thomas, Apostle
27 St. John, Evangelist and Apostle
28 The Holy Innocents, Martyrs
31 Watch Night

ABC—American Baptist Churches; AG—Assemblies of God; CC—Christian Church (Disciples of Christ); CN—Church of the Nazarene; EC—The Episcopal Church; Lu—Lutheran bodies; PCUS—Presbyterian Church in the United States; RCA—Reformed Church in America; SBC—Southern Baptist Convention; UCC—United Church of Christ; UMC—United Methodist Church; UPC—United Presbyterian Church in the U.S.A.

### Four-Year Church Calendar

|               | 1977        | 1978        | 1979        | 1980        |
|---------------|-------------|-------------|-------------|-------------|
| Ash Wednesday | February 23 | February 8  | February 28 | February 20 |
| Palm Sunday   | April 3     | March 19    | April 8     | March 30    |
| Good Friday   | April 8     | March 24    | April 13    | April 4     |
| Easter        | April 10    | March 26    | April 15    | April 6     |
| Ascension Day | May 19      | May 4       | May 24      | May 15      |
| Pentecost     | May 29      | May 14      | June 3      | May 25      |
| Trinity Sunday| June 5      | May 21      | June 10     | June 1      |
| Thanksgiving  | November 24 | November 23 | November 22 | November 28 |
| Advent Sunday | November 27 | December 3  | December 2  | November 30 |

### Forty-Year Easter Calendar

| | | | | | | | |
|---|---|---|---|---|---|---|---|
| 1977 | April 10 | 1987 | April 19 | 1997 | March 30 | 2007 | April 8 |
| 1978 | March 26 | 1988 | April 3  | 1998 | April 12 | 2008 | March 23 |
| 1979 | April 15 | 1989 | March 26 | 1999 | April 4  | 2009 | April 12 |
| 1980 | April 6  | 1990 | April 15 | 2000 | April 23 | 2010 | April 4 |
| 1981 | April 19 | 1991 | March 31 | 2001 | April 14 | 2011 | April 24 |
| 1982 | April 11 | 1992 | April 19 | 2002 | March 31 | 2012 | April 8 |
| 1983 | April 3  | 1993 | April 11 | 2003 | April 20 | 2013 | March 31 |
| 1984 | April 22 | 1994 | April 3  | 2004 | April 11 | 2014 | April 20 |
| 1985 | April 7  | 1995 | April 16 | 2005 | March 27 | 2015 | April 5 |
| 1986 | March 30 | 1996 | April 7  | 2006 | April 16 | 2016 | March 27 |

### Four-Year Jewish Calendar

|                                      | 1977         | 1978        | 1979         | 1980         |
|--------------------------------------|--------------|-------------|--------------|--------------|
| Purim                                | March 4      | March 23    | March 13     | March 2      |
| Passover                             | April 3      | April 22    | April 12     | April 1      |
| Shabuoth (Revelation of the Law)     | May 23       | June 11     | June 1       | May 21       |
| Rosh Hashanah (New Year)             | September 13 | October 2   | September 22 | September 11 |
| Yom Kippur (Day of Atonement)        | September 22 | October 11  | October 1    | September 20 |
| Sukkoth (Thanksgiving)               | September 27 | October 16  | October 6    | September 25 |
| Simhath Torah (Rejoicing in the Law) | October 5    | October 24  | October 14   | October 3    |
| Hanukkah                             | December 5   | December 25 | December 15  | December 3   |

Holidays begin at sunset on the evening before the date given.

### Traditional Wedding Anniversary Identifications

| | | | | | | | |
|---|---|---|---|---|---|---|---|
| 1 | Paper   | 7  | Wool   | 13 | Lace    | 35 | Coral    |
| 2 | Cotton  | 8  | Bronze | 14 | Ivory   | 40 | Ruby     |
| 3 | Leather | 9  | Pottery| 15 | Crystal | 45 | Sapphire |
| 4 | Linen   | 10 | Tin    | 20 | China   | 50 | Gold     |
| 5 | Wood    | 11 | Steel  | 25 | Silver  | 55 | Emerald  |
| 6 | Iron    | 12 | Silk   | 30 | Pearl   | 60 | Diamond  |

### Colors Appropriate for Days and Seasons

**White.** Symbolizes purity, perfection, and joy and identifies festivals marking events, except Good Friday, in the life of Jesus: Christmas, Easter, Eastertide, Ascension Day, Trinity Sunday, All Saints' Day, weddings, funerals.

**Red.** Symbolizes the Holy Spirit, martyrdom, and the love of God: Pentecost and Sundays following.

**Violet.** Symbolizes penitence: Advent, Lent.

**Green.** Symbolizes mission to the world, hope, regeneration, nurture, and growth: Epiphany season, Kingdomtide, Rural Life Sunday, Labor Sunday, Thanksgiving Sunday.

**Black.** Symbolizes mourning: Good Friday.

## Historical, Cultural, and Religious Anniversaries in 1977

5 years (1972). *February 17:* President Nixon leaves for eight-day China visit. *March 22:* Senate approves constitutional amendment banning discrimination on the basis of sex. *April 16:* Apollo 16 moon mission begins. *May 22:* President Nixon begins seven-day Russian visit. *June 17:* five men apprehended by police when attempting to bug Democratic offices at Watergate complex. *June 29:* Supreme Court rules that death penalty is cruel and unusual punishment. *August 11:* last U.S. combat troops leave Vietnam. *December 7:* Apollo 17 in last moon mission. *December 26:* President Truman dies.

10 years (1967). *June 5:* six-day war between Israeli and Arab forces. *July 23:* racial violence in Detroit. *October 21–22:* antiwar protests in Washington, D. C. *December 3:* Dr. Christiaan N. Barnard performs first successful heart transplant.

15 years (1962). *January 31:* Cuba expelled from O.A.S. *February 20:* Col. John H. Glenn, Jr., first American to orbit the earth. *May 31:* Adolf Eichmann hanged for role in Nazi extermination of six million Jews. *June 25:* Supreme Court bans New York school prayer. *July 10:* Telstar launched. *October 11:* Vatican Council opens. *October 22–November 20:* Cuban missile crisis.

20 years (1957). Common Market established. Congress passes first civil rights legislation. *January 4:* Eisenhower Doctrine proposed. *September 24:* federal troops protect school integration in Little Rock. *October 4:* U.S.S.R. launches Sputnik I.

25 years (1952). Nasser leads army coup against King Farouk. Mau Mau attempts to oust whites in Kenya. *February 6:* Elizabeth II succeeds George VI. *November 4:* Eisenhower elected president. *November 16:* hydrogen bomb testing near Eniwetok.

50 years (1927). Mao Tse-tung leads peasant uprising in Hunan province. *May 20:* Lindbergh begins transatlantic solo flight in *The Spirit of St. Louis.*

*August 7:* International Peace Bridge between U.S. and Canada opened. *September 18:* C.B.S. begins radio network. *November 13:* Holland Tunnel between New York City and New Jersey opened.

75 years (1902). First International Arbitration Court opens at the Hague. *May 20:* Cuban Republic inaugurated. *August 11:* Oliver Wendell Holmes, Jr., appointed to the Supreme Court.

100 years (1877). Edison invents phonograph. Reconstruction Era officially ends. Henry M. Stanley traces Congo River.

150 years (1827). John Keble writes *The Christian Year.* Ludwig van Beethoven and William Blake die. Sir Joseph Lister born. *July 4:* New York State abolishes slavery.

200 years (1777). Congress submits the Articles of Confederation to the states for ratification. Henry Clay born. *June 14:* Continental Congress adopts the Stars and Stripes. *July 31:* Lafayette joins the Colonial forces. *October 4:* Washington establishes winter quarters at Valley Forge. *October 17:* Burgoyne's surrender at Saratoga marks turning point in the American Revolution.

250 years (1727). Thomas Gainsborough born. Sir Isaac Newton dies.

300 years (1677). William Penn frames first charter separating church and state at Quaker colony of West Jersey. Baruch Spinoza writes *Ethics* and dies.

400 years (1577). Peter Paul Rubens born.

450 years (1527). Sack of Rome under Charles of Bourbon. John Rut seeks Northwest Passage. Nicolo Machiavelli dies.

500 years (1477). Titian born.

550 years (1427). Thomas a Kempis writes *The Imitation of Christ.*

650 years (1327). Meister Eckhart dies.

700 years (1277). Toledo Cathedral begun.

750 years (1227). Genghis Khan dies.

1450 years (527). Reign of Emperor Justinian begins.

1700 years (277). Mani, founder of Gnostic sect of Manichaeism, dies.

## Anniversaries of Hymns, Hymn Writers, and Composers in 1977

20 years (1957). Death of James A. Blaisdell (b. 1867), American Congregationalist and educator, author of "Beneath the forms of outward rite"; Jean Sibelius (b. 1865), Finnish composer of "Finlandia," hymn-tune for "Be still, my soul," "This is my song," and "We would be building."

25 years (1952). Death of Francis H. Rowley (b. 1854), American Baptist, author of "I will sing the wondrous story"; William J. S. Simpson (b. 1860), author of "Cross of Jesus, cross of sorrow."

30 years (1947). Death of Maurice Frederick Bell (b. 1862), British Anglican and hymnist, translator of "Hail thee, festival day" and "The glory of these forty days"; Percy Carter Buck (b. 1871), British hymnist and organist, composer of hymn-tunes MARTINS ("Sing alleluia forth") and MONT RICHARD ("Dear Lord, whose loving eyes can see," "Not always on the mount may we," and "Ride on, ride on in majesty"); Sydney H. Nicholson (b. 1875), British organist, composer of hymn-tunes BOW BRICKHILL ("We sing the praise of him who died"), CRUCIFER ("Lift high the cross"), LYTLINGTON ("God be in my head"), and others; J. Henry Showalter (b. 1864), composer of hymn-tune MOHLER ("With thankful hearts, O Lord, we come").

40 years (1937). Writing of "O day of God, draw nigh" by R. B. Y. Scott (b. 1899), Canadian-born clergyman and educator; "Put forth, O God, thy spirit's might" by Howard Chandler Robbins (1876–1952), American Episcopalian.

50 years (1927). Composing of hymn-tune CHARTERHOUSE ("O God of light, thy Word, a lamp unfailing" and "O Son of Man, our hero strong and tender") by David Evans (1874–1948), Welsh organist and educator. Writing of "My Master was so very poor" by Harry Lee (1875–1942), American poet; "Come, O Lord, like morning sunlight" by Milton S. Littlefield (1864–1934), American Congregationalist and hymnologist. Birth of Catherine Bonnell Arnott, American poet, author of "God who stretched the spangled heavens" and "O Christ, who came to share our human life"; Basil E. Bridge, author of "The Son of God proclaim." Death of Frederick C. Maker (b. 1844), British musician, composer of hymn-tunes MELROSE ("God send us men"), REST or WHITTIER ("Dear Lord and father of mankind" and "O thou whose gracious presence blest"), ST. CHRISTOPHER ("Beneath the cross of Jesus"), and WENTWORTH ("My God, I thank thee"); Herbert B. Turner (b. 1852), American Congregationalist, composer of hymn-tune CUSHMAN ("We would see Jesus").

75 years (1902). Composing of hymn-tune WELWYN ("Lord God of hosts, whose purpose, never swerving" and "O brother man, fold to thy heart thy brother") by Alfred Scott-Gatty (1847–1918), British musician. Writing of "Have thine own way, Lord" by Adelaide A. Pollard (1862–1934), American writer; "Judge eternal, throned in splendor" by Henry Scott Holland (1847–1918), British Anglican. Death of George William Warren (b. 1828), American Episcopalian organist, composer of hymn-tunes ECCE AGNUS ("Behold the lamb of God") and NATIONAL HYMN ("God of our fathers" and "Heralds of Christ").

100 years (1877). Composing of hymn-tunes BREAD OF LIFE ("Break thou the bread of life") and CHAUTAUQUA ("Day is dying in the west") by William F. Sherwin (1826–1888), American Baptist choral director; PAX TECUM ("Peace, perfect peace") by Charles J. Vincent (1852–1934), British organist. Writing of "Who is on the Lord's side?" by Frances Ridley Havergal (1836–1879), British poet. Birth of Thomas Curtis Clark (d. 1953), American poet, author of "Where restless crowds are thronging"; Henry Sloane Coffin (d. 1954), American Presbyterian, author of "O come, O come, Emmanuel"; Grace Noll Crowell (d. 1969), American poet, author of "Because I have been given much"; Robert Guy McCutchan (d. 1958), American hymnologist, composer of hymn-tune ALL

THE WORLD ("Let all the world in every corner sing"). Death of George N. Allen (b. 1812), American educator, composer of hymn-tune MAITLAND ("Must Jesus bear the cross alone"); Henry Williams Baker (b. 1821), British Anglican, author of "The king of love my shepherd is," "O God of love, O king of peace," etc., and composer of hymn-tune STEPHANOS ("Art thou weary"); Charles W. Everest (b. 1814), American Episcopalian, author of "Take up thy cross"; Caroline M. Noel (b. 1821), British poet, author of "At the name of Jesus"; Alexander R. Reinagle (b. 1799), British organist, composer of hymn-tune ST. PETER ("Father whose will is life and good," "From thee all skill and science flow," "How sweet the name of Jesus sounds," "In Christ there is no east or west," etc.); John H. Stockton (b. 1813), American Methodist, author and composer of "Come, every soul by sin oppressed."

150 years (1827). Composing of hymn-tune HENDON ("Take my life, and let it be" and "Christ, of all my hopes the ground") by H. A. Cesar Malan (1787–1864), Swiss author of more than 1,000 hymns and hymn-tunes. Publication of "Bread of the world in mercy broken," "God, that madest earth and heaven," and "The Son of God goes forth to war" by Reginald Heber (1783–1826), British Anglican. Writing of "New every morning is the love" by John Keble (1792–1866), British Anglican; "Ride on, ride on in majesty" by Henry H. Milman (1791–1868), British Anglican. Birth of John Baptiste Calkin (d. 1905), British organist, composer of hymn-tunes NOX PRAECESSIT ("Lamp of our feet" and "Walk in the light") and WALTHAM ("Fling out the banner" and "I heard the bells on Christmas day"); Catherine Winkworth (d. 1878), British author,

translator of "All my heart this night rejoices," "Now thank we all our God," "Praise to the Lord, the almighty," etc. Death of Ludwig van Beethoven (b. 1770), German composer whose themes were adapted for many hymn-tunes including HYMN TO JOY ("Joyful, joyful, we adore thee" and "Sing with all the sons of glory"); William Blake (b. 1757), British poet, author of "And did those feet in ancient times" and "To mercy, pity, love and peace."

200 years (1777). Composing of hymn-tune MEIRINGEN ("All hail the pageant of the years") by Christian G. Neefe (1748–1798), German musician. Birth of Thomas Campbell (d. 1844), British poet, composer of hymn-tune SAGINA ("And can it be that I should gain").

250 years (1727). Birth of Samuel Stennett (d. 1795), British Sabbatarian Baptist, author of "Majestic sweetness sits enthroned" and "On Jordan's stormy banks I stand." Death of William Croft (b. 1678), British organist, composer of hymn-tunes HANOVER ("O worship the king" and "Ye servants of God"), ST. ANNE ("Lamp of our feet," "O God, our help in ages past," and "O where are kings and empires now"), and ST. MATTHEW ("Come, let us rise with Christ our head," "O Spirit of the living God," and "Thine arm, O Lord, in days of old").

300 years (1677). Publication of "Fairest Lord Jesus, ruler of all nature" in *Münster Gesangbuch*. Death of Johann Franck (b. 1618), German statesman and poet, author of "Deck thyself, my soul, with gladness" and "Jesus, priceless treasure."

750 years (1227). Birth of Thomas Aquinas (d. 1274), Italian scholastic philosopher, author of "Humbly let us voice our homage."

## Quotable Quotations

### JANUARY

1. We are made wise not by the recollections of our past but by the responsibilities of our future.—George Bernard Shaw.

2. The greatest temptation of religion is to become worship-centered instead of service-centered.—Charles L. Allen.

3. What is beautiful is a joy for all seasons.—Oscar Wilde.

4. God in Christ is God challenging me to decision.—Emil Brunner.

5. A man can no more possess a private religion than he can possess a private sun and moon.—G. K. Chesterton.

6. There are a great many things which the Lord will put up with in the human heart; but there is one thing he will not put up with—second place.—John Ruskin.

7. These are the good old days we will be longing for a few years from now.—John L. Sutter.

8. The greatness of life consists not so much in doing so-called great things but in doing small things greatly.

9. Some people carry their religion on their backs like a burden when they should carry it like a song in their hearts.—Ronald E. Terry.

### February

10. Whatsoever a good man does, he cannot do more than he owes to God.—William Manson.

11. The way we treat our fellowman is the way we treat God.—Teilhard de Chardin.

12. You can never give another what you have found, but you can make him homesick for what you have.—Oswald Chambers.

13. We are shaped and fashioned by what we love.—Johann Wolfgang von Goethe.

14. We must come to see that the end we seek is a society at peace with itself, a society that can live with its conscience.—Martin Luther King, Jr.

15. There is no better exercise for the heart than reaching down and lifting somebody up.—John Andrew Holmes.

16. Men become what they are, sons of God, by becoming what they are, brothers of their brothers.—Martin Buber.

17. The shadows will be behind you if you walk toward the light.

### March

18. He who has only himself for his goal has a void.—André Gide.

19. To believe in God is to know that all the rules will be fair and that there will be wonderful surprises.—Mary Corita.

20. Any crisis may be the hour when God gives birth to new dimensions in our lives.—C. Neil Strait.

21. It is poor preparation for your first Sunday in eternity to have misspent your last Sunday on earth.

22. Nothing requires a rarer intellectual heroism than willingness to see one's own equation written out.—George Santayana.

23. Jesus Christ is offered to men, first and foremost, not as a problem but as a solution.—William Temple.

24. The Christian belief in Christ's divinity began not as an intellectual theory but as the impact of an experience.—A. M. Ramsey.

25. We will be unfettered to the secrets of the stars in thy good time.—John Drinkwater.

26. The crucifixion of Jesus set men thinking more than anything else that has ever happened to the human race.—Donald M. Baillie.

27. In the semblance of the gardener, God walked again in the garden in the cool, not of the evening, but of the dawn.—G. K. Chesterton.

### April

28. The primary evidence provided by the apostles is not what they said but what they became.—Elton Trueblood.

29. The great difference today is not between believers and unbelievers but between persons who care and persons who do not care.—Abbe Pierre.

30. If God could turn some of us inside out he might send us to turn the world upside down.—Leonard Ravenhill.

31. The tragedy of life is what dies inside of people while they still live.—Albert Schweitzer.

32. Lighthouses don't toot horns; they just shine.—Dwight L. Moody.

33. All that is required to be done could easily be done if only people would rise up and play their part, not bothering who gets the glory of it.—Blaise Pascal.

34. The more the local church reaches out in mission the more it must reach within for resources.—Charles Forman.

35. An atheist may be simply one whose faith and love are concentrated on the impersonal aspects of God.—Simone Weil.

36. Our race, like that of the migrating birds, cannot live and perform all its functions in one climate but must take a periodic flight to another homeland.—H. Richard Niebuhr.

### May

37. A man's religion is, properly speaking, what has right of way over every other thing including even life itself.—Lesslie Newbigin.

38. You can give without loving, but you cannot love without giving.—Amy Carmichael.

39. Faith sees the invisible, believes the incredible, and receives the impossible.—Susan Kirk.

40. Our work for peace must begin within the private world of each of us.—Dag Hammarskjöld.

41. The life that is too busy for worship is busier than God intended it to be. Work is life's eminent duty, but worship is life's preeminent dynamic. To divorce one from the other is to court disaster, for while work exhausts power, worship renews it.—Stuart Holden.

42. Making sense of life means ultimately and always making sense of death.—J. S. Whale.

43. Suffering presupposes love.—Jürgen Moltmann.

44. Of all men the Christian man is the freest.—Martin Luther.

45. The resurrection is not just a personal survival: it is a cosmic victory.—James S. Stewart.

### June

46. Inexperience is what makes a young man do what an older man says is impossible.

47. Essentially it is the God-relationship that makes a man a man.—Søren Kierkegaard.

48. To realize the worth of the anchor we need to feel the storm.

49. A sovereign remedy for self-righteousness is the vision of God and his righteousness.—Ernest Fremont Tittle.

50. Christianity's mission in the world is not to save civilization but to save men.—Halford E. Luccock.

51. A friend is someone who leaves you with all your freedom intact but who obliges you to be fully what you are.—John L. Heureux.

52. Lord, help me to resist the temptation to make a molehill simply by adding a little dirt.

53. Doubt of any sort cannot be removed except by action.—Thomas Carlyle.

### July

54. The years teach much which the days never know.—Ralph Waldo Emerson.

55. That religion will conquer which can render clear to popular understanding some eternal greatness incarnate in the passage of temporal fact.—Alfred North Whitehead.

56. Make yourself an honest man and then you may be sure that there is one rascal less in the world.—Thomas Carlyle.

57. Do not have your concert first, then tune your instruments afterwards. Begin the day with the Word of God and prayer, and get first of all in harmony with him.—J. Hudson Taylor.

58. Most of God's troubles with laborers in his vineyard is absenteeism.

59. Every cubic inch of space is a miracle.—Walt Whitman.

60. The really happy man is the one who can enjoy the scenery when he has to take a detour.—Freeman Wesley Moore.

61. A man needs to feel something in this slippery world that holds.—Herman Melville.

### AUGUST

62. Liberty is always dangerous, but it is the safest thing we have.—Harry Emerson Fosdick.

63. The devil may set the world on fire, but the framework of the universe is fireproof.

64. A man who lives right and is right has more power in his silence than another has by his words.—Phillips Brooks.

65. There is another man within me that's angry with me.—Thomas Browne.

66. Man sees the deed, but God knows the intention.—Thomas a Kempis.

67. The gospel of Christ knows no religion but social, no holiness but social holiness.—John Wesley.

68. Our religion begins as a domestic affair and ends in a foreign policy.—Arthur Whitham.

### SEPTEMBER

69. The larger the island of knowledge the greater the shoreline of mystery.—Ralph W. Sockman.

70. A true life is at once interpreter and proof of the gospel.—John Greenleaf Whittier.

71. The more often one surrenders to a failing the more difficult does it become to do anything else.—George A. Buttrick.

72. There are a good many pious people who are as careful of their religion as of their best service of china, only using it on holy occasions, for fear it should get chipped or flawed in working-day wear.—Douglas Jerrold.

73. When we study the life of Christ we are in fact seeing God focused in a human life.—J. B. Phillips.

74. As a candle shines only when that of which it is made is being spent, so life is only real when it is being spent for others.—Leo Tolstoy.

75. Anything large enough for a wish to light upon is large enough to hang a prayer upon: the thought of him to whom that prayer goes will purify and correct the desire.—George Macdonald.

76. We must not only sit in heavenly places; we must work in unheavenly places.—Harry Emerson Fosdick.

### OCTOBER

77. God is complete for himself while for us he is continually being born.—Teilhard de Chardin.

78. God's love for poor sinners is very wonderful, but God's patience with ill-natured saints is a deeper mystery.—Henry Drummond.

79. Truth unveils itself to him who lives well, prays well, and studies well.—St. Augustine.

80. Ordinary people at all levels help each other to be more supernatural than each could have been alone.—Evelyn Underhill.

81. To tell the whole story of Jesus' love and power would exhaust the capacities of the universe.—William Temple.

82. Religion is either a dull habit or an acute fever.—William James.

83. There comes to every man a midnight of the soul when he must unmask.—Søren Kierkegaard.

84. In his holy flirtation with the world, God occasionally drops a handkerchief. These handkerchiefs are called saints.—Frederick Buechner.

### NOVEMBER

85. Love is exclusively a person.—Norman Grubb.

86. The church is the union of those who love for the sake of those who suffer.—Clarence J. Forsberg.

87. Failure doesn't mean God has abandoned you; it does mean God has a better idea.

88. It is wisdom to live the greatest possible number of good hours.—Ralph Waldo Emerson.

89. We are not saved by faith and works but by a faith that works.—Martin Luther.

90. Your will is the real you; surren-

der there and God has you.—François
Fénelon.

91. I know that God is in the Bible
because when I study it he comes out
of the Bible into my life.—E. Stanley
Jones.

### December

92. Better not to live than not to
love.—Henry Drummond.

93. The light that shows our sins is
the light that heals us.—George Fox.

94. A Christianity that does nothing
and costs nothing and suffers nothing is
worth nothing.

95. Was the message of the angels
only a meaningless platitude or was it
a promise to which we may turn with
certainty as a beam of light in a dark-
ening world?—Oswald C. J. Hoffmann.

96. The darkest night has shining
stars in it.

97. The best gifts are always tied with
heartstrings.—*Oregon Jesuit.*

98. We accept ourselves though we
are unacceptable.—Paul Tillich.

99. The future is something which
everyone reaches at the rate of sixty
minutes an hour, whatever he does,
whoever he is.—C. S. Lewis.

100. Real generosity toward the future
lies in giving all to the present.—Albert
Camus.

## Questions of Religion and Life

These questions may be useful to
prime homiletic pumps, as discussion
starters, or for study groups.

1. What traits of personality should
be characteristic of Christians?

2. What is meant by the words "to
die with dignity"?

3. What biblical guidelines relate to
social drinking?

4. How can I decide between right
and wrong?

5. Is world hunger too large a problem for Christians to handle?

6. Should pornographic literature be
suppressed by the courts?

7. What are the values of creative
tension?

8. In what respects are our worship
services similar to those in the early
church?

9. Is capital punishment a cruel and
unusual punishment?

10. Compare missionary activity of today and past generations.

11. Are there realistic bases for Christian optimism?

12. How may church people help the
retarded?

13. If the apostle Paul were to preach
in my church next Sunday, what might
be his topic?

14. How important to the church are
church-related colleges?

15. Explain the phrase "conviction of
sin."

16. In what ways does the church conform to the world?

17. Should Christians fear death?

18. How may our family life be
strengthened?

19. What is "the prophetic mission
of the church"?

20. Does biblical paraphrasing corrupt
the biblical text?

21. How can smokers be persuaded to
be more considerate of nonsmokers?

22. What can the church learn from
the occult?

23. Interpret the humanity of Jesus.

24. What are the motivations of
Christian charity?

25. What are the Christian implications of abortion?

26. Can we trust Russia?

27. What is "unconditional grace"?

28. Does the Constitution protect the
rights of atheists?

29. Should I distrust mystical experience?

30. How can I know if I am saved?

31. How may I be freed from a sense
of despair?

32. What were the methods Jesus used in training his disciples?

33. What is beauty?

34. What can the church do about violence?

35. Define "spiritual maturity."

36. For Christians is the Old Testament expendable?

37. How may I know God's will?

38. What is religious pluralism?

39. What did Jesus teach concerning heaven and hell?

40. Why do many churches have steeples?

41. How may the "success" of a revival be determined?

42. How can I learn to love and accept myself?

43. What are the psychological values of humor?

44. Should we hesitate to indoctrinate our children?

45. Who speaks for the church?

46. Are "acts of God" a threat to faith in God?

47. Are we spending too much on church buildings?

48. Is America a Christian nation?

49. Relate Christ's cross to the believer's salvation.

50. What significance does the church attach to Candlemas Day?

51. Are psychiatry and Christianity antagonistic?

52. What is the role of emotion in Christian experience?

53. Why are some leaders in the women's liberation movement critical of the Bible?

54. Why has death become a prominent theme in contemporary religion and culture?

55. What is new in contemporary forms of worship?

56. Can individuals influence public life?

57. How many women hold high administrative positions in American churches?

58. Have we lost our commitment to the great commission?

59. Are some vocations more Christian than others?

60. Why does the New Testament speak of death as sleep?

61. How may I discipline my life?

62. What can be done about morally offensive television programs?

63. What can be done about the growing problem of child abuse?

64. What evidences apart from the Bible are there for the existence of God?

65. How does God call people into full-time Christian work?

66. How can I make people like me?

67. Is it a denial of our faith in life after death to mourn those who die?

68. What does the Bible teach about speaking in tongues?

69. Are we expecting government to do too much for us?

70. What is the function of symbolism in religion?

71. What purpose lay behind Christ's dramatic entry into Jerusalem?

72. Why do whites seem to expect blacks to take initiatives for improved racial relationships?

73. What are the advantages and disadvantages of spontaneous prayer?

74. Is plea bargaining a weakness in our system of criminal justice?

75. Does the display of the American flag in worship compromise the separation of church and state?

76. Are statistics a valid evidence of a church's achievement?

77. How may our obsession for sex be Christianized?

78. Should I forgive someone who doesn't want to be forgiven?

79. What Christian witness can I offer a person suffering a terminal sickness?

80. What are the values of tradition in religion?

81. How politically oriented should the pulpit be?

82. What are the best times and places for private prayer?

83. Explain when righteous wrath might be justified.

84. Is preaching central in public worship? If not, what is?

85. Can you give me any rules of thumb for resisting temptation?

86. What significance do American Jews attach to the State of Israel?

87. What portions of the New Testament have been most effective in evangelism?

88. Has polarization increased or decreased within America?

89. Has the generation gap about which so much was written a few years ago been closed?

90. What did we learn from Vietnam?

91. Is the traditional Christian teaching concerning divorce too arbitrary?

92. In what ways does the work of a military chaplain differ from that of a parish pastor?

93. How may I start and encourage family worship in our home?

94. What in balance have been the positive and negative consequences of busing to achieve racial integration in public schools?

95. What is the doctrine of the second coming? Relate it to Christian faith and practice.

96. How vigorously should Christians seek to evangelize Jews?

97. Can the custom of saying grace before meals become too casual and meaningless?

98. How do we judge among conflicting interpretations of Old Testament prophecy?

99. How can Christianity help me to face and to accept tragedy?

100. What did the apostle Paul mean by "the crucifixion of the flesh"?

## The Idea Box

DIAL-A-STORY. There really are few new ideas, but there are a few people who take old ideas or at least the basic concept and relate them in significant new ways to the people with whom they work. We are aware of "Dial-a-Devotional," "Dial-a-Prayer," and similar helpful ministries. A grandmother in Petersburg, Virginia, recognizing that children receive instruction through many forms of media and knowing that children are fond of telephoning, developed "Dial-a-Story," and there were more than 50,000 children who dialed for a Bible or Bible-related story in a ten-month period.—John A. Barker. American Baptist Churches, Valley Forge, Pennsylvania.

PHONE CALLS FROM PIERRE POCEAUX. At the time of the children's sermon a telephone near the pulpit rings. I pick up the receiver and engage in a one-sided conversation with an imaginary boy named Pierre Poceaux, a French Arcadian (Cajun) who lives along a Louisiana bayou. This children's sermon format captivates the imaginations of the children—and adults—in the congregation. All that is needed is a telephone,

the recorded sound of a telephone ringing, a sermonette in the form of a telephone conversation, and of course an imaginary boy who fits your local scene and loves to call at the right time on Sunday mornings to talk with the pastor.—Roger H. Grummer, Grace Lutheran Church, Houma, Louisiana.

WORSHIP-BY-PHONE. Shut-ins, hospitalized members, and others unable to attend church are able to listen to our worship services by means of the Conference Call arrangement with the telephone company. Before the time of worship a Conference Call operator of the telephone company connects those wishing the service on a particular Sunday, and I have a few moments to extend personal greetings. Then the telephone line is switched to the public address system for the service of worship. Worship-by-phone is available to twenty-five or more persons each Sunday at a nominal service fee. The church furnishes small telephone amplifiers so listeners do not need to hold receivers and so others with them may also listen. I should be pleased to send detailed information to churches making such a request to me.—Donald E. Mayer, Hope United Church of Christ, 6273 Eichelberger St., St. Louis, Missouri 63109.

ELDER ADULTS SUNDAY. Congress has authorized Mother's Day and Father's Day, and we have Children's Day. But the Columbia Baptist Church, Seattle, Washington, has Elder Adults Sunday which not only honors its elderly but also provides an opportunity for the distribution of literature and information concerning the aging.—*American Baptist Input.*

BOOK DISPLAY. Members of our Christian Education Committee compiled a list of books and in cooperation with a local supply house displayed new books on tables in the church. Parishioners were invited to browse before and after our worship services and to purchase books for the church library or for personal use. In this way the number of books in the church library is greatly enlarged by the addition of recent titles. —F. Freddie Griffith, Madison Park Christian Church, Quincy, Illinois.

THE LITTLE COMMUNION. For persons wishing to partake of Holy Communion more frequently than the four scheduled observances each year our church provides communion following each of our worship services on Sunday. This "little communion," as it is called—although no communion is little—takes about ten minutes and ministers on successive Sundays to a varying number of communicants. Persons attending are frequently those at a point of decision or passing through a period of distress, trouble, or sorrow.—Linn Creighton, Presbyterian Church, Flemington, New Jersey.

AUGUST HOLIDAYS. July has the Fourth, February has President's Day, and January has New Year's Day. But poor August has no holidays. So in August we celebrate meaningfully three great days that are deserving of a double commemoration. One Sunday we desig-

nate with appropriate decorations and worship as "Thanksgiving in August," another as "Easter in August," and a third as "Christmas in August."—Eugene W. Ebert, First Presbyterian Church, Alliance, Ohio.

THE TRINITY REGISTER. Under this title the Trinity United Methodist Church, Youngstown, Ohio, in its newsletter "Trinity Chimes" lists family concerns according to the following headings:

*We rejoice in the Christian baptism of . . .*

*We rejoice in receiving into the Christian fellowship of the church . . .*

*We rejoice in the Christian marriage of . . .*

*We rejoice with the parents in the birth of . . .*

*We express our sympathy to the family of the following member of our church who has entered into rest . . .*

*We express our sympathy to those who have lost a loved one not a member of our church . . .*

CHURCH CALLING. In order that our members might know one another more intimately than by way of news items, church dinners, and casual conversations after church, we provide those willing to cooperate envelopes containing the names, addresses, and telephone numbers of four church families whom they then visit. This deepens and strengthens our Christian fellowship. Those participating report back to the church office and often request additional envelopes.—J. Edward Krueger, United Church of Christ, Wahpeton, North Dakota.

MIRROR ROOM. A profile of the local church and in a sense of the church universal is to be found in the mirror room or communications center of our church. The room is an extended bulletin board on which are put photographs of members and church activities, church members in the news, attendance and financial reports and charts, monthly calendars of church activities, reports from mission fields, and exhibits of various kinds. Space is provided where parishioners may post items of mutual interest. The displays are changed continually in order that the mirror room may be a week-by-week part of the church life.—David R. Bushnell, Grace United Church of Christ, Duquesne, Pennsylvania.

MORTGAGE OFFERING. On Mortgage Reduction Rally Day each member of the Peace Baptist Church, Detroit, Michigan, is urged to contribute an additional dollar specifically for the lowering of the indebtedness of the church.

NAME TAG SUNDAY. On the third Sunday of each month we encourage our people to wear a simple name tag which the church provides. The tags help the worshipers to learn names and assists newer people to become acquainted with the church family.—C. Neil Strait, Taylor Avenue Church of the Nazarene, Racine, Wisconsin.

MONEY-BACK GUARANTEE. While preparing my Loyalty Sunday sermon I read the words "put me to the test" in Mal. 3:10. On Sunday I said that God means for us to return a tithe for his work and will bless the lives of all who so respond to his call. I challenged the congregation to tithe for one year with the promise that if at the end of that period they did not feel their stewardship had enriched their spiritual lives they might reclaim their gifts. This challenge was accepted by many of our families, the increase in pledges has been noticeable, and many lives and the life of the church have been transformed. —Joe A. Harding, Central United Protestant Church, Richland, Washington.

SHEPHERDS. "Operation Brotherly Love" is an outreach and shepherding program involving many of our members. Several families are assigned to a man and his household. They call in the fall and introduce the church and its work and make periodic check-ups to learn of any spiritual needs to which, like good shepherds, they may respond with the love and concern of Christ and his church.—Richard Sutherlin, Central Christian Church, Clovis, New Mexico.

PROVE THE TITHE. On the last Sunday of our annual stewardship month emphasis is placed on the stewardship of our money by asking each member to give a tithe or 10 percent of a week's gross income to the church. Prior to "Prove the Tithe Sunday" posters announce this annual stewardship effort, the support of our people is solicited in a letter to all members, and the young people in our Sunday school classes circulate sign-up sheets and encourage wide participation. On this Sunday our offering is sometimes doubled and is usually 50 percent larger than on other Sundays. We believe this activity helps our people to know the joy of giving.—Max R. Hickerson, Clovernook Christian Church, Cincinnati, Ohio.

BIBLE DISPLAY. Members and friends of the church bring old and new Bibles to our worship service on Bible Sunday and display them on tables at the back of the sanctuary. The collection includes large and small editions in ancient and modern languages and designed for many purposes. During the following week the Bibles are placed in the window of a local bookstore, and the public is reminded of the heritage of God's printed word.—Walter B. Pruett, United Methodist Church, Aledo, Illinois.

COLONIAL WORSHIP. America's Christian heritage is celebrated at the First Presbyterian Church of Mount Pleasant, New Jersey, when the pastor, Jack Van Ens, wears a wig, glasses, and greatcoat and mounts the pulpit to deliver a sermon after the manner of a preacher of the Revolutionary period. On one occasion he based his sermon on "The Dominion of Providence over the Passions of Men" by the Rev. John Witherspoon, a signer of the Declaration of Independence. The members of the church, whose records go back to 1730, dress appropriately for heritage services in colonial garb and worship by candlelight in an unheated sanctuary.

SEASONAL CHALLENGE. As a way of identifying with the less fortunate, the Centenary United Methodist Church, Richmond, Virginia, challenges its members to attempt to buy their food during the period of Advent with the amount of money that a family receiving welfare would have allotted to them for the purchase of food under the food stamp program.—*Virginia Advocate*.

GIANT CHRISTMAS CARD. The members of our young adult class design a large card on poster board, mount appropriate pictures with attractive lettering, and display it on the first Sunday in Advent. The church people are invited to sign the card and make a contribution to the church equal to the cost and mailing of sending individual cards to their church friends. A copy of the giant card is sent in our weekly church paper to every church home just before Christmas.—David McGregor, First Cumberland Presbyterian Church, Columbia, Tennessee.

## Daily Bible Reading Guide for 1977

JANUARY. **Our one prayer: remembering to pray for all the saints in all the world.** *1:* John 17:11–26; *2 (Sunday):* John 11:1–44; *3:* John 14:12–24; *4:* John 15:1–11; *5:* John 16:16–33; *6:* Matthew 6:1–18; *7:* Matthew 7:1–12; *8:* Matthew 8:1–13; *9 (Sunday):* Matthew 18:15–35; *10:* Matthew 23:1–14; *11:* Mark 11:12–25; *12:* Mark 14:32–42; *13:* Luke 6:12–38; *14:* Luke 9:18–27; *15:* Luke 9:28–43; *16 (Sunday):* Luke 11:1–13; *17:* Luke 18:1–14; *18:* Luke 18:31–43; *19:* Luke 21:29–38; *20:* Acts 1:12–26; *21:* Acts 4:23–37; *22:* Acts 10:1–8; *23 (Sunday):* Acts 10:9–33; *24:* Acts 12:1–17; *25:* Romans 8:22–39; *26:* Ephesians 3:1–21; *27:* Ephesians 6:1–24; *28:* Philippians 4:1–23; *29:* Colossians 4:1–18; *30 (Sunday):* I Thessalonians 5:1–28; *31:* I Timothy 2:1–8.

FEBRUARY. **Our one call: remembering that our peace is found only in doing his will.** *1:* Deuteronomy 6:1–25; *2:* Deuteronomy 3:1–20; *3:* Joshua 24:14–28; *4:* Ruth 1:1–18; *5:* I Kings 18:21–39; *6 (Sunday):* Psalms 119:1–24; *7:* Psalms 119:25–48; *8:* Isaiah 2:1–4; *9:* Isaiah 6:1–8; *10:* Isaiah 45:1–25; *11:* Isaiah 55:1–13; *12:* Jeremiah 29:1–14; *13 (Sunday):* Ezekiel 33:1–16; *14:* Joel 2:12–32; *15:* Matthew 22:1–22; *16:* Mark 1:14–28; *17:* Mark 10:17–31; *18:* Luke 12:1–12; *19:* Luke 14:1–14; *20 (Sunday):* Luke 14:15–35; *21:* John 4:1–26; *22:* Acts 8:26–40; *23:* Acts 16:1–18; *24:*

Romans 5:1–21; *25:* II Corinthians 5:1–21; *26:* II Timothy 2:1–26; *27 (Sunday):* Titus 2:1–15; *28:* Revelation 22:1–21.

MARCH. **The Lord's people: remembering those who love the Lord regardless of race, color, or creed.** *1:* Leviticus 19:1–18; *2:* Leviticus 19:30–37; *3:* Deuteronomy 26:1–11; *4:* Deuteronomy 26:12–19; *5:* Proverbs 22:1–29; *6 (Sunday):* Proverbs 25:1–28; *7:* Malachi 2:1–10; *8:* Matthew 5:21–48; *9:* Matthew 25:31–46; *10:* Mark 3:19–35; *11:* Mark 12:28–44; *12:* Luke 10:25–37; *13 (Sunday):* John 13:31–38; *14:* Acts 11:1–30; *15:* Acts 17:22–34; *16:* Romans 12:1–21; *17:* Romans 13:1–14; *18:* Romans 14:1–23; *19:* Romans 15:1–13; *20 (Sunday):* I Corinthians 8:1–13; *21:* I Corinthians 13:1–13; *22:* Galatians 3:1–29; *23:* Colossians 3:1–17; *24:* I Thessalonians 3:1–13; *25:* I Thessalonians 1:1–10; *26:* Hebrews 13:1–8; *27 (Sunday):* I Peter 1:1–25; *28:* I Peter 4:1–11; *29:* I John 2:1–11; *30:* I John 4:1–21; *31:* I John 5:1–5.

APRIL. **Our one atonement: remembering the passion and death of our Lord.** *1:* Psalms 130:1–8; *2:* Luke 19:1–28; *3 (Sunday):* Luke 19:29–48; *4:* Luke 20:1–47; *5:* Luke 21:1–28; *6:* Luke 22:1–13; *7:* Luke 22:14–53; *8 (Good Friday):* Luke 23:1–38; *9:* Luke 23:39–56; *10 (Easter):* Luke 24:1–35; *11:* Acts 2:14–36;

*12:* Acts 3:1–26; *13:* Psalms 111:1–10; *14:* Psalms 31:1–24; *15:* Acts 10:34–48; *16:* Acts 17:1–15; *17 (Sunday)*: Acts 26:1–23; *18:* Romans 3:1–31; *19:* Romans 10:1–21; *20:* I Corinthians 1:1–31; *21:* Isaiah 43: 1–13; *22:* Isaiah 53:1–12; *23:* Ephesians 1:1–14; *24 (Sunday)*: Ephesians 2:11–22; *25:* Colossians 1:1–29; *26:* Hebrews 2:1–18; *27:* Hebrews 9:1–28; *28:* Jude 1–25; *29:* Revelation 5:1–14; *30:* Isaiah 35: 1–10.

MAY.    **Our one hope: remembering his promise to endue all true believers with the power of his Holy Spirit.** *1 (Sunday)*: Psalms 49:1–20; *2:* Psalms 51: 1–19; *3:* Psalms 71:1–24; *4:* Luke 24:36–53; *5:* Daniel 12:1–13; *6:* Matthew 6: 19–34; *7:* Matthew 28:1–20; *8 (Sunday)*: Mark 12:13–27; *9:* Luke 3:15–22; *10:* John 3:1–21; *11:* John 3:22–36; *12:* John 5:19–30; *13:* John 9:1–41; *14:* Acts 2:1–13; *15 (Sunday)*: John 10:1–42; *16:* John 16:1–15; *17:* John 20:19–31; *18:* Acts 2: 37–47; *19:* Acts 24:10–27; *20:* Romans 1: 1–17; *21:* Romans 4:1–25; *22 (Sunday)*: I Corinthians 15:1–34; *23:* I Corinthians 15:35–58; *24:* II Corinthians 4:1–18; *25:* Ephesians 4:17–32; *26:* I Thessalonians 4:1–18; *27:* I Timothy 6:12–21; *28:* I John 1:1–10; *29 (Sunday)*: I John 2:12–29; *30:* I John 3:1–24; *31:* Revelation 21:1–27.

JUNE.    **Our one goal: remembering the true meaning and purpose of life.** *1:* II Kings 23:1–25; *2:* Psalms 1:1–6; *3:* Psalms 40:1–17; *4:* Psalms 66:1–20; *5 (Sunday)*: Psalms 84:1–12; *6:* Psalms 92: 1–15; *7:* Matthew 7:13–29; *8:* Matthew 10:16–33; *9:* Matthew 16:13–28; *10:* Mark 2:1–12; *11:* Luke 6:39–49; *12 (Sunday)*: Luke 12:13–40; *13:* Luke 15: 11–32; *14:* Luke 18:15–30; *15:* John 4: 27–42; *16:* John 6:47–71; *17:* John 15: 12–27; *18:* John 17:1–10; *19 (Sunday)*: Acts 1:1–11; *20:* Acts 4:1–22; *21:* Acts 20:17–38; *22:* Acts 22:1–21; *23:* Romans 8:1–21; *24:* I Corinthians 10:1–15; *25:* I Corinthians 14:1–20; *26 (Sunday)*: Ephesians 1:15–23; *27:* Ephesians 2:1–10; *28:* Ephesians 4:1–16; *29:* Philippians 2:1–13; *30:* Philippians 3:8–21.

JULY.    **The one God: remembering that we owe him our freedom and our loyalty.** *1:* Exodus 19:1–9; *2:* Exodus 20: 1–17; *3 (Sunday)*: Deuteronomy 32:1–14; *4:* I Chronicles 29:10–20; *5:* Psalms 24: 1–10; *6:* Psalms 89:1–18; *7:* Isaiah 61:1–11; *8:* Isaiah 64:1–12; *9:* Ezekiel 18:1–23; *10 (Sunday)*: Ezekiel 18:24–32; *11:* Daniel 3:1–18; *12:* Daniel 3:19–30; *13:* Daniel 6:1–18; *14:* Daniel 6:19–28; *15:* Jonah 1:1–17; *16:* Jonah 2:1–10; *17 (Sunday)*: Jonah 3:1–10; *18:* Jonah 4:1–11; *19:* Matthew 25:14–30; *20:* Luke 4:31–42; *21:* John 8:25–36; *22:* Romans 6:1–23; *23:* Romans 7:15–25; *24 (Sunday)*: I Corinthians 6:1–20; *25:* Galatians 5:13–26; *26:* Galatians 6:1–18; *27:* II Timothy 1: 1–18; *28:* Hebrews 12:1–13; *29:* Hebrews 13:9–25; *30:* I Peter 2:1–10; *31 (Sunday)*: I Peter 2:11–25.

AUGUST.    **Our own discipline: remembering that in him we live and move and have our being.** *1:* Job 23:1–17; *2:* Psalms 94:1–23; *3:* Proverbs 3:1–12; *4:* Isaiah 1:1–20; *5:* Isaiah 40:18–31; *6:* Matthew 17:1–13; *7 (Sunday)*: Ezekiel 3:1–27; *8:* Zechariah 4:1–10; *9:* Malachi 3:1–18; *10:* Matthew 19:16–30; *11:* Matthew 20:1–16; *12:* Mark 8:31–38; *13:* I Corinthians 11:23–34; *14 (Sunday)*: II Corinthians 12:1–10; *15:* Titus 3:1–15; *16:* Hebrews 10:19–39; *17:* Hebrews 11: 1–16; *18:* Hebrews 11:17–40; *19:* James 1:1–27; *20:* James 2:1–26; *21 (Sunday)*: James 3:1–18; *22:* James 4:1–17; *23:* James 5:1–20; *24:* I Peter 4:12–19; *25:* Revelation 2:1–8; *26:* Revelation 2:8–11; *27:* Revelation 2:12–17; *28 (Sunday)*: Revelation 2:18–29; *29:* Revelation 3:1–6; *30:* Revelation 3:7–13; *31:* Revelation 3:14–22;

SEPTEMBER.    **Our one work: remembering that we are workers together with him.** *1:* Genesis 1:1–31; *2:* Genesis 2:1–25; *3:* Deuteronomy 10:12–22; *4 (Sunday)*: I Chronicles 28:9–21; *5:* Psalms 34:1–22; *6:* Psalms 37:1–22; *7:* Psalms 37:23–40; *8:* Ecclesiastes 9:7–18; *9:* Haggai 2:1–9; *10:* Matthew 5:1–20; *11 (Sunday)*: Matthew 21:18–32; *12:* Matthew 24:36–51; *13:* Mark 10:32–52; *14:* Mark

13:24–37; *15:* Mark 14:1–9; *16:* Luke 6:1–11; *17:* Luke 10:38–42; *18 (Sunday):* Luke 12:41–48; *19:* John 6:16–29; *20:* John 21:15–25; *21:* Acts 9:1–9; *22:* Acts 9:10–31; *23:* Acts 9:32–43; *24:* I Corinthians 3:1–23; *25 (Sunday):* I Corinthians 4:1–21; *26:* I Corinthians 16:1–24; *27:* II Corinthians 1:1–24; *28:* II Corinthians 6:1–18; *29:* II Corinthians 8:1–24; *30:* II Timothy 4:1–8.

OCTOBER. **The one word: remembering that he has nowhere left himself without witness.** *1:* Deuteronomy 4:1–14; *2 (Sunday):* Deuteronomy 8:1–20; *3:* Deuteronomy 11:18–32; *4:* Joshua 1:1–9; *5:* I Kings 8:1–21; *6:* I Kings 8:22–36; *7:* I Kings 8:37–53; *8:* I Kings 8:54–66; *9 (Sunday):* Psalms 11:49–72; *10:* Psalms 119:73–96; *11:* Psalms 119:97–120; *12:* Psalms 119:121–144; *13:* Psalms 119:145–176; *14:* Jeremiah 15:1–21; *15.* Jeremiah 23:18–32; *16 (Sunday):* Ezekiel 2:1–10; *17:* Ezekiel 12:17–28; *18:* Ezekiel 37:1–14; *19:* Matthew 22:23–46; *20:* Matthew 24:1–35; *21:* Mark 4:1–20; *22:* John 1:1–18; *23 (Sunday):* John 5:31–47; *24:* John 12:20–50; *25:* John 15:1–11; *26:* John 17:10–26; *27:* Acts 18:1–28; *28:* Galatians 1:1–24; *29:* I Thessalonians 2:1–20; *30 (Sunday):* II Timothy 3:1–17; *31:* Hebrews 4:1–16.

NOVEMBER. **The one thanksgiving: remembering in all things to give thanks.** *1:* Exodus 23:1–13; *2:* Exodus 23:14–25; *3:* Leviticus 26:1–13; *4:* I Chronicles 16:7–36; *5:* Nehemiah 8:1–12;

*6 (Sunday):* Psalms 11:1–7; *7:* Psalms 33:1–22; *8:* Psalms 50:1–23; *9:* Psalms 65:1–13; *10:* Psalms 116:1–19; *11:* Jeremiah 33:1–11; *12:* Matthew 9:1–17; *13 (Sunday):* Matthew 9:18–38; *14:* Matthew 11:1–19; *15:* Matthew 11:20–30; *16:* Luke 17:1–19; *17:* Luke 24:36–53; *18:* John 6:1 15; *19:* II Corinthians 9:1–15; *20 (Bible Sunday):* Psalms 67:1–7; *21:* Psalms 68:1–35; *22:* Deuteronomy 28:1–14; *23:* Psalms 107:1–22; *24 (Thanksgiving Day):* Psalms 100:1–5; *25:* Isaiah 12:1–6; *26:* Isaiah 42:1–16; *27 (Sunday):* Ephesians 5:1–21; *28:* I Timothy 4:1–16; *29:* Revelation 7:1–17; *30:* Romans 15:1–13.

DECEMBER. **The one Savior: remembering the unspeakable gift of our one Lord and Savior.** *1:* Psalms 46:1–11; *2:* Psalms 118:1–29; *3:* Isaiah 9:1–7; *4:* Isaiah 11:1–10; *5 (Sunday):* Isaiah 25:1–12; *6:* Isaiah 40:1–17; *7:* Isaiah 52:1–15; *8:* Isaiah 59:1–21; *9:* Jeremiah 23:1–8; *10:* Jeremiah 33:12–26; *11:* Daniel 2:1–30; *12 (Sunday):* Daniel 2:31–49; *13:* Nahum 1:1–15; *14:* Zechariah 9:9–17; *15:* Zechariah 11:1–17; *16:* Zechariah 12:1–14; *17:* Zechariah 13:1–9; *18:* Zechariah 14:1–21; *19 (Sunday):* Malachi 4:1–5; *20:* Luke 1:1–25; *21:* Luke 1:26–38; *22:* Luke 1:39–56; *23:* Luke 1:57–80; *24:* Matthew 1:18–25; *25:* Luke 2:1–20; *26 (Sunday):* Matthew 2:1–12; *27:* Matthew 2:13–23; *28:* Luke 2:34–52; *29:* Mark 9:1–13; *30:* I Timothy 1:1–17; *31:* I Peter 3:18–22. —American Bible Society.

# SECTION II. Vital Themes for Vital Preaching

**January 2. Awareness of Time (New Year's Sunday)**

TEXT: Ps. 90:12.

I. An awareness of time should teach us to make an effort to complete every task lest it never be finished. Although it may not be possible to complete every task we begin, we should make every effort to move toward the goal of completion.

II. An awareness of time should cause us to place a proper value on the use of time. We must be careful to choose what we are going to do, for time does not allow us to do everything. We should do the things that really matter. Like Martha in Luke 10:40 we can become "cumbered about much serving."

III. An awareness of time should cause us to come to the close of each day with the assurance that all is right between us and our fellowman. Is there a restoration to be made? Is there a breach to be mended? Is there a quarrel to be settled? (See Rom. 12:18.)—Thomas B. Stevenson.

**January 9. It's the Life that Counts**

TEXT: Matt. 7:21.

On Christmas we celebrate the birth of Christ and marvel that such a person could have made his appearance on earth in the first place. At Easter time we celebrate the victory of Christ over death, an event that we call the resurrection and without which there would

be no Christian church today. But we need a third major Christian holiday to celebrate the life that Jesus lived between Bethlehem and Calvary. Without the life that Jesus lived his birth would have no special meaning and his resurrection would have been an absurd impossibility.

I. With us too it's the life that counts: not our birth, high or low; not our looks, good or bad; not our money or prestige or race or position.

II. It's our life that counts: not our professional beliefs, nor the forms of our worship, nor the church in which we have our membership. It is how we live, above all else, that counts.

III. Everywhere in scripture the testimony is the same: nothing we say or believe or do amounts to anything unless our lives possess integrity, sensitivity, unselfishness, the forgiving spirit, that undiscourageable goodwill toward men that we call Christian love.—Ivan B. Bell.

**January 16. Trust in God**

TEXT: Ps. 118:8–9.

I. Trust in God means belief in God —a consciously sought, clearly faced, factually grounded, intellectually trustworthy conviction that God is the supreme fact and factor in human life and history.

II. Trust in God means faith in God —a belief in him so strong, so vital, so certain that you are willing to let it guide your life.

III. Trust in God means confidence in God—a confident knowledge, born of your own experience that he can be depended upon, that he knows and cares, that he is sufficient for all things, that you can put the hand of your life in his outstretched hand and go where he leads.—Harold A. Bosley.

## January 23. The Practice of Prayer (Week of Prayer)

I. Pray where you are. God is present everywhere and ready to listen.

II. Pray when possible in a quiet spot where you can be alone. It is well to fix your mind deliberately on God, apart from confusing distractions.

III. Pray to God simply and naturally as to a friend. Tell him what is on your mind. Get help from the prayers of others.

IV. Pray remembering the good things God has done for you. Count your blessings from time to time and give thanks for them.

V. Pray for God's forgiveness for the unworthy things that you may have done. He is near to a humble and contrite heart.

VI. Pray for the things that you need, especially those that will make your life finer and more Christlike.

VII. Pray for others, remembering the situations they confront and the help they need.

VIII. Pray for the world in its needs, asking God to bring better things and offering your help to him.

IX. Pray that God's will may be done in you and in the world. His purposes are deeper and wiser than anything we can imagine.

X. Pray and then start answering your prayer.—Carl J. Sanders.

## January 30. The Master's Joys
Text: John 15:11.

I. *Jesus found joy with his family at Nazareth.* There had to be so much love and laughter and happiness in that home, or he would never have prayed to God as his Father and introduced a new kind of kingdom patterned after the human family.

II. *Jesus found joy in a good meal.* Some of the greatest lessons he taught were spoken as he broke bread and drank wine with his friends around the dinner table.

III. *Jesus found joy in the laughter of children.* He watched them dancing in the street and compared the new kingdom of love to the happiness of these children.

IV. *Jesus found joy in friendship.* The hours spent with Mary and Lazarus and Martha in Bethany were treasured moments snatched from the busy ministry he came to fulfill.

V. *Jesus found joy in his work.* He took seriously the task God called him to do, but the touch of humor was always there, even when he was teaching and healing and challenging enemies.

VI. *Jesus found joy in his vacations.* When he was physically exhausted from the pressures of the crowds that pushed in upon him he would get into a boat and pull away from the shore on Lake Galilee, as he was lulled to sleep by the lapping of the waves.

VII. *Jesus found joy in helping fallen men stand on their feet.* His most beautiful parable about a father's love that forgives and welcomes home a penitent son closes with the preparations for a veal barbecue and a dance to celebrate his homecoming.—Ira E. Williams, Jr.

## February 6. Christ's Call to Discipleship
Text: Luke 9:59–60.

I. Have you ever thought how often Jesus' first word to a person was an imperative verb? People came to him seeking his help, and he immediately challenged them to act. So he spoke to Peter and Andrew to come and follow, to the servants at the marriage feast to fill the water pots, to the woman at the well to give him to drink, and to the impotent man by the pool to rise and walk.

II. When we honestly come face to face with Jesus Christ, he calls us to follow him. As we obey and follow we will grow in certain insights of faith and qualities of Christian character, but these come as we walk after him. Too many of us are holding back, trying to develop the convictions and receive the gifts of love and joy and peace before our commitment to him. It cannot be done.

III. The Christian life will be a transforming experience for any person who determines to answer Christ's call to follow. For the most part it will mean the doing of simple and good daily duties. It will mean the worship of God on Sunday with his people. It will include the study of God's Word and daily serious prayer to him. It will include acts of kindness and of love. It will be the simple and yet basic matter of following on the way. Commonplace as the road may appear it will lead us to the heavenly city.— William E. Sanders.

## February 13. Three Perspectives (Race Relations Sunday)

SCRIPTURE: Luke 10:25–37.

In Jesus' story of the good Samaritan he illustrated three perspectives on life.

I. There were the thieves who robbed the traveler on the lonely, thug-infested road to Jericho. Like those who deliberately exploit the poor, their attitude was: "What's yours is mine. I'll take it."

II. There were the priests and the Levites who passed by, refusing to get involved with a bleeding man in a ditch. Like those today who are so busy (going to a prayer meeting or running an evangelistic service?) that they just ignore the poor, their attitude was: "What's mine is mine. I'll keep it."

III. There was the good Samaritan who stopped, looked, and acted; who picked up the wounded man and ministered to him; who took him to the inn and paid the bills and promised to come back and take a continuing interest. His attitude was: "What's mine is God's. I'll share it."—Leighton Ford.

## February 20. Christian Gentlemen (Brotherhood Week)

TEXT: I Cor. 10:31.

I. When others are engaged in conversation, do I go up to them, rudely interrupt the conversation, and start talking to one of the parties without due regard to the other person or persons involved?

II. Am I careful to be gentlemanly with reference to remarks I might make to someone in the presence of several others—remarks that might be filled with "little" insults, seasoned with the attitude, "Now's my chance to put him in his place" or "Now's my chance to get a good laugh"?

III. Am I always gentlemanly in regards to showing concern and thoughtfulness to other persons, regardless of their status or position?

IV. Am I gentlemanly in times of pressure and in other difficult situations?

V. Am I gentlemanly to the extent that I always show appreciation for the things people do for me, regardless of how small they may be, and am I thoughtful enough to express thanks to those who befriend me?—O. W. Polen in *Church of God Evangel*.

## February 27. What Is the Church? (Lent)

TEXT: I Cor. 12:27.

I. The church is basically and simply the community of Jesus, not an institution or program, but a group of people who have heard about him, who know him and have responded and keep on responding to him in such a way that they become his "body," the means by which his spirit lives on and influences our lives and the lives of others and the world around us in our day.

II. The church is the responsive and responding community, the community in which Christ is honored, in which and by which his gospel, the good news of God's love, is proclaimed, by which his love for all men and his concern for the last and the least is expressed.

III. When the church is the church, it responds in faith to a God who can be trusted, come what may; it responds in celebration, reminding itself over and over again in the act of worship of all that this faith means; it responds in proclamation, sharing its faith with all who will heed and listen; and it responds in obedience, doing his work, challenging the power of evil, binding up the wounds of men and nations, giving of itself in service to others, helping when others won't help, and caring when others fail to care.—Edward C. Dahl.

## March 6. The Encouragements of Faith (Lent)

SCRIPTURE: Heb. 11:1–10.

The persons named in Heb. 11 had faith enough to try even when they were not sure they would succeed.

I. Faith in "impossible dreams" has changed the world. Often such dreams have brought ridicule to those who held them. But their faith enabled them to work on, and finally they became victorious.

II. Faith in God enables us to undertake the task of trying to live like Jesus Christ. When Toyohiko Kagawa tried, he was called "God's fool." When Albert Schweitzer tried, he was criticized for giving up a notable career in music and philosophy for work as a medical missionary.

III. Faith in God supplies the hope which enables us to be more than conquerors. The risk of failure is dispelled. Faith encourages us to try.—E. Paul Hovey.

## March 13. The Prayer of Jabez (Lent)

TEXT: I Chron. 4:10.

Hidden away among the genealogies in I Chron. 4:10, like a lovely flower in an unexpected place, is the story of Jabez. In the prayer of this young man and God's response to him, there is a formula for blessing and power as fresh and effective as it was 3,500 years ago. There are five characteristics of Jabez revealed in his prayer.

I. A heartfelt desire to know the blessing of God: "O, that thou wouldest bless me indeed."

II. A divine dissatisfaction with narrow horizons: "And enlarge my coast."

III. A determination to witness the power of God: "And that thine hand might be with me."

IV. A dependence upon the protecting grace of God: "And that thou wouldest keep me from evil."

V. A deep sense of the exceeding sinfulness of sin: "That it may not grieve me."—Harold R. Crosser.

## March 20. They Were There (Lent)

I. There was a thief who cursed God and cursed his fate. Are we like him?

II. There was another criminal who was repentant and anxious to be forgiven. Are we that man?

III. There were soldiers who claimed detachment and thus found amusement in the grisly business of crucifixion. Have we, like them, exploited goodness and truth?

IV. There was a centurion whose mind was open and whose heart was touched and changed by the heroism of Jesus. Are we sensitive to the deep meaning of the cross, even as this soldier was?

V. There were civic leaders, officials, and teachers who ridiculed Jesus, trying to make themselves look good while making him look bad. Has false pride distorted our understanding of what is just and right?

VI. There were humble friends, followers, and loved ones who were overcome by sorrow at the spectacle of Jesus' hurt. Do we likewise perceive life's tragic dimension and weep with those who weep, finding ways to bear others' burdens and share their grief.—John H. Townsend.

## March 27. The Cross as Challenge and Conviction (Passion Sunday)

TEXT: Heb. 12:2.

I. The cross must always be borne voluntarily. If we bear the cross we take it without compulsion. If Jesus had called legions of angels to defend him, his victory would have been temporary, not permanent. He could have escaped the cross by compromising with the truth. He might have exercised political expediency and not have come in conflict with the existing authority. He might have remained in retirement beyond the Jordan and not have faced the entrenched ecclesiastical power which resided in Jerusalem.

II. The cross is a challenge to the lonely way. Jesus trod the winepress alone. His family did not understand him. The city in which he was reared was ready to ostracize him. In the crucial hour of his need even his most trusted disciples forsook him and fled. The multitudes followed him, but when he told them that those who would come after him must eat his flesh and drink his blood, which meant that they must share his hardships and sufferings, they also turned back and went no more with him.

III. The cross must become the supreme passion of our souls. When Jesus went unflinchingly to Jerusalem in the face of certain death, it was only because he cherished an enduring cause. (See John 18:37.) Jesus loved the truth and man's salvation more than his own life. Death was not defeat but victory.—Fred R. Chenault.

## April 3. Appeal from the Cross (Good Friday)

TEXT: John 19:28

I. This cry shows to us the humanity of our Lord Jesus together with his infirmities.

II. This word, almost a prayer, tells us of the humiliation of our Lord Jesus.

III. This cry instructs us as to the price that God paid for redemption.—William R. Taylor.

## April 10. Resurrection and Change (Easter)

SCRIPTURE: Matt. 28:1–10.

I. *The resurrection is the grand reversal.* The early believers did not say with dismay, "O look what the world is coming to"; rather they said with delight, "Look what has come into the world—Jesus Christ is alive!" They saw the ruins, but they saw the resources which could reconstruct the ruins. They saw sin abounding, but they rejoiced in grace abounding. It was assurance that allowed the pivot of history to swing from blank despair, from the failure of moral nerve, and from futility and frustration and fatalism to faith and confidence.

II. *The resurrection is the glorious report.* The living Christ went to his own. He went to those who knew him, who trusted him, and who loved him. He met them on the way. On this resurrection day we do more than commemorate a historic fact. We celebrate a present reality. The early Christians believed that Jesus was alive not because they couldn't find his body; they believed he was alive because they met him, the living Christ, on the way. Jesus met them. There is more on this day than thinking of the proofs and evidences that he came out of that grave. That is conclusive. The Lord Jesus is alive, and he meets his own on the road, and he says to them, "Hail!"

III. *The resurrection is the great release.* In the resurrection of Jesus Christ there is a spiritual dynamic. There is a vital thrust. There is a powerful propulsion which through the Holy Spirit takes hold of human beings who are surrendered to Jesus Christ and lifts up that which is limpid and languid and lethargic and lifeless and lazy and lackadaisical. There is something in the resurrection of our Lord Jesus Christ from the dead which picks us up out of the doldrums, out of this self-centeredness which is such a tragic curse at the heart of so many of our lives, and which releases us, sets us free, sends us going on our way. Jesus said to his disciples: "Go, tell my brethren. Let them know that I am alive and I will meet them in Galilee." —David L. Larsen.

## April 17. I Didn't Know That!

SCRIPTURE: I Cor. 1:17–25.

Jesus revealed some things about life that man either had not learned or refused to accept. And somehow we haven't fully learned them yet.

I. Did you know that good does not always triumph in this life?

II. Did you know that life's greatest achievements have the greatest price tags?

III. Did you know that religion is not necessarily a synonym for Christianity?

IV. Did you know that man is a strange mixture of good and evil?

V. Did you know that God loves us anyway?

VI. Did you know that while Jesus' death was condemning sin it was also placing a premium upon the sinner?—Jerry Hayer.

### April 24. The Ministries of Silence
TEXT: Rev. 3:20.

I. Silence does not mean meditating on the words of a good book, although that may be one of the things we do in the silence. Silence does not mean reading prayers or even composing our own, although that also may be of great help. Silence is waiting all alone for the word of God to come. Only in the silence can God speak. Only in the silence can man hear.

II. In silence the noisy machinery of argument is shut down, the clangor of discussion dies away, and the need to put up a better case vanishes. In silence God who is already there is allowed to come to the surface of the conscious mind. He leads us back onto the path we have chosen but have abandoned. He restores to us our peace and joy. He asserts his will as we already know it and leads us into a new and deeper commitment to it.

III. We continually ask for more knowledge and deeper insight. Most of us already know enough about God. Our need is to let him have his way. Sometimes our greatest step forward is to stand still. I already know that God is absolute compassion, that he is eternally my father, and that he bleeds to bring the whole world into the kingdom of love. What I need is silence in which I can allow these things to become my peace, my joy, and my commanding concern.—D. Bruce Johnson.

### May 1. Guidelines for Christian Families (National Family Week)
TEXT: Ps. 133:1.

I. A family should endeavor to eat together—at least one meal a day.

II. A family should share the work of the household.

III. A family should make time for fun together.

IV. A family should make time for prayer together.

### May 8. Achieving Happiness at Home (Mother's Day)
TEXT: Ps. 127:1.

Happiness at home is not assured by the acquisition of material things. It is not assured by any rearrangement of outward circumstances. Some would have us believe that all one has to do to bring a spirit of tranquillity into the home is to acquire a finer house and new furniture or to change one's brand of detergent, coffee, tobacco, or breakfast cereal. I wish it were as simple as that, but it isn't.

I. *We must learn to control our tongues*. If we are going to achieve a harmonious, emotionally stable family life, we've got to discipline our wayward tongues. This will not be easy, for at home we tend to relax and get off our good behavior. We grow careless and say things to members of the family that we would never think of saying to total strangers on the outside. It is a great pity. Let every member of the family make the psalmist's prayer his own daily petition: "Set a watch, O Lord. before my mouth; keep the door of my lips" (Ps. 141:3).

II. *We must learn the art of putting ourselves in the other person's place*. Sometimes I think our world needs empathy more than it needs sympathy. We must try imaginatively to exchange places and look at life through the other person's eyes. It is amazing how one can live with someone for years in the intimacy of married life without coming within a thousand miles of ever learning how life seems to that individual or what he or she wants from life.

III. *We must carry into this relationship the same graces that we practice away from home*—graces like courtesy, politeness, patience, considerateness, thoughtfulness, and appreciation. We practice these graces in our outside business and social contacts, but when we get home we "let down." We relax on those finer qualities of character which are essential to success in any human relationship. If it is right to practice good manners in the presence of outsiders, is it not right that we should practice them even more faithfully in the company of those whom we profess to love best?

IV. *We must cultivate the forgiving spirit.* (a) He who harbors resentment in his heart contributes to domestic tension. An unforgiving, retaliatory spirit has turned many a lovely home into an unbearable relationship.

(b) We must cultivate a readiness to seek forgiveness. Some are more willing to forgive others than they are to seek pardon for themselves when they are in the wrong. In our family relationships we are bound to make mistakes, for none of us is perfect, and when we are at fault we ought to have the grace to confess it and ask forgiveness.

(c) To ask forgiveness requires humility. It isn't easy to confess one's own sins and mistakes. It is much easier to point the indicating finger at others and confess their sins. We are too proud to acknowledge that we are wrong, too proud to "break down" and confess quite frankly our own guilt and shortcomings.

V. In the creation and preservation of family life, God is the first essential. However well we master other techniques, if he is left out, we are inviting failure.

(a) The best insurance against a broken home is vital religion. Nothing is more calculated to stabilize the family, reduce friction, and dispel tension. When the apostle Paul listed the "fruit of the Spirit," he named the qualities which are essential to domestic bliss: love, joy, peace, patience, kindness, goodness, faithfulness, gentleness, self-control (Gal. 5:22, RSV).

(b) Let us invite God into the family circle. Let us bring all under the sway of his gracious lordship. There is no problem of home life too great for him to handle. He can patch up any rift, straighten out any tangle, restore any fellowship, and dispel any misunderstanding. His wisdom, guidance, and power can make of any home a "gate of heaven."—William M. Elliott, Jr.

## May 15. The Poor Rich Man
SCRIPTURE: Mark 10:17–22.

The scripture tells the story of what is commonly referred to as the "young rich man." A closer look at the context reveals a depth of poverty.

I. *There was poverty of spiritual depth.* This man was not acquainted with the Master's will. No amount of riches can compensate for a poverty of spiritual things.

II. *There was a poverty of sharing.* This man was "saddened" when Christ suggested that he "sell all." He did not realize that a man's wealth is figured finally in terms of what he gives, not in what he keeps.

III. *There was a poverty of service.* What he had, he was not using. And what is not used—be it time, talent, or treasure—will come to naught.—C. Neil Strait.

## May 22. What the Church Should Be
TEXT: Jer. 50:2.

I. *Seeker of truth.* The church has nothing to fear from the pursuit of truth. Indeed the church should insist on the vigorous search for truth. (See John 8:32.)

II. *Covenant community.* The church should not be viewed as just another voluntary organization. The church is different. Membership in the church should mean more than a club membership. Church membership should be thought of more as membership in a family. The church should be a fellowship characterized by mutual love and concern. It should be a community of people living in a covenant relationship to God and to each other.

III. *Covenant community in mission.* The church does not exist for itself but rather as God's servant people in the world. No matter how rich the internal life of a congregation, a church is not whole unless it reaches out in ministry. The church should be in mission in its local community—transforming, redeeming, challenging, and reconciling—and in mission to the larger society to which it belongs.—Lovett Hayes Weems, Jr.

## May 29. In Joyous Remembrance (Memorial Day)
Text: Deut. 8:2.

I. Memory is the bridge of thought and life spanning the yesterdays, joining the todays, in the spirit of oneness and continuity. Much of our religious life is remembering.

II. Memory deepens our reverence and joy in our priceless heritage.

III. A joyous memory may add insight, wisdom, and understanding to life.

IV. Memory must be selective. We are often told that we must also know how to forget. How tragic it is when the sacred library of memory seems to be filled only with old griefs, hurts, or words of life's defeat. Life is too joyous to carry over into the tomorrow excess baggage that we just do not need.

V. A covenant of memory gives us a word of hope and of life. Memory recalls the blessed dead who filled life with victory and hope.—Frank A. Court.

*The Sower Went Out to Sow*
## June 5. Formula for Soul Growth
Scripture: Matt. 13:3–9.

I. I will allow Christ to control my total life.

II. I will commune with Christ daily in prayer.

III. I will worship God faithfully in his sanctuary.

IV. I will let Christ speak daily from his holy scriptures.

V. I will enlarge my capacity to love God, my fellowman, and myself.

VI. I will invest at least a tithe of my time and talent in specific Christian service each week.

VII. I will give at least a tenth of my income to my church and other humanitarian causes.

VIII. I will seek the help of my brethren lest I fail to fulfill these disciplines.—Robert W. Rae.

## June 12. How Children Grow (Children's Day)
Text: I Pet. 2:2.

I. Out of the cradle there is outreach, little arms reaching out, a mind reaching out, a heart reaching out, and growth takes place as there are loving parents to answer that outreach.

II. The child learns by participation and sharing in the environment of a family. That is why the environment for healthy growth takes in discipline, love, understanding, and primarily the sense of expectation that the child shall learn to participate.

III. The child grows into becoming, absorbing knowledge until it becomes insight and understanding.

IV. A child grows through overcoming. A wise parent doesn't always smooth the way for the child.

V. Life grows by reaching upward to the spiritual through the tug of dreams and high views. Life's imperative is always to grow.

## June 19. Our Father (Father's Day)
Scripture: Matt. 6:9–13.

*used*

If we are to pray and live as we should, we must grasp the implications of God's gracious fatherhood.

I. As God's adopted children we are loved no less than is the one whom God called his beloved Son (Matt. 3:17; 17:5). In some families containing natural and adopted children the former are favored above the latter, but no

*6-5-77*
*AM*

such defect mars the fatherhood of God.

II. We are God's heirs. Adoption in the ancient world was for the securing of an heir, and Christians are joint heirs with Christ of God's glory (Rom. 8:17).

III. We must honor our Father: the center of our concern must be his name, his kingdom, and his will.

IV. We must love our brothers by care and prayer for them. The Lord's Prayer schools us in intercession for the family's needs: "Our Father . . . give us . . . forgive us . . . lead us . . . deliver us."

V. So we need faith in Christ, confidence and hope in God, a purpose of obedience, and concern for fellow Christians if we are to say "our Father" with true meaning.—J. I. Packer.

### June 26. How to Get Rid of Painful Memories

TEXT: Phil. 3:13–14.

I. Forgive yourself of that which has hold of your memory. If it's nagging you, most likely it's something you wish you could live over so you could change it. You can't. It's behind you. So forgive yourself and start over.

II. Get busy doing God's work. If you have time to brood, then this memory will come back strongly. Take away that chance. Fill your waking hours with efforts for God and by his inspiration be a living channel for him to reach others. Work, think, sacrifice, serve in his name. Drive out the memory with fatiguing work.

III. Practice the continual art of forgiving others. It is an art, you know. It's that quick spirit of love that says "I forgive" before the mind has a chance to think of some advantage that might be gained by holding back the forgiveness. It's that grace of God coming through human relationships to grant the immediate forgiveness that Christ granted us. When asked, forgive.

IV. Become an overt soul-winner for Christ. No matter what other work you do for him, take on the regular burden of speaking to people about their souls.

Let others know that you're ready any time to pray with them, counsel them, and help them find the answers to their soul's problems. Be a representative for God and "an ambassador for Christ."— Dan Harman.

### July 3. What Is Freedom? (Independence Sunday)

TEXT: Jas. 2:12.

I. Freedom is the source of all that is best and worst in man.

II. Freedom is subject to limits in order to safeguard the freedom of others.

III. Freedom is the basic condition for the growth of knowledge, culture, religion, and whatever else elevates and liberates man.

IV. Freedom increases human dignity when it is based on intelligence and aims at the good of another and not exclusively of self.

V. Freedom can be suppressed as effectively by mob rule as by dictatorship.

VI. Freedom is better served by sacrifice than by self-indulgence.

VII. Freedom calls upon those in authority to give the "benefit of the doubt" to those who would use it.

VIII. Freedom is from God. Its responsible use can exasperate, fatigue, and gratify, but no one who savors the values of the human spirit would forego its splendid challenge for a life of undisturbed ease.—Richard Armstrong.

### July 10. Doubt and Unbelief

TEXT: Mark 9:24.

Christ never failed to distinguish between doubt and unbelief.

I. Doubt is can't believe; unbelief is won't believe.

II. Doubt is honesty; unbelief is obstinacy.

III. Doubt is looking for light; unbelief is content with darkness.—Henry Drummond.

### July 17. The Challenge of Jeremiah

SCRIPTURE: Jer. 1:1–10; 37:1–38:28.

I. Jeremiah felt a deep sense of direction from God. Do you?

II. Jeremiah wanted God to speak through him. Do you?

III. Jeremiah listened to God's plan for his life. Do you?

IV. Jeremiah was ready to speak the advice of the Lord, even though it didn't please the people. Do you speak and live as Christ wants or do you give in to popular opinions?

V. Jeremiah didn't hesitate to talk to leaders wherever they served. Do you take the easy path and leave the popular government leaders and religious leaders alone?

VI. Jeremiah didn't let punishment for service to God shut him up. Do you avoid Christian service for fear you might be unpopular or misunderstood?

VII. Jeremiah went on "telling forth" the unusual message of God. Are you determined to tell the unusual message of God—the truth as revealed in his Son Christ Jesus? The truth of Christ is strange to the world, but it is life, the only life, both now and for eternity.

VIII. Jeremiah's warnings of the results of disobedience are found in Jer. 39. Is there a warning here for you? Only you and God know all your sins. —Danny E. Bush.

### July 24. How God Heals
TEXT: Luke 5:17.

I. Through physicians and surgeons and the wonderful means of medical science God heals. Dr. Walter Bradford Cannon, a noted physiologist, writes, "All the healing forces are laid up in the body ready to go into operation when needed."

II. God's healing grace comes through mental suggestions. The mind has a great influence over the body.

III. God brings healing when we surrender "our fears, resentments, self-preoccupation, and guilt which produces disease."

IV. God heals by the direct touch of his spirit upon our bodies.

V. His final cure is the resurrection when our mortal bodies put on immortality. When our infirmities are not healed we need to remember that God will give us the grace and power to use them. That often requires even more grace than does healing.—E. Stanley Jones.

### July 31. Christian Faith and Christian Action (Transfiguration Sunday)
TEXT: Luke 9:43.

I. This is the way Jesus ministered among the people the day after he had experienced the transfiguration, one of the most mysterious moments of his life.

(a) The transfiguration cannot be explained; it can only be sensed. There on the mountain Jesus, accompanied by three disciples, had retired to pray. As he prayed his whole appearance changed. He seemed to glow with a strange light as he conversed with Moses and Elijah, who, long dead, appeared "in glory," as the scripture describes them.

(b) The very next day, as they were coming down from the mountain, they were met by a large crowd. Out of the crowd rushed a man, demanding that Jesus heal his epileptic son.

II. The glory of the transfiguration and the miserable demands of the crowd —only within the Christian understanding of God is such a contrast tenable.

(a) There are religious people who see God only in the quiet, refined surroundings of tranquillity and peace. To them the transfiguration by itself is a symbol of all that is holy. Where there is peace, there is God.

(b) There are others who find the ultimate good in the midst of people where need is fulfilled. Where wounds are assuaged, where want is satisfied, there is God.

(c) I would suggest that Christ stands in the midst of both worlds, worlds of peace and confusion, and reconciles them in his love. His cross draws together the dirt and suffering and death of this world's experience and the peace that comes only from above—and we have new life in him.

III. Christians often deny themselves the blessing of entering into this new life in Christ because like many other religious people they pull these two experiences apart. Some Christians say that life in Christ is a life of prayer; others say it is a life of faithful service.

(a) Membership in the Christian fellowship implies that we seek to be at home in both worlds, not that we attempt to walk astride both in impossible tension. We must beware of separating Sunday, the Lord's Day, as we call it, from the rest of the week, as if the other six were not his. Rather in our life there must be a melding, a bringing together of our total experience and total dedication.

(b) We are a fellowship that is committed to do all things in the name of God, whether it is our work, our play, our leisure, our worship. As children of God we live in God's world, and we live in order to reflect our creator both in our persons and in society. Prayer and social action must not be an either/or proposition. Nor are they greater and lesser good. Together they are the means by which God's grace flows into the life of the world.—John M. Burgess.

## August 7. A Sacrifice and a Shrine

TEXT: Luke 21:3–4.

Archibald Rutledge said, "Wherever there is a sacrifice there is also a shrine."

I. Wherever we make an unselfish sacrifice we build a shrine in our own souls.

II. Wherever we make a sacrifice we build a shrine in the souls of others.

III. Wherever there is a sacrifice we build a shrine in society.

## August 14. The Remnant

TEXT: Matt. 7:14 (NASB).

I. That text is discouraging! We want crowds for we measure success by numbers. If "everybody's doing it" we must get with it. The hard fact is, as scripture says, the broad road leads to destruction and many travel it.

II. Jesus never put much faith in crowds even though one of his temptations was to do so. He put faith in twelve men and trusted the future to those few. When almost everyone left him except the twelve, he asked, "Will you also go away?"

III. It is simply amazing what just one person can do when led by God: William Carey in modern mission, William Wilberforce against human slavery, Martin Luther in church reformation, Frances Willard for temperance, John Howard in prison reform, Robert Raikes in the Sunday school movement, and Florence Nightingale in nursing. God has always used "the remnant," and he continues to do so today.—Leonard Campbell in The Upper Room.

## August 21. The Joys of the Ministry

I. The joy of dialogue. Dialogue is being in touch with another human being. It is listening and talking and sharing with another the trivialities and extraordinary happenings of our lives. Few people have such a unique opportunity to share in dialogue as the minister. The parish minister is in dialogue with people as a preacher, a counselor, and a teacher.

II. The joy of caring. Most ministers enter the ministry because they care about people and because they know that God cares about people. Caring is not exclusive to the ministry, but the clergyman has a rather unique opportunity to be present with people not only in the everyday events of life but also at the crucial moments of human existence.

III. The joy of tradition. I know of no title that I deem more honorable than that of minister of the church of Jesus Christ. It is not fair to compare vocations. In the sight of God each man's labor is as worthy as the next, but I take pride in the heritage of my calling. I am part of the lineage of men whose lives have determined the course of history. It is a humbling realization for a minister to reflect on the succession in which he stands.—Russell Crossley.

## August 28. Pioneers

TEXT: Heb. 12:1–2 (MOFFATT).

I. If we are to pioneer with Jesus in

a new age and in an ever-changing environment, we will need not only faith in him but also his pioneering spirit. For from him we learn that pioneering is more than cutting down primitive forest. It is a quality of spirit essential in dealing with life.

II. Jesus described the citizen of the kingdom as one who was able to bring out of his treasures things both old and new. The pioneer must be able to find new solutions in new circumstances. He learns to prefer new answers and attitudes if they are better suited to new situations. Good pioneers learn to combine the wisdom and experience of the past with a willingness to discover new insights and understandings.

III. The pioneer in the faith, like Jesus, learns to choose and to prefer what will best serve the cause of Christ in new and changing experiences. Jesus does not ask us to forsake the faith of our fathers. He does ask us to pioneer with him in making it a living faith which motivates and gives direction to life. By his own definition he came that people might have more abundant life —life in all its fullness.

IV. The pioneer must prepare for those who will come after. We have the assurance of Jesus that he is the way, the truth, and the life. What better legacy can we leave than to make provision that he will be known by the rising generation, those who will come after our own?

V. Pioneering with Jesus keeps us aware that our God is not too small to span barriers of race, class, color, sex, and income. There are abundant signs that churches are increasingly ready to pioneer with one another in preparing for a better world ahead without claiming that Jesus is a private, exclusive possession of any one of them.

VI. You and I are meant to be joyful pioneers. Jesus did what he did "for the joy that was set before him."

VII. Keeping our eyes on him, we are reminded that his pioneering and ours does not end with life on this earth. For he is the pioneer who passed through the gates of death and returned victorious with news of the continuing life beyond.—William W. Davis.

## September 4. The I.Q. of a Christian
TEXT: Jas. 3:17.

The *interior quality* or I.Q. distinguishes a Christian as "sterling" distinguishes silver.

I. The I.Q. of a Christian is marked by *a sensitivity to a higher righteousness*. The higher righteousness always tries to reproduce the spirit of a law; the lower righteousness is satisfied with its letter. The Old Testament rule was that the worshiper was to bring a tenth of his income as his offering. Surely no one should imagine that anything less than that is required of a Christian. But let us not imagine that mechanically to set aside one-tenth of our income for the Lord and then be stingy and narrow and selfish with the rest meets the higher righteousness when it means "one-tenth is his; nine-tenths is mine." The higher righteousness says: "It's all his. I'm only a steward of it."

II. The I.Q. of a Christian is marked by *private prayer and personal devotion*. The interior quality of a Christian is marked by a pattern of regular, personal, and private communion with the Father in fair weather as well as foul and without ostentatiousness or those vain repetitious and well-worn phrases that many use.

III. The I.Q. of a Christian is revealed by *ethical obedience to God*. Ethical obedience is the place where all may begin in the Christian life and beyond which none can go. It means obedience in all of life's relationships.—Raymond E. Balcomb.

## September 11. Believing in Love
TEXT: Song of Solomon 8:7.

I. I believe in love in its most earthy pleasures. If God made man and woman to cleave one to the other and planted in them a primitive urge to give themselves one to the other, he must have meant it to be good. Certainly he sanctified it above all physical acts and made it the means whereby new life was born.

II. I believe in the love of things. The good Lord must have loved things because he made so many things, even good juicy steaks. When he placed man among things and made him dependent upon things, he must have dropped in him a little bit of his own love of things. Were it not for his love of things man might still be wallowing in the midst of primeval mud. But instead man shares in the divine urge to create. Look at him in his basement workshop hammering, sawing, painting, calling to his wife to see his creation, and proudly putting it out where all can see while his wife primps and patches and sews and irons and comes forth with a creation on Easter Sunday like the queen of heaven entering into the court of all saints.

III. I believe in an intellectual love. You find it in the mental curiosity of research, in the boy looking for a particular kind of round, red pebble on the seashore, in the scientist looking for the neutron, in the military intelligence officer seeking to understand the enemy, in the man who reads a murder mystery or prays to understand the will of God. Is the satisfaction more self-fulfilling than that of a seeker after the truth who has grasped a bit of the universe and knows he knows and knowing it loves the knowledge and the source of all wisdom—God?

IV. I believe in spiritual love, which is purely and simply a relationship devoid of the motive of reward or punishment and based upon the affinity of the divine for the divine, whether it be the divine affinity of two souls in a community of saints or the response of the spark in our human clod which lightens up in the presence of the Light of the world. This love is not based upon anything we get or anything we give; it just is. I believe in Original Love.—Ensworth Reisner.

## September 18. The Exclusiveness of the Kingdom

TEXT: Matt. 7:14.

Jesus was observing fact, not stating his desire, when he said, "The gate is narrow and the way is hard, that leads to life, and those who find it are few." There is a certain inevitable exclusiveness about the kingdom of God. It is perhaps the most exclusive society of all! The exclusiveness of the kingdom of God belongs to us and not to God. From the point of view of God's desire, the kingdom is intended to be inclusive. The invitation is open to all, but the response is such that only a few find it. Why is this?

I. Life in the kingdom calls for choice. As creatures who are made in the image of God we possess the freedom of choice. If we are to live in the kingdom we must choose to live in the kingdom. We must choose initially, and we must choose repeatedly. This is a law of life.

II. Life in the kingdom calls for commitment. It doesn't require much of a man to be a Christian, but it does require all there is of him. Lack of that kind of commitment in nominal Christians accounts for the contemporary recession of Christian influence. God will not do our work for us. Our pious prattle will not substitute for costly commitment.

III. Life in the kingdom calls for courage. When one enters the kingdom of God he then lives in two worlds. As Jesus said, "You are in the world but not of the world." This kind of bi-worldly existence produces an inevitable loneliness which requires strong courage. It is the courage required of a Christian merchant who refuses to operate his business on all seven days of the week. It is the courage required of the Christian young person who refuses to follow the crowd when all his friends worship popularity. It is the courage required of a Christian mother who refuses to turn her home into a cheap night club or to live in shallowness all her days. It is the courage required when our trust is placed in God, not in money or status or people.—John W. Meister.

**September 25. What Makes a Church Great?**

I. *Great in spirit.* When its warmth of fellowship is apparent to all who worship there, it possesses a warmth which blesses all who come.

II. *Great in love.* Its love abounds toward Christ and toward sinners. The members love one another with deathless devotion.

III. *Great in compassion.* Its heart reaches out to suffer with those who need its ministry. Only by having a compassion of heart can a church be great. As one has well said, "A passionless church is a passing church."

IV. *Great in consecration.* It withdraws itself from the world with its fashions and its fads; its members live a consecrated life; it has no place for worldliness and for human aspirations.

V. *Great in loyalty.* It is loyal to Christ. It is loyal to his Word. It is loyal to "the faith once delivered unto the saints." Its members are loyal to the Lord and to his church by their dedication of time, of talents, and of treasure.
—J. D. Grey.

**October 2. Feed My Sheep (World Communion Sunday)**

Scripture: Ezek. 34:2–3; John 21:15–19.

I. The struggle for food is not new. The Bible records one famine after another. Almost every generation has experienced some degree of famine. Following World War II mankind felt that at last the battle against hunger was being won. In the '50s and '60s we saw bumper harvests in many nations. All this optimism turned to despair as the '70s have become a decade of mass hunger and starvation.

II. Intellectually we know the situation is real, but in our hearts it is not so real. Intellectually we read God's Word through the prophet Ezekiel, in the gospel of John, and the other writings of the Bible, but does the message become real? How can we comprehend the world hunger situation and believe on Jesus Christ and obey his commands if we continue to live our self-centered and wasteful ways? What are we saying about his Word if we continue to overeat and then buy diet pills and dietary foods?

III. We are called to "feed my sheep." How do we respond to the feeble cries for help? We need to respond to their need with food in one hand and the Bible in the other. "Feed my sheep" includes both the physical sense and the spiritual sense. Most of the starvation today is centered in the non-Christian nations. We must give them physical nourishment for their bodies and spiritual food for their souls. We can no longer accept exclusive attitudes of self-righteousness.

IV. If we are the "elect" in God's universe, it is because he has chosen us to serve. The time has come when all Christians must take their commitment to Jesus Christ and his command seriously. Let us unite in common concern and effort to provide both the physical and spiritual nourishment desperately needed by at least one-third of the world's population. We need constantly to remind ourselves that "we are our brother's keeper." We can no longer be passive and indifferent to the needs of others.—H. Richard McClain.

**October 9. Living in Christ**

Text: Phil. 1:21.

I. Living in Christ means understanding who Satan is and believing that the message of scripture about Satan is meant to be taken seriously and at face value.

II. Living in Christ means that we consciously build one another up in the faith. Christians are expected to strengthen, counsel, and pray for one another.

III. Living in Christ means sharing Christ. The church as the body of believers is equipped to do this. Christians should be past caring about their own well-being. They obey, because a disciple always obeys his master and because of an overwhelming desire to share with another valuable human being the life-giving love of Jesus.

IV. Living in Christ means worshiping through a total yielding of ourselves to him. Worship goes beyond lip service on Sunday mornings. It includes the daily awareness of God in our lives and listening to him through prayer and scripture.

V. Living in Christ keeps the Christian from being afraid. Satan will work on Christians, just as he worked on Jesus. But the surrounding strength of Christ is the armor of God and cannot be overcome. The Christian church at this moment in history has a magnificent opportunity to teach, to love, to heal, and to liberate those who have been caught in the forces controlled by Satan. —Roger C. Palms. Adapted from *The Christian and the Occult.* Reprinted by permission of Judson Press.

### October 16. Witnessing Laymen Make Living Churches (Laity Sunday)

I. *Be a witness.* Tell of ongoing encounter with the living God. Share the joy of Christ through your life.

II. *Be an evangelist.* Tell of the mighty acts of God in the lives of people. Have a loving concern for others and invite them into the church.

III. *Be a shepherd.* Minister to the needs of committed church members. Seek to restore all those who have begun to stray.

IV. *Be a teacher.* Help train those in the household of faith. Christian knowledge is essential for enduring faithfulness.—Kermit Long.

### October 23. The Fairness of God

Text: Heb. 6:10 (tev).

The God we worship and serve is not an unfair, unrighteous (kjv), or unjust (rsv) God. One evidence that he is not unfair is the fact that he will not forget. Three things are suggested in this text that he will remember.

I. He will not forget or overlook (rsv) the *work* we do. Others may overlook it but not God. Ours may be a big

job or a little one. Whether big or little, he will not overlook what we do. Anything we do for him and for our fellowman in his name is never forgotten or overlooked. If faithful we receive his commendation at the end of the journey, and his "well done" should be sufficient reward.

II. He will not forget or overlook the *love* we show for him or for our fellowman in his name. When we came into union with the resurrected Christ we were brought into union with *agape* or love. "God is *agape*" (I John 4:8, 16). His love should reach out through us to all kinds of men and women. God will not forget or overlook any expression through us of his love for those about us.

III. God will not forget or overlook the *help* we give or have given to fellow Christians and, we could add, to any person who is in need. Such help is a product of our love for them. This love for them in turn is a product of his love for us and for them. He wants to love fellow believers and all men through us.—T. B. Maston.

### October 30. Words! Words! Words! (Reformation Sunday)

I. The Word of the Lord filled Jeremiah. (a) God called Jeremiah through his Word (Jer. 1:4–5)—calling words.

(b) God's Word broke down Jeremiah's excuse (v. 7–8)—vain words.

(c) God spoke through Jeremiah with power (v. 9–10)—powerful words.

II. Jesus fulfilled (filled full) the words of scripture. (a) God promised a Savior through his Word (Luke 4:18–19)—calling words.

(b) Many make excuses for not believing the promises of God's Word (v. 24–29)—vain words.

(c) Jesus is the Word which was promised. He gives it body (v. 21)—powerful words.

III. We must be filled with the Word of God. (a) God's Word calls us to exercise love in all things (I Cor. 12:31)—calling words.

(b) Without love our words are noisy gongs and clanging cymbals (I Cor. 13:1–3)—vain words.

(c) God's Word communicated in love changes loves (v. 4–13)—powerful words. —Donald R. Haase.

## November 6. Alcohol in and out of Church (World Temperance Day)

SCRIPTURE: Rom. 14:10–21 (NEB).

In Romans 14 Paul gives some timeless principles of Christian conduct which apply to the consumption of beverage alcohol.

I. He said, "Don't judge." This is sound because only God can judge aright. Since we must all face the judgment and answer to God for ourselves, we are not to judge our neighbor who drinks or does not drink.

II. Paul admonishes us to be considerate of our weaker brother. We dare not become a stumbling block, a hindrance to faith, a *skandolon* to him. We are to encourage and build him up. This may call for refraining from practices which would weaken or ruin his faith. Paul wrote, "It is right not to eat meat or drink wine or do anything that makes your brother stumble" (v. 21).

III. Another Pauline principle is the sacred nature of our bodies. We are told that they are the temple of God's spirit which lives in us. Scripture warns, "If anyone destroys God's temple, God will destroy him" (I Cor. 3:17). Modern medicine has taught us the harm that drinking does to the brain, our reflexes, and our inhibitions. Overwork, overeating, lack of exercise, inadequate sleep, and drinking alcohol can hurt the body and constitute a sin against its Maker. We are to take care of our bodies. Abstaining from beverage alcohol is part of that discipline.

IV. A fourth biblical principle is self-control. The Christian is not to be a slave to anything or anyone less than Christ. He will not be enslaved by any habit. We all know that a man often begins by taking a drink and ends by having drink take him. The Christian duty is self-restraint. We are free to abstain.—Alton H. McEachern.

## November 13. Paul's Formula for Giving (Stewardship Day)

I. For a Christian to give is nothing less than an obligation. (See Rom. 15:27; Gal. 2:10.)

II. Even if the gift be handed to an official of the church, it is nonetheless given to God. (See II Cor. 8:5.)

III. The pattern and example of giving is Jesus himself, who, though he was rich, for our sakes became poor. (See II Cor. 8:9.)

IV. In such giving two things happen: (a) Our love is turned into action and stops being mere words. (See II Cor. 8:8.)

(b) The unity of the church is demonstrated in which it is impossible for some to have too much while others have too little. (See II Cor. 8:10–15.)

V. Giving should be regular. (See I Cor. 16:1–2.)

VI. It should be proportionate to a person's resources to help those who have nothing. (See I Cor. 16:1–2; II Cor. 8:12–15.) There is no credit in making oneself destitute; and there should be no pleasure in leaving oneself in luxury.

VII. It should be willing and joyous. It must not be given as an extortion. God loves a cheerful giver. (See II Cor. 9:6–11.)

VIII. It must be universal and not left to the few.

IX. Any gift to the poor is a thanksgiving to God. (See II Cor. 9:12.) No one can show gratitude to God better than by helping others.

X. The sight of such generosity and responsibility for others is a powerful commendation of Christianity and brings glory to God. (See II Cor. 9:13–15.)

XI. Paul makes careful arrangements for the administration of the fund. (See II Cor. 8:16–24.) There must be no room for any suggestion of dishonesty.

XII. Arrangements are made to have the gift delivered personally. (See II Cor. 8:22–24.) If possible the giving must be person to person.—William Barclay.

## November 20. The Best Kind of Living (Thanksgiving Sunday)

TEXT: I Cor. 14:17 (PHILLIPS).

I. Thanksgiving helps to make the best kind of living because an appreciative person is one who is glad for everything God gives.

II. Thanksgiving, not once a year but daily, makes for the best kind of living because each day brings something new to acknowledge with thanks.

III. Thanksgiving is the best kind of living because it places us in the best of company: the poets who wrote our psalms of praise, the companions of the Spirit who showed forth God's praise with their lips and in their lives, and Jesus who in his sacrament of love first gave thanks.—David A. MacLennan.

## November 27. The Salvation Christ Brings (Advent)

SCRIPTURE: Rom. 13:11–14.

Advent is our reminder that Jesus Christ, Son of God, is the firstborn of all creation. He is the Savior. He is kindness and salvation. The Son of God came on earth and entered human history to renew the world from within and to be for the world an abiding source of supernatural life.

I. Christ saves us from living our lives according to the lowest denominators of existence.

II. Christ saves us from our own dark follies: a lifetime of swords and spears and training for war.

III. Christ saves us from a lifetime of darkness: lust and quarreling and jealousy.

IV. Christ saves us from the merely pragmatic life: we are to be instructed in Christ's ways and walk in Christ's paths.—*Dimension*.

## December 4. Advent Penitence (Advent)

TEXT: Luke 3:8.

I. Christmas is and, I hope, will be this year a time of penitence of *metanoia*.

II. A time when we test our lives and the life of our societies by the incarnate life of Christ.

III. A time when we realize that only a radical change in our minds and attitudes and so of our styles of living and of our economic, political, racist, and sexist structures will enable us to face our present threats to survival.

IV. A time when we remember with Dietrich Bonhoeffer in the midst of his doomed existence in the prison of tyranny: "It is not some religious act which makes a Christian what he is but participation in the suffering of God in the life of the world. This is *metanoia*."

V. A time when in penitence we confidently turn away from the fear of threats to survival to the joy of living with and for others in the freedom and unity which Christ brought and brings at Christmastide.—Philip A. Potter.

## December 11. What Is the Spirit of Christmas? (Advent)

TEXT: Luke 2:14.

I. It is the spirit of song. Christmas is a festival of song and a time when Christendom praises God.

II. It is the spirit of youth and a time when we become young again.

III. It is the spirit of playtime when we lay aside the more sordid things, our worries and cares, and play.

IV. It is the spirit of giving and a time when it is more blessed to give than to receive.

V. It is the spirit of love and a time when the love of God and the love of our fellowman prevail over all hatred and bitterness and when our thoughts and deeds and the spirit of our lives manifest the presence of God.—George F. McDougall.

## December 18. Christmas Is for Loving (Advent)

TEXT: I John 4:16.

I. Christmas provides us with the medicine of love. Christmas is for loving! It is a spring from which joy flows, and anyone can drink from that spring. It all started with God's love for us.

The loving still goes on, and whether you are alone at Christmas or not, God is with you. He loves you and me. That's the initiative taken by a loving God at Christmas.

II. There is the human response. Christmas is for loving him. The beauty of the manger scene moves us to reenact it in pageantry and song. The Christmas carols are our love songs addressed to God the Father who has so loved us in Jesus.

III. Christmas is for loving others. And we love especially the needy, whoever they are. And here love is blind. It doesn't calculate; it doesn't ask too many questions. All it wants to know is if there is genuine need.—Thomas A. Whiting.

### December 25. The Gifts We Give (Christmas)

TEXT: Matt. 7:11.

I. We give gifts from the heart when we give love, joy, understanding, appreciation, tolerance, and above all the joy of being alive.

II. We give gifts of the mind when we give ideas, truth, dreams, poetry, words of understanding and love.

III. We give gifts of the spirit when we give the gifts of prayer, aspiration, peace, and faith.

IV. We give the gift of ourselves when we give the words of joy, laughter, inspiration, encouragement, and guidance.

V. We make a gift to the community when we have the gift of a good personality, a worthy self.—Frank A. Court.

# SECTION III. Resources for Communion Services

## SERMON SUGGESTIONS

**Topic: Let's Celebrate!**
TEXT: Rev. 14:6–7.

I. Let's celebrate and give glory to God that he gave us Christ.

II. Let's celebrate the glory of God's love which Christ embodied and which finds strange and life-changing focus in the death of Jesus on the cross.

III. Let's celebrate our forgiveness.

IV. Let's celebrate the tremendous fact that we are "members of the mystical body of thy Son, the blessed company of all faithful people and heirs of thine everlasting kingdom."

V. Let's celebrate the fact that because of God's grace we have passed from death into life.—David A. MacLennan.

**Topic: The Table Fellowship**
SCRIPTURE: Mark 14:22–26.

I. As Christians we live between two great feasts. We look back to the Lord's Supper in the upper room. We look forward to the marriage supper of the lamb in heaven. We look back in faith. We look forward in hope. All the eating and drinking we do between the two ought to be motivated by his love for us and as a manifestation of our love for him. As Christians all eating and drinking can be with Jesus and ought to be done in faith, hope, and love.

II. If we take seriously the fact that all our eating and drinking should be done for the glory of God, that Jesus Christ is the unseen guest at every meal, and that it is by his grace we are provided day by day our daily bread, we will find two things happening to us.

(a) Our common meals will take on the overtones of a sacramental experience in terms of person-to-person relationships.

(b) Our sacramental meal, the Lord's Supper, will take on the overtones of responsible service to be rendered in a secular society, simply because we are God's people, committed and consecrated to doing his will in all of life.

III. Here we are with Jesus in the upper room. He is the host. We are the guests. The table fellowship reaches its climax when he lifts his eyes to heaven and gives thanks: "Blessed art thou, O Lord our God, King of the universe, who bringest forth bread from the earth. Amen." Then he breaks the bread, saying, "This is my body broken for you . . . and this cup is the new covenant in my blood shed for you." From his hands we receive the bread. From his hands we receive the cup.

IV. When you take these elements what do they mean to you? What difference does the sacrament of Holy Communion make in your life? Suppose you had decided to sleep this morning and missed this observance of the Lord's Supper. Would there be something missing in your life? Or to approach it more positively, you are here and in a few moments we will eat and drink together. What will be yours that would not have been yours had you not been here? Who is to say that eating and drinking with Jesus and his disciples must mean this or must mean that and no more or no less? Who is to say that the Lord's Supper must mean the same thing each time you partake?

V. To save the table fellowship from being dead liturgy or vain repetition, there are three things you must do.

(a) You must come in a spirit of repentance. Sin short-circuits contact with the God of all grace. "If I regard iniquity in my heart, the Lord will not hear me" (Ps. 66:18).

(b) You must come in faith. "Without faith it is impossible to please him. For whoever would draw near to God must believe that he exists and that he rewards those who seek him" (Heb. 11:6).

(c) You must come expectantly. "Blessed are those who hunger and thirst for righteousness, for they shall be satisfied" (Matt. 5:6).

VI. What the Lord's Supper will mean to you will depend on the clarity with which you define your need. Shift your mind into neutral and nothing will happen. There is nothing magical about the elements themselves. If you are honest with yourself and you say, "Dear God, this is where I am, and this is where I need help," then you will not go away disappointed.—Walter L. Dosch.

## Topic: The Dimensions of Communion
TEXT: Luke 22:19.

I. The look *backward* that is a time of remembering Jesus Christ.

II. The look *inward* that release may come to you through confession and forgiveness.

III. The look *upward* for communion and fellowship with the living Christ.

IV. The look *outward* to find oneness with your fellowman.

V. The look *forward* for confidence and hope for the future.—Robert P. Bunch.

## Topic: The True Nature of the Lord's Supper

I. The Lord's Supper is a divine institution and not a human device. It is the Christ's appointment to meet his people every first day of the week. Jesus said just before his death, "I will not drink henceforth of this fruit of the vine, until that day when I drink it new with you in my Father's kingdom" (Matt. 26:29). Today in the kingdom, which is the church on earth, he meets with us about his table of remembrance.

II. The Lord's Supper is a social institution. "For as often as ye eat this bread, and drink this cup, ye do shew the Lord's death till he come." In other words this is not simply an individual observance; it involves the entire church. Therefore, we have the exhortation found in Heb. 10:25: "Not forsaking the assembling of ourselves together, as the manner of some is; but exhorting one another: and so much the more, as ye see the day approaching." What more impressive sight is there than to observe a great host of people in meditation and worship as they participate in the simple but scriptural memorial of the Lord on each Lord's Day?

III. The Lord's Supper is a symbolic participation in the death of Christ. "The cup of blessing which ye bless, is it not the communion of the blood of Christ? The bread which we break, is it not the body of Christ?" (I Cor. 10:16.) In the act of Communion, obedient men and women are related to the death of their Lord, the death that he chose in order to liberate them from their sins. Our meeting with Christ at his table becomes a pledge of our faithfulness to him.

IV. The Lord's Supper confirms the new covenant in Christ. "This cup is the new testament in my blood: this do ye, as oft as you drink it, in remembrance of me." The Christian is in a covenant relationship with Jesus. The covenant has been confirmed and ratified by the blood of Christ; hence it can never be made void. For this reason the Christian does not live a speculative and uncertain life.

V. The Lord's Supper is a proclamation. "For as often as ye eat this bread, and drink this cup, ye do shew the Lord's death till he come." This means that as we gather about the table of remembrance we say to the world, "Christ died for our sins according to the scriptures." And if one absents himself from the table of memory, his sermon remains undelivered. "For he that eateth and drinketh unworthily, eateth and drinketh damnation to himself, not discerning the Lord's body. For this cause many are weak and sickly among you, and many sleep" (I Cor. 11:29–30). —Ard Hoven in *The Lookout*.

### Meditation: How Zacchaeus Remembered Christ

There is a legend about Zacchaeus which says that when he was old and still living in Jericho, he left his house every morning at dawn. After a bit he returned in a calm and entirely happy frame of mind. This routine never varied, and the result never failed. His wife wondered about it, and one day stole after him. She saw him go straight to the sycamore tree in which he sat the first day he saw the Lord. Once there he took a jar, filled it with water, and carried it to the tree. After working the soil and pulling out a few weeds, he watered the roots of that tree. Then he went back home and from his home went out to serve both God and man.

This legend of Zacchaeus reveals that he worked hard to keep certain precious memories alive and refreshed. He used a little ceremony to strengthen his life before going out to strengthen other lives. The result was that it made a difference in his own spirit, in his relationships, and in his daily life.

Communion, the taking of the bread and the cup in remembrance of Jesus, is much like that experience of Zacchaeus. It is our opportunity to renew certain precious memories. It is a simple ceremony which has the effect of strengthening our lives in order that we might strengthen others. It makes a difference, if we allow it, in our own spirits, our relationships, and our daily walk. Frequency of participation is important, for a cumulative effort is realized. The Lord's Supper in which we share is one essential component for growth in the Christian life.—John H. Townsend.

### Topic: Around the World in Sixty Minutes

Text: Matt. 24:14.

In a service of Christian worship we move in imagination and concern around the world within the hour usually devoted to our chief business as children of God. This is brought home to us vividly in the central service of Christian worship, the Lord's Supper.

I. At the Lord's table we are linked with persons of all races, cultures, and nations who confess that Jesus Christ is Lord.

II. In praise and prayer we encompass humanity through our intercessions.

III. In worship we are united to participate in the world mission of the gospel.

IV. At the Lord's table we remember that, while Christ died for us as individuals, he died for all, and we return to our homes and vocations as world citizens, inclusive and world-minded in our love.—David A. MacLennan.

### Meditation: Does Anyone Care?

In some way or other, in either an articulate way or an unspoken way, all of us ask: "Does anybody really care about me? My friends have done their bit, and my family has shown me their love and affection. But does anything at the heart of things care whether I live or die, or am happy or unhappy, or make the most of life or a mess of life? Does anybody care?" Then the words of Jesus come to us, "This is my body which is given for you," and we take it in our hands and we feel it, and somehow or other we know that somebody cares that much. Some ask the question, "Can my sins ever be blotted out?" No matter how sophisticated we may be and no matter how conditioned we may be to the idea of sin as a part of human nature, nevertheless we do not like our sins and we are not proud of them. And there comes a time in everyone's life when he says, "Can these mistakes that I see so plainly now, these wrongs and these sins, can anything be done to offset them in the balance of life?" And the words come, "My blood was shed for the remission of your sins." Don't ask how. The mystery of one man's sacrifice somehow outweighing the balance of all men's sins is not for our analysis. When we hear the words and see the cup and drink the wine, somehow or other we have the assurance that our sins are forgiven.—Theodore P. Ferris.

## ILLUSTRATIONS

DIVINE DEPTH. A symbol has divine depth in the sense that it refers to a multiple aspect of reality. It is a vehicle which carries past and present making; it is both form and content, a thing and a sign; it binds the world of things to the world of man's innermost consciousness, and does it by way of an external reference. A symbol is like everything else in the universe—it points beyond itself. The great symbols of tradition are not arbitrary or accidental. They are profoundly embedded in the divine depth of life where man and God meet. —Samuel H. Miller.

EXPECTANCY. A. E. W. Mason says of Francis Drake that he always looked out on life as though he expected doors to be open before him through which he would pass to magic realms and great experiences. That being so we are not surprised to learn that of magic realms and great experiences he knew more than most. It is that spirit of expectancy that matters in spiritual things as in everything else. And we do well to remind ourselves that in other lives, if not in ours, miracles akin to those wrought while our Lord was in the flesh continue to be wrought and that some who sat where we sit were delivered from their weaknesses, strengthened to bear their burdens, and received a vision of the service they might render. It all happened where we now are and during the experience which we are sharing today. And it happened to them because they came believing that, whoever else would be there, Jesus would be there.—Roderick Bethune.

INSTRUCTIONS. They that receive the Lord's Supper are, before they come, to prepare themselves thereunto by examining themselves of their being in Christ; of their sins and wants; of the truth and measures of their knowledge, faith, repentance, love of God and the brethren, charity to all men, forgiving those that have done them wrong; of their desires after Christ; of their new obedience; and by renewing the exercise of these graces by serious meditation and fervent prayer. During the time of receiving the Supper they are with holy reverence and attention to wait upon God, heedfully to discern the Lord's body, affectionately to meditate on his death and sufferings, hungering and thirsting after Christ, feeding on him by faith, receiving of his fullness, trusting in his merits, rejoicing in his love, giving thanks for his grace, renewing their covenant with God and their love to all the saints.—Martin Luther in *The Larger Catechism*.

ONENESS IN CHRIST. Jesus brought into the world a whole new idea of oneness. The world into which he was born was falling apart into broken and brittle groups, each seeking some advantage at the expense of the other. He did not separate people with the barbed-wire entanglements of political, religious, racial, or economic frontiers. In Christ there is neither Jew nor Gentile, bond nor free. Titian gives him the likeness of an Arab; Tintoretto paints him as an Italian; Murillo presents him as a Spaniard; Rubens gives him the physiognomy of a peasant of Flanders Field, but he is the same in them all. He is a Greek in

Antioch; he is a Latin in Rome; he is a Slav in Moscow; he is an Anglo-Saxon in Washington, but he is the same to them all. To Dante he was a redeemer; to Tennyson he was a revealer of immortality; to Francis Thompson he was the Hound of Heaven; to Lincoln he was a lover of the lowly.—Joseph R. Sizoo.

ENABLEMENT. Because there are days in the experience of us all when things have gone wrong and we have known defeat and are feeling utterly depressed; days when, seeing in Christ what we might have been, we are sick at heart because of what we are; when we are so conscious of failure, of the sorry tragic mess in which we have landed ourselves, and of our grieving of the holy and loving Spirit of God that we doubt whether we can ever be forgiven or whether there can ever now be any restoration of the years that the locust hath eaten—because of that we need this great heartening trumpet-note to come breaking across the confusion of our souls: "He is able to save to the uttermost!" It is the word of the Lord, and it is here in the sacrament for you. Blessed be his glorious name.—James S. Stewart.

## PRAYERS

DRAW NIGH TO US. Almighty God, seen by the pure in heart, known by the childlike spirit, and near to those who come in desperate need: draw nigh to us as we approach thy mercy seat that, hearing thy voice and seeing thy face, we may be inspired by a sense of thy living presence.

We come conscious of the gulf that separates our foolish ways from thy holy purposes. Created with souls in touch with the Infinite, spirits that can soar aloft to regions where angels love to dwell, and minds that can comprehend the deep and hidden things of life, we have lived within the bounds of the material; spiritual blindness, sin's nemesis, hath overtaken us.

"Who shall ascend unto the hill of the Lord or who shall stand in his holy place? He that hath clean hands and a pure heart; who hath not lifted up his soul unto vanity, nor sworn deceitfully." We have no answer in ourselves, O God; no easy word of pardon and no facile promise of forgetfulness can ease our inner torment when we have betrayed our ideals, tarnished our characters, and acquiesced in evil. We need the grace of a new beginning, the liberating power of sins forgiven, and the assurance of a broken relationship restored.

In the breaking of bread, in communion with the saints on earth and in heaven, may we experience that peace which the world can neither give or take away. We ask this through him who made of human life a sacrament, of thorns a crown, of a cross a throne, and through whom we rise from the tomb of our dead selves glorious and triumphant.—Murdo Ewen Macdonald.

PRAYER OF CONFESSION. O God most gracious, who of thy great mercy hast called us again unto the table of our Lord, we humbly confess that we are unworthy of the least of thy benefits.

We come to pay our vows unto the Lord, and we find ourselves confronted and rebuked by the memory of the vows we have taken and our utter failure to fulfill these vows. We have promised so much and performed so poorly. We have promised to be Christ's faithful disciples to our life's end, but we have ceased to listen when his truth became too searching, and we have turned back from following when the way grew hard.

We come to seek thy presence, yet in the clear light of thy glory revealed in Jesus Christ we stand revealed, just as we are. We set Christ's patient love for us over against our faltering love for him; his forgetfulness of self against our own lives so self-centered; his humility against our foolish pride; his triumphant faith against our doubts and fears.

We come to enter into fellowship with thyself through Jesus Christ. What communion can there be between sinful man and God most holy or between the frail creatures of a day and the eternal

God? With shame we remember how Christ came to make possible such communion. He came to be like us that we might become more like him, yet how unlike him we are. He came to share our life that we might learn to share with him the very life of God, and how far we are still from thy kingdom of love and joy and peace. Have mercy upon us, O God. Create in us the clean heart without which none can stand in thy sight, and so bring us to share with thee the bread and wine of heaven.— R. Leonard Small.

WORLD COMMUNION.      Almighty God, our heavenly Father, we look to thee in faith and expectancy, with gratitude and love in our hearts, with eagerness and adventure in our spirits. Grant to us in this hour of worship an immediate and fresh sense of thy presence here. In the fellowship of the faith may we focus upon thee and the things eternal and find that meaning which thou art seeking to reveal to us for our life's direction and strength.

Wilt thou bless our praise and our worship as we give our gratitude to thee for thy wonderful goodness. Wilt thou teach us truly to understand and deeply appreciate the good of this our life. May we thank thee as the author of all that is meaningful and fine and good. In the thought of thee may we take new heart, achieve new confidence, and find new strength for the problems, the testings, the decisions, and the struggles that make up our days. Give us new heart and new hope that we may dare to believe in good things in the days to come. And as thou canst make all things work together for good if we but love thee, so may we believe deeply in life and may our praise and prayer be filled with courage and confidence.

We lift our prayer for thy people all about this earth on this World Communion Sunday. We rejoice in the privilege of this global fellowship of faith. Let thy cause move forward in the light of thy leading and in thy strength.

Wilt thou bless our deeper life of prayer as we open our spirits to thee. May we truly speak with thee day by day as a man speaks with his friend. May we trust the leading thou dost give us and dare to follow the light that we have, even when we are encompassed by so much of the darkness of uncertainty.

Grant us the courage to take the next step that thou art showing to us. In this time of worship may the sacrament be a means of bringing us very close to thee, mindful that we have a Savior, conscious of his wonderful love. May we take on new courage and rejoice in thy wonderful saving goodness. Let thy blessing be upon all thy people in this world, those who do not call upon thee in faith as well as those who do. Let thy purposes move through the hearts of men. Grant that this world may learn the lessons of truth and light and may advance to better days and better things. Let thy Spirit touch the troubled and sore spots of turmoil. Deliver us from the evils that constantly beset us, and make of us new persons in Christ. Grant that we may help create such a climate of goodwill, acceptance, and understanding that men may truly learn to live together in the light of thy truth.— Lowell M. Atkinson.

# SECTION IV. Resources for Funeral Services

## SERMON SUGGESTIONS

**Topic: Assurance of Immortality**
TEXT: Job 14:14.

This anguished cry of Job echoes in the hearts of men today as it has in every age. Disguise it as we may, we are preoccupied with thoughts of death and immortality. Mankind hungers for life, is apprehensive of death, and longs for an answer to the ancient question, "If a man die, shall he live again?" Job's question, our question, receives varied responses.

I. For some, death is the final solution. When our last breath is drawn and the last heartbeat stifled, that is the end. The brief span of our life on earth, with its joys and sorrows, its triumphs and tragedies, and its victories and failures, is closed by death. That is all; there is nothing more. From darkness we come; into darkness and oblivion we depart.

II. There is another response to the question. Immortality, some believe, is indeed the persistence after death of the living soul or spirit of man. But such survival is not as an identifiable, individual personality that man survives beyond the grave. The soul is received and merged with the universal eternal consciousness or spirit we call God. There will be no meeting of husbands and wives, no reunion of children and parents or friends, and no communion with the saints or with the great spirits of antiquity, as comforting and desirable

as one would expect that to be. In short there will be no discrete identities in the life after death. All will become part of the universal, all-embracing spirit.

III. Christianity clearly offers the assurance of immortality. (a) Jesus spoke of life after death in simple, familiar, and domestic terms. "Set your troubled minds at rest. Trust in God always; trust also in me. There are many dwelling places in my Father's house; if it were not so I should have told you; for I am going there on purpose to prepare a place for you." Those dear dead of ours and we ourselves do not at death simply vanish into darkness and oblivion. There is a destination, an arrival, and a welcome already prepared and waiting.

(b) What life after death is like we do not know or need to know. It is the "undiscovered country from whose bourn no traveler returns." So as another has said, "It is unwise to claim knowledge of the furniture of heaven or the temperature of hell." We do not know the details, but we accept the truth. In the end we must and do accept the Christian assurance on trust, trust in the wisdom and love of our heavenly Father.—Benjamin F. Holme.

## Meditation: Beyond the Door

"In my Father's house are many rooms." What Jesus is evidently trying to tell us is simply that heaven is a dwelling place where the souls of the redeemed are with God. It is a place of peace and joy where God rules in love and where sin is not known. In the Book of Revelation, John becomes more specific and adds that tears, sorrow, and pain do not exist there.

Such a description might fit any place where God's rule is fully accepted. Pain and sorrow are most often the results of man's departure from God's ways. Even death entered the world through sin.

Perhaps, in the terms Jesus used, you can think of this life as being lived in a small room. We have to love it because it is a place of familiar surroundings. We feel secure within its walls. But this earthly room of ours has only one door, and that door is marked death. What lies beyond is strange and unknown, and therefore we may be afraid of it.

In God's time that door opens, and his hand beckons us through. We shrink from it, but there is no choice. His loving call must be obeyed. When we pass through that door which we feared so much, we find ourselves in a larger room where there is glorious light and a sense of peace, where God's love prevails and where sin is unknown. There we are to be forever with the Lord.— Albert P. Stauderman.

## Meditation: How the King of Glory Comes

I am sure that we meet a larger self at death because sometimes by accident and sometimes in moments of spiritual exaltation we occasionally break through to it even now. I believe it is possible in this life to enter into it much more often and much more vividly than we suspect. This is, I think, what Christ taught. His kingdom of heaven, that life more abundant, was an experience of the present—an intensification of this existence, not something of the faraway uncertain future. Our lack of understanding has pushed this bright and beautiful possibility further from us until, at last, we have thrust it over the rim of death, there to await us in the next world, while all the time, did we but guess it, it is here at our very elbows. For the most part we go at half-pressure through a play world, but sometimes some poignant love, joy, beauty, or suffering lifts up the everlasting gates of our blindness and the King of Glory comes in. He will never come in a timid, artificial, selfish, and ease-loving existence. It is when ease and safety are torn away and we are stripped to the very bare bones, stripped to the very soul, that the soul emerges triumphant. Better still it is when we voluntarily strip ourselves of the little selfish timidities for a great cause that this mysterious King of Glory comes in most radiantly. The saints and mystics knew this. They were not in pursuit of a pale negation; they were furiously and gloriously crucifying the smaller self that the larger might be set free. They knew that they would never find what they were seeking in a hideous, exotic pursuit of happiness and comfort or in frightened attempts to escape suffering. It is to be found in love, that splendid and reckless outpouring of self for someone or something other than ourselves. In beauty, when it stabs us awake to the marvels all about us and when the awakening brings with it a certain wildness and intoxication, a madness of joy, before which all the small hothouse artificialities are swept away. In truth, that deep simplicity which thrusts one down into the still fastnesses of the spirit where God is to be met. And finally it is found in that courage which knows it is infinitely better to die at full breath of vivid unselfishness, rather than live on in a dreary ease and safety.

More and more frequently individuals are breaking down the hard barriers and driving through to that increased vitality which is the hidden possibility of us all and which already many of us have experienced in fleeting moments. With this larger life there must come an ever-growing realization of worlds beyond our present one—worlds which are ours to inherit someday, as the blue sky is the heritage of the unsuspecting caterpillar. With this fuller realization it is possible that the world-old enemy of mankind, the fear of death, is to be vanquished. The time may not be far off when to lose a friend by death will be hardly more than to have him cross the ocean when our own passing will be merely the happy setting sail for a new country. It may be that at last death itself is dying.—Howard Thurman.

## Topic: Waiting for the Setting Sun

SCRIPTURE: Ps. 69:3; Luke 12:35–48.

In a very personal way the sun is going to set for each one of us someday. There will come a time when we will have seen our last sunrise, and we shall meet our Lord face to face. What shall we tell him when we meet him? Shall we tell him that we are "weary with crying," our throats parched, and our eyes have grown dim waiting for our God, as the psalmist said? Shall we explain how we took his gift of life and sat it out on a park bench for a lifetime just waiting for something to happen or that we took his gift of life and did nothing with it because of the barbarians? How should we be awaiting? What should we be doing while we are waiting? It's not wrong to wait, but it makes a big difference what we are doing while we are waiting. There are certain things that we would like to have him find us doing.

I. We would like to have God find us with our work completed. Life for so many of us is filled with loose ends. There are so many things left undone and things half done, the things put off and the things not even attempted.

II. We should like God to find us at peace with our fellowman. It would be a haunting thing to pass from this world with bitterness toward some other man, whether that person be wife or husband, child or parent, neighbor or president. To meet the Lord with a grudge on our lips is to deny all that the Christian faith stands for. No man should let the sun go down upon his wrath, says Ephesians, especially the last sun of all, and who knows when that will be.

III. We should like to have God find us at peace with ourselves. This may be harder than it sounds. Psychiatrists tell us that many mental troubles begin because we do not love ourselves enough. We are told to love our neighbors as ourselves, but some of us can't even love ourselves.—C. Thomas Hilton.

## Meditation: End and Beginning

It is always a solemn moment "when that which drew from out the boundless deep turns again home." On the one hand is the eternity from which we came and on the other the echoless shore from which there is no return and into which we all vanish. During a brief period of consciousness we cross the gap between what was and what is yet to be. Ordinarily we think of death as an end, but in reality it is a beginning.

When the larva weaves the gray mantle about itself it doubtless thinks of it as a shroud, but when the moth bursts forth into newness of life to flit from flower to flower drinking the sweet nectar and to soar into the sunlit heights, that which we thought was a casket has proved to be a cradle. It was not the end of life but the beginning of more glorious life.

If unborn twins could discuss their approaching birth they would no doubt say: "For us it will be the end. When we are separated from the source of our food, warmth, shelter, and protection, we shall perish." But that which they thought would be the end proves to be the beginning.

Saddened as we are by the separation from a loved one we must think of it as the beginning of a finer, richer life for him. It has been planned that way by an all-wise Father since before "the morning stars sang together and all the sons of God shouted for joy."

If God is able to create as wonderful a thing as a human personality, we must agree that he knows the best disposition to make of it. Surely the passing of our friend marks the beginning of greater fulfillment.

The fleeting and temporary nature of life drives us back to a contemplation of God as the embodiment of stability and permanence. "Before the mountains were brought forth, or ever thou hadst formed the earth and the world, even from everlasting to everlasting thou art God."

## ILLUSTRATIONS

DEATH THE GATE TO LIFE. It comes with shadowed face, but it opens doors for life above and beyond it. If nothing ever passed away, how would the new find room and foothold? If old forms, like buried seeds, were not dissolved, how would the life-germ at the heart be set free? The outworn in everything becomes a hindrance. The garments of mortality grow old. "Come," says Death, and his voice is kind and his shadowed face is tender, "take them off; there are new ones within. I am only a servant. Life and Love are my masters, but they cannot reclothe even a buried seed—except it die."—Gaius Glenn Atkins.

CHILDREN OF GRIEF. The Bible does not make light of sorrows. Its heroes have their troubles. Call the roll of its sons and daughters and you will find that at some time each one of them was a child of grief. In the Bible sorrow is real and sorrow is positive. When Rachel weeps for her children, the scene is real. When David goes into the room in the tower over the gate and utters his pitiful lament over Absalom, the Book does not describe his anguish as an illusion. Paul's hunger and thirst, and stripes and shipwrecks, and perils and imprisonments were not the vain froth of a mortal mind.—Edwin Holt Hughes.

PRELUDE. The apostles spoke of death, not with a full stop, not with a question mark, but with an exclamation point. "Death is swallowed up in victory!" And this was no sudden access of optimism or flash of pious hope. Were they not the men who had seen Jesus die? And if he could die and lie there in a rocky tomb, what hope was there for continued life for the rest of us? The one reason for their astounding reversal of belief, for the exclamation point in their assertion of eternal life, was that they had seen or heard that this same Jesus had risen from the dead. Therefore, although the darkness of death continued to descend on them, one by one, they knew that it was the prelude to the world of light. For them as for all who made this leap of faith, "the darkness was passing away," for the true light was now shining, the light "that shines more and more unto the perfect day."—David H. C. Read.

A BLOOMING DEATH. A stranger, seeing a gardener cut down a century plant after it had bloomed, inquired: "Why cut it down? Wouldn't it revive after it has had a little rest?" "No, the old plant's done for. Might have lived to be a hundred if it hadn't up and bloomed." "Does blooming always kill then?" "Yes, in this country anyhow." "Then why didn't you cut it back and keep it from blooming?" "A bloomin' death, to my way of thinkin', is a mighty sight better'n a no-account life!"

LIGHT AND DARKNESS. Out of the darkness and horror of Calvary came the voice of the crucified saying, "Father, into thy hands I commend my spirit." And the dark was no longer dark, for he was with his Father. He had come from God, and he went to God. So also those who walk with God in this earthly pilgrimage know from blessed experience that he will not abandon his children who trust in him. In the night of death his presence will be "better than light and safer than a known way."—John Sutherland Bonnell.

ACCEPTANCE. A theological scholar died at the untimely age of 46. Among those who mourned was a three-year-old boy, the playmate of his little daughter. He felt perplexed and indignant over what had happened to Wendy's daddy. When his mother told him that Wendy's daddy was with God, the little lad replied in tones of infinite acceptance and understanding, "Oh, then he's still real."

AFFIRMATION OF FAITH. A woman was driven to despair by the death of her husband and daughter in an automobile accident. Although her friends comforted her and she tried very hard to keep her courage, she kept sinking lower every day. Finally she walked out the door of her house and down the road in complete desperation. She would just keep wandering and not care what happened to her. As she walked, a passage from the Apostles' Creed kept coming to her mind over and over, until finally its full force hit her and she heard herself saying aloud: "It's really true! It's really true!" The words that she had remembered were "I believe in God the Father Almighty, Maker of heaven and earth." She said to herself: he is an Almighty Father, and if he can take care of heaven and earth, he can take care of my daughter and husband, and he can take care of me. She returned home and began to live life anew.—William J. Vamos.

AFRAID OF GOD. A young soldier in a military hospital heard the doctor on his evening rounds say to the nurse, "I am afraid by the time I get back in the morning this one will be gone." After the doctor had left the ward, the boy, who now realized that he was dying, began to ask for a chaplain. When a chaplain could not be found, the head nurse went in to talk to him. She said, "What is the matter?" The boy said, "I heard the doctor say that I am going to die, and I am afraid." The nurse said, "Afraid? What is there to be afraid of?" The boy said. "I'm afraid of God." The nurse said, "Afraid of God who sent his Son into the world to die for you?"—Charles H. Buck, Jr.

RELIGION WITHOUT TEARS. A generation which wishes for a religion without tears must find it difficult to adjust its beliefs to the teachings of the New Testament and to the facts of life. Bereavement is the sharpest challenge to our trust in God; if faith can overcome this, there is no mountain which it cannot remove. And faith can overcome.—W. R. Inge.

THE FATHER'S CARE. If you are a parent, you have seen little miracles of love born into your home. You have held them in your arms and played with them on your knee. You have felt their little fingers wrap themselves around your heart. You love them more than you love yourself. Having brought them into being, can you think of yourself as ever consenting to their annihilation? Not until you can see yourself blotting out these little ones and throwing them on the dustheap of oblivion have you any right to believe that God will surrender his children to the grave. We must believe in eternal life if we believe in the God and Father of our Lord Jesus Christ.—John A. Redhead.

ADEQUACY. When W. E. Sangster, England's great Methodist preacher, lay dying with muscular atrophy, he wrote me a letter. In it he said: "All my life I have preached that Jesus Christ is adequate for every crisis. I have but a few days to live, and oh, Billy, Christ is indeed adequate in the hour of death. Tell everyone it is true. Tell them from me that God is wonderfully near his children as they come to the end of life's road."—Billy Graham.

# PRAYERS

THOU ART ETERNAL LIFE. God all-glorious, ever-blessed, forever self-giving, we come from thee, we belong to thee, and we are destined for thee. Thou art the life eternal, and we live only as we live in thee and thou in us. Apart from thee, O God, there is no real and enduring life. Take these fugitive and fragmentary days, we humbly pray, and lift them into the rhythm and wonder of thine abiding life.

Grant us, O God, to the measure of our capacity, the joy of thy self-giving love, thy moral creativeness, and thy spiritual fellowship. Though our outward man perish, may our inward man be renewed day by day, until death itself is dead, and this dim mortal has put on immortality. Redeem us to thyself, O Lord; by thy grace reckon us dead unto sin and alive unto thee forevermore.

Teach us, O God, that we live in thee here and hereafter; show us that the love we know on earth abides in thee. Take from our hearts all that hinders love or mars fellowship that we may know the glory and prophecy of our lives. Unite us with thyself and with those whom we have loved in the holy communion of the immortal life.—Joseph Fort Newton.

OASIS IN A DRY LAND. O thou in whom are found the origin and destiny of life, we draw near to thee with the assurance that thou wilt draw near to us. We praise thee that even in sorrow we can give thanks. We thank thee for the light of thy eternal presence shining through the shadows of this hour. As in this time we sense our weakness we are grateful for the strength of thine everlasting arms. For thy Word which is as a well of living water springing up into everlasting life we give thee thanks. As we drink deeply of its meaning may it be as an oasis for our spirits in a dry and thirsty land. We thank thee for the life that has been lived so graciously in our midst for so many years. We praise thee for thy love that nothing in this world or in the world to come can separate us.

Help us to realize that this crisis in our earthly pilgrimage that we call death can teach us so much of life. May we be faithful to the stewardship of sorrow that is committed to us with this hour. May we deepen down into him who is our life. May we listen in the depths of our being for "deep speaking unto deep." As we are sensitive to the eternal present in the temporal may we have courage to live not as those without hope but as those with a living hope. In all kinds of weather help us to follow patiently the north star of thy eternal purpose.—John Thompson.

ABOVE THE SHADOW. Almighty and everlasting God, the Lord of our life and death, we desire to acknowledge thee in all our ways and in all the events which befall us. In sorrow of heart, yet in quietness and confidence, we have gathered for these last solemn and tender offices of faith and love. Lift us above the shadow and the sadness of mortality into the light of thy countenance and the comfort of thy presence. Speak to us thy word of peace as we stand now in the presence of death. It is thine own hour. The loneliness and the silence thou hast made. But thou canst do thy children no harm. In sorrow as in joy, in loss as in gain, and in life as in death we confess thee to be good. Thou art the Lord of life; we trust in thee through Christ.—John Hunter.

# SECTION V.  Resources for Small Groups

## BACKGROUND MATERIALS

GOD'S BEST INSTRUMENT.    Sometimes people find it difficult to witness alone: they do it best in small companies. Others are often touched not alone by Christian character or experience of an individual kind but by seeing Christian relationships in operation. Here the small group seems to be God's best instrument to get people started and to help them grow. A young woman who had rather reacted against traditional religion has been attending one of these groups now for a couple of months and writes saying, "Everything is so much more exciting and important and happy now." This new experience has come to her largely through the kind of friendship and fellowship she has found among other people who attend that group. Are you part of such a company? Are you making faith real to others in this available fashion? Or do you say, complacently and smugly, that the "old ways" are good enough for you? Business can't say that. Education can't say that. Science can't say that. Why do you keep your religion in the horse-and-buggy days when you are missing the needs of thousands who will not go with you at your jog-trot pace but might join you if you would shift your gears and learn something new with which to confront the people of a new time?— Samuel M. Shoemaker.

SENSE OF MISSION.    The personal sharing groups have not only become the source of new vitality for the church; they have also provided a new sense of mission for the leaders. In and through the groups the leaders come to know people in ways they could scarcely have previously imagined. Enabled by the group situation to give up the role of authoritative leader, encouraged by the group process to really listen to what is being said and what is being meant, supported by the group in his own failures and encouraged by the group as it supports wavering faith and nudges the recalcitrant toward growth, the group leader rediscovers the opportunity for nurturing spiritual growth and so recaptures the joy of ministry.— Robert C. Leslie in *Sharing Groups in the Church* (Nashville: Abingdon Press, 1971).

A GROUP'S CONTRACT.    The following list gives some possible areas of a group's contract with each other. Remember, a contract among group members is specific, and it has to be one that is arrived at by the entire group members who are willing to commit themselves to it for a specific time. It says something definite about the purpose of the group meeting week after week, a purpose that each person is willing to commit himself to for a specific period of time. And contracts evolve as the group, by consensus, sees its purpose change.

1. Be on time for all group meetings.

2. End the meeting on time.

3. Stay for the entire meeting.

4. No one person should dominate the conversation; everyone should be given an opportunity to speak.

5. The discussion should be kept on the right track. Chasing rabbits is fine if you are after rabbits.

6. There should be no whispering in the group. If someone has something to say, it should be said to the entire group.

7. Absences must be kept to a minimum.

8. The group is bound by confidentiality. What is said in the group remains there.

9. Listen to what is being said. If you don't understand something, say so. You owe it to yourself and to the group to be clear on all points.

10. There are no spectators in the group, only participants.

11. The focus is on affirming people, not on destroying them.

12. Don't leave a person hanging at the end of a session. Allow time to clear up any agenda items.

13. Be flexible, even with your guidelines.—William Clemmons and Harvey Hester in *Growth through Groups* (Nashville: Broadman Press, 1974).

## DISCUSSION SUGGESTIONS

**Topic: Characteristics of the Church Group**
RESOURCE: Acts 2:44–45; 4:32, 34–35.
I. A learning group.
II. A loving group.
III. A praying group.
IV. A witnessing group.
V. A sharing group.
VI. A power-filled group.
VII. A praising group.
VIII. A respectful group.
IX. A thankful group.
X. A happy group.—Howard D. Berglund.

**Topic: Basic Christian Principles**
I. The fatherhood of God.
II. The brotherhood of man.
III. The value of every individual as a child of God.
IV. The law of love as the law of life.
V. The way of service as the way of life.
VI. The kingdom of God as the goal of life.

**Topic: Perspectives of the Last Supper**
I. The backward look to the Last Supper and to Calvary: "This do . . . in remembrance of me" (I Cor. 11:25).
II. The forward look to the bridal supper of the Lamb in the perfected kingdom: "Till I come" (Rev. 2:25).
III. The feeding upon Christ by faith: "Take, eat; this is my body" (Matt. 26:26).
IV. The church as the body of Christ: "As my Father hath sent me, even so send I you" (John 20:21).
V. The eucharist or the church's thanksgiving in the confession of the Redeemer's name.
VI. The real presence of the Lord himself as surely as on that last betrayal night, sealing his promise to believers and giving himself unto his own.—Nathaniel Micklem.

**Topic: The People of God**
I. We are a forgiven people.
II. We are a redeemed people.
III. We are a chosen people.
IV. We are a covenant people.
V. We are a servant people.
VI. We are a called people.

**Topic: Christian Commitment**
I. Christian commitment is made to a Person.
II. Christian commitment is to the will of God.
III. Christian commitment is to the kingdom of God.
IV. Christian commitment is made to maximum efficiency. The objective of genuine evangelism is not just more Christians but more effective Christians.

V. Christian commitment is to spiritual growth.

VI. Christian commitment is made to disciplined living.—W. Fraser Munro.

**Topic: Galatians: The Book of Religion**

I. The religion of change (Chapter 1).

II. The religion of liberty (Chapter 2).

III. The religion of faith (Chapter 3).

IV. The religion of heirs (Chapter 4).

V. The religion of love (Chapter 5).

VI. The religion of support (Chapter 6).—Derl G. Keefer.

**Topic: Aspects of Corporate Worship**

I. The spirit of obedience.

II. The spirit of reverence.

III. The spirit of communion.

IV. The spirit of fellowship.

V. The spirit of sacrifice.

VI. The spirit of celebration.

VII. The spirit of edification.—Luther D. Reed.

**Topic: Christian Growth**

I. Prerequisite for Christian growth. (See John 15:1–11.)

II. The need for Christian growth. (See I Cor. 3:1–4; II Pet. 1:3–11).

III. The goal of Christian growth. (See Eph. 4:11–16; Phil. 3:12–16; I John 3:1–3.)

IV. Overcoming hindrances to growth. (See I Cor. 2:1–5; II Cor. 4:7–11, 16.)

V. The place of the Holy Spirit in growth. (See John 16:12–15; Rom. 8:26–27; Gal. 5:16–17, 22–25.)

VI. Resources for Christian growth. (See Phil. 4:4–9; Col. 3:1–4, 12–17.)

VII. Tensions and Christian growth. (See Rom. 12:1–2; Jas. 1:2–8, 12.)

VIII. Growth in our relationships. (See Rom. 12:9–21.)

IX. Growing as witnesses. (See Matt. 5:13–16; Acts 8:4–6; Rom. 1:14–17.)

X. Accepting the challenge to grow. (II Tim. 1:6–10; 2:1–7.)

**Topic: On the Nature of Religion**

I. Religion as ecstatic emotionalism. (See I Cor. 13:1.)

II. Religion as intellectualism and speculation. (See I Cor. 13:2.)

III. Religion as working energy. (See I Cor. 13:2.)

IV. Religion as humanitarianism. (See I Cor. 13:3.)

V. Religion as asceticism. (See I Cor. 13:3.)

VI. Religion as perfect love. (See I Cor. 13:4–10.)—James S. Stewart.

**Topic: Christian Marriage**

I. To cherish a mutual esteem and love.

II. To bear with each other's infirmities and weaknesses.

III. To comfort each other in sickness, trouble, and sorrow.

IV. In honesty and industry to provide for each other and for their household in temporal things.

V. To pray for and encourage each other in the things which pertain to God.

VI. To live together as heirs of the grace of life.

**Topic: Prophetic Emphases**

I. Amos: God's plumb line is swinging. (See Amos 5:23–24.)

II. Hosea: God's divided heart. (See Hos. 11:8.)

III. Micah: What does God require? (See Mic. 6:8.)

IV. Isaiah: God our refuge and strength. (See Isa. 37:33, 38.)

V. Zephaniah: The wages of sin. (See Zeph. 3:1–2.)

VI. Jeremiah: Accepting the inevitable. (See Jer. 27:12–14.)

VII. Habakkuk: The song of the nightingale. (See Hab. 3:17–18.)

VIII. Unknown prophet: Redemption and restoration. (See Isa. 52:8–9.)

IX. Malachi: First things first! (See Mal. 1:6.)—John Calvin Reid.

**Topic: Highlights of the Book of Revelation**

I. The aim of hope: Faithful obedience to the limit. (Chapters 1–3.)

II. The endurance of hope: The

church in conflict. (Chapters 4–5, 10–14.)

III. The dark side of hope: The judgment of the nations. (Chapters 6–9, 15–19.)

IV. The goal of hope: The coming of Christ and his kingdom.—George R. Beasley-Murray.

## Topic: Questions People Ask

I. Since I have become a Christian and have separated myself from my former friends, I find it very hard to witness to them effectively. What should I do?

II. Some of the people I talk with about holy living insist on seeing verses of scripture before they will accept any new ideas about Christian living. Are there some verses that I could use with them?

III. In some people who profess to being cleansed and filled by the Holy Spirit I see evidence of pride and selfishness. I am tempted to think that they are not sincerely involved in their relationship with Christ. Are they really hypocrites?

IV. After I have been forgiven and cleansed and have walked with God, is it still possible for me to sin and be lost?

V. When the Holy Spirit cleanses a man from his inner infection, making him "whole" or "entire," does the cleansing reach to all of man's attitudes or only to those which he knows need the Spirit's cleansing?

VI. What if a person wants only to be saved? Does everybody have to take the full course? What does "holiness without which no man shall see the Lord" (Heb. 12:14) have to do with it?

VII. Although I have experienced forgiveness for my sins and have received the inner cleansing which the Holy Spirit provides, I have times of doubt and of feeling pretty low. What is the matter with me?

VIII. I have heard that some groups teach that speaking in "tongues" is the proof of being filled with the Holy Spirit. Are such "tongues" the evidence of being Spirit filled?

IX. What is the "sin against the Holy Ghost" which the Bible teaches is unpardonable?—Donald M. Joy in *The Holy Spirit and You.*

## Topic: Christian Courage

I. The courage to be uncomplaining.
II. The courage to be uncompromising.
III. The courage to be uncomfortable.
IV. The courage to be uncluttered.
V. The courage to be uncompetitive.
VI. The courage to be unself-conscious.
VII. The courage to be unconquerable.
VIII. The courage to be uncritical.
IX. The courage to be unconventional.
X. The courage to be uncontrollable.

## Topic: The Way Out

I. The way out of anxiety and into trust. (See Phil. 4:6–7.)

II The way out of bewilderment and into certainty. (See II Cor. 4:6, 8, NEB.)

III. The way out of boredom and into joyous adventure. (See Matt. 16:24–25.)

IV. The way out of despair and into hope. (See II Cor. 4:8–9, PHILLIPS.)

V. The way out of doubt and into faith. (See Mark 9:24.)

VI. The way out of fear and into courage. (See I John 4:18, PHILLIPS.)

VII. The way out of sin and into salvation. (See John 14:5–6.)

VIII. The way out of temptation and into victory. (See I Cor. 10:13.)—William Fisher.

# SECTION VI. Resources for Lenten and Easter Preaching

2-27-83 AM.

**Topic: How Was Jesus' Death Different?**

TEXT: Luke 23:33.

I. One reason for Jesus' death being different is that his death was *planned*.

(a) His death was promised throughout the history of the Hebrews, and thus his death was the fulfillment of prophecy. Jesus always referred to his death as being in accord with the scriptures. The cross was a divine plan from the foundation of the world.

(b) Because the cross was planned, the death of Jesus was voluntary. The cross was no accident. Jesus was not the victim of his environment. He was always master of the situation and reminded the people that he laid his life down on his own accord and that no one took away his life. This was God's work of salvation, and he was obedient to that will.

II. Jesus' death is different because it had a *purpose*. (a) The cross was a place of sacrifice. His death was an offering for sin. No other death had this meaning or purpose. For some years now we have been emphasizing the love of God to the exclusion of the other side of God, his justice and holiness. God is a God of love, but God is a just and holy God. When we go against God we are subject to God's wrath.

(b) This penalty of death was taken by God in the person of Christ on the cross. Christ was our substitute. As the Bible says, "There is no redemption without the shedding of blood." A price was paid for our sins in terms of the lifeblood of Jesus. Jesus said he came to earth to give his life a ransom for many.

(c) Because of the cross the way is open for man's return to God. Now he can be reconciled. God will accept him, forgive him, and love him. But the question is whether modern man wants to be forgiven and wants to be accepted by God as his child.

III. Jesus' death was different because of the *person* on the cross. (a) This really made the difference in the three crosses on Good Friday. Two were only men. In the middle there was a man but more than a man. Here was the Son of God who repeatedly prayed as a son, "Father." The unbiased Roman soldier exclaimed when Jesus died, "Truly this was the son of God!" Wasn't Paul right when he wrote, "God was in Christ reconciling the world to himself"? There is no other way to explain the perfect life, the absolute poise, and the beautiful death of Jesus. We come to the conclusion that on this cross was God in Christ, the Messiah, Lord, and Redeemer.

(b) If Jesus is God on the cross suffering and dying for us, there comes a deep sense of gratitude that calls us to follow and be his slaves forever. Such love demands all we have and are. Gratitude wells up within us, and we cannot be satisfied until we surrender all.

IV. The greatest reason for Jesus' death being different from all other deaths in history was the fact that his death did not last but three days. All other men died and stayed dead. On Good Friday we watch him die as one of three on crosses. We need this experience of death with him, for if we die with him we shall also live with him when he rises on Easter. So this is not only a remembrance of the world's quite unique death, but it is an occasion for our dying to self and sin. How glorious will Easter then be. We shall have new life, new beings in Christ.—John R. Brokhoff.

## Meditation: A God-Given Way of Seeing

When Jesus utters these words that move us so deeply, "Father, forgive them; for they know not what they do," what happens then is not something like a miracle of self-control. What happens is not anything that has to do with our will power. What happens is a miracle of a new, God-given way of seeing. The person who is given this ability to see past the filthy surface and see the children of God despite the distortion can also see love.

We Christians are promised this transformation of our way of seeing people, and we are promised it in a totally new way. For now when we are faced by those who do us wrong we must say and we are privileged to say: "Jesus Christ died for this man who is cheating us, this woman who vents her unaccountable hatred upon us, this person who is defrauding us; he bought him dearly, he has surrounded him with his love." The person who accepts the cross in this way when he faces stormy passages with his fellowman, and accepts the gift of this way of seeing—in other words, the person who sees the mystery of sonship to God in the other person— that person ceases to be merely an echo of such conflicts; he stops merely reacting to them. On the contrary, the creative impulse of love comes into his life. The point is that one of the persons in conflict must begin to love. Then he will be in for a surprise at how much will be changed.

That's why the moment in which this word from the cross was spoken is so tremendous. Here was one capable of loving because he saw his haters and his enemies in a wholly new way. And since that moment a wholly new power has entered into the world. It is available to every one of us.—Helmut Thielicke in *Christ and the Meaning of Life*.

## Topic: What the Cross Accomplished

I. The death of Christ may be described as an *expiation* for sin, for it was a divine act which renders the punishment of sin unnecessary.

II. It was a *vicarious* death. He died "for us," "for our sins," "in our stead." He was forsaken of God that we might not have to be forsaken.

III. It was a *representative* death. The Lord Jesus Christ is in very truth, by the original law of the universe, the representative of mankind.

IV. It may be described as a *ransom*— an act of God by which we are delivered or redeemed from the calamities which threatened us so long as we were exposed to the punishment of sin, and by which we are also delivered or redeemed from those moral and spiritual evils from which there was no escape through the restoration to us of the life of God.

V. It was a *satisfaction* to the righteousness of God in whatever sense the punishment of the guilty can be spoken of as a satisfaction to the righteousness of God.

VI. It was a *sacrifice* for sin—an acknowledgment, such as we could never have made for ourselves, of the greatness of our guilt and an actual submission on our behalf to the penalty of guilt.

VII. It was a *propitiation* for sin—a propitiation originated and effected by God himself, an act done in our name and ultimately carrying our submission with it.—R. W. Dale.

**Topic: What the Centurion Saw**

TEXT: Mark 15:39.

What was it that this centurion saw that might have caused him to speak in this way?

I. He saw a *love* so great and unquenchable that it could grant forgiveness to its persecutors and revilers: "Father, forgive them, for they know not what they do."

II. He saw a *hope* for the future so confident that it could say with assurance to a condemned felon, "Truly, I say to you, today you will be with me in paradise."

III. He saw a *faith* so immense and undiscourageable that it could exclaim at the end of this agonizing experience, "Father, into thy hands I commit my spirit."—Edward C. Dahl.

**Topic: Peter's Role in the Crucifixion**

I. Peter's role in the crucifixion was first to try to save Jesus from it. That would seem to be a praiseworthy role, but instead of praising Peter Jesus rebuked Peter for it. "Get thee behind me, Satan!"

(a) Why did Jesus then rebuke Peter so vehemently? It was because Peter was opening up again a question that Jesus had settled when he resisted the temptation to become a political messiah.

(b) Strange that what had been proposed first to Jesus by the evil one should now be proposed by implication by a beloved follower and friend, the first one that he might get Jesus in his power, the other by his friend that Jesus might be saved from crucifixion.

(c) Had Jesus refused the suffering that lay ahead for him as Messiah, he would have had nothing to give to those who themselves must suffer in physical suffering or in the attacks of unworthy or ignorant people. "His hands were mighty with saving power because they were scarred" (Luccock).

II. The role Peter played in the crucifixion was next to try to save himself from any acknowledged association with Jesus.

(a) This is Peter's denial. There was the courtyard and the fire and the bystanders and the maiden and Peter's three denials that he did not know Jesus or had anything to do with him.

(b) Luke tells us that as Peter made his most vehement denial Jesus passed along the corridor above him and looked at Peter with a look that was so much wounded love rather than condemnation that it broke Peter's heart and released his tears. He went out and wept bitterly.

III. There then began for Peter in his remorse what led to Peter's ultimate role in the crucifixion.

(a) Peter who had tried first to save Jesus from it and then to save himself from it made the discovery of a saving power through the crucifixion and what ensued from it that was for him and all mankind.

(b) For Peter personally this was effective in the beautiful scene where corresponding to the three denials by Peter there were to the risen Lord the three affirmations of loyalty and love in response to the question, "Simon, lovest thou me?"

(c) Peter was restored to the confidence of the group of disciples and the early church. He was restored to confidence in himself and given a new commission which was to preach the one whom he had denied. He preached Jesus Christ, crucified and risen, and he did it with such boldness that they took knowledge of him that he'd been with Jesus.—Charles L. Seasholes.

**Topic: The Meaning of the Cross**

I. The symbol of a great sacrifice, something done there in a moment of time to remind us of our immeasurable debt to those who have gone before us and with their lives paid a price to enrich us and redeem us.

II. The symbol of a great trust. Jesus died that day in the calm confidence that this world was God's world and that nothing could ultimately work in God's world but God's way, his truth, and his righteousness.

III. The symbol of a great confidence

in us, in human beings, in human nature. We marvel at the faith of Christ that he could believe so greatly in man. While the cross reveals the evil in men, at the same time it pays enormous tribute to our eternal greatness.—J. Wallace Hamilton.

## ILLUSTRATIONS

UNIQUE.    Where is there to be found in the world, amid the weavings of beautiful thoughts touching the nature of God and human destiny, anything like Christianity? There is no story like it, though many stories have a certain resemblance to it, likely enough when we remember the heart has always cried out for salvation and a deliverer. But this story is not one of many. That God placed himself in the hands of his sinful creatures for them to work on him, stripping him of glory, of strength, of dignity, of support; that God himself at the last should be forsaken of God and that he should rise triumphant, returning to a world that cast his out—there is no other story like this.—A. E. Whitham.

THE OLD EXPECTATIONS.    Christ burst the bonds of the old expectations when he hung upon the cross. Expected king he was, but unexpectedly prepared to rule in love and even suffering and not in arrogance. Expected man of power he was, but unexpectedly prepared to use that power patiently and quietly within the free hearts of his people. Expected man of authority he was, but unexpectedly prepared to exercise it in his kingdom forever. Through the cross God burst the bonds of the old expectations, quenched the old and feeble glory, and put in its place a new and unfading light.—W. Sibley Towner.

HE EMPTIED HIMSELF.    His pockets were empty. He who owned eveything put himself at the mercy of friends and enemies alike. He who owned everything had to borrow everything. When he was born his parents borrowed a stable. When he needed money it came from the fish's mouth. The roofs under which he slept were borrowed. His grave was borrowed. The only thing he had that was his very own was the cross. In the highest sense this too was borrowed. The cross was not his but ours. The greatest stooping from heaven to earth was when he became obedient unto death, even the death of the cross.— R. Earl Allen.

ACTION OF THE CROSS.    The living Christ who died has destroyed my guilt and brought me to God. That is not the action of the resurrection but of the cross. I believe that the divine power in him which wells up in my faith, rather than the irrepressible vitality of his divine "nature," is the power by which Christ rose. But it is still more the power by which he gained his finished victory on the cross. Without the primary theology of the cross the resurrection of Christ would have no more value than a reanimation.—P. T. Forsyth.

BY HIS WEAKNESS.    God allows himself to be edged out of the world and onto the cross. God is weak and powerless in the world, and that is exactly the way, the only way, in which he can be with us and help us. Matt. 8:16 makes it crystal clear that it is not by his omnipotence that Christ helps us but by his weakness and suffering.— Dietrich Bonhoeffer.

PARABLE.    In the South Pacific about 2,000 miles west of Chile is an island called Easter. It received its name because it was on Easter Day, 1722, that it was discovered by the Dutch explorer Roggeveen. What makes Easter Island remarkable are the unusual stone monuments found on it, huge statues going back many centuries, the full story of which is still a puzzle to anthropologists.

That island has always struck me as a parable of what Easter is in the lives of all too many Christians, a strange place worthy of an occasional visit but having no relationship with the real world around it. I am not referring to the commonly noted fact that so many people visit the church only on Easter. I am referring to the less noted but much more tragic fact that so many Christians visit Easter only once a year and then in a way which is detached from their daily lives in the world.— Howard Hageman.

EXPLAINING EASTER.    A man wrote to Albert Einstein to ask him if he could not describe the theory of relativity in simpler words so that he might at least catch a glimpse of the meaning. Einstein wrote back that he could not do what was requested, but if the man would come to Princeton and call on him, Einstein thought he could play it on his violin. That's about all we can say to those who demand that Christians describe or prove Easter. Why do we believe in eternal life? Because we believe in life. And we believe in life because of Jesus. Look at Jesus. Humanity has always hungered and thirsted for a knowledge of itself, and God has replied by giving to us Jesus. In him we see God. In him we see ourselves. In him we see life given meaning by God. —John M. Burgess.

TOUCH ME IN THE MORNING.    Once more at Easter time the lilies have bloomed just as they have so many years before. Once more the trees have issued their blossoms and leaves just as they have so many years before. Once more at Easter time the promise of spring has come just as it has so many years before. And once more at Easter time we need his touch. Touch me and tell me that love is better than hate. Touch me and convince me that right is stronger than wrong. Touch me and assure me that life has conquered death.— Jerry Hayner.

ETERNAL TRUTH.    If Easter means anything to modern man it means that eternal truth is eternal. You may nail it to the tree, wrap it up in grave clothes, and seal it in a tomb; but "truth crushed to earth, shall rise again." Truth does not perish; it cannot be destroyed. It may be distorted; it has been silenced temporarily; it has been compelled to carry its cross to Calvary's brow or to drink the cup of poisoned hemlock in a Grecian jail, but with an inevitable certainty after every Black Friday dawns truth's Easter Morn.—Donald H. Tippett.

## PRAYERS

PRAYER.    Almighty and everlasting God, out of whose goodness and mercy we are privileged to meet in this appointed place of worship, grant that we may experience a satisfying spiritual encounter.

We thank thee, O God, for the beauty and sacredness of life. Give us to know thy will for our lives that in our daily deliberations and decisions we may worthily magnify thy holy name, through Jesus Christ our Lord. We praise thee for the prophets and sages of every generation. We are most grateful for Jesus of Nazareth in whose ministry and message we find the true meaning of life and the hope of salvation. Grant that as we enter upon these days of Lent, days of special reflection and preparation for Easter, we may become more intimately acquainted with the Lord of life. Increase our appreciation of him and of the church. Help us see the church as the continuing and transforming power of Christ in the world. Help us see the church as the "precious remnant," the "gathered community," a people dedicated to doing the will of Christ. Strengthen thy church that the world may yet believe.

Bless us in our worship today. Keep us mindful of previous failures as well as present achievements. Increase our vision and strengthen our faith. Increase our loyalty and multiply our devotion. May we continue to give ourselves joyously to the challenge of this our beloved church. Give us a new awareness of thy presence. Comfort the afflicted and bereaved. Arouse the complacent. Humble the conceited. Strengthen the faithful. Forgive us our sins and remember them no more. Visit us with thy healing presence and redeeming love.—G. Curtis Jones.

PRAYER.    O God, our true life, in whom and by whom all things live: thou commandest us to seek thee and art ready to be found; thou biddest us knock and openest when we do so. To know thee is life, to serve thee is freedom, to enjoy thee is a kingdom, to praise thee is the joy and happiness of the soul. We praise and adore thee; we worship thee, we glorify thee, we give thanks to thee for thy great glory. We humbly beseech thee to abide with us, to reign in us, to make these hearts of ours a holy temple, a fit habitation for thy divine majesty. O thou maker and preserver of all things, visible and invisible, keep, we beseech thee, the work of thine own hands, for we trust in thy mercy alone for safety and protection. Guard us with the power of thy grace, here and in all places, now and at all times, forevermore.—St. Augustine.

EMMAUS COMPANION.    Gracious Lord, we remember that thou didst accompany thy two disciples as they journeyed to Emmaus. We too have a journey; we have a pilgrimage to perform. Our Emmaus is a distant though happy land. Do thou go with us, O Lord. Be our companion. Guide us, uphold us, strengthen us, make our hearts to burn within us, and evermore manifest thyself to our souls in gracious and in heavenly power.

# SECTION VII. Resources for Advent and Christmas Preaching

## SERMON SUGGESTIONS

**Topic: To Magnify the Lord**
TEXT: Luke 1:46.

To magnify means to enlarge. We magnify an object in order to see it clearly. To magnify the Lord is to see him and to help others see him more distinctly. What joy could come to our homes and to our community if each of us made it the primary purpose of his life to magnify God.

I. To magnify the Lord requires the ability to know God. One cannot adequately magnify that which he does not see clearly. To this end life says, "Stop, look, and listen." We are a society of activists; to be up and doing is our theme. We take literally the counsel, "Be ye doers of the word and not hearers only." We acknowledge that worship is a prelude to activity; but our danger is as much on the other side, that we become doers without listening. A prelude to wise action is the injunction, "Be still and know that I am God."

II. To magnify the Lord requires praise. The acts of God in history are good news. Men who believed that God had acted had something to report. "Get you up to a high mountain, O Zion. Herald of good tidings, lift up your voice with strength." There is much hunger in the world, and it is not limited to lack of bread. We live in the midst of starved spirits. The emptiness many experience is caused by their inability to hear or assimilate the truly good news. To magnify the Lord is "to proclaim liberty to the captives . . . to give them a garland instead of ashes."

III. To magnify the Lord requires the upgrading of personality at every opportunity.

(a) Paul said to the Corinthians, "Do you not know that you are God's temple, and that God dwells in you?" He was talking of the church, but the fact is also personal. To magnify the Lord is to acknowledge the divine miracle in every life.

(b) How shall we upgrade personality? How shall we increase another's self-respect?

(1) One way is to acknowledge and have faith in whatever goodness he already possesses. Jesus found in downgraded lives something to build upon. It was so with the much-married woman at the well, the adulteress, the tax cheater, and the demon-possessed who lived among the tombs. By implementing the positive and by complimenting the good, Jesus brought to the surface more of goodness and so upgraded life. It is the lift that many need, and it is one way to magnify the Lord.

(2) If we would upgrade personality we will respond to every man's predicament with kindness. In our fast-draw and bargain-driving society, people, including some of our neighbors, are starved for kindness. Kindness upgrades

both the giver and receiver and so magnifies the Lord.—Wesley P. Ford.

## Meditation: Consecrating the Commonplace

The agonies of the Christmas sermon are not entirely avoided even if our hapless season churchgoer stumbles into an evangelical setting. There, though rationalistic shreddings of the New Testament account of the incarnation are rigorously excluded, often an iconoclasm is promoted that leaves the congregation only slightly less unsettled. The preacher inveighs against all the unbiblical trappings that have accumulated around the Savior's cradle: the carols that do not express precise scriptural teaching; the emphasis on material gift-giving; the pagan Christmas tree; the gluttonous centrality of the Christmas dinner and the anthropocentric family reunions; the stress on our own children instead of on the Christ Child; and the evil genius of the whole occasion: Santa Claus. Depending upon the closeness of his confessional and temperamental alignment with Cromwellian times, the evangelical pastor may even give the impression that Christmas should be radically deemphasized—or done away with altogether. After all the holiday is nowhere commanded or even recommended in scripture; and look at the appalling ways in which non-Christian Western society has secularized it since the eighteenth century.

Seen as the fulfillment of the deepest longings men have brought to expression in their myths, the Christmas story is not to be set over against the traditional lore of the Christmas season. Indeed that lore, when properly understood, will reinforce and heighten the truth of the incarnation itself. The traditional carols will be listened to more closely, and even the most "secular" will yield the eternal message. The Christmas tree will inevitably and properly suggest the one who grew to manhood to "bear our sins in his body on the tree, that we might die to sin and live to righteousness." Family reunions will point to the truth that where two or three are gathered together, there Christ is in the midst, as well as to the family of the redeemed, the clouds of witnesses, and the church triumphant that we shall ourselves join by God's grace before many more Christmases have passed. The dinners and the parties will speak of the Christ who hallowed feasts when he walked this earth and who constitutes "living bread come down from heaven." The centrality of children at this blessed season should remind us that childlike faith before the mysteries of the incarnation is a requisite for participation in his kingdom. And even (or especially?) the archetypal and ubiquitous Santa Claus, who comes from a numinous land of snow-white purity to give gifts to those who have nothing of their own, proclaims to all who have ears to hear the message of the entrance of God into our sinful world to "give gifts to men." —John Warwick Montgomery.

## Topic: The Wisdom of the Wise Men

TEXT: Matt. 2:10.

I. The magi were busy at their daily—or nightly—tasks when they saw the star. Even today daily fidelity gives men a quicker awareness of truth.

II. The magi were foreigners, a reminder that Christianity was not a cult of Judaism any more than it is an American commodity for export or for state occasions: Christianity is a world-wide faith.

III. The magi acted with abandon, not caution. They did not call a study conference or appoint a committee to consider all the angles; they simply got up and followed a star.

IV. The wise men did not come to Bethlehem to criticize, to scoff, or to argue; they came to worship. Are we as wise as they?—George A. Buttrick.

## Meditation: Christmas for Grownups

"Christmas is for children!" Sometimes this provides grownups with justification for extravagant or sacrificial giving. Or it offers them license for savoring unembarrassed the storybook joy and excitement of Christmas without having to take seriously its real-life implications or even to realize that there are any. Without self-consciousness we describe the incarnation with baby talk of littlest lambs and littlest angels and in fact imprison Christmas in perpetual babyhood. We do not celebrate a cradled baby George on Washington's Birthday or a beardless, bouncing Abraham on February 12. Why a fixation with the baby Jesus and lullabies on his birthday? Why not, just once, a grownup Christmas for grownups? Why not a Christmas of the virile Christ of Galilee, the Christ of compassion, the Christ of deliberate choice at cost, the Christ of the cross, the Christ of total relevance? Why not, instead of a too-comfortable, old-shoe Christmas, one that refreshingly pinches just a little?—*Christian Herald.*

## Meditation: Unfolding the Mystery

Christmas means nothing to life if it is only poinsettias upon an altar and a festival reserved within the walls of a church. No, indeed. The mystery of God is embedded in the whole of existence, in every thought, in every undertaking, and in every shred of human consciousness upon this planet. Christ's work in this world is to unfold that mystery, to lift the labor of each day's talk to the grandeur of the eternal design, and to pierce the prison walls of the self-enclosure with the liberating wonder of his divine existence. To be the stewards of such a mystery is to give scale to everything that a man does and to give it dimension and love, ultimate meaning and purpose. It matters not at all what a person's occupation is or his livelihood or profession. Whatever it is to which he devotes his life and his leisure can be put into consonance with the sacred way of God, that "way" which the scriptures called "the way of holiness." Christ walks in our midst to illumine that for all of us, and we walk after him with the light shining through our pace, giving dignity to every step, and peace in every hope.—Francis B. Sayre.

## Topic: Advent Themes

1. *Repentance.* This is not simply penitence, feeling sorry for sin, nor is it remedying faulty behavior, turning from sin. It is not a condition for getting into the kingdom of God; rather it is the kingdom of God, the rule of God in the heart and in life, the prerequisite for the repentant and the new God-directed mind that turns from sin daily to the grace of God in Jesus Christ with faith and love.

2. *The Forerunner.* He was not simply the law before the gospel in Christ. He too summoned men and women to turn to God through the power of the good news that in Jesus of Nazareth God's kingdom was breaking in, moving men to repentance.

3. *The Christ.* As in all true preaching, the figure of Jesus Christ is central. Again this is not by merely predicting that he will be born, for all of the gospel texts of the New Testament were written long after his earthly sojourn. The recurrent word is that in Jesus Christ, God has kept the promise which he made to his Old Testament people and his grace and the gift of the new life are there in his Christ, the anointed.

4. *The Second Coming.* Advent preaching is preparation indeed for the second coming of Christ, the return to judgment, and the equipping of the Christian in faith and life to be ready for the end time. The preacher is not to frighten his hearers into watchfulness but to hold the completed atonement of Christ before them as the power for their watchful waiting and their stewardship of the time that is at their disposal.

5. *The Old Testament.* The covenant God of his people in the Old Testament preserves them in faith through the promise and the gift of his Son the Redeemer whose completed work the people of the New Testament celebrate with the witness of their joy.

6. *Joy.* It remains important for the entire season that the mood of violet or purple paraments and penitence do not cancel out the tiptoe-expectation of

the coming of the kingdom and the power of the promise to replace the anxieties of this present time with faith and joy.

7. *Faith.* Advent is the time of hope. Linked with it is faith, the confidence that God keeps his promises and has already done so in his Christ. Therefore the preacher has to be sure that his people are hearing the gospel of the one resource of faith, hope, and joy for the Christian believer.—Richard R. Caemmerer in *Preaching Helps.*

## ILLUSTRATIONS

ADVENT CANDLES. In the use of four candles for the season there has been a specific meaning placed on each candle. The first has been called the Prophecy Candle, opening up the period of waiting. The second is the Bethlehem Candle, symbolic of the preparations being made to receive and to cradle the Christ Child. The third is the Shepherd's Candle. This typifies the act of sharing Christ. And the fourth is the Angels' Candle, the candle of love and final coming. These candles usually are white. A fifth candle placed in the center of these candles is red. This is the Christ Candle, the last candle to be lighted on Christmas Eve.—*A Book of Advent.*

INCIDENT. Halford E. Luccock, shopping at Christmas time, bumped into a lady and spilled her packages in every direction. He helped her gather them up and apologized. She said: "Oh, how I hate Christmas. It turns everything upside down." Dr. Luccock simply remarked that this is just what it is made for.

ESSENTIAL SPIRIT. The Christmas season is the most human and kindly of seasons, as fully penetrated and irradiated with the feeling of human brotherhood, which is the essential spirit of Christianity, as the month of June with sunshine and the balmy breath of roses. —George W. Curtis.

MAGIC. The joy of brightening other lives, bearing others' burdens, easing others' loads, and supplanting empty hearts and lives with generous gifts becomes for us the magic of Christmas.— W. C. Jones.

THE MIRACLE OF CHRISTMAS. The legend tells that when Jesus was born the sun danced in the sky and the aged trees straightened themselves and sent forth the fragrance of blossoms once more. These are the symbols of what takes place in our hearts when the Christ child is born anew each year. Blessed by the Christmas sunshine, our natures, perhaps long leafless, bring forth new love, new kindness, new mercy, and new compassion. As the birth of Jesus was the beginning of the Christian life, so the unselfish joy at Christmas shall start the spirit that is to rule the new year.—Helen Keller.

WHAT IS CHRISTMAS? Christmas is the air of excitement everywhere, the happy, pushing holiday crowds, the sharp fragrance of pine, the winking glint of tinsel. Christmas is the pulsing of the human heart, quickened again with hope. It is the warm handclasp of friends, dancing anticipation in the eyes of a child opening a present. It is a candle glowing in a window, welcoming a stranger—welcoming the Christ.

KEEPING FAITH IN CHRISTMAS. If we would be faithful to the spirit of Christ without which Christmas would be a pagan charade, we must get up off our calloused knees and throw away our Palestinian tourist brochures and sing of the Christ who comes, who has come and will come—now and forever.— William Robert Miller.

THE CHRISTMAS RUSH. An ancient legend tells how the devil became alarmed at the manner in which the whole world was becoming fascinated with the story of the coming of Christ. So charmed were men by the beauty and simplicity of the lovely Christmas tale, so thrilled by the glitter and glamour of the season, so entranced by the music that filled their children and homes, that he was deeply concerned lest all the world should turn in faith to the Savior. Some strategy must be planned that would thwart the acceptance of faith in Jesus Christ. The answer finally accepted was the invention of the Christmas "rush." The devil would send his emissaries abroad everywhere to keep people so busy with the outward celebrations of the season, so absorbed with the feasting and the revelry, so caught up in the whirl of buying and wrapping gifts, that the inner glory of it would go unnoticed. The plan was perfect. His Satanic Majesty has almost succeeded in his plan.—Clifford Ansgar Nelson.

VIGNETTE. One December afternoon many years ago a group of parents stood in the lobby of a nursery school waiting to claim their children after the last pre-Christmas class session. As the youngsters ran from their lockers, each one carried in his hands the "surprise," the brightly wrapped package on which he had been working diligently for weeks. One small boy, trying to run, put on his coat, and wave, all at the same time, slipped and fell. The "surprise" flew out of his grasp, landed on the tile floor, and broke with an obvious ceramic crash.

The child's first reaction was one of stunned silence. But in a moment he set up an inconsolable wail. His father, thinking to comfort him, knelt down and murmured: "Now it doesn't matter, son. It doesn't really matter."

But his mother, much wiser in such affairs, swept the boy into her arms and said: "Oh, but it does matter. It matters a great deal." And she wept with her son.—William Muehl.

## PRAYERS

HIS COMING. Almighty God, we give thee thanks for the mighty yearning of the human heart for the coming of a Savior and the constant promise of thy Word that he was to come. In our own souls we repeat the humble sighs and panting aspirations of ancient men and ages and own that our souls are in darkness and infirmity without faith in him who comes to bring God to man and man to God. We bless thee for the tribute that we can pay to him from our very sense of need and dependence and that our own hearts can so answer from their wilderness the cry, "Prepare ye the way of the Lord." In us the rough places are to be made smooth, the crooked straight, the mountains of pride brought low, and the valleys of despondency lifted up. O God, prepare thou the way in us now and may we welcome anew thy holy Child. Hosanna! blessed be he who cometh in the name of the Lord.—Samuel Osgood.

EXPRESSIONS OF LOVE. At the approach of the Christmas season, our Father, we seek thy presence, thankful beyond words for this beautiful time of the year, for all it means in happiness to little children, and especially for the joy it brings to all. Thou hast been our guide in years past when we created our traditions for this season. Every year they have taken on more meaning and become living symbols of our loyalty and love for each other and our devotion to Christ.

O God, thou wouldst have us explore new ways of adding meaning to these days when love is warmest in our hearts and for expressing our love to thee especially through our concern for thy little ones. The great power of love which this season calls forth has never been given adequate expression. After we have done all the customary things, there seem to be great unused energies of good left over, unexpressed. We would not be unaware of the lives about us that are hungry for love as some are for food, but neither would we burden others with sadness which would mar the perfect joy of these days.

We pray, our Father, for the peace and calmness that come from the indwelling of thy spirit. Let no business of preparations mar the serenity and evenness of our disposition. Let no attention to details keep us from being constantly aware of the supreme meaning of these days. May we be delivered from all temptation for elaborate externals or outward show. May we never depart from the beauty of simplicity. O God, may we have inexhaustible reserves of good humor and patience and understanding that we may bring to a clearer, warmer glow the flame of devotion and renew in the hearts of children and of all people the desire to make these blessings available for all children of men.—Lulu Snyder Hamilton.

PRAYER.    O God, for whose spirit our world hungers and thirsts, bless with peace and righteousness the world as the season of goodwill comes upon us. Let thy spirit rule among the nations that concord and mutual service may be established and that the mind of Christ may bind people with people and race with race in brotherhood. Support all those at this season who think and plan to give happiness to others. Help us all to be mindful and considerate of them. Abundantly bless those in whose hearts there is little room for joy because sorrow has come to them. Grant that in the knowledge of Christ's comfort they may find the peace that knows no end.—Morgan Phelps Noyes.

PRAYER.    Eternal God, we pray that in this hour of devotion and prayer we may be made aware of thy nearness to us. In so many ways thou dost come to those who have ears to hear and eyes to behold. Today we pray that thou wilt come to each one of us in the joy and blessed mystery of Christmas.

We thank thee for him who came forth from thee, who was thyself made flesh to dwell with us and to reveal to us thine heart of love and the glory of all things noble, holy, and beautiful. He is our guide, our savior, our comrade, and our hope.

We confess our halting witness to the brotherhood that he taught and to the peace and goodwill of which the angels sang on the first Christmas morn. Wilt thou raise up statesmen who shall point the way and lead the nations of the world to peace and brotherhood that thy kingdom may come and thy will be done on earth as it is in heaven.

And now in this holy season wilt thou guide each one of us to true happiness that there may not only be cheerfulness in the outer man but also a deep and abiding peace within our souls. As the shepherds of old came wondering and adoring, so may we. And as wise men came worshiping and bringing their gifts, so may we bring the gold, the incense, and the myrrh of our love to the cradle of the Christ Child.—Philip E. Gregory.

# SECTION VIII. *Evangelism and World Missions*

## SERMON SUGGESTIONS

**Topic: An Evangelistic Ministry**
TEXT: Acts 20:24.

I. *Evangelism must be first.* (a) By evangelism I mean "offering the good news of the forgiveness of sins in Jesus Christ to those who do not have it and urging them to accept it." That must take priority; it must be the overriding theme of all that I do in my ministry.

(b) We often get sidetracked by substituting function for goal. Counseling is important. Worship and education are important. The church as the body of Christ needs to be nurtured and built into a strong body. But counseling, worship, and education are functions of the body as it lives and grows. We want the body to be healthy so we can do a job, and God gave his body, the church, the job he wanted it to do: "Be my ambassadors, my instruments, my witnesses to reach out to the world." That's the overarching goal or purpose.

II. *Evangelism must be personal.* Evangelism is offering good news to the people, not just proclaiming it into space without concern for a target. People want personal attention. They want a gospel that is applied to their individual and personal needs.

III. *Evangelism must be whole.* Man is more than a body. He is a person with mental and spiritual, psychological and social needs as well as physical. Evangelism—that offer of good news, forgiveness, life, and salvation—must take into consideration the whole man with all of his needs. It must deal with his life situation, without, however, forgetting the spiritual.

IV. *Evangelism must be for everyone.* (a) Evangelism is not only the concern of the pastor but of every Christian, every man, woman, and child who knows Jesus Christ as Lord and Savior. Every Christian is a priest, we have said since the Reformation, who can read his own Bible and say his own prayers, but we need to apply that also to sharing his faith with others.

(b) We have sought to equip and build the body but have lost the purpose of doing it—to equip for witness. That is the task of the pastor or the teacher and that is the goal of worship and education—to motivate and prepare for outreach. When your ministry captures that vision you will be able to experience the meaningful, exciting, happy ministry that I think St. Paul had.—Erwin J. Kolb.

**Topic: The Great Commission**
SCRIPTURE: Matt. 28:16–20.

I. Christ claimed to have been given *all* authority in heaven and on earth.

II. Therefore he sends the church to make disciples of *all* the nations.

III. He bids those he sends to transmit to these disciples *all* his teaching.

IV. He promises to be with his people

66

*all* the days, even "to the end of time."
—John Stott.

## Topic: How Is the Christian Faith Caught?

I. *Build a relationship*. Develop a friendship, not just to exploit it, but for its own sake. And as you let yourself be known, it is a Christian "you" that is known. And this surely includes your faith.

II. *Listen and then listen some more*. Careful listening reveals another person's true interests, concerns, and even needs. Good listening is a simple way of saying, "I care about you." And listening earns the right to speak.

III. *Try "we" rather than "you."* This is an echo of Jesus' incarnation. If your friend opens his life a crack to you, you might open yours a bit to him. For the realization that you, a Christian, also have needs and problems which the biblical message of redemption has really spoken to you about, will open the possibility that maybe it could really speak to your friend's needs as well. Don't be afraid to share a little of yourself.

IV. *Pace yourself*. Don't rush another person into making a decision he is not ready to make. Convictions need to grow. Create an openness and a curiosity to know more, and then keep the relationship open for the next chat.

V. *Keep to the basics*. Weird religious puzzlers are really not important. They may just be "conversation stoppers." Admitting that you don't know some things is disarming. It may also be true. But come to the person of Jesus Christ as soon as possible. Jesus Christ is the place to center the conversation.

VI. *Mark the path to discipleship*. Make clear what becoming a Christian means. Soft-pedaling the demands is foolish. People want someone worth believing in these days. Let the cross and the resurrection make their impact. Explain what commitment means and does not mean. Let your friend see what Christian faith "feels like" by sharing in a small group, maybe a social group of friends in your home or apartment. Bring him to church if he's ready for it.

VII. *Avoid the irrelevant*. Pious clichés put people off. So does legalism. "No thanks, I don't do that: the Lord took away the desire for that when I opened my heart to him." Do you know how this sounds to a non-Christian? Denominational disagreements are pointless. If you use any printed matter, make sure it is not loaded with the writer's bias. A New Testament in modern English is better.

VIII. *Pray and then pray some more*. The "birth from above" is God's business, and if he does not create the new life, you can't. Prayer helps to correct your own attitudes. But avoid putting your friend under a kind of awkward discomfort by informing him that you are conspiring with God for his capitulation. Jesus says, "Pray in secret."

IX. *Let each commitment be unique*. So your friend doesn't weep the way you did. The point is, does he truly acknowledge Jesus Christ as his own Lord and Savior? And does he commit his whole life to this Jesus Christ? If he does, then let the experience be truly and uniquely his, not an echo of yours. Not everyone comes the same route. When James and John heard Jesus say, "Follow me," they just got up and followed him. And they kept on following him too.

X. *Follow up*. And this means whether the response is positive or negative. If the answer is "no," then your friendship should not be ended. After all you were trying to share your faith, not win a scalp. And being able to accept a "no" with kindness and love may be the most effective way to keep open the door to a later reconsideration. And if the response is "yes," then stay with your friend while he learns his first lessons in his new family and while he learns how to tell his friends and his family what has happened to him.—Harold N. Englund.

TEXT: Matt. 3:11.
## Topic: A Christian's Initiation

I. We enter the church by a process of initiation that establishes a unique relationship to God for all time. We join a society to whose rules we promise obedience. Yet initiation into the church is far more than a voluntary joining of a society of like-minded people. In fact we do not join the church so much as we are joined into it. In our Christian initiation it is God who takes the initiative. The church is his family and "household of faith."

II. Though all men are children of God, in our initiation into his church we become so in a unique way. By his gracious act he adopts us into that family as sons and heirs, joint-heirs with his Son Jesus Christ. By his free gift we are "born anew" and made living members of his family by the Holy Spirit that he imparts. And to those who remain faithful in this relationship he pledges an inheritance that is nothing less than eternal life.

III. A Christian so initiated may at some later time of course break his promises or neglect to fulfill them. He may even deny his Christian name. But he can never break or give back or exchange the mark of his family relationship. A wayward son is still a son. His birth in the family of God can never be undone, never repeated. It is in truth an "everlasting benediction."—*The Worship of the Church*.

**Topic: The Perils of Evangelism**

I. *Shallow optimism.* The "new evangelism" tells us that our task as evangelists is simply to announce to men that they are redeemed. Therefore they may go and live like it. We are told: "The redemption of the world is not dependent upon the souls we win for Christ. There cannot be individual salvation. Salvation has more to do with the whole society than with the individual soul. We must not be satisfied to win people one by one. Contemporary evangelism is moving away from winning souls one by one to the evangelization of the structures of society." Billy Graham says this is like telling the prodigal that he has no need to return to his father and home. He may make himself comfortable in the pigpen. This unwarranted optimism pulls the stinger of personal and mass evangelism.

II. *Foreboding pessimism* leaves man to conclude that there is "no exit" from our dilemma. Here the humanist might well echo Shakespeare's Hamlet: "The time is out of joint. O cursed spite that ever I was born to set it right!" The times have always been out of joint and will always be out of joint so long as men are out of fellowship with their Maker and with their fellowmen.

III. *Indifference of believers.* James S. Stewart writes, "The real problem of Christianity is not atheism or skepticism, but the nonwitnessing Christian trying to smuggle his own soul into heaven." We are all aware of this mentality.—Alton H. McEachern.

## ILLUSTRATIONS

"SO I SEND YOU." I personally believe that our failure to obey the implications of this command is the greatest weakness of evangelical Christians in the field of evangelism today. We do not identify. We believe so strongly and rightly in proclamation that we tend to proclaim our message from a distance. We do not dive in to rescue them. We are afraid of getting wet and indeed of greater perils than this. But Jesus Christ did not broadcast salvation from the sky. He visited us in great humility.—John Stott.

LOCATION. During the days of the Welsh Revivals a man from London went by train to Wales to investigate and to see for himself what was taking place. As he left the train at a certain station he saw a policeman standing in the village square. Thinking to ask him for directions, he said, "Where is the revival?" The man in blue drew himself up to his full height, patted his chest, and said, "The Welsh Revival, sir, is under these buttons."—C. Reuben Anderson.

THE OLD DOCTRINES.    The doctrines, which are so hopelessly old-fashioned we don't say much about them any more, try to express this truth on which the New Testament insists from its first page to its last: a man can change; he need not stay as he is. *Repentance* means that a man can turn away from sin. No matter how long he has been sinning, he need not go on sinning. *Conversion* means that a man can face about from darkness to light. *Regeneration* means that a man can be born anew even when he is old. *Sanctification* means that a man can become holy and can bring his thought, his emotions, his imagination, and his will into harmony with the will of God.—Frank Halliday Ferris.

FULL-ORBED EVANGELISM.    Jesus Christ is both Savior and Lord. As Savior he speaks to the person in need. As Lord he speaks to the structure in sin. A full-orbed program of Christian evangelism embraces the conversion of persons and of structures to Jesus Christ. A program that limits itself either to persons or structures is a perversion of the gospel, not simply a limited understanding of it. If the Christian faith is to make a difference in the human family it won't happen by maintaining church hierarchies. It will happen as Christians learn that they all belong to the same group of servants of Jesus Christ, then get organized to perform with power as his servants in the service of humanity.—Francis X. Pirazzini.

PASSION FOR SOULS.    The joy of catching a soul is unspeakable. When we have got one soul we become possessed by the passion for souls. Get one and you will want a crowd. Why should a man apologize for leading his fellows to the running waters and the bracing air of the open moor? Ours is the Pentecostal inheritance. Let us assume the Pentecostal attitude of zealous and hungry reception.—John Henry Jowett.

SHARING THE CROSS.    In the thirteenth century there lived in Spain a young man by the name of Ramon Lull. He was a member of the court of James I of Aragon and there enjoyed a position which provided many opportunities for pleasure. Eventually he tired of that quality of experience. He decided that he would retire to a monastery. There he spent his days in quiet meditation, but at night he would go into the town nearby where he enjoyed worldly pleasures. The day came when this bored him, and he became dreadfully unhappy. Soon he found that his sleep was being disturbed by dreams in which he would hear voices calling him to a life of service to mankind. In one dream Christ appeared to him, asking him to accept the gifts of the spirit, gifts of inner peace. He awakened shouting: "I don't want to do it! I don't want to do it!" Then one night Christ appeared to Ramon Lull and without a word put the cross into Lull's hands, looked him in the eyes, and turned away. Lull awakened with a start and said aloud: "To think that I should help Christ carry his cross in the work of the redemption of mankind. This I will do." Straightaway he went out to live as he believed Christ would have him.—Homer J. R. Elford.

BELIEVING IN MISSIONS.    I have never met the man who has seen Christian missions in action who didn't believe in missions. Missions are schools and hospitals, for example, and the man who says he doesn't believe in schools and hospitals is not talking religion or irreligion; he is talking nonsense. Missions are a nurse who slogs through the mud of a Fijian village in the dark of night to deliver a baby on the floor of a one-room shack. I'm at a loss to know what it means to say that one doesn't believe in this kind of work that saves lives. Is it conceivable that any sane man should contend that this is not worth doing? This is the shared life, and no other religion that the world has ever seen knows anything about it. It is the life that Jesus lived and still lives.—Charles H. Buck, Jr.

GIFT OF LOVE. There is only one missionary attitude and action that is appropriate to facing the global realities of today, which, like dumb idols, are so irresponsible and inhuman. It is love. "Many gifts, one Spirit"—yes. But let us not forget, as Paul reminds us, that however diverse our gifts may be, the one gift we must all have if the others are not to become sterile and idolatrous is the gift of love.—Philip A. Potter.

MANIFESTATION OF GOD. The missionary movement is inseparable from the very nature of the Christian faith. This remains true however much we may recognize the values in non-Christian religions. Some of them are today experiencing a renaissance. This is apparently due in considerable part to their identification with the regnant nationalisms. To be truly an Indian, it is urged, is to be loyal to Hinduism as the indigenous faith of India. To be a patriotic Burmese likewise is to be a Buddhist. To be a good Pakistani is to be a Moslem. But even if we gladly and gratefully acknowledge these religions to be great manifestations of man's search for God, there is still the final fact that they do not have Jesus Christ as the manifestation of God to man. That is the uniqueness of the Christian faith. If it is true for any man, it is true for every man. Jesus Christ is the Light of the world, not just of America or Europe. That is the heart of the Christian faith. To hold that faith is to be committed to a worldwide mission of the Christian church.—Samuel McCrea Cavert.

MISSIONARY HEN. In Gloucester, England, in an old-fashioned garden and orchard there stood this quaint marker, dated December 21, 1869:

"Here lies Tidman's missionary hen,
Her contributions, four pounds, ten;
Although she is dead, the work goes on,
As she has left seven daughters and a son,

To carry on the work that she had begun.
So be it."

Here is the story behind the marker. A man named Tidman lived in a little village. He longed to do something for the London Missionary Society in its program of world evangelization. He had little funds to give and so decided that one of his hens should belong to the society and that all of the eggs which she laid should be sold and the money given to the missionary society. Before the hen died the money amounted to four pounds, ten shillings (about $23). But that was not all. The hen sat on eight eggs which hatched, and these too were assigned to be the property of the missionary society. In time they brought in a large amount of money.—C. Reuben Anderson.

INNER VOICE. At the General Conference of the Methodist Church in 1924 E. Stanley Jones was made a bishop and was within hours of his consecration. I heard him tell about the sleepless night he spent after his election. He said that in the night the Inner Voice had spoken to him, saying, "Stanley, if you decline this honor, I'll let you walk with me through Asia." It was enough. He declined the bishop's chair. The Inner Voice proved right. Not Asia only but the world!—Paul S. Rees.

ARTICLES OF FAITH. Give your heart to the friend and lover of men, who died on the cross to redeem us from eternal woe, and you will find such peace and sweetness as you have never imagined.

The conversion of one immortal soul on those foreign shores awakens in me a deeper emotion than all the beauties of the glorious land of America.

I do not know that I shall live to see a single convert, but notwithstanding I feel that I would not leave my present position to be made a king.

I was never deeply interested in any matter and prayed earnestly for it but at some time, in some way, the answer came. And yet I have had so little faith.

I am not tired of my work, neither am I tired of the world; yet when Christ calls me home I shall go with the gladness of a boy bounding away from his school.

Death will never take me by surprise —I feel so strong in Christ. He has not led me so tenderly thus far to forsake me at the very gate of heaven.

The result of our travels and toils has been the wisest and best possible— —a result which, if we could see the end from the beginning, would call forth our highest praise.—Adoniram Judson, American missionary in Burma from 1814 to 1850.

WITHOUT HELP OR HOPE.    Physical misery is everywhere out here. Are we justified in shutting our eyes and ignoring it because our European [and he might have said, American] newspapers tell us nothing about it? We civilized people have been spoiled. If any one of us is ill the doctor comes at once. If an operation is necessary the door of some hospital or other opens to us immediately. But let one reflect on the meaning of the fact that out here [in Africa] millions and millions live without help or hope of it. Every day thousands and thousands endure the most terrible sufferings, though medical science could avert them. Every day there prevails in many and many a far-off hut a despair which we could banish. Will each of my readers think what the last ten years of his family history would have been if they had been passed without medical or surgical help of any sort. It is time that we should wake from slumber and face our responsibilities.—Albert Schweitzer in *On the Edge of the Primeval Forest.*

# SECTION IX. Children's Stories and Sermons

## January 2. The Man Who Kept Christmas

Once there was a man who so enjoyed the spirit of Christmas that he decided to keep it always. So he put it in a large jar and set it on the mantelpiece, where it gave a lovely glow all through the Christmas season.

Soon after however there was quite a to-do, what with packing away the lights and ornaments and the manger scene and getting the tree out of the house without its shedding too many needles. Somewhere along the line the jar with the Christmas spirit disappeared, and no one seemed to know where it had gone.

Months later when rummaging about the attic the man discovered the jar once more, and he was shocked to find the glow was gone. All that remained was a small, hard, black clinker that rattled thinly as he shook it. The man brought the jar downstairs and regarded it thoughtfully for a long time. Then he decided to do something about it. Before he went to bed that night he got a little brown paper bag and filled it with some odds and ends he hadn't used for months. During the days that followed he distributed these odds and ends as he went about his daily duties: a pinch of good cheer here, a wish of goodwill there, some charity, some thoughtfulness, and some love. And lo, one night he came home to find his jar of Christmas spirit glowing as brightly as ever, shedding its radiance throughout the house and into the dark night beyond. And ever since he has kept the spirit of Christmas glowing every day.—*The Gold Star Family Album.*

## January 9. Climbing a Mountain and Living a Life

Where would you be if you had gone as high as a man can go and still have his feet on the earth? You would be on top of Mt. Everest, the highest mountain in the world.

The first American to climb to the top of the world's highest mountain was Jim Whittaker. It took him six weeks, and he lost thirty pounds. He had to brave strong winds and temperatures as low as thirty degrees below zero!

When the mountain-climbing team left the United States, each man was asked this question, "Will you get to the top?" Most answered, "I hope so" or "I'll surely do my best." Jim answered, "Yes, I will."

Jim knew that he could never do it alone, and he did not do it alone. He needed not only good equipment but also good partners. He had many partners at the beginning of the climb, but one by one they had to drop back. When Jim Whittaker finally reached the top, there was only one partner still with him—his native guide, Nwang Gombu.

Jim Whittaker needed equipment in order to climb Mt. Everest. So too do you need equipment in order to live your life. You won't need strong ropes to help you live as much as you will need a strong faith in God. Without this faith you'd give up and quit. Some people do. And you won't need the mountain climber's spiked boots; you'll need something at the opposite end of your body—a head filled with the results of a good education. With faith in your heart and facts in your head, you'll have some mighty fine equipment for living your life.

And you'll need partners. Jim Whittaker had many partners at the lower levels, but one by one he lost them as he climbed onward and upward until at the top he had only one partner left —his guide.

So it is in life. You have many partners now. You have God as your guide. You have your parents, your teachers, your minister, and your friends. But as you go on in life these good partners will leave you for one reason or another. And finally at the end of your life you will have only one partner left, the one who will never leave you—your guide who is God.

So let him be your very best partner and guide right now!—James N. Urquhart.

## January 16. Overcoming Obstacles (Missionary Day)

When William Carey was a young man in England in the 1770s he felt the unbelievers in other lands should also hear the good news about Jesus. But in those days missionaries did not go out to other lands to preach the gospel. At a church council meeting the bishop said to Carey, "If God will see fit to convert the heathen he will do it without your help or mine." The bishop was wrong, of course. There were many more obstacles in William Carey's life, for even his own family was against his going out. In 1793 he went to India and spent many years there as a missionary.

Carey is considered by many to be the greatest missionary since the apostle Paul. They had one thing in common— obstacles all the way, and yet they went right ahead serving the Lord. Is there an obstacle in your life? Will you overcome it and serve the Lord?—Martha Janzen in *Rejoice!*

## January 23. The Christian's Stabilizer

Norfolk Island in the Pacific Ocean is the home of a bird called the tropic bird. These large white birds with their long, red tail feathers make nests on the cliffs. The long tail feather acts as a rudder to keep the bird on course over the long miles of flying over the sea. If this red tail feather is lost for any reason, the bird becomes unbalanced and unstabilized in flight—virtually helpless.

Faith in God is a Christian's stabilizer. It enables us to know right from wrong, to overcome temptation, to help others by our love and understanding, and to steer a straight course with God. The stronger our faith becomes the truer the course we steer. However if our faith becomes weak we begin to wobble; and if it is lost we flounder and sink into sin, becoming unsure of our direction.—Winifred G. Walker in *The Upper Room.*

## January 30. Cheating Ourselves

In days when ocean travel was a matter of weeks, an inexperienced passenger made a crossing with no food except the crackers and cheese he had brought aboard. After the vessel had docked at his destination, he learned that the price he had paid for his ticket included all meals en route. He had thought he was practicing economy, but he had gone to needless expense and had forfeited varied meals for the crackers and cheese he ate alone.

On the journey of life many persons defraud themselves by accepting short rations for mind and emotions. When one gives his attention to that which is less than the best, he is cheating himself. When worthwhile books, new or old, are available in paperback or may be borrowed from public libraries, one who limits his reading to the trivial dulls his taste and degrades his mind.

It pays to give honest thought and consideration to our style in Christian living. We need to ask ourselves, "If I get what I want, will I want what I get?"—Elinor Lennen.

## February 6. He Heard His Mother Pray

Abe Lincoln was only nine when his mother, Nancy Hanks Lincoln, died. Nine years seems a brief allotment for a mother to impress a child for life, but so deep was the influence of Nancy on the impressionable Abe that in later life Lincoln declared, "All that I am or hope to be, I owe to my angel mother."

Why was Nancy Lincoln so special to her son? She was just an ordinary woman given to the hard labors of a rugged frontier. Her life was brief and simple, but impressions she made upon the heart of her son truly lasted.

Abe Lincoln's mother taught him by precept and example the simple principle of prayer. Little Abe had knelt at his mother's knee. He had heard his mother talk with God. Years later he said: "I remember my mother's prayers and they have always followed me. They have clung to me all my life."—Lawrence R. Giles.

## February 13. The Face of Christ (Race Relations Sunday)

Turgenev once dreamed that he was in a wooden church where waxed candles burned. As he stood among many fair-haired Russian folk, a man came up and stood behind him. Turgenev sensed that the man was Christ. Then, overwhelmed by curiosity and awe, he looked at his neighbor. He saw "a face like all men's faces." The Christ was "an ordinary, ordinary man!" That could not be! But the writer turned away. Then he knew that the peasant standing beside him was none other than Christ. He made another effort to control himself, but then he was haunted by "the same face" with its "everyday though unknown features." The novelist's heart sank, and he came to himself. Only then did he realize "that such a face—a face like all men's faces—is the face of Christ."—Woodrow A. Geier.

## February 20. Using His Talent

Through the summer months the minister of a Scottish seaside parish held worship services in the local schoolhouse. There being no regular pianist, he would ask for volunteers from the congregation to accompany the hymns. On this particular Sunday no one responded to his appeal. Finally a small girl piped up, "My daddy can play the piano." Sure enough, after a little hesitation, her father came forward, sat down at the piano, and began to play the opening hymn—with one finger. He never missed a note and his timing was perfect. The minister learned afterward he was a well-known surgeon from a nearby city. There were probably other worshipers present who were better players. But as a dedicated Christian this surgeon was accustomed to giving any talent he possessed—making no excuses that he had not more to offer.—J. M. Orr.

## February 27. Keeping Lent (Lent)

There is a story of a Jewish ghetto in east Europe that had all the businesses and crafts except a watchmaker. People's clocks and watches played out for want of attention. Their rabbi kept insisting that the members of his congregation wind their watches and keep them running, even though they were inaccurate. One day a watchmaker arrived from another community. Everyone rushed to him to get his timepiece fixed. But the only ones he could repair were those that had been kept running. The abandoned clocks and watches had grown too rusty to be saved. It is so with keeping Lent. To neglect consideration of the passion of Christ is to collect rust in our Christian works.—*South Carolina Methodist Advocate*.

## March 6. His Life for Hers (Lent)

The sister of a young boy was gravely ill. Blood for transfusion was desperately needed to implement the hope that she might yet survive. The parents had donated all the doctors would allow. The only donor at hand was the young brother. Father and mother took him aside and asked if he would be willing to give his blood to help save his sister's life. The boy was thoughtfully silent. Thinking that he had not understood, they made the request again. Still silence, and then the lad said "Yes."

Wishing to relieve the youngster of any alarm during the procedure, the doctor gave him a light anesthetic. As he returned to consciousness, the father and mother were at his side to tell him of their love and gratitude for his generosity in giving his blood to save his sister's life. Again there was no immediate response. As they continued to speak of their love to their little boy, he finally looked up at his parents and said, "But I thought you asked me if I were willing to give my life."—Glenn B. Ogden.

## March 13. Branded for Jesus (Lent)

Branding was an important aspect of ranching in the West, particularly in the days of the open range. The brand on cattle or less frequently on horses was proof of ownership at the time of the roundup.

Branding was important in other ways in biblical times. Captives were frequently branded with the name of their captor. Similarly slaves sometimes had the name of their owner branded or stamped on them. Similarly those who have been captured by Christ, those who have become his slaves, have his mark branded or stamped on them. (See Gal. 6:17.)

For Paul these brands or marks of ownership by the Lord were his scars. Our brands are not physical brands or marks. There may be some people in the world who suffer physical punishment for their obedience to Christ, but that is not true of you or me.

However that which is inner cannot help but manifest itself outwardly. Can those about us in the home and on the street, where we work and where we play, see some of the marks of Jesus in our lives? Have we really been branded by him and for him?—T. B. Maston.

## March 20. The Family Table (Lent)

Jesus spent a good deal of time around family tables not only with good friends like Mary, Martha, and Lazarus but also with "tax collectors and sinners." For him the table seemed to be a symbol of the large family into which God called us all—saints and sinners, sweet and sour. Just before his death Jesus and his disciples celebrated the Passover by gathering around a table to break bread and share a common cup. For Christians this event became the sacrament of the Lord's Supper. This sacrament renews commitment to Christ and creates fellowship among the communicants.

Our family tables stand as symbols of God's all-encompassing love, drawing us together and breaking down the barriers that divide us.—Wayne C. Rollins in *These Days*.

## March 27. The Passionflower (Passion Sunday)

In 1610 an Italian ecclesiastic and historian, Giacomo Basio, received drawings of a flower described as "stupendously marvelous" from a Mexican Augustinian friar, Emmanuel de Villegas. Basio was captivated by the flower's symbolic resemblance to the passion of Christ and felt it was his duty to present it to the entire world as an example of the Creator's work. The extraordinary arrangements of the plant's floral parts began to take on a host of associations appropriate to the Lenten season which leads up to Easter.

The bud of the flower represents the Eucharist; the parts of the floral envelope, the petals and sepals, represent the ten faithful apostles of Christ; the corona represents the crown of thorns; the five stamens represent the hammers or wounds; the three styles represent the nails and the three bracts on the peduncle, the trinity. In addition the half-opened flower represents the star of the East, and the long roots descending into the earth symbolize the triumph over

hell and signify Christ's resurrection.—
Edward S. Ayensu in *Smithsonian*.

## April 3. The Guest (Lent)

A pious father always closed grace
for the evening meal with these words:
"Come, Lord Jesus, be our guest and
bless what thou hast provided." "Papa,"
said the little son, "every evening you
ask Jesus to come and be our guest, but
he never comes." "My son," replied the
father, "we can only wait. But we know
that he will not despise our invitation."
"Well, then," asked the little fellow, "if
we expect him to come and have dinner
with us, why don't we set a place for
him at the table?" And so to save further embarrassing questions, the father
permitted the boy to set a place at the
table. Just then a knock came at the
door. When they opened it a poor helpless waif stood shivering in the cold.
The son thought for a moment and
finally said, "I guess Jesus couldn't come
today, and so he sent this poor boy in
his place." With little further conversation the little beggar boy was brought
in and set at the empty place at the
dinner table.—John W. Wade.

## April 10. Candles at Dawn (Easter)

The Church of the Holy Sepulchre in
the heart of the city of Jerusalem this
year will blaze forth the glory of the
resurrection.

In the center of that huge pile of
stone is a magnificently wrought sepulchre. Here in the tomb of Joseph, tradition tells us, Christ was laid.

At arm's height, in the wall of this
tomb, there is a tubelike opening.
Created from alabaster, it is about six
inches in diameter. It literally invites
one to thrust his hand and arm into
the opening. And that is what happens
at daybreak each Easter morning. There
is a tremendous sentiment related to
this. For in this act a miracle occurs.
Here is the impressive story.

Youth all over Palestine are waiting
at dawn. One young man, considered
most worthy, is privileged to reach a
candle into the alabaster opening in the
sealed tomb. His arm and hand tarry

within the empty sepulchre for a moment, and then he draws it forth. His
candle has been lighted from within.

As he turns to light the outreached
candles held by other lads, he shouts,
"Hallelujah, Christ is risen!"

These young men now hurry as ra-
pidly as lighted candles will permit to
the doorways of the cathedral. Here
eager young men are waiting with their
candles, also to hear the glad tiding,
"Hallelujah, Christ is risen." Then off
they run to street ends, to villages along
highways, and to town centers, each with
the shout, "Hallelujah, Christ is risen."

And waiting in towns and villages are
more expectant lads with their unlighted
candles. Then they in turn to small,
narrow streets and doorways with their
"Hallelujahs." It is all an impressive
yearly event on Easter morning. The
lighting of the candles becomes an unforgettable symbolic act which carries
its message to every portal and home in
the land.—F. B. McAllister.

## April 17. Courageous Witness

When Chrysostom appeared before the
Roman emperor charged with being a
Christian, the emperor threatened him
with banishment if he would not renounce Christ. Chrysostom replied,
"Thou canst not banish me, for the
whole world is my Father's kingdom."

"Then I will take away thy life," said
the emperor.

"But thou canst not," was the reply,
"for my life is his with Christ in God."

"I will take away thy treasure."

"Thou canst not for my treasure is in
heaven where my heart is."

"Then I will drive thee away from
man and thou shalt have no friend left."

"Thou canst not," again said Chrysostom, "for I have one Friend from whom
thou canst never separate me. I defy
thee for thou canst do me no harm."

## April 24. The Briar and the Rose

Once there was a briar growing in a
ditch, and there came along a gardener
with his spade. As he dug around it
and lifted it out, the briar said to itself:
"What is he doing that for? Doesn't he

know I am only a old worthless briar?"

But the gardener took it into the garden and planted it amid his flowers while the briar said: "What a mistake he has made! Planting an old briar like myself amid such rose trees as these!"

But the gardener came once more and with his keen-edged knife made a slit in the briar and budded it with a rose, and by and by when summer came lovely roses were blooming on that old briar.

Then the gardener said, "Our beauty is not due to that which came out of you but to that which I put into you." —Mark Guy Pearse.

## May 1. Enough for Now

A small girl was asked to recite Ps. 23 in a church school program. She rehearsed it beautifully at home; however, in front of the congregation she became speechless and frightened. All that she could say was "The Lord is my shepherd, I shall not want." Her teacher tried to whisper the words, but she became more confused. Tears began to roll down her cheeks. Then, just before running off the platform, she hastily added, "And that'll be enough for now." —Jack Naff.

## May 8. Story of a Bad Boy

The highest mountain in the state of New York is called Mt. Marcy. That name seems strange because it was named after a town's "bad boy," a boy that had the reputation of being incorrigible and was nicknamed "Wild Bill." The honor of having the highest mountain named after him would never have come if it had not been for a modest schoolteacher who, when the rest of the community considered Bill incorrigible, refused to believe it. She was of the opinion that he was not really a bad boy at all and that he did have a potential. Her faith in Bill led her to make a risky investment in him.

For more than a decade she spent many hours each day with "Wild Bill," many of them annoying and seemingly unrewarding, but she persisted, never losing faith in Bill. It took a long time

for the investment in the boy to pay any dividends at all, and then one day a few of Bill's contemporaries caught the enthusiasm of the schoolteacher for Bill, and they suggested his name for a public office and to their amazement he was elected. After that it was not long until in rapid succession he was chosen the Governor of the State of New York, then a United States Congressman from that state, a second term as Governor, and then to the United States Senate where he did yeoman service as one of the greatest in his day in the Senate.

And so when they came to name their highest mountain, they selected the name not of the town's "bad boy" but the most beloved man in the state for that great honor. It would never have been called Mt. Marcy if it had not been for a modest, small-town schoolteacher who steadfastly refused to underestimate Wild Bill Marcy. Underestimate no man for there is no man without his hour, not even Wild Bill Marcy.— Donald H. Tippett.

## May 15. A View from Space (Rural Life Sunday)

The space flights to the moon and the visitation to its surface by man will perhaps rank as the greatest achievement of this century. This milestone has allowed man to peek into a little more of God's creation, a part of which has mystified every generation since time began for them.

Perhaps this successful venture has achieved another purpose in that it has shown earth as God's garden spot of the universe by comparison with the other bodies within vision. Unquestionably it has also proved that his creation of earth was unique in relationship to those other bodies we have learned about from the many scientists who have long studied them. As man has been able to photograph earth from out in many thousands of miles in space, what a different sphere indeed it presents to any other body we have so far been able to study.

How much more now the stirring words of Ps. 24 mean as we read, "The earth is the Lord's and the fullness thereof; the world and they that dwell therein." The firmament indeed showeth his handiwork.—James G. Goodwin in *Sunshine Magazine*.

## May 22. Lost Treasures

In the Valley of the Kings at Luxor in Egypt, which has been called the "city of the dead," the elaborate tombs all tend to follow the same pattern. The excavated entrances at the base of the mountain open into long corridors hewn out of solid rock and lead downward toward the rooms containing the treasures buried with dead monarchs.

Nearly all these foyerlike corridors in the pitch blackness come upon perpendicular pits carved out of the rock with straight up and down sides and deep enough to kill him who falls into them.

Thus the trap was designed to take the life of any would-be grave robber. The latter was common in the ancient world because of the custom then to bury the precious possessions of the deceased with him.

Only one ancient tomb has been unearthed whose valuables were still intact. In other words all of the care of the ancients to prevent their graves from being robbed was for naught. It is believed that the very people who dug the tombs robbed them or that succeeding monarchs learned the secret and had the tombs robbed in their behalf.

Men have always had trouble making their treasures secure. Whatever earthly treasure one accumulates, it must be observed that perfect security for it is impossible. Jesus made this observation in Matt. 6:19-20.—Franklin Owen in *Western Recorder*.

## May 29. The Lonely Drummer Boy

Marching in the Memorial Day parade was a little drummer boy about seven years old. For some reason he had fallen about 200 feet behind his unit of children. He was also at least 200 feet ahead of the next unit. Up the avenue he marched unconcerned that he was all by himself. Unintentionally he was a star. Groups of people applauded as he

went by, but he didn't seem to notice. He was altogether intent on playing his drum as best he could, continuing to march on all by himself.

The lad had a message for me and for us. He kept on going. When we feel lonely it is not the time to sit down and wring our hands.

He didn't worry what others said. When Christian principles call us to march alone we must not worry what others think. He continued to drum his best. When we can't keep up with others there is no reason to do less than our best. God wants the best from us, and he helps us accomplish it whenever we need to walk alone. He cares for us then as always.—Eugene W. Ebert.

## June 5. The Head of Lincoln

Gutzon Borglum, the sculptor, was working on a head of Abraham Lincoln. Each day he chipped away the stone, and each day it was the task of a cleaning woman to sweep up the pieces and carry them off. Amazed, she watched the head of Lincoln emerge under the sculptor's hands until at last, when the work was almost finished, she could hold in her wonder no longer. "Mr. Borglum," she said, "how'd you know Mr. Lincoln was in that stone?"

## June 12. Children God Used (Children's Day)

Have you noticed how many times in the Bible children have been used by God to help others?

Just think what might have happened if Miriam had not watched over her baby brother Moses. If Miriam had not been there, the baby might have been found by soldiers of the king and taken away to be killed.

Samuel was given the task of helping Eli in the temple.

A young girl helped her Syrian master, Naaman, by telling him that Elisha, the prophet, would be able to cure him of his disease.

David was the youngest son of eight, and yet he was the one who with the help of God fought and killed the giant.

A young boy offered his picnic to

Jesus to feed 5,000 people. Two loaves and five fish were given; they seemed so little, but the boy gave them gladly and Jesus was able to feed all the people with them.—Gillian Leech.

## June 19. The Fourth Astronaut

When an oxygen tank exploded aboard Apollo 13 in April 1970, the lives of four astronauts hung in the balance for four anxious days. Worldwide attention was focused on the plight of astronauts James Lovell, Fred Haise, and John Swigart. Special prayers were offered in churches throughout the world. Thirteen nations, including the Soviet Union, offered assistance in the rescue mission.

During the time of the rescue effort, the father of one of the astronauts stated in an interview that there was a fourth astronaut riding in the capsule with them. He was referring to God. When asked if he thought God played a role in the recovery, one of the astronauts replied that he had prayed, and he believed God had directed them.

God directs us today just as he directed his people long ago. As long as they obeyed him, he promised to guide them in their battles.—John A. Ishee in *Home Life*.

## June 26. An Eagle among the Chickens

A young farm boy found an egg in the desert. He brought it home and put it in the chicken coop where one of the chickens hatched it. As the bird grew it was obviously different from the other chickens, but it acted like the rest. It pecked at corncobs and scratched for grain. But this bird was not a chicken; it was an eagle. What a pathetic sight to see this proud monarch of the skies scratching and pecking like a chicken. One day the boy took the eagle to the top of a mountain and hurled it over a cliff. The eagle was afraid and momentarily panicked. It spread its wings. The wind came up under them. Its descent was suddenly arrested. It began to glide and rise and fall with the air currents. Then it flapped its wings and began to climb toward the sun. It swooped and soared. It circled over the boy's head.

Then it disappeared over the horizon.

Men are like that. We are appalled at the man who lives like an animal. He is dirty, self-centered, and vulgar. His life is wholly lacking in discipline and morals. What is it that is so appalling about such a person? Man is not just another animal. Man is destined and intended for a higher kind of existence than that. The man who lives like an animal is like the young eagle that looks so pathetic among the chickens.—Warren E. Shaw.

## July 3. A Voice from the Sky

I saw a little old sparrow down on the sidewalk, hobbling along. One wing drooped. It went over into a corner next to the church door. Eddies of bitter wind choked with street dust, and flying gum wrappers almost blinded the sparrow. "I'm all alone and so sick and no one really cares. If I die I'll just lie here until they sweep me away into the gutter. Who will go to my funeral?" So the sparrow thought, never expecting a reply which came from the downcast sky. "Me. I'll go to your funeral, little sparrow," said the Lord.—Merton S. Rice.

## July 10. An Experience under the Stars

Long ago a young man sat alone under the evening sky. The sheep he was tending gathered quietly beside a little stream and settled for the night. The young shepherd watched as the sun sank slowly in the west, painting the sky with the hues of the desert sunset. Gradually more and more stars appeared, and before long the sky seemed to be studded with sparkling jewels. The Milky Way made a path of glory across the sky. The beauty and wonder of the night filled his soul to overflowing. He burst forth spontaneously, "The heavens declare the glory of God and the firmament sheweth his handiwork."

The words of the shepherd-psalmist concerning God and the starry heavens were truer than he himself had any way of knowing. With his unaided eyes he could see between 2,000 and 3,000 stars on a clear night. During the course of a year of sheepherding, he could have seen about 6,000 different stars. How many stars are there that he could not see? In one star city, our own Milky Way, there are millions of stars, and the largest telescope has found nearly two million star cities.

An experience under the stars can enlarge one's conception of God. Back of the great plan which one sees enacted in the heavens is a great planner. The order and dependability which allow astronomers to predict the course of the stars with precision far off into the future are expressions of the trustworthiness of the master designer and builder of the heavens.—Howard J. Clinebell.

### July 17. The Stubborn Horse

A horse received a hero's tribute in Oviedo, Spain. It was credited with having saved several lives because it stubbornly refused to enter a tunnel. The driver of the horse and cart, a local baker, exhorted the stalled animal to move along. But it would not budge. Meanwhile a long line of impatient motorists on the road between Ciano and La Nueva was being held up. Before the horse could be removed by force, the tunnel collapsed.

We can profit in many ways by observing and heeding the instinct of animals. In its limited way it is one more manifestation of the wisdom of the Creator working through nature. The more aware we become of the many and varied forms in which the Lord reveals his creative power for the benefit of mankind, the closer we will draw to him. And the more effectively will we cooperate with him in applying his love and truth to every facet of daily life. —The Christophers.

### July 24. He Remembered His Brother

Once a cold, hungry boy, dirty and dressed in rags, wandered into a mission in his slum neighborhood. The mission workers took the boy in. They bathed him and dressed him in clean clothes. Then they set him in front of a warm heater and fed him a good, hot meal. After thanking them for their help, he left.

Within a few minutes he was back and with him was a smaller boy, dirtier than he had been. The smaller boy was his little brother. He had brought his brother to the people who had expressed love to him. He wanted his brother to have the things that he had found.

John and Andrew had followed Jesus. They had heard him speak and had accompanied him to the place he was staying. They spent the whole day with Jesus. Can you imagine what spending a whole day with Jesus would be like?

Like the poor boy, they must have experienced things that they had never dreamed of. Like the boy, they wanted others to know what they had discovered. Andrew "first findeth his own brother Simon" and told him, "We have found the . . . Christ."

Like the boy who wanted his brother to have food and clothing, Andrew wanted his brother to experience the teachings and love of Christ. Because of Andrew's concern, Peter became one of Jesus' disciples.—Charles and Nancye Willis in *Home Life*.

### July 31. A Matter of Caring

Babe Ruth had hit 714 home runs during his career, and this was one of his last full major league games. It was the Braves versus the Reds in Cincinnati. The great Ruth was no longer as agile as he had once been. He fumbled the ball, threw badly, and in one inning his misplays were responsible for most of the five runs scored by Cincinnati. As he walked off the field after the third out and headed toward the dugout, a crescendo of yelling and booing reached his ears.

Just then a boy jumped over the railing and with tears streaming down his face threw his arms about the knees of his hero. Ruth didn't hesitate for one second. He picked up the boy, hugged him, and set him down on his feet, patting his head gently. The noisy fans stopped booing, and a silent hush enveloped the park. The scene of one little boy who cared about the feelings of another human being melted the hearts of the crowd.—Alfred J. Kolatch in *Guideposts*.

## August 7. Judging by Appearances

Lizards are generally a fearsome-looking lot. Some look like snakes with no feet at all, and some run along the ground on their hind legs looking like birds of prey. Many have the remnants of a third eye which was once located in the top of their head, and some are able to glide through the air. Some can travel backward or forward like a worm, and most of them can break off their tail any time they need to escape. And one kind of lizard looks for all the world like the dragons of mythology, growing to twelve feet in length and using its long whiplike tail to cut down foes.

Yet of all these 2,500 kinds of lizards only two are poisonous: the Gila monster of America's southwest and its cousin, the Heloderm of Mexico. All the rest are nonpoisonous, and many of them are easily tamed, can learn simple tricks, and will answer to calls.

We must be careful not to judge others by appearances but remember that their worth is judged only by God. —Max L. Batchelder in *The Lookout*.

## August 14. God-Pleasers

Anyone who follows the world of athletics knows what a crowd-pleaser is. He or she is that athlete who not only plays the game with extraordinary skill but also does everything with a flair of excitement. The spectators love it. Perhaps that is why I have seen Willy Mays receive a stout round of applause for striking out! He could do even that with class.

I suppose that most of us would like to be crowd-pleasers and be lauded by the masses. But through Paul's reflection on his own ministry he calls us to be God-pleasers instead. His words suggest that we cannot be both.

People of faith have long known the struggle of trying simultaneously to please both God and man. And a real struggle it is! But it is a struggle in which we are keeping good company for Paul knew it too. Note that the passage (I Thess. 2:1–8) in which he proclaims his speaking to please God is the same one in which he reminds the Thessalonians of his gentleness with them. Clearly he realized that we please God the most when we love people the best. For love is the connecting link which keeps us in touch with both God and others. And which keeps life worth living too.—Donald F. Becker.

## August 21. Parable

Behold a ball team went forth to play a game. Just as the umpire was saying "Batter up" the catcher for the home team arrived and took his place. The center fielder didn't arrive until the second inning. The first baseman didn't show up at all but later sent his regrets and said that he had to go to a chicken dinner at Aunt Mary's. The third baseman didn't show because he had been up late the night before and decided to sleep late. The left fielder felt the need to visit another ball game across town. A shortstop was present but had left his glove at home. Two players were away on a weekend trip and could not make it but were there in spirit.

Verily, when the pitcher went into the box, he looked around for his teammates and lo, his heart was heavy for their places were empty. But the game was announced and the visitors were in the stands, so the game had to go on.

So the pitcher tightened his belt, stepped into the box, and did his best to serve as pitcher, first baseman, and third baseman. There were boos from the stands while the home team was badly beaten.

Verily, verily, when the absent members of the defeated team had lost, decision was made to get a new pitcher, but who really lost the ball game?— Hugh Smith.

## August 28. Holy Ground

What would you say Sunday morning if an usher met you at the church door with these words: "Take off your shoes. This is holy ground." There was a time when removing the shoes was a mark of respect. It is to this day in some oriental churches. Perhaps such an act of respect would help us to get more out of our church services. It would serve to remind us to leave the world behind us when we enter God's presence. The sense of reverence might help us to expect the transforming power of God from this service. "Be still and know that I am God" reminds me to listen if I am to receive. Isaiah went to the temple expecting to meet God. The result? He saw the power and glory of God. He saw himself for what he was—a sinner in need of forgiveness. He was forgiven, and God's cleansing fire took away his sin. He dedicated his life to God. When the Lord's call to service came he was ready. "Here am I. Send me!"—Ada B. Hoelscher in *Family Devotions*.

## September 4. Jephthah's Promise

This story of Jephthah and his daughter—how tragic it is! Jephthah had been made the battle leader of Israelites in a war against their most dangerous enemies. Before the battle Jephthah made a promise to God. If he could only win the battle, so Jephthah promised, then he would sacrifice to God the first thing which came out to meet him when he returned home. No doubt Jephthah thought a dog or some other household animal would trot out to meet him. But it was his only child! As she came rushing out proudly and happily to welcome her father home from the battle, suddenly Jephthah remembered his promise to God.

We all make promises which later seem foolish. We do things or say things which are unkind or thoughtless. We fall into bad habits. But no matter how much we get mixed up in our lives, God loves us and can help us find the way out. No matter how much trouble we cause ourselves, God can help us to live bravely through our mistakes and even to become through them more useful to him.—Stephen Greene.

## September 11. The Live Helicopter

Believe it or not, there is a live helicopter with humming wings that flap so fast that you have to look twice to see them and with color so pretty that it glows! What is it? A hummingbird!

This tiny bird is really God's wonder. Who else could make a bird so tiny that it weighs no more than a lemon drop? Who else could make a bird so small that it can fit in a nest that is the size of a marshmallow! And who but God could make a bird with green feathers that seem to turn to shimmering gold before your very eyes? Who but God could make a bird with a ruby-red throat that sparkles in the sun like a jewel?

But the tiny hummingbird is blessed even more! It is blessed with strange and wonderful wings, and with these wings that can beat so fast that they look like a blur it can make a strange humming noise—just like a helicopter. It can even flutter in the air, right over a blooming bush or pretty flower, and fly back and forth, just like a helicopter.

The tiny hummingbird is a live helicopter, all right, which God created long, long before man even thought of machines with wings.—Clare Miseles in *Sunshine Magazine*.

## September 18. Rewarding Another Person

Do you remember the story of Queen Esther and Mordecai?

At one time Mordecai learned of a plot to kill the king. He was able to reveal the plot and thus save the king's life. The deed was recorded and then forgotten.

One night the king could not sleep. He ordered the book of records to be read to him. When the men read about Mordecai, the king asked, "Has he been rewarded?" The men answered, "He has not been." In the morning the king called Haman, his favorite official, and asked, "What should I do for the man I want to honor?"

Haman thought: "The person the king wants to honor must be me. What would I like to have the king do for me?" Quickly he answered. Imagine his disappointment when he was told to carry out his suggestions for Mordecai.

Jesus asks us to do by choice what Haman did unwittingly. What do you wish someone would do for you? Do it for someone else.—Ruth Conrad Leichty.

## September 25. New Salem Postmaster

When he was 24, Abraham Lincoln served as the postmaster of New Salem, Illinois, for which he was paid an annual salary of $55.70.

The New Salem post office was closed in 1836, but it was several years before an agent arrived from Washington to settle accounts with ex-postmaster Lincoln, who was a struggling lawyer and not doing too well.

The agent informed him that there was $17 due the government. Lincoln crossed the room, opened an old trunk, and took out a yellowed cotton rag bound with string. Untying it, he spread out the cloth, and there was the $17. He had been holding it untouched for all the years. "I never use any man's money but my own," he said.

## October 2. Fighting for Crumbs

A loaf of bread bounced from a basket as a baker's truck turned the corner too quickly. When the loaf hit the pavement a crumb broke off and lay beside it.

Almost instantly three sparrows made a swoop for the crumb. When the contest was over two of the birds flew away without a bite, and the other one carried off a meager breakfast. The loaf was untouched, unnoticed.

The crumb was worthwhile as a pickup; it was nothing as a prize. Just a little wider range of vision, just a little more faith, and each bird would have been satisfied. How often our own eyes are blurred to our own opportunities while we fight for crumbs.—Arnold Healy.

## October 9. Why Pain?

The usefulness of pain was illustrated by a Chicago *Daily News* account relating the misfortunes of a ten-year-old girl who was unable to feel painful injuries. From infancy she had suffered cuts, burns, and even fractures of both legs without knowing it. Scorching dishes felt only pleasantly warm to her. Doctors predicted that she would be lucky to escape premature death. "She will not have a pain in the side to tell her about an inflamed appendix, a pain in the arm to warn of a heart attack, or a headache to show hypertension," the article pointed out. "Pain is our built-in safeguard."

Some forms of pain are agonizing, to be sure, especially when they go beyond the warning point and develop into a chronic affliction. However we can often do much to minimize serious injury by paying attention to the advance warning of pain that God permits for our protection.—The Christophers.

## October 16. Bonsai Trees

An interesting feature of Japanese horticultural artistry is the production of dwarf bonsai trees. In a Tokyo flower shop featuring dozens of these trees I had a feeling of looking at a forest through the wrong end of my binoculars. Although bonsai are true trees, which may live a century or more, they attain a height of only about two feet. They grow from seeds in small pots containing too little soil to nourish their branches. Buds are nipped off and constant pruning, shaping, and training are required. The grower ties branches with string, places lead weights at their tips, and takes pains to hinder normal growth and keep them stunted.

What is art in a flower shop becomes just ugly pettiness in Christian lives when we pluck the buds and blossoms of generosity and joyful giving before they can beautify our lives and bring God's blessings.—Naomi Ruth Hunke in *Open Windows*.

## October 23. The Proud Frog

An old fable of a frog shows the danger of being too eager for the approval of men. The frog arranged to journey south for the winter with two wild geese. He found a string and requested that each goose hold an end. The frog held the middle of the string in his mouth. As they sailed away through space they passed over a field where an admiring farmer looked up and asked, "Who invented that?" The frog could not miss the chance to claim credit, so he answered, "I invented it." He lost his grasp on the string, of course, and the geese went on without him. The frog who could not humble himself was humiliated—and very dead from the hard fall.—Elinor Lennen.

### October 30. A Strange Bible

The Gangster's Bible was the name given to a manuscript acquired by Dr. Edgar J. Goodspeed at the University of Chicago around 1930. It was a ninth-century Greek lectionary of the gospels. It came to Dr. Goodspeed from either the Greek treasurer or cook of the notorious Colosimo restaurant in Chicago, a place usually kept closed by the police. This splendidly miniatured lectionary, originally written in Greece, had in some way come into the possession of this person and had been used for a strange purpose. It was kept in a trunk but was brought out when the gangsters wished to initiate a new member or swear to some new feud or vendetta—to take the oath upon.

When the city journalists learned the story of this manuscript, they appropriately called it the Gangster's Bible. Dr. Goodspeed said that a new side of gangsterism had been revealed. Even gangsterism has its sanctities!

Actually this is a tribute to the Bible. This particular use of it may raise questions for us, but it also speaks of the nature and influence of the Bible. Apparently these gangsters understood that the Bible represented truth, honor, integrity.—Herchel H. Sheets in *Wesleyan Christian Advocate.*

### November 6. Millions of Galaxies

Did you ever look up at the cloudless night sky bristling with pinpricks of light and wonder how many million stars you could see?

Well, the answer is that it isn't even remotely a million. In fact a person with good eyes can see only about three thousand at best—without a telescope of course.

And all the stars we can see with our naked eyes are in our own galaxy, the Milky Way, although that galaxy is itself made up of millions of stars, and there are millions of such galaxies in the universe.

Our own galaxy looks something like a pancake, with our solar system about halfway out toward the edge. We see a band of white—the "Milky Way"—when we look lengthwise back through the center of the "pancake."

The brightest star you can see is fifty-four trillion miles away, and if it should explode at this instant you wouldn't see the explosion until 1987.

God created the universe on a scale difficult for man fully to comprehend. How fortunate that he made the pathway to salvation clear and simple to follow.—Max L. Batchelder.

### November 13. Treasures (Stewardship Day)

In the middle of the third century, Lawrence, a deacon in the church at Rome, was so effective that the congregation grew swiftly through his efforts. The pagan officials became so alarmed that they seized Lawrence, planning to execute him to prevent further growth of the church. They hoped also to confiscate huge treasures that the church had reportedly accumulated. The persecutors searched Lawrence's residence and the church but could find no treasure. Then Lawrence was subjected to torture to force him to reveal where the treasure was located. Finally he agreed to show them the church's treasure if the persecutors would accompany him to the church on the next day. When the doors were thrown open, the persecutors saw nothing but a large gathering of the poor and downtrodden members of the congregation. "These," said Lawrence, "are the treasures of the church." In their rage the pagans immediately executed the saintly deacon.—John W. Wade.

## November 20. The Pilgrims' Friend (Thanksgiving Sunday)

One spring morning an Indian named Squanto came out of the woods and found a small colony of white men—the Pilgrims who had survived the first winter after landing at Plymouth Rock in 1620.

Had he been a man who nursed grudges, he might have faded silently into the forest until he gathered enough braves to sneak back and wipe out the palefaces. The seed of hatred had been sown in his heart by a greedy British sea captain who had sold him into slavery in Spain. Later Squanto escaped to England. He was home again only through the kindness of a man who befriended a forlorn human being in a strange land and in so doing planted the seed of love. He chose to remember goodness rather than evil—to let the seed of hatred die and the seed of love flourish in its place.

As Squanto approached the group of Pilgrims, he astonished them by calling to them in English. Soon he was showing them the hunting, fishing, and farming skills of the Indians. He became their friend.—*Sunshine Magazine.*

## November 27. God the Source (Advent)

While I was growing up we lived close to an uncle who was a successful fruit grower. He sold thousands of bushels of fruit, but his pride and joy was the big luscious Elberta Peach. I moved away, and it was several years before I visited my uncle again. I was shocked when I saw what remained of his orchard. "What happened?" I asked him. Sadly he told me that one year the crop was bad, and the next year it was worse. Greatly distressed he contacted the county agricultural agent who, after investigation, told my uncle: "Mr. Roberts, you've made a fatal mistake; you've paid too much attention to the fruit and have given no attention to the trees." He continued, "Take care of the trees and the fruit will be inevitable." My uncle's eyes lighted up as he talked with me and he said: "Oral, I'm putting in a new orchard. This time I'll take care of my source."

Phil. 4:19 records that God is the source of your total supply. Things and people are instruments only. If you cultivate your relationship with God, the supply of your needs will naturally follow because God as source controls the harvest.—Oral Roberts.

## December 4. Let Your Light So Shine (Advent)

One of the songs I remember from boyhood Sunday school days had the refrain, "Brighten the corner where you are." Those words came to me when we drove to the Cape Hatteras National Seashore in North Carolina and climbed 268 steps to the top of Hatteras Lighthouse, 191 feet above the mean high water mark. Built in 1870 at a cost of $150,000, Hatteras Light is a warning to ships at sea, reminding seamen of the treacherous shoals which extend nine miles out to sea. More than 500 ships of many nations have foundered at or near Cape Hatteras, earning for the area the sinister reputation of "Graveyard of the Atlantic."

Hatteras Light today, thanks to a lamp system producing a beam of 250,000 candlepower, is visible 20 miles to sea and under especially favorable atmospheric conditions has been observed 51 miles at sea. That is some beacon!

Our Lord spoke of his followers as beacons of light and as candles lighted and placed upon a stand, not hidden under a bushel. By being faithful to the highest we have known, by living in a manner worthy of Christ, and by giving ourselves in love for those in need we shine like beacons and fulfill our calling as Christians. What light is shining from your life these days?—Roger S. Nicholson.

## December 11. Holy Tree (Advent)

A legend comes down to us from the early days of Christianity in England. One of those helping to spread Christianity among the Druids was a monk named Wilfred (later Saint Wilfred).

One day, surrounded by a group of his converts, he struck down a huge oak tree, which in the Druid religion was an object of worship.

As it fell to the earth the oak tree split into four pieces, and from its center sprang up a young fir tree. The crowd gazed in amazement.

Wilfred let his ax drop and turned to speak. "This little tree shall be your holy tree tonight. It is the wood of peace, for your houses are built of the fir. It is the sign of an endless life, for its leaves are evergreen. See how it points toward the heavens? Let this be called the tree of the Christ Child. Gather about it not in the wilderness but in your homes. There it will be surrounded with loving gifts and rites of kindness."

And to this day that is why the fir tree is one of our loveliest symbols of Christmas.—*Guideposts Magazine.*

## December 18. The Man Who Is Different (Advent)

Jesus was different from anyone who has ever lived. In some ways he was the same as we, but if you think about it you'll see how he was better than everyone. As a baby he startled a king, as a boy he puzzled the lawyers, and as a man he ruled nature, walking on the waves and making the storm cease. He healed many people without medicine and didn't ask for money for the help he gave.

He never wrote a book, but thousands of books have been written about him. He never wrote a song, but more songs have been written about him than about anyone else. He didn't start a college, but all the schools together have not gathered as many students as he has had. He never called an army or fired a gun, but no leader has had more volunteers than he.

The Devil could not overcome him, death could not destroy him, and the grave could not hold him. He was rich, but for our sake he became poor, so poor that he slept in a borrowed manger, he cruised on the lake in someone else's boat, he rode on another man's ass, and he was buried in another's tomb.

Boys and girls, you'll never meet anyone quite like him.—Ronald Armstrong.

## December 25. Light on the Manger

The children were arranging the figures of Mary, Joseph, and the Christ Child in the little manger scene. They lighted two tall candles and carefully tried them in various positions until the light fell exactly where they wanted it. One child excitedly said, "Be sure that Jesus shows!"—Nancy Gibbons Zook.

# SECTION X. *Sermon Outlines and Homiletic and Worship Aids for Fifty-two Weeks*

## SUNDAY: JANUARY SECOND

### MORNING SERVICE

**Topic: The Gifts of Faith (Epiphany)**
SCRIPTURE: Matt. 2:1–12.

Matthew tells us that sometime after the birth of Jesus Christ—perhaps as much as two years—wise men from the east came to worship him. From the Bible story we know very little about the wise men. We do not know that there were three who brought the gifts. And we are not even told that they were kings or, for that matter, when they arrived in Bethlehem. It is likely, in view of their long journey and of Herod's command that all children under two years of age were to be killed, that they arrived when Jesus had already become a young child.

I. The fact that the story provides so little information about the wise men shows that Matthew's interest is not focused upon the wise men themselves. Rather he is interested in the fact that the Gentiles came to worship the Jewish Messiah. He is also interested, perhaps above all, in the gifts that they bore.

(a) It is easy to see why gold is an appropriate gift for Jesus Christ. Gold is the metal of kings. Thus the gold that was presented to Jesus acknowledged his right to rule. Jesus Christ was a king, as the wise men knew. He was the King of kings. Hence the wise men pointed to his future kingship by their gifts of pure gold.

(b) It is also easy to see why frankincense was a significant gift. Frankincense was a type of incense used in the temple worship. For one thing, it was mixed with the oil that was used to anoint the priests of Israel. For another, it was part of the meal offerings that were offerings of thanksgiving and praise to God. Frankincense gave the offering its most pleasant odor. Thus it was probably of frankincense that Paul was thinking when he compared the gifts of the Philippians to such a sacrifice, calling them "an odor of sweet smell, a sacrifice acceptable, well pleasing to God" (Phil. 4:18). In presenting this gift the wise men pointed to Christ as our great priest, the one whose whole life was acceptable and well pleasing to his Father.

(c) Just as gold speaks of Christ's kingship and rule and frankincense speak of the perfection of his life, so myrrh speaks of his death. Myrrh was used in embalming. By any human measure it would be odd, if not offensive, to present a spice used for embalming to the infant Christ. But it was not offensive. Nor in this case was it odd. It was a gift of faith. We do not know precisely what the wise men may have known or guessed about Christ's ministry, but we do know that the Old Testament again and again foretold his suffering. He was to die for our sin. It was the gift of myrrh that symbolized this part of his ministry.

II. We have looked at the spiritual significance of each of the three gifts given to Jesus by the wise men, and yet the study would be incomplete unless I were also to take you to one other verse that bears upon the gifts of the wise men.

(a) The verse from Isa. 60 occurs in the midst of a great prophecy of the coming of Jesus Christ in glory at the end of this present age. The chapter begins, "Arise, shine; for thy light is come, and the glory of the Lord is risen upon thee" (v. 1). It continues by showing that the nations shall come to Christ's light "and kings to the brightness of his rising" (v. 3). Then comes v. 6: "The multitude of camels shall cover thee, the dromedaries of Midian and Ephah; all they from Sheba shall come; they shall bring *gold and incense,* and they shall show forth the praise of the Lord."

(b) Do you see the importance of this verse? When the Lord Jesus Christ returns a scene will be enacted that will be similar to the coming of the wise men to Bethlehem at his first coming. He will reign in power. Gifts will be given to him. But when the gifts are presented they will not be gold, frankincense, and myrrh. They will be gold and frankincense only. Myrrh speaks of suffering. But when the Lord Jesus Christ died on the cross, he suffered once and for all for sin. Hereafter there will be no more need for his suffering.

(c) Do you see that truth clearly? You should, for it is the true meaning of Christmas. Jesus Christ came to earth to die. That was his mission. He died for our sin. Now those who believe on him wait for his second coming in glory.

(d) The world has so many false ideas of Christmas. For some persons it is only a story that is somehow meant to glorify babies and motherhood. For others there is the false idea that we must do something for God, like that Christmas song "The Little Drummer Boy" that suggests that Jesus will smile at us if we play him a tune on our drum. Oh, no! Jesus does not need to have us play him a tune on our little drums. He does not need anything that we can produce. But we do need him. We need a Savior. To understand Christmas is to come believing that.

III. We are able to bring nothing to the Christ who is our Savior. But there is one sense which is an exception to that. We must come with our faith, for we must come believing. Moreover there is a sense in which by faith we too may present the gifts of gold, frankincense, and myrrh.

(a) Myrrh is also a symbol of your death and of the spiritual death that should come to you for your sin. You lay it at Christ's feet and say: "Lord Jesus Christ, I know that I am less perfect than you are and am therefore a sinner. I know that I should receive the consequence of my sin which is to be barred from your presense forever. But you took my sin, dying in my place. And I believe that. Now I ask you to accept me as your child forever."

(b) You may come with your frankincense, acknowledging that your life is as impure as the life of the Lord Jesus Christ is sinless. The Bible teaches that there is no good in man that is not mixed with evil. But it also teaches that Christ comes to live in the believer so that the good deeds produced in the life of a believer by the indwelling Christ become in their turn "an odor of a sweet smell, a sacrifice acceptable, well pleasing to God."

(c) You may come with your gold. Gold symbolizes royalty and rule. Thus you acknowledge the right of Christ to rule your own life. You say: "I am your child, and you are my Father. Direct my life and lead me in it so that I might grow up spiritually to honor and to serve you accordingly."— James Montgomery Boice.

## Illustrations

PRESENT TENSE. George Fox, a man of energy and courage, had grasped a great idea, the idea that Christian experience could be couched in the present tense. He was able to arouse men and women in a remarkable way by the direct question, "What canst *thou* say?" He discovered the power which always emerges when men move over from speculation to experience and when they provide a verification of the reality of what they experience by the only evidence which is convincing, the evidence of changed lives.—Elton Trueblood.

LOOKING FOR GOD. Christianity tells us that to find God we do not start by looking within ourselves. We look *backward* to the astonishing story of Israel which culminates in the Christ-event. We look *upward* to where a Man sits at the right hand of the Father. We look *forward* to the return of Jesus in the very body which was once nailed to the cross, a glorified body yet the same body which had been buried and resurrected. Only after looking backward and upward and forward do we look down into our believing hearts where Christ by his spirit is now living.—Vernon C. Grounds.

## Sermon Suggestions

GOD AND HIS PROMISE. Text: Josh. 1:5. (1) This promise presents the eternal God as the link between the dead and the living. (2) This promise presents the faithful God as the link between the past and the future. (3) This promise presents the unchangeable God as the link between the known and the unknown. (4) This promise presents the all-sufficient God as the link between the small and the great.—R. A. Finlayson.

IS THERE SUCH A THING AS LUCK? Text: Luke 10:31. (1) One of the bewildering facts of life is that many important happenings seem to come by luck. (2) Luck will endanger our lives if we count on it or if we use it as an alibi for our failures. (3) The existence of luck can bring out faith and courage within us. We develop faith when we are willing to take a chance. If life were a sure thing we would have little need for faith. (4) This is a law-abiding universe, and life is governed not by luck but by the laws and purposes of God. (See Gal. 6:7.) (5) God has a plan and purpose for every life, and whatever breaks into our lives nothing can defeat us if we are faithful to God. (6) Whatever seems to happen by luck, it is well always to take the long view. (See Luke 16:10–31.) —Charles L. Allen.

## Worship Aids

CALL TO WORSHIP. "Know therefore that the Lord thy God, he is God the faithful God, which keepeth covenant and mercy with them that love him and keep his commandments to a thousand generations." Deut. 7:9.

INVOCATION. Our Father, we thank thee for thy Word and for the eternal truths which guide us day by day. We thank thee most of all for the living word, Jesus Christ, and the sureness of his presence. Teach us how to turn unto thee so that thy thoughts may be our thoughts and thy ways our ways.

OFFERTORY SENTENCE. "Thy prayers and thine alms are come up for a memorial before God." Acts 10:4.

OFFERTORY PRAYER. Our Father, we bow in humble gratitude that as a new year dawns we may call on thee to guide, strengthen, bless, and forgive, and that through these gifts we may share thy love with all who call upon us and thee.

PRAYER. Our Father, amid the fears and frustrations that haunt us at this year's beginning, let us hear thy counsel and let us feel thy comfort. May there be inroads of thy strength in our lives to make us conquerors in the times of crisis. May there be wells of spiritual reserve in our souls for the valleys through which we will surely walk. And may there be deposits of divine guidance firmly planted in our minds for the times of decision that will be ours.

Help us, Father, to face the future with definite courage and with deep commitment. Grant to each of us a sensitive heart: a heart of true concern that will respond to the hurts and ills of those about us.

We ask, Father, for wisdom in the hour of opportunity and for patience in the moment of failure. May we ever remember that thou art the craftsman of life and that we are thy tools. Help us to be ready instruments of thy Spirit. May we be unafraid to assume the tasks placed upon us by thy will.

May this year be one of victory through venture and one of accomplishment through action. May we be assured of the prodding of thy Spirit when we choose the path of indifference.—C. Neil Strait.

*1-8-78 P.M.*

## EVENING SERVICE

### Topic: Believing in Providence
TEXT: Gen. 50:20.

I. Believing in providence will build confidence that the days of our years have purpose and meaning. Joseph was confident that it was not so much his brothers who sold him into Egypt as it was God had used his brothers to send him into Egypt to accomplish a larger purpose. There is a caring hand which directs the destiny of our lives.

II. Believing in providence builds confidence that in 1977 there can be no accidents but only purposes in our lives. Obviously that good will not always be immediately discernible. There come into our experience those things we would rather not admit, and we are forced to cry out to God, "Why?" But if we believe that there are not accidents but that what God ordains for us is right, we will be kept from bitterness and resentment.

III. Believing in providence builds confidence in the dynamics of divine guidance. This does not mean that when you stand at the crossroads of some decision you are going to hear a voice, "This is the way, walk ye in it." Many times I have been faced with a decision and have said, "Lord, if you would only speak with a voice that I could hear!" But I have never heard any voice from heaven. Most often he guides us as we expose ourselves to his word in our time of prayer and in our experiences of worship. Make diligent use of the means of grace.

IV. Believing in providence builds confidence that God, because he is God, can turn scandal into blessing. What Joseph's brothers did to him was sin. It was evil and they knew it and they admitted it. That was the scandal. But God turned it into a blessing: "You meant it for evil, but God meant it for good." God is able to make the wrath of man to praise him (Ps. 76:10). In the crucifixion our sins nailed Jesus to the cross, and that was evil. That we should so deal with God's best gift to earth is a scandal upon history. But on Good Friday God was able to take the evil deed of crucifixion and make it the means of our salvation.

V. Believing in providence builds confidence that the resounding fury of hate and rejection is not the final or ultimate sound. It was not in the ears of Joseph or in the ears of Jesus, nor will it be in our ears so long as we do not lose faith that God has a forgiving and loving purpose to be achieved through us. Love endures when tongues have ceased and prophecies have failed.

VI. Believing in providence builds confidence that God will provide the resources to accomplish his purposes. We can say with Paul, "I can do all things through Christ who strengthens me," because we know that God will supply all our need according to his riches in glory by Christ Jesus (Phil. 3:13, 19). To save many people alive God sent Joseph to administer the resources of Egypt. Joseph recognized that in the providence of God he had become an agent for his brothers' good. In days when problems confront us we need to make use of our resources that will enable us to be both grateful and generous.

VII. Believing in providence builds confidence that history is moving forward toward an ultimate goal. God's changeless purpose will reach its consummation when every knee shall bow and every tongue confess that Jesus Christ is Lord, when the kingdoms of this world become the kingdom of our Lord and of his Christ, and when he shall reign as King of kings and Lord of lords forever and ever. Then and only then will faith experience fully what it has embraced when it received Christ as Savior. Contrariwise, then and only then will unbelief become aware of what it has forever forfeited.—Walter L. Dosch.

## SUNDAY: JANUARY NINTH

### MORNING SERVICE

**Topic: Authority and Freedom**

SCRIPTURE: Rom. 8:1–4.

"Freedom" is a great Christian word. Jesus promised that when he sets men free they are free indeed, and Paul begged his readers to stand fast in the freedom for which Christ had set them free. What is the freedom of a Christian man? It emerges clearly when we consider the mutual relations of the words liberty, tyranny, and authority.

I. *Freedom from tyranny.* The New Testament seldom, if ever, speaks of our Christian "freedom" without indicating the "tyranny" from which we need to be delivered in order to enjoy it. There are three major tyrants from which Christ can set us free. They concern the past (our guilt), the present (our self), and the future (our fears). Only when these tyrannies are broken are we free to find our true selves in the uninhibited service of God and of men.

(a) It is freedom from guilt which is meant by freedom from the law. When Paul declares that the Christian is "not under law," he is not saying that we are delivered from its *requirements* but from its *condemnation.* God condemned sin in the flesh of Jesus in order that we might be freed from the law's condemnation and freed also to meet the law's requirements. (See Rom. 8:1–4.)

(b) By freedom from self we mean Christ rescuing us from the prison of sin which is, in fact, our self-centeredness. To live for self is bondage and death; to die to self and live for others is liberty and life.

(c) It is obvious that we cannot be free to live as children in God's family if we are paralyzed by fear. All fear inhibits freedom. Nobody is truly free who is afraid, whether our fears are rational or irrational, sophisticated or superstitious.

(d) One of the most thrilling notes of the gospel is the freedom from guilt, self, and fear which Christ offers us today. By his death our guilt can be expunged. By the power of his resurrection we can be turned inside out, from self to unself. And his exaltation to God's right hand assures us that all the ogres of which we are afraid are under his feet. Once freed from these tryants, we are free for God and men, to give ourselves away in service.

II. *Freedom under authority.* Tyranny and authority are two very different things. If freedom is impossible without deliverance from tyranny, it is equally impossible without submission to authority. Tyranny destroys freedom; authority makes it possible. There are two major spheres of personal life in which freedom and authority appear to be incompatible but in which each actually depends upon the other. One is intellectual (freedom of thought) and the other moral (freedom of behavior).

(a) *Intellectual freedom.* (1) People ask how, if we are obliged by any authority (pope, church, Bible, or state) to believe something, we can ever be intellectually free. This is to misstate the problem. There is only one authority under which the mind can find its freedom, and that is the authority of truth itself. Intellectual freedom is not identical with "free thought," that is, the liberty to think and believe absolutely anything whatsoever. To believe nothing is to be in bondage to meaninglessness. To believe lies is to be in bondage to falsehood. To believe facts is the only bondage which, in reality, is freedom. And this is so whether the facts are those of science or of scripture, e.g., that the earth is round or that God is love. We are free to deny these truths, as flat-earthers do on the one hand and atheists on the other. But such freedom is a bondage to illusion.

(2) A useful analogy may thus be drawn between scientific research and biblical research, which indicates the proper relation between human reason and divine revelation. For scientific and biblical research are both investigations into divine revelation. Both scientist and Bible student have their data given to them by God, in the first case in nature, in the second in scripture. We cannot alter these data. This is, if you like, the "tyranny" of truth. The task of the scientist is to observe, to weigh and measure, to interpret and to systematize. Similarly the task of the Bible student is to ponder, to interpret, to relate, and to systematize. But in both cases the function of our reason is not to stand in judgment upon revelation but to sit in humility under it. Only so can we maintain our intellectual integrity and find our intellectual freedom.

(b) *Moral freedom.* (1) The case is similar with moral freedom. People say that they cannot be morally free if they are obliged by authority to behave according to certain standards any more than they can be intellectually free if they are obliged to believe certain propositions. But God's revelation is a revelation of what is good as well as of what is true and thus imposes upon us limits of behavior as well as of belief.

(2) Perhaps no words arouse more

hostility in the human breast than the three monosyllables "thou shalt not." Yet such restrictions are essential for true freedom. Freedom to indulge in sin is no more true freedom than freedom to believe a lie. Indeed freedom to believe a lie is bondage to fantasy, as freedom to indulge in sin is bondage to sensuality. Intellectual freedom is found only in truth and moral freedom is found only in righteousness.

(3) The reason is that this is how things are in God's moral world. This is how he has made human beings. As the only person who knows how a machine works best is its maker, so the only person who knows how a human being functions best is his Creator. And the moral law of the Bible is the Maker's instructions for his own creatures. The moral law, far from being an alien code imposed upon us against nature, is the only behavior code which is adapted to our nature and by which we find our human freedom.

(4) Paul assures us that, even in the case of pagans, "what the law requires is written on their hearts" (Rom. 2:15). Thus God wrote his moral law both on tablets of stone and on tablets of flesh, both objectively in the Bible and subjectively in men's hearts. There is therefore a vital correspondence between divine law and human nature. It is true that fallen human nature is hostile to God's law, but in being so it is hostile to its own true welfare and freedom. Moral liberty is found in obedience not disobedience, in self-denial not self-indulgence.

(5) So Jesus calls us not only to come to him if we are heavy-laden, in order to lose our burdens, but also to take his yoke upon us and "learn" from him. To assume his yoke is to submit to his authority as our teacher and Lord, to believe his instruction and to obey his commands. He rescues us from tyranny but places us under authority. The beautiful truth is that both the loss of the one and the gain of the other lead to the same result: "rest for your souls." The true liberty of a Christian consists on the one hand of freedom from the

tyrannies of guilt, self, and fear and on the other of freedom under the authority of Christ as teacher and Lord.—John Stott.

## Illustrations

VULNERABLE STRENGTH. We must remember that we are tempted through our gifts. The person with charm will be tempted to use that charm "to get away with anything." The person gifted with the power of words will be tempted to use his command of words to produce glib excuses to justify his conduct. The person with a vivid and sensitive imagination will undergo agonies of temptation that a more stolid person will never experience. The person with great gifts of mind will be tempted to use these gifts for himself and not for others, to become the master and not the servant of men. It is the grim fact of temptation that it is just where we are strongest that we must be forever on the watch.—William Barclay.

LIMITATION AND OPPORTUNITY. Life is a landscaping job. We are handed a site, ample or small, rugged or flat, picturesque or commonplace, whose general outlines and contours are largely determined for us. Both limitation and opportunity are involved in every site, and the most unforeseeable results ensue from the handling—some grand opportunities are muffed, and some utterly unpromising situations become notable. —Harry Emerson Fosdick.

## Sermon Suggestions

HOW CAN WE KNOW GOD'S WILL? Text: Jas. 4:15. (1) Rest on the *character* of God who never wills anything contrary to his character. (2) Look to the *call* of God through his Word, through prayer, and through the voice of conscience. (3) Look to the *counselors* of God and confer with those whose counsel you trust. (4) Remember *consecration* is part of God's divine direction. (5) *Circumstances* are sometimes God's way of showing you your course.—William McLeister 2nd.

DO ALL THINGS HAPPEN FOR THE BEST FOR GOD'S CHILDREN? Text: Rom. 8:28 (AV). (1) Accident vs. plan in the creation and the direction of the world. (2) Accident vs. plan everywhere in nature. (3) Accident vs. plan in personal and national life. (a) The Bible indicates that God cares for his children. (b) The Bible indicates that men have been puzzled by the seeming indifference of God to his children. (c) The Bible indicates that God has purpose in life making it possible to believe both in his loving care and in his discipline in this preparatory school we call human life. (See Deut. 8:4; Ps. 94:12; Prov. 3:11; John 15:2; Rev. 3:19.)

## Worship Aids

CALL TO WORSHIP.
Come, you who are weak,
  but would be made strong;
Come, you who are weary,
  but want a new song.
Come, you who are seeking
  the joy of creation,
Come into the fellowship
  of this congregation—
Who also are seeking,
  even as you,
The heart of the good,
  the noble, and true;
In times overwhelmed
  by furor and strife
To find God revealed
  in everyday life.
—Thomas Roy Pendell.

INVOCATION. Eternal and ever-blessed God, come to us this day as we wait upon thee; and banish every evil thought, and restrain every wandering thought, that we, being pure in heart, may see thee.

OFFERTORY SENTENCE. "What shall I render unto the Lord for all his benefits toward me? I will pay my vows unto the Lord now in the presence of all his people." Ps. 116:12–14.

OFFERTORY PRAYER. Help us to remember, O Lord, that a life is a more persuasive testimony than words, that deeds are more effective than arguments, and that these gifts are only a portion of the loyalty thou dost require of us.

PRAYER. From thee, our God, we receive everything, through thee all is possible for us, and for thee we want to live. From thee comes the joy of each day and the blessings that light our road, from thee the splendors of the earth and the friendships of men, from thee the flights of enthusiasm and the need of adoration, from thee the Christian family and the treasures it transmits, from thee the Book which we would absorb, from thee the master who has conquered our heart. We thank thee, Lord, for all thou givest us. And it is through thee that we accomplish each step of the way; through thee that we lift ourselves after a fall and set forth once more ever stronger; through thee that our indolence may be changed into life, our doubt into faith, our despair into hope. Through thee we are each moment brought back, understood, consoled. O God, we recognize everywhere the touch of thy hand. And it is for thee and in turning toward thee that our life takes on meaning; for thee that it is worthwhile having arms, a heart, and a brain; and for thee to seek, to suffer, to wait. For thee, since thou art our reward and the goal of our journey, there is no enemy that we dare not face, no peril that we would not wish to surmount, and no sacrifice for which we are not ready. O God, all we have and the little that we are, we give for thee.— Philippe Vernier.

## EVENING SERVICE

### Topic: To Whom Does God Tell His Troubles?

God shares his problems especially with those who love him above all. He makes his troubles known particularly to these because they are in position to hear him clearly and to care.

I. God told, and yet tells, his sorrows to Jesus. The Son responded magnificently. The weight of God's burden was upon Jesus when he preached his first sermon in his home synagogue at Nazareth. He read a passage from Isa. 61 and declared that God had sent him to aid the poor, the captives, the blind, and the oppressed. Jesus had God's approval ("This is my beloved Son; listen to him"), among other reasons because he heard and responded to God's troubles, giving himself in life and death to lighten the load on God's heart.

II. God has told, and yet tells, his problems to the church, the new body and instrument of Christ in the present world. People often insist that the church "stay out of trouble," away from controversial issues. That of course is not intended to be, for that would mean the church's removal from God's troubles in the world. The effect of that counsel also would be to prevent the church from places like the one where the cross was first raised and where the impact of the cross should be brought today.

III. God shares his problems particularly with individual Christians who are deeply dedicated to him. The prime example of this is of course Christ. "No man ever spoke like this man!" reported officers who had been sent to arrest Jesus (John 4:46). "And never man listened as this man listened," observed Frank Laubach, pointing out that Jesus spoke so powerfully because he listened to God so intently.

IV. God is telling his troubles to the world outside the church, and the world is hearing, in some instances hearing exceedingly well. Indeed the world of sports and institutions of government have run ahead of the church in implementing more just treatment of minority and ethnic groups.

V. God desires us to bring to him every significant problem that we have, and he graciously hears and helps us. He depends on us to help him in the tribulations he has and will have until all persons accept his way of love and righteousness and all the world is made whole in him.—Herschel T. Hamner in *The Methodist Christian Advocate*.

# SUNDAY: JANUARY SIXTEENTH

## MORNING SERVICE

**Topic: Evangelism, Unlimited (Missionary Day)**

TEXT: Matt. 28:18–20.

I. "All authority"—*unlimited jurisdiction*. (a) The risen Christ stands before these eleven "unlearned" disciples on a mountain in Galilee. They all worship him, but "some doubted" (v. 17). Christ meets that doubt with one of the most daring statements ever uttered: "All authority in heaven and on earth has been given to me" (RSV).

(b) The best the great conquerors and world empires could hope for was to control the entire earth. Even this goal remains unrealized in human history. But Christ possessed—and still does—all the power which rules the heavens and all the power which rules the earth. This includes, among other things, absolute power of command and unrestricted use of personnel, resources, and finances. Thus he immediately commands, "Go ye therefore . . . ."

II. "All nations"—*unlimited ethnography*. (a) I am tempted to say that the command of Christ has no geographic limitations. Surely imaginary lines drawn by man—or even marine and terrestrial boundaries set by God—should restrict neither him who has "all authority" nor those whom he has sent "into all the world."

(b) The original words require us to think in ethnographic rather than geographic terms. The ethnic or racial groups throughout the world are infinitely complex. A whole science of ethnology has been developed to describe these races according to language, color, features, stature, physiology, etc. But no matter how science describes the races, Christ's answer is the opposite of the Sanskrit *neti*: "Yes, that is what I mean—make disciples of that nation, that race, those people."

(c) No matter how much the learned of our age contend that certain ethnic groups should be left undisturbed in

their "cultural innocency," Christ disagrees. He commands us to make disciples among them and to baptize them in a special name. That name is one, yet it is said to be "of the Father and of the Son and of the Holy Spirit" (RSV). Our service cannot be nameless, void of initiation rites, nor free from enlistment of "learners" in the school of Christ, his church.

III. ". . . teaching them to observe all that I have commanded you"—*unlimited curriculum*.

(a) The actual teachings of Christ can be recorded in such a small space that the record would hardly deserve to be called a book. Yet we who have spent a lifetime trying to fathom the depths of those teachings begin to understand what John meant when, in reference to the acts of Christ, he said, "Were every one of them to be written, I suppose that the world itself could not contain the books that would be written" (RSV). More books have been written and more speeches made on the subject of Christ than on any other subject. Yet we are left with the keen consciousness of the inexhaustibility of that theme.

(b) Still we have a mandate not only to "teach" all that he has commanded but also to "observe" all that he has commanded. Until all nations learn to observe all he has commanded, our curriculum is not complete.

IV. "I am with you alway"—*unlimited continuity*. (a) Christ's coming to earth did not leave heaven empty. He referred to himself as resident in heaven even while he talked to Nicodemus in Jerusalem. Similarly his return to heaven did not leave his disciples orphans. The Book of Acts is full of what Christ did in heaven and on earth after he disappeared in the cloud above Mount Olivet. The departing Christ said, "I am with you."

(b) The Western world has spent so much time in search of the "historical Jesus." Would that we could be inspired to spend the same energies in pursuit of the "everlasting Christ." His presence is with us "alway" (Greek: "all the days"), "even unto the end of the world." What our Lord did 2,000 years ago in that far-off country of Palestine was only introductory to what he did through his disciples in the Book of Acts and what he wants to do for us and through us.

(c) A king's duties begin when he goes through the coronation and assumes his position on the throne. Christ did that after his ascension into heaven. His real rulership began then. Acts tells us what he did in the first century. Hebrews tells us what he continues to do in all centuries, if we will only obey him. Would that we could see him at work at the right hand of God as king, priest, and commander of his army on earth! Would that our eyes should be opened like those of Elisha's servant, so we could see that Christ is with us now! —Bronell Greer.

## Illustrations

THE MASTER'S LOVE.     Jesus loved men not because they were attractive and beautiful and free from faults but because his love went out to those who needed love, rather than to those who deserved it, and because it was his very nature to love. He loved quarrelsome fishermen, squalid profiteers, men and women who had scarred the night with sin, and Pharisees who patronized him. Men's enmity inflicted the wounds of the cross, but it was our Lord's love which made him receive them. By the way in which he endured the worst pain that men could inflict upon him, he showed the depth, tenderness, and constancy of his love for them.—Hedley Hodkin.

GUIDELINES.     Those who are serious about their faith do not confuse it with other beliefs, loyalties, or practices, or mingle them together indiscriminately, or pretend they are alike, of equal merit, or mutually compatible if they are not.

Those who are serious about their faith make high demands of those admitted to the organization that bears the faith, and they do not include or allow to continue within it those who are not fully committed to it.

Those who are serious about their faith do not consent to, encourage, or indulge any violations of its standards of belief or behavior by its professed adherents.

Those who are serious about their faith do not keep silent about it, apologize for it, or let it be treated as though it made no difference, or should make no difference, in their behavior or their relationships with others.—Dean M. Kelley in *Why Conservative Churches Are Growing*.

## Sermon Suggestions

THE UNWEARIED WELL-DOER.     Text: II Thess. 3:13. (1) There must be a perpetual replenishing of the spiritual life so that we receive power through prayer. (2) There must be a learning of the ways of loyalty by which we are given the strength to do and to endure to the end. (3) There must be the lift of a great fellowship. (4) There must be the assurance that beyond our human uncertainties is the divine certainty.—Lowell M. Atkinson.

SOMETHING MORE.     Text: Phil. 1:9. (1) Abounding love toward God. (2) Abounding love toward neighbors. (3) Abounding love toward enemies.—Walter L. Dosch.

## Worship Aids

CALL TO WORSHIP.     "Trust in [God] at all times; ye people, pour out your heart before him: God is a refuge for us." Ps. 62:8.

INVOCATION.     Merciful God, forgive the halting nature of our discipleship. We confess that so little of thy love has reached others through us and that we have borne so lightly wrongs and sufferings that were not our own. We confess that we have cherished the things that divide us from others and that we have made it hard for them to live with us. And we confess that we have been thoughtless in our judgments, hasty in condemnation, grudging in our forgiveness. Forgive us, we beseech thee.

OFFERTORY SENTENCE. "Therefore, my beloved brethren, be ye steadfast, unmoveable, always abounding in the work of the Lord, forasmuch as ye know that your labour is not in vain in the Lord." I Cor. 15:58.

OFFERTORY PRAYER. God of our fathers, dearly do we cherish the blessings which thy church brings to us and dearly do we covet the privilege of sharing through these gifts the proclaiming of thy Word until all of the earth shall praise thee.

PRAYER. O God, who art from everlasting to everlasting, the creator and upholder of all things, the source of life and light: thy ways are not as our ways nor thy thoughts as our thoughts; thy judgments are unsearchable, and thy ways past finding out. Thou hast never left the world which thou hast made: day by day thou dost sustain it, bringing forth out of thy treasures things new and old. The seasons are thine with their changing beauty; the wealth of the earth is thine in its manifold splendor; all this thou hast given to man for him to use it and rejoice, seeing in it the bounty of thy love. Throughout the ages thou hast led our race along the upward path, encouraging us by thy many gifts, schooling us by the discipline of suffering. Thy wisdom has been our guide; thy love has overruled our folly and sin. Thou hast raised up great leaders in time of need, thou hast inspired explorers in every realm of knowledge, and in every age thou hast made known thy law that in the fear of thee is the beginning of wisdom and that without righteousness no nation can be great.

## EVENING SERVICE

Topic: Keys to Continuous Revival

The New Testament church had a sustained evangelism. Luke records that "the Lord added to the church daily" those who were being saved. Luke also notes outstanding characteristics of the church which were the keys to this unending harvest of souls. God's people carried with them the reasons for daily tallying of saved persons.

I. It was a *telling church*. They testified to Jesus' death and its meaning to them. They explained that Jesus was God come to deliver them from sin and to remove the guilt of past evil behavior.

II. New Testament Christians *studied* diligently. They gleaned every bit of truth the apostles taught them. They had an open ear to all spiritual information. Doctrine stirred no fear within them. They relished knowledge about Jesus.

III. The early church was known for its close *fellowship*. There was a quality of togetherness about them best described as a friendly acceptance and a loving concern. The popular thing was to eat together. Everyone was included—saint and sinner.

IV. New Testament Christians drew upon the resources of God by means of *prayer*. Prayer was not spasmodic but habitually meaningful. The initial warriors of God made no claims to rugged individualism. They admitted their inadequacies in persuading men about the lordship of Christ.

V. *Miracles* took place among the believers in Luke's day. Immediately our thoughts fly to physical healings. This is indeed the miraculous work of God. One lady said, "The greatest miracle I've ever seen is when God forgives and changes a sinner." Both are acts that anyone will agree are out of the ordinary. These strange events convince men of the genuineness of God's activity and power in the church. One conversion naturally results in another and another. The Bible shows us that God reveals himself through mighty deeds.

VI. The first church of Christ was a *generous* church. It has been said that the initial Christian community was communistic. The grammar of the Greek implies rather that the church members thought of their material assets being at the disposal of God. When a temporal need arose, God's people naturally and willingly sold their belongings to meet the situation.

VII. The first Christians *praised* God. Every opportunity that presented itself found these people worshiping. Worship was dynamic for them. It was packed full of praises to God. The Christians continually lifted the eyes of the world to the God who had changed their lives. Their gratitude expressed relief from guilt and heartfelt love for the Savior. Credit was correctly placed in the hands of the Crucified.

VIII. Ask anyone around in A.D. 50 and he would tell you, "These Jesus-people are *joyful* all the time." It was a quality that drew people to them. Luke paid them a high compliment when he reported they "did eat their meat with gladness."

IX. The early church was *united*. This means more than being together in proximity. Church members pulled in the same direction, achieving the identical purpose—evangelism.

X. Continuous revival happens because a church has "favour with all the people." William Barclay characterizes the New Testament church as "people whom others could not help liking." It was an *attractive* church.—Lyle Pointer in *The Preacher's Magazine.*

## SUNDAY: JANUARY TWENTY-THIRD

### MORNING SERVICE

Topic: Faith, Health, and Healings
TEXT: Matt. 9:22.

What is the relationship between religion and health or, to put it another way, between faith and healing? How does one sort it all out as a person who is both a man or woman of faith and also the child of a scientifically oriented world?

I. Perhaps the first thing for us twentieth-century Christians to note is that the ministry of Jesus appears to have been to a large extent a healing ministry. The blind, the lame, the deranged, and the ill march through the pages of the gospel record, together with tidings of the relief and release they found in Jesus.

(a) When John sent his disciples to ask Jesus who he really was, Jesus replied, "Go and tell John what you have seen and heard: the blind receive their sight, the lame walk, the lepers are cleansed, and the deaf hear, the dead are raised up, and the poor have good news preached to them."

(b) Matt. 9 is a typical passage from the gospels and could be replaced by many another chapter. In it the dead or apparently dead, "sleeping" child is restored to life and health, a woman is healed of a long-term disorder, and two blind men find it possible to see again.

(c) In these and similar incidents Jesus connects the healings accomplished with "faith." In similar vein Matthew says of our Lord's return to Nazareth, "He did not do many mighty works [referring to healing miracles] there because of their unbelief."

(d) Is this picture of Christ, the divine physician, merely symbolic? Is it simply the Bible's way of making the point that Jesus was and is the bringer of new life and health to the human soul? Or is it the picture of one who had the power to change and alter men's bodily states as well as to guide their souls?

II. Both possibilities are valid, and we do not have to choose between them. He did bring new life and health to men's spirits, and he still does. He did and still does minister to men's bodies as well as to their souls.

(a) Now as then our bodily states are quite clearly and intimately connected with our attitudes. "Take heart . . . your faith has made you well," says Jesus to the woman in the crowd. "According to your faith be it done to you," he says to the blind passersby. Everything scientific research has learned in recent years about the psychosomatic aspects of medical treatment bears witness that this intuition of Jesus is actually a law of health.

(b) I see this universal law at work when, as a frequent hospital visitor, I watch some people recover from serious and crippling illness when they find it possible to face their disability in a mood of trust and confidence, while others don't make it through a similar crisis because they become obsessed by fear, grief, and hopelessness.

(c) Our faith or lack of it makes a difference over the long pull. To believe that there is a power greater than us on which we can depend for help and health and strength; to place ourselves in the hands of a God who cares, cherishes, and forgives; to act on the assumption that the universe is basically trustworthy and that life is, in spite of all its agony, a precious and blessed gift; to feel that our lives and our reactions can be built into and share the will and purpose of the Creator; to live by the law of love and self-giving and trust rather than by the chaos of fear and selfishness and hate—this is indeed a source of health and healing. Thus our bodies are given power to resist and to recuperate. Albert E. Day was right when he insisted that health is maintained and healing takes place when one becomes "a God-trusting, God-expectant, God-cooperative person"—in other words, when faith is at work.

III. Can we always expect God to protect us from diseases? Do we have a right to ask that our prayers be automatically answered whenever we pray for health? What shall we make of the healings that do take place and also of those that don't? Isn't it possible to claim too much?

(a) There are some prayers that I find it very difficult to make and others that I do not think ought to be made at all. But I have no hesitation about praying in faith for wisdom, courage, healing, and strength. I know that people cannot automatically expect to be instantaneously healed by faith or the laying on of hands or prayer or anything else and that even those who appear to be healed in this manner seldom are permanently cured.

(b) I believe that we have a right to pray for healing and to pray in faith believing that our faith and that of the patient will become a powerful force for health. We pray in the conviction that faith can and does move mountains but in remembrance also that it couldn't and didn't remove a hill named Calvary.

(c) There are times when God has other plans for us and for those we love. We were not meant to live forever here on earth and quite probably we were not even meant to have an easy and painless life. St. Paul wrestled with a bodily affliction which he calls his "thorn in the flesh." It greatly troubled him and hampered his work, and he tells us how he prayed over and over again to be released. The answer God gave was "No, but my grace is sufficient for you instead." "Father," said Jesus, "if it be possible, let this cup [of suffering and death] pass from me; nevertheless, not my will, but yours be done."

(d) At the end of all our asking, faith will say, "Whatever happens, O eternal Friend and Supporter, I place and leave my body and my life itself in your hands in trust and confidence." "Prayer's greatest healing is therefore not healing but the courageous and creative acceptance of the terms of mortal life. True prayer does not evade pain but gains from it insight, patience, courage, and sympathy; and at long last makes it an oblation to God. True prayer does not sidestep death but greets it. This is healing beyond healing. By this prayer we are more than conquerors!" (George A. Buttrick.)—Edward C. Dahl.

## Illustrations

EARLY CONVERSION. Robert Rodenmayer tells of a funeral he conducted for a couple who had lost their only child, a little girl, almost overnight: "After the funeral I went back with them to their house. They were poor people—the man worked in the local mill—and had very little to go on. We sat in the kitchen and made some coffee. Nobody had much to say. In fact on such occasions one feels that he ought either to remain silent or to say as simply as possible the best thing he knows. So I tried. I said I believed that it was impossible for any person to move outside of the circle of God's loving concern. I could not say exactly where their child was, but I was sure about God. It was as if the circle of God's love were like the circumference of a wheel; somewhere within it was this man and this woman and their child. They meet, as the spokes do, in the hub of the wheel which is the reality of God and his compassion."—Irving D. Larson.

HEART OF THE MYSTERY. Dust of the earth, troubled by dreams, swept by the storms of beauty and madness, lured by inaccessible truths and tortured by innumerable illusions, seeking peace and making war, with incredible courage and awful fears, curious beyond measure, saint and devil by turn, man stands at the heart of the mystery—and finds in himself the center of all uncertainties.—Samuel H. Miller.

## Sermon Suggestions

DAY-BY-DAY CHRISTIAN LIVING. Text: Rom. 12:11-13 (MOFFATT). (1) Keep alive that loyalty with which you began: "never let your zeal flag." (2) Don't lose your enthusiasm for Christ and his mission: "maintain the spiritual glow." (3) Meet the needs of God's children and share the Good News with everyone: "serve the Lord." (4) Be radiant, avoiding a sad countenance or "piosity": "let your hope be a joy to you." (5) Practice Christian disciplines: "be steadfast in trouble, attend to prayer, contribute to needy saints, make a practice of hospitality."

WHAT HAPPENS WHEN WE PRAY. (1) We identify ourselves with the Christian

way of life. (2) We acknowledge kinship with all of God's creation. (3) We know that the influence for good of a prayerful person expands. (4) We find that prayer releases divine energy through the person who establishes fellowship with God. (5) We learn to love and that we can conquer through love. (6) We gain peace of mind and find quietness. (7) We feel the touch of God's hand. (8) We learn to listen and to know the joy of following our Master's leading.—Mary West.

## Worship Aids

CALL TO WORSHIP. "Oh that men would praise the Lord for his goodness, and for his wonderful works to the children of men! For he satisfieth the longing soul, and filleth the hungry soul with goodness." Ps. 107:8–9.

INVOCATION. O God our Father, who dost dwell in the high and holy place, with him also that is of a humble and contrite heart: grant that through this time of worship in thy presence we may be made the more sure that our true home is with thee in the realm of spiritual things, that thou art ever with us in the midst of our common walk and daily duties, and that the vision of the eternal may ever give meaning and beauty to this earthly and outward life.

OFFERTORY SERVICE. "We then that are strong ought to bear the infirmities of the weak, and not to please ourselves." Rom. 15:1.

OFFERTORY PRAYER. Our heavenly Father, help us to remember that though Christ does offer his companionship, yet to us belongs the decision as to whether or not we will follow him. May we through these gifts and our witness share with all the world the blessedness that comes to us through thy grace.

AN AFFIRMATION OF FAITH. We believe in the discipline of the soul which results in creative Christian living.

We believe that through prayer and

worship we increase the effectiveness of our faith.

We believe that we must transform the experiences of worship and prayer into a powerful witness for Christ.

We believe that this witness becomes meaningful when it is a shared witness in all areas of our lives.

We believe that this means a daily giving of ourselves for Christ as a token payment of the debt we owe for what he did for us and continues to do for us.

We believe that through the means of Christian stewardship and tithing we express our devotion to our Lord in a tangible act of love through giving.

We believe that through the shared, corporate experience of worship and fellowship in the church we discover some of the means which enable us to give expression to these fundamental beliefs. —Chester E. Hodgson.

## EVENING SERVICE

**Topic: Worship as Expression**
TEXT: Ps. 95:6.

I. Worship may be defined as the expression to God of our gratitude for the life that comes from him. In this definition we see that worship has to be expressed.

(a) Until we worship by some act, some word, or some thought, worship is no more possible than is conversation without the use of the mind to form the thought, the voice to enunciate the words, or the will to bring the word into being.

(b) Our bodies and minds are necessarily involved with the material world in worship. We have to choose a time for it, a place for it, and a method for it. The best place for worship is in church. It can rise spontaneously and be offered in the quietness of one's own room, or in the garden, or on the golf course, but this is most unusual. Church is the place. If you don't worship there, you won't worship anywhere.

II. Worship has to be expressed to God. (a) Maybe that is the trouble with modern worship: we don't believe in

God. That is certainly true for the atheist, the agnostic, and the fool. "The fool hath said in his heart, there is no God." But don't be a fool. The earth is a fact; so is space and time and so is life. And where it all comes from is God. He is the Creator, and him we worship.

(b) To the Christian, God is much more than a creator: he is the Father. Christ came to reveal that God is "our Father which art in heaven." And so we think of God in that way and are thus able to worship the object of our being —with love.

III. Worship has to be the expression of gratitude. (a) It may be that you don't feel grateful for life. Then why do you hang on to it the way you do and try to enhance it? Of course we love life. We can't get enough of it. Then why don't you show your gratitude? You may say: "But that's not necessary. God knows I am grateful." Yes, but it needs to be expressed.

(b) Consider your own experience. Certainly if you are a father you have been aware of the joy of life expressed in the everyday experience of your own children and their pleasure in the good things you have made possible for them. But suppose they never expressed their gratitude to you by an outward sign. Something would be missing, wouldn't it? But remember when your child climbed into your lap, hugged you, and said, "Daddy, I love you." That was real expression.

(c) That is what we mean by worship, and it adds to our relation with God just as it adds to our family. We worship God: to express our love and gratitude to him, to adore his splendor, and to join ourselves with him who is our Father and our life. In doing this we gain as much as we give. We express our love, but in doing it we feel expressed the love of God for us; we adore his splendor only to discover that we are made splendid by our adoration; we join ourselves to him only to find that God has in some mysterious way joined himself to us and made us stronger than we were.—James Stanley Cox.

*Acts 20:28  Feb 6 - '77* (handwritten)

# SUNDAY: JANUARY THIRTIETH

## MORNING SERVICE

**Topic: Gifts of the Church**

I. The church's first gift to men is *a grand faith to live by*. This is important, for a man requires a faith to live by if he is to live at all. We do not live by our negations but by our affirmations, and the Christian church offers men a mighty affirmation to live by, the faith that in Jesus Christ of Nazareth almighty God acted decisively and definitively to reconcile the world unto himself and to give the world knowledge of his character and purpose.

II. The church's second gift to men is *a magnificent purpose to live for,* namely, the extension of God's rule and reign among men, the kingdom of God. A purpose that makes sense gives life dignity and meaning and direction and power—the upbuilding, the extension, and the furthering on earth of God's kingdom in the hearts and lives and world of men is the church's second offer to men.

III. The church's third gift to men is *a divine fellowship to live in*—the church militant, expectant, and triumphant; the church visible and invisible; the divine fellowship that is "the communion of saints," embracing past, present, and future, and time and space and eternity.

IV. The church's fourth gift to men is *inexhaustible resources to live on* as they make their pilgrimage through the days of their years.

(a) The Bible is the first resource, the Bible which is "the word of God, which speaks with the wisdom of God, which shows men the way of God, which teaches men the will of God, and which equips men for the work of God."

(b) Prayer is the second inexhaustible resource. "Seeking God, listening to God, is an important part of the business of human life: and this is the essence of prayer," Evelyn Underhill reminds us. "We do something immense, almost unbelievable, when we enter that world of prayer, for then we deliberately move out toward that transcendent being whom Christianity declares to be the one reality: a reality revealed to us in three ways as a creative love, a rescuing love, and an indwelling, all-pervading love, and in each of these three ways claiming and responding to our absolute trust. Prayer is the give-and-take between the little souls of men and that threefold reality."

(c) As in prayer we go to God, so in sacrament God comes to us. The sacramental system of the church is the third resource for living Christianly that the church offers men.

(d) The Holy Spirit, the gift of its presence and indwelling, is the fourth great resource the church offers men.

(e) The fifth inexhaustible resource that the church offers men, and perhaps the most wonderful gift of all, is grace, which, in Bishop Brent's words, "is not the infusion of some mysterious spiritual property, which God having imparted leaves the recipient to make use of by himself; grace is the gift of God's personal working in the life through the indwelling Spirit."

V. The fifth gift of the church to men is *the Lord Christ,* God's Son, as savior, companion, friend, to grow up with and to grow old with, to walk through life with, to suffer with, to rejoice with, to die with, and with all one's strength to follow and serve, to love and to adore. —Frederick W. Kates.

## Illustration

MARTIN LUTHER KING, JR.     Martin's life, like all of ours, was a human life. Like ours, it was prone to human weaknesses, disappointments, failures. Yet he had faith, and that faith made him strong. He had love, and that love spilled over to all humankind. He was always and achingly conscious of those who most needed love—the oppressed, the poverty-stricken, the victims of hatred and hunger—and he courageously undertook, through his life's work, the ransoming of these neediest of God's children and our brothers and sisters. —Coretta King.

## Sermon Suggestions

THREE KINDS OF CHRISTIANS. (1) Some Christians make Christ sick. (See Rev. 2:1–7; 3:14–22.) (2) Some Christians please Christ. (See Rev. 2:8–10; 3:7–8.) (3) Some Christians about whom Christ has mixed emotions. (See Rev. 2:14–15; 2:20; 3:1.)—Raymond E. Balcomb.

JOY IN THE LORD. Scripture: Phil. 1:21–30. (1) Joy in life (v. 21). (2) Joy in faith (v. 25). (3) Joy in the gospel (v. 26). (4) Joy in the spirit (v. 27). (5) Joy in persecution (v. 28). (6) Joy in death (v. 21). (7) Joy in heaven (v. 23).—Ed Irwin.

## Worship Aids

CALL TO WORSHIP. "Thy word is a lamp unto my feet, and a light unto my path. I have sworn, and I will perform it, that I will keep thy righteous judgments. Quicken me, O Lord, according unto thy word." Ps. 119:105–107.

INVOCATION. Almighty God, fountain of all good, kindle in us insight and aspiration, that this hour of prayer may be a moment of time lived in eternity. Open our ears that we may hear. Soften our hearts that we may receive thy truth. Reveal thyself to us here that we may learn to find thee everywhere.

OFFERTORY SENTENCE. "Unto whomsoever much is given, of him shall be much required: and to whom men have committed much, of him they will ask the more." Luke 12:48.

OFFERTORY PRAYER. Help us, dear Father, to be cheerful givers of our time, means, talents, and self to the Master that he may use us in the upbuilding of his kingdom.

PRAYER. Infinite Source of all knowledge and truth, free us who cannot free ourselves from this sense of futility and incompleteness that surges like angry waves against the foundations of our faith.

Whence comes this protest against the tragedies of life? Hast thou not created our wills and framed the nature of our thoughts? At dawn our spirits soar, our hearts grow brave, and our assurance seems secure. Then in the heat of the day our insufficiency creeps over us and confronts us with overpowering reproach. To what end were we born?

If doubts rise in us, are they apart from thy creation? Our years seem like sands that run out before life has taken on dignity or ultimate significance. We feel terribly alone and far from home. Is there no place in the universe where love and friendship have abiding value? Oh, help us to have faith that thy purposes are beyond defeat.

We need faith that we may help those friends of ours who find no meaning in the music of life. We have no fear of death, but we would discover the significance of life. Beauty grows old; love is taken from us by death; truth remains obscure.

Yet in the sunset's splendor we know that after the darkness shall come again the dawn. Grant to our hearts that light shall enable us to share with those who see no gleam beyond the night and who have found no word by which to name thee.

For the sake of the unbelieving give us faith. Keep us loyal to our earthly tasks in order that through our faithfulness others may come to faith. We pray for light for one step ahead, truth by which to make today's choice, and courage for the present duty. So do we place our lives in thy keeping, O thou the light of all our days.—Ralph S. Harlow.

## EVENING SERVICE

### Topic: Digging Wells in Dry Places
TEXT: Ps. 84:5–6.

Sooner or later everyone walks through this valley of Baca. Some walk in it longer and more frequently than others, but all must walk it sometime. It is thrust across the pathway of life which moves to God and glory. And the way we travel through the dry, dusty, thirsty, agonizing valley is a revelation of what we really are. For human personality there are three consequences for men who go through the valley of Baca.

I. Some people go through the valley and are utterly defeated. Life holds nothing good. Baca destroys them. They find nothing rewarding, discover no new truth. It is an arid, agonizing experience, and their souls wither and die. Life holds nothing fresh. They give up. They are destroyed, embalmed bodies traveling life's highway.

II. There are others who are not greatly weakened by the valley of Baca. They merely endure and emerge unchanged. They go on as before. They derive no added power, no new insight, no remodeling of character, no reinforcement of personality. They simply pass through the burning, desolate valley and keep on going as before.

III. There are those about whom the psalmist sings, "As they go through the valley of Baca they make it a place of springs." They do not merely accept the difficult experience. They do not simply endure the tough, agonizing ordeal. They produce something from it. They dig wells in the hard, dry soil of life until they reach the depths, for faith is there. They satisfy the thirst for truth and righteousness, for God is there. They make the desert bloom by the spring of life's creativity. They make Baca a permanent gain for themselves and, having triumphed, enrich the whole world. They leave wells of refreshment for all whom their lives touch.—Edward L. R. Elson.

## SUNDAY: FEBRUARY SIXTH

### MORNING SERVICE

Topic: **Help Me! I Feel Lonely**
TEXT: John 16:32.

I. How do you define loneliness? One must distinguish between loneliness and solitude. For our use solitude is to be geographically alone. This can be helpful or harmful. Loneliness is to be spiritually or relationally alone. And this can occur whether other people are present or not. The dictionary distinguishes loneliness as being depressed by a sense of being alone. Loneliness is a sense of having inadequate relationships with others.

II. There may be many reasons or contexts for loneliness. Loneliness is not contingent upon time. It is possible to be lonely in the most busy times. Furthermore loneliness is not synonymous with being separated from people. Perhaps loneliness is more evidenced in crowded cities than anyplace else. This is why we speak about the "lonely crowd."

(a) Even in the finest families and within the deepest friendships at times we hide from each other. We all pull into our shell, build separating walls, and cut ourselves off from others. We fail to communicate with each other. There are constant doubts and fears which we hide from each other. Often we want to share but cannot seem to know how to articulate our deepest longings.

(b). Circumstances may cause loneliness. There are some life events which just lay the banana peels on which we slip into loneliness.

(1) There are some events in life and some times in life when circumstances dictate our being alone, and we allow the alone to become loneliness.

(2) There is a loneliness sometimes caused by nonconformity. The crowd makes its demands loudly and clearly, but if one is to be a person, an individual with integrity, he sometimes must stand against the crowd. And loneliness may result.

(3) There is loneliness which sometimes comes to the person who has huge decision-making responsibility. In terms of our human relationships there is a loneliness in making great decisions which affect others. It is said that the office of the President of the United States is the loneliest position in the whole world.

(c) There is a basic loneliness which no contact with others can cure, and that's the loneliness resulting when man tries to live without God. Man must live in relationship with God. St. Augustine said it best: "Thou, O Lord, hast made us for thyself and our hearts are restless until they rest in thee." I convey my conviction that there is no real meaning in life apart from God. The chief manifestation of loneliness in our society today may be the huge number of persons who are expressing meaninglessness—the purposelessness of life.

III. You have to choose how you will face up to the loneliness which inevitably threatens you and every man. I would like to make five simple suggestions.

(a) Discover God. God became a person in Jesus Christ that we might know him and that he might make himself known to us.

(1) In knowing Christ we know the answer to our loneliness. We know that God understands our loneliness because Jesus was lonely. He experienced the depths of loneliness that no one of us will ever experience. Christ was rejected by men. He subjected himself to the loneliness of complete death, not only that he might communicate to you and me that he understands our loneliness, but also that he might give an answer.

(2) In Christ we can see the difference between solitude and loneliness. Jesus appreciated solitude, but he disliked loneliness. You and I will never be as lonesome as Christ was on Good Friday morning. He took our loneliness for us. In Christ God is communicating this to us.

(b) Discover the church. It is important to be a part of God's people on earth. God does not intend that we live in a vacuum but that we be involved with a community of his followers, to understand and experience belonging as we participate in a fellowship of Christians.

(c) Discover the needs of other people in the world. God made us to be related to others in his world. We must understand a crucial truth here that loneliness is not answered if we want to be with others just for our good. Loneliness is answered only if we want to be with others for their good.

(d) Discover purpose. This seems to be a natural result of knowing God, the church, and the needs of others. When Jesus was most alone he expressed his purpose of life, "I have overcome the world" (John 16:33). Use your alone times to struggle to know your useful purpose. This is when to be alone becomes useful solitude.

(e) Discover yourself. (1) Do not be afraid to analyze honestly why you feel as you do when loneliness seems to be squeezing in. And don't hesitate to seek to know yourself.

(2) Loneliness really is a kind of walking death, for it means separation from fellowmen and separation from real communication with God. But it need not be that. For in Jesus Christ the walls of separation are torn down. Jesus expressed it, "I am not alone, for the Father is with me." And you are never alone.—Thomas L. Jones.

## Illustrations

THE NEIGHBOR'S CORN. A novelist, Susan Glaspell, told of a farmer named Ira who prided himself on the quality of the corn he grew. But when anyone asked him for some of the seed, he replied, "I guess it's all spoke for this year." But the season came when the corn did not keep its quality. One afternoon Ira discovered why. The winds were blowing the pollen from the neighbor's corn across the fence and onto his fields. He deliberated a few moments, then gathering a sack of his prize corn, he started out of his house. When his mother asked him where he was going, he replied that he was going to teach the neighbors on both sides how to grow corn. When she was curious to know what had made him change his mind, he replied, "Because I can't have good corn while their corn is poor."—Gene E. Bartlett.

VOICE IN THE NIGHT.    A mother put her daughter to bed in an upper berth on the child's first train trip. "Good night, dear," she whispered. "God will watch over you."

About a half hour later when silence had descended over the car, the little girl called, "Mother, are you there?" "Yes, dear," her mother replied. A little while later the child called, "Daddy, are you there too?" "I'm here," said her father. "Go to sleep." After this had been repeated several times, a sleepy passenger finally lost patience and shouted: "We're all here, little girl. Your father, your mother, your brothers and sisters and your aunts and your uncles. Now go to sleep and let me alone!"

There was a brief silence. Then in a tremulous voice the child called, "Mother, was that God?"—Kenneth L. Dodge.

## Sermon Suggestion

IN ONE EAR AND OUT THE OTHER.    Texts: Prov. 20:12; Jer. 6:10; Matt. 11:15. (1) Listen with interest to what our fellow-man and to what God is saying. (2) Listen selectively, choosing to whom we will listen. (See II Tim. 4:3–4.) (3) Listen with concentration and develop the ability to hear. (See Rev. 2:7.)—Frank H. Epp.

## Worship Aids

CALL TO WORSHIP.    "We have thought of thy lovingkindness, O God, in the midst of thy temple. According to thy name, O God, so is thy praise unto the ends of the earth." Ps. 48:9–10.

INVOCATION.    Almighty God, the giver and lord of life: we bless and praise thee for thy merciful keeping and gracious care, for all the gifts of thy providence and grace, and for all the blessings which manifest thy fatherhood. We thank thee for the faith which sustains us, the hopes which inspire us, and the light by which we daily walk. We thank thee for Jesus Christ, who, by the life he lived, the temptations he conquered, the gospel he taught, and the cross he bore, has brought us nigh to thee and closer to one another.

OFFERTORY SENTENCE.    "Verily I say unto you, Inasmuch as ye have done it unto one of the least of these my brethren, ye have done it unto me." Matt. 25:40.

OFFERTORY PRAYER.    Dear Father, may we ever give thee a definite, consistent, and heartfelt service.

PRAYER.    Father in heaven, whose mercies fail not: we come to thee with praise on our lips and with thankfulness in our hearts.

We thank thee for this holy day, for the peace of worship, for the joy of communion, for liberty of access to thy throne of grace, and for all the blessings bestowed upon us in Jesus Christ.

We thank thee that thou art not far away from any one of us, that our faintest sigh is heard of thee, that though we cannot behold thee with the outward eye we may commune with thee in spirit and see thee with the eye of faith.

We thank thee for all things bright and beautiful around us, for the face of nature and the sweet faces of those we love, for holy memories of loved ones in thy safe keeping, and for the great and good who, having lived in thy fear, have entered into rest.

We thank thee for the great and good still with us, for those whose example inspires us with pure desires and worthy ambitions, and we bless thee for all the silent workers who in quiet homes and in silent ways do thy will and bring thy kingdom into the hearts of men.

We thank thee for the faith we have

and for the mercies thou hast still in store for us, and we beseech thee that thou wouldst continue thy work of grace in our hearts, supplying all our needs in Christ Jesus and working in us both to will and to do of his good pleasure. —James Burns.

### EVENING SERVICE

**Topic: The World God So Loved**
TEXT: John 3:16.

I. God must love the world of beauty for he leaves it everywhere. (a) Ralph S. Cushman wrote a poem in which he wondered if this side of heaven were so beautiful with all of the glory of nature, the purple of the violet, the delicate tinge of the magnolia blossom, blue waves beating on a cliff, and the fragrant scent of a pine tree in the summer sun, then how beautiful must heaven be on God's side.

(b) If God loves beauty so that he leaves it everywhere in his great created world, is not salvation responding to the challenge of beauty and trying to make life within reflect life in all of its beauty without?

II. God loves law and order. (a) We trace his way through the scientist's quest and know that God's laws are dependable. The stars come nightly to the sky, cause and effect are never separated, the hand of God is steady and sure. In the midst of change God is unchanging.

(b) Isn't salvation living with eternal ways in the midst of life's changing days? Emerson put it, "Listening to what the centuries say as against the hours."

III. God loves wholeness. In the Bible it is called the "grace of God."

(a) In every situation there is life's healing touch. We find it in nature as the ravages of war are soon covered by green, growing things. We find it in

disease as the forces of the body rush to do battle with the intruder.

(b) Isn't salvation to bring our broken dreams, our thwarted hopes, and our dissipated lives back into the wholeness of God, allowing his grace to heal the broken and bruised life? Isn't this our thought in regard to Christ? When man was far from the thought of God, he sent Christ as his final word of love and mercy. In the words of the scripture, "Not that we loved him, but that he loved us and sent his Son to be the propitiation for our sins." "We touch him in life's throng and press and we are whole again."

IV. God does not intend to leave our world as it now is. (a) Scientists tell us that we live in an expanding universe. Creation is not finished, and the last chapter has not been written.

(b) We sense God in the battle of life everywhere. His presence is made known by beds of pain, testing, moments of trial, temptation's fatal hour, and life's most bitter defeat. God is on every battlefield, being crucified again in the horror of it as youthful lives are smothered out before dreams come true. He tramps the city street where youth betrays his dream, where old age can only wait, and where life everywhere has a devaluated sign of cheapness. He calls again through Calvary the enduring value of life repeating the phrase, "You were bought with the price of all I had in the gift of Christ."

(c) Isn't salvation throwing yourself wholeheartedly on God's side in the struggle of life between good and evil? There is no neutrality. The everlasting choice is before us. Salvation's joyful sound and the joy bells of heaven ring only as someone responds to the deathless challenge of Christ, "Take up your cross and follow me."—Frank A. Court.

## SUNDAY: FEBRUARY THIRTEENTH

### MORNING SERVICE

**Topic: Love Story**
TEXT: John 1:12–13.

The Bible, instead of being a book of prohibitions, is primarily a love story. Reduce it to its basic components as you do the story plot of any great novel, and you'll come up with four central themes and variations on those themes.

*Theme One.* "In the beginning God." He personally created the most beautiful world that mind could imagine. Then as the final act of his creation he brought into being a man and a woman who were touched with the quality of his own image. How he loved these two people! How he enjoyed his conversations with them, as he entrusted to Adam and to Eve the responsibility of overseeing all of his great creation. He had a plan for their lives, as he has a plan for yours. The Bible describes the deep, everlasting love of your creator-sustainer God who yearns to be in personal contact with you. He still has a plan for your life.

*Theme Two.* (a) Something has gone wrong with this romance. This same God who implanted in Adam and Eve and in you his very own image gave, as part of that image, the capacity for you to go your own way independent of him. Few are his restrictions of the person who truly understands who God is. They don't even seem like restrictions. They're the guidelines of a loving Father who knows how his son and daughter function best. They're designed to free you to an exhilarating lifestyle.

(b) Yet you can choose to break your relationship with your loving, creating, sustaining God. And you've made this choice. You've made it through Adam and Eve who disobeyed. They actually disobeyed because of their unbelief. They didn't believe that God had leveled with them when he instructed them that he knew what was best. Satan, a delightful, pleasing, seductive person, constantly whispers in your ears: "My way is better and a way of life to its fullest. Be free of the limitations God has placed upon you." So Adam and Eve broke the heart of their lover-God and in the process shattered their own hearts.

*Theme Three.* (a) It comes almost instantaneously in its muted, quiet promise that one will come who will crush the head of the tempter. The theme builds through the Old Testament narrative of God at work in the lives of individuals and a nation, both of which alternate tender response with harsh rebellion.

(b) The Bible says God still loves you, no matter how messed up your life is or how self-sufficient you appear to be. The Bible says that God went to the cross for you. His name is Jesus. (See I Pet. 2:24.) He rose from the dead in victory over what has gone wrong. He loves you so much that he has taken upon himself the penalty which you already have partially experienced, perhaps are experiencing now, or will experience in the future. He desires to make you anew. He wants you to become his new creation. That's why he says you need to be born again through the blood of Jesus Christ through the power of his Spirit.

*Theme Four.* (a) God never rapes anybody. His love woos. God never makes false promises, telling you that he'll take away all your problems if you come to him. He does promise you his peace which will calm your troubled, resistant heart. He promises you his strength to meet the difficulties of day-in, day-out existence, difficulties which are the direct or indirect result of the buildup of sin through centuries of human rebellion.

(b) He says: "This life isn't that long. There's a life to come. You'll live seventy, eighty, or ninety years and then step into my direct presence forever. Do you take me at my word? Will you experience the over eight thousand promises that I have for you? My love is total. It's complete. It's lasting. Granted, it does have its conditions. My love will never fail you. But for you to fully experience it you'll need to say you're sorry. It's that I want to forgive you. I don't love you any less when your back is turned on me. But we can't have restored relationship unless you'll turn and come and let me hug you. Let me show you how much I love you, how thoroughgoing my acceptance is, and how there's nothing in the world you've done that was not nailed to the cross along with me. Turn your back on that stubborn, arrogant, passive resistance. Put your trust in me. I'm not trying to bombard you with a grocery list of dogmatic facts about myself. You'll get to know me better as the years go by, as we have friendship and fellowship together. Come right now just as you are. Let me heal your broken, battered spirit. Let me give you strength for the problems which won't go away but can be handled with my help."—John A. Huffman, Jr.

## Illustrations

TWO MEN IN CHURCH. A church in Africa was in the midst of a worship service. Suddenly there appeared a man dressed in torn, dirty, smelly clothes. The usher said to him, "Why don't you sit down on the floor next to the door?" At least there the wind could waft away the smell, he thought. After awhile the poor man left.

Then came a man dressed in a fine suit, a white shirt, and tie. Everyone knew immediately that he must be a very important person. The usher invited him to sit on the front row in the church.

After the service the pastor invited the man in the fine suit for dinner. When the first dish of food was passed, the guest put the food into one of his suit pockets. When the next dish was passed, he put that food into another suit pocket. The pastor could hardly bear to see the fine suit ruined by the dripping grease. Finally he burst out, "What are you doing?" The guest replied: "Obviously you did not invite me. You invited my suit. So I am feeding my suit."—John F. Carrington.

DISCRIMINATION. If you discriminate against me because I am dirty, I can wash myself.

If you discriminate against me because I am bad, I can reform and be good.

If you discriminate against me because I am ignorant, I can learn.

If you discriminate against me because I am ill-mannered, I can learn to behave.

But if you discriminate against me because of my color or race, you discriminate something God gave me and over which I have no control.

## Sermon Suggestions

SOMETHING TO LEAN BACK ON. Text: II Tim. 1:12. (1) You can lean back on the spiritual nurture of your childhod and youth. (2) You can lean back on a faith that has been tested in history. (3) You can lean back on the personal experience of God in your life. (4) You can lean back on the promises of God.— A. Hayden Hollingsworth, Jr.

THE GREATEST OF THESE. Text: I Cor. 13:13. (1) Love is superlative. (2) Love is selfless. (3) Love is sacrificial.

## Worship Aids

CALL TO WORSHIP. "O love the Lord, all ye his saints: for the Lord preserveth the faithful. Be of good courage, and he shall strengthen your heart, all ye that hope in the Lord." Ps. 31:23–24.

INVOCATION. Beget in us a thirst for thy presence. Kindle in us the impulse to pray, tear out our pride, rip away our fear, and persuade us to kneel in our need that we may rise in thy strength. Grant that we may show our love for thee by working loyally toward justice in every touch of man upon his fellowman. In this church grant that we may willingly become a part of that body wherein again the Lord is made flesh and dwells on the earth.

OFFERTORY SENTENCE. "Offer the sacrifices of righteousness, and put your trust in the Lord." Ps. 4:5.

OFFERTORY PRAYER. O eternal God, may these gifts represent an inner commitment to love thee above all else and to love our brethren in need because they are loved by thee.

PRAYER. Lord of history, hear us as we cry out for integrity in our government, for justice in the courts of law, and for equality in human rights. Make us aware of what history has to teach us about life so that the old mistakes may not be repeated.

Lord of all nations, hear us as we plead for understanding among all mankind, for a world able to settle differences without arms, and for compassion as a people toward other people. Convict us to hear the voices from the perimeters of the Third World and from every place where people live in the hideousness of dehumanization.

Lord of conscience, we admit that honesty is often the exception rather than the rule, that suffering and pain really do not impress us, and that technology has overwhelmed our sense of responsibility and dulled our reverence for life. Speak to our faltering consciences. Cleanse them so that we may hear and speak the truth again.

Lord of life, we affirm your creation and its potential for our lives, your love and mercy we have all experienced, and your claim on our lives in the person of Christ. Call us then to be creators, changers, and helpers; and renew in us a sense of commitment that would enable us to hear your word giving life in the midst of death.—David F. Weyant.

## EVENING SERVICE

**Topic: Acting Like Christians**

Living as a Christian means exhibiting many facets of God's grace in our hearts, all of them the outgrowth of Christian love and all of them polished and brightened by practice. These graces are the outward expression of an inner Presence and attitude, the putting into practice of those things we know are good and right.

I. *Sympathy*. There is hardly a day that we do not come in contact with someone who has been buffeted by the winds of adversity. All around us there are those who sorrow, who are suffering from illness, poverty, despair, bereavement, or other troubles. How utterly unchristian to be indifferent toward this suffering. True sympathy is begotten by love and expressed at the personal level. The Christian, having experienced the comfort of the Holy Spirit, should know how to sympathize with others. (See II Cor. 1:4.)

II. *Compassion*. There is a distinction between sympathy and compassion, for compassion involves depth of understanding—one sinner's being sorry for another sinner's plight. Compassion looks deep into the heart, suffers with and understands the need of the other person, and communicates that understanding. Compassion ignores the unlovely as it sees God's image in most unlikely places.

III. *Courtesy*. Courtesy is the art and grace of treating others with respect and understanding—just as we would like to be treated. It is politeness in the face of provocation, the turning of the other cheek when we have been offended. Courtesy involves the soft answer that can turn away wrath. It is observance of the niceties of social intercourse in the midst of trying circumstances. Only too often unhappy situations develop because of the lack of common courtesy. That this should be true where Christians are concerned is a travesty, reflecting dishonor on the very name Christian.

IV. *Patience*. Impatience has dimmed the witness of many a Christian. How often we must distress our Lord by our impatience with others. Some people seem slow, inarticulate, and inept—just the way we appear to our Lord perhaps. And he is infinitely patient with us.

V. *Tact*. Frankness is not always for the glory of God. I have known some Christians who have prided themselves on being frank, and I have known some who have been hurt by this frankness. Telling the truth can be done in love, taking into consideration the feelings of others. Tact is that grace which enables us to sense the feelings of others and to act toward them or communicate with them in a way that preserves human dignity.

VI. *Forgiveness*. Without a spirit of forgiveness human relations cannot be maintained at the Christian level. We live in the light of God's forgiveness, and it is an attitude that God requires of us. Forgiveness involves shedding the robe of self-righteousness and being clothed with the humility that is a part of true Christianity.

VII. *Practicality*. We often are sound in theory but fail at the point of implementation. To many of us the Christian graces are nebulous attributes that we expect in others but fail to exhibit ourselves. Practicality involves helping people in the place where they need help. It is not just a kind word but also a kind act where that act can do the most good. Where food is needed, give food. Where clothing is needed, give clothing. Where comfort, sympathy, courtesy, and patience are needed, show these. The apostle James admonishes us: "Be ye doers of the word, and not hearers only, deceiving your own selves." Acting like a Christian means just that. —L. Nelson Bell in *Christianity Today*.

# SUNDAY: FEBRUARY TWENTIETH

## MORNING WORSHIP

**Topic: When Morality Turns Sour (Brotherhood Week)**

SCRIPTURE: Ps. 1; Luke 18:9-14.

I. Consider the Pharisee. (a) The Pharisee was an impeccably moral person. What he said about himself was undoubtedly true. He avoided evil behavior. He did not extort, deal unjustly, commit adultery, nor compromise with the Romans for a living as did the tax collectors. Although it was not prescribed by Jewish law, he fasted twice a week as an act of self-mortification for the sins of the people. He not only gave a tenth of his products of the soil and his animals as a tithe to the Lord, as the law prescribed, but went beyond the law in tithing even what he bought from others. This Pharisee is obviously a moral, upright, conscientious person, devout in the pursuit of his faith.

(b) There is something very unbecoming about this Pharisee. I have met him in other people and find him unbearable. It is impossible to get along with him, and you cannot help but wonder what cruel act he will perpetrate next upon others in the name of his high moral code. He is a moral man whose morality has gone sour.

(1) The Pharisee picked out a number of sins of which he was not guilty and decided that this made him a moral person. Then to reassure himself of his good opinion of himself he reminded himself of the religious duties he fulfilled.

(2) Morality goes sour when our morality makes us self-righteous. The Pharisee becomes a very unlovely and unloving person as he makes odious comparisons of himself with others. His own morality begins to turn sour as he feels compelled to take note of the sins of another standing by.

(3) Morality goes sour when our morality separates us from other persons. The Pharisee thanks God he is not like other men and particularly not like the tax collector. We can see him gathering his arms tightly about himself in separateness from other persons. His morality had given him a sense that he was too good to associate with other persons.

II. Consider the tax collector. (a) What is the preservative needed to keep our morality fresh, creative, and vital? The answer is to be found in the vignette Jesus gives in the picture of the tax collector. The point to the scene is not that he really was not so bad after all but what his attitude was. Recall that he prayed, "God, be merciful to me a sinner!" In that one sentence lies the secret to a wholesome moral life.

(b) The mistake of the Pharisee was in forgetting his common kinship with the tax collector as a fellow sinner. Forgetting that reality he mistakenly prayed, "God, I thank thee that I am not like other men." His morality was turned sour when he failed to realize that indeed he was like other men.

(c) Recognizing our common kinship with all others as sinners we recognize our common need to live our lives daily in reliance upon God's mercy. When we rely upon God's love for us as we are rather than upon so many good deeds we have done, that milk of human kindness flows fresh and free. We marvel at God's accepting love and find our way to accepting others. We love because we have first experienced his love for us. Knowing God's forgiveness, we move toward forgiving others. Not relying on our own will to keep us moral, we find a divine will at work in our lives to surprise us with acts of compassion and righteousness beyond our own ability.—Colbert S. Cartwright.

## Illustrations

BORN TO BE BROTHERS. While Generals Lee and Grant were conferring at Appomattox Courthouse, some of the Union officers were looking up old friends who had been on the other side. They returned, as the conversation ended, bringing with them some Confederate officers who wanted to pay their respects to Grant, among them General James Longstreet. Grant and Longstreet had graduated from West Point only a year apart; the last time they had seen each other was before the war when Grant had been in St. Louis on business and had sat down with Longstreet to a game of cards known as "brag." Now Grant took Longstreet warmly by the arm and said, "Let's have another game of brag to recall the old days." Longstreet was moved by the incident, and telling about it later he could only say, "Why do men fight who were born to be brothers?"—Raymond E. Balcomb.

GODLY GRIEF. In the early days of Hitler's movement in Germany, a handful of young fanatics planned and carried out the assassination of Walter Rathenau, a high government official, the first Jew in public life to lose his life under the Hitler movement. When the young men were apprehended and placed in prison one of them received a very strange note. It was actually written to his mother by the mother of Rathenau, the man who had been killed. Rathenau's mother said in her note that she was writing to express her sympathy. She said that while she grieved for her son who had been killed, her pain surely was not as great as that of being the mother of a boy who was one of the killers. The note was sent on to prison, and the young man reading it was amazed. What kind of person could write such a note? What kind of faith was this! He began to study the Jewish religion, seeking an answer. Upon his release from prison after some years, he escaped from Germany and joined the French Foreign Legion. Wherever possible he visited the places associated with Jewish history. He learned to speak and to write the language. Over a period of years he associated himself closely with the Jewish people, their plight, their hopes, and their fears. Then he dropped out of sight. Not even his friends knew where he was. But one day walking on the dock of a port in southern France a war correspondent who had known this young man saw a familiar figure pass, dressed in the working clothes of a porter. He followed and finallly approached him and asked the question. Yes, it was the same man. He took him inside where the story could be told. The German had deliberately taken this job in a seaport in order that he might be the go-between to help persecuted Jewish families escape from Germany. Already he had helped over three hundred find their way to freedom. Over the years this man had made a complete turn-around. The assassin was seeking to make restitution for his crime. It stands as a true reminder of the words Paul wrote centuries before, "Godly grief leads to repentance."—Gene E. Bartlett.

## Sermon Suggestions

BEYOND AN EYE FOR AN EYE. Text: Matt. 5:38–39. (1) The Christian is to go beyond reaction to response. (2) The Christian is to go beyond consideration of outward acts to a regard for the inward disposition or spirit from which they arise. (3) The Christian is to go beyond retaliation to where we share the life and spirit of God.—Charles L. Seasholes.

LIVING BY THE GOLDEN RULE. Text: Matt. 7:12. (1) The gentle approach brings peace. (2) The tolerant attitude brings understanding. (3) The way of suffering brings understanding. (4) Sacrifice brings restitution.—Philip E. Gregory.

## Worship Aids

CALL TO WORSHIP. "Hereby perceive we the love of God, because he laid down his life for us: and we ought to lay down our lives for the brethren. Let us not love in word, neither in tongue; but in deed and in truth." I John 3:16, 18.

INVOCATION. Eternal God our Father, who art from everlasting, thou hast made us and not we ourselves. Thou hast set us never far from thee, that we, thy children, may learn the ways of freedom and choose thee with all our hearts. Grant us now thy Holy Spirit that confident in prayer we may worship thee with gladness and become as little children before thee.

OFFERTORY SENTENCE. "Therefore, as ye abound in every thing, in faith, and utterance, and knowledge, and in all diligence, and in your love to us, see that ye abound in this grace also." II Cor. 8:7.

OFFERTORY PRAYER. O God, help us so to practice by our gifts and our lives the divine principle of goodwill that in our homes, our communities, and among all the nations of the earth, men may enjoy the boon of peace.

PRAYER. O eternal and merciful God, you are a God of peace and love and

unity and not of the discord and confusion which, in your righteous judgment, you have permitted to happen. This world has become divided and broken in that it has forsaken you. For you alone can create and sustain unity. In its own wisdom this world has fallen away from you, especially in those things which pertain to your divine truth and to the blessedness of our souls. As in its own so-called wisdom the world comes to shame by its being torn apart, so may it return again to you who love unity. We poor sinners, to whom you have graciously granted that we acknowledge this condition, beseech and implore you: through your Holy Spirit bring together again all that is scattered; unify what is divided; and make it completely whole. Grant therefore that we turn to your unity, seek your truth, and avoid all discord. So may we become of one will, one knowledge, one disposition, and one understanding that relies upon Jesus Christ our Lord. In the harmony of unity may we praise and adore you, the heavenly Father of our Lord Jesus Christ.—World Council of Churches.

## EVENING SERVICE

### Topic: Drawn by the Spirit

SCRIPTURE: Acts 2:1–11.

The Holy Spirit lifts people who are lonely, grief stricken, depressed, sad, and unhappy; he lifts them into relationship with a warm other person. That warm other person may by all measures be a totally opposite kind of person having a different cultural background, a different political persuasion, or even a different language. But the language of compassion, of empathy, and of love, which is the language of the Holy Spirit, is universal, and translation is not needed.

I. The experience of danger draws people together, and the Holy Spirit is active when there is danger. The Holy Spirit would have us keep a light heart and an open mind as we struggle through these heavy times. One can easily turn very foul and bitter about the realities of life. Christians are called to be loving in an unlovable situation. Those of you who have felt the danger or the damage of life but still remain unhateful have experienced the Holy Spirit as strongly as anyone on that first day of Pentecost.

II. The experience of tragedy and death draws people together, and the Holy Spirit is active when tragedy and death strike. Often when some sort of ultimate tragedy strikes, families and friends are able to bind up old wounds and use the situation to begin anew. It is amazing how many times a funeral will bring together people who haven't seen each other in years—and bring them together on a very meaningful basis, working through a tragedy together. In such circumstances the Holy Spirit is active.

III. The experience of beauty draws people together, and when we are open to seeing or hearing beauty we are open to receiving the Holy Spirit. The Holy Spirit works through beauty, through creativity, and through man's ability to transcend himself and do something greater than he thought he was capable of.

IV. The experience of birth and new life draws people together, and the Holy Spirit is active in the renewal of life. These events bring families and friends together in a Pentecost experience. But new life is more than an infant child. New life is discovering after all that you're not dead, that your life has not collapsed as you thought it would, and that in fact you have the courage to live through a painful confrontation. New life is the discovery that life can be new.

V. The experience of worship draws people together, and the Holy Spirit is here in worship. All sorts of different people gather to worship the same Lord. And when we worship together we experience the Holy Spirit as he comes to judge us, to cleanse us, to forgive us, and to heal us.—Craig Biddle III.

## SUNDAY: FEBRUARY TWENTY-SEVENTH

### MORNING SERVICE

Topic: On Being Wrong (Lent)
Scripture: Acts 8:9–24.

I. Simon Magus, although converted to Christianity, remained a sorcerer or magician. This meant that he wielded considerable influence over the Samaritans among whom he lived, seeming even to have the ability to cast spells and perform miracles. The stirring preaching of the apostle Philip attracted Simon, however; he was baptized and immediately began being an evangelist in his own right. It looked as though this man would make his mark as a leader of the early church. But Simon had it all wrong. He missed what Christianity was about, mistaking the gifts of God for tricks of the magician's trade.

II. With great eagerness and excitement Simon rushed to the apostles—money in hand.

(a) His fistful of money was urged upon Peter. Recoiling from him, Peter responded, "Your silver perish with you, because you thought you could obtain the gift of God with money!" Peter's choice of the word "gift" in this situation meant something totally free, something which could not be bought. Further reprimanding him, Peter went on to say, "You have neither part nor lot in this matter, for your heart is not right before God."

(b) He then called for repentance, letting Simon realize in no uncertain terms that he was emphatically wrong in equating God's grace with a magician's trickery. No amount of money could take the place of a humble and contrite heart. No selfish desire to manipulate God ever could put a person in the Christian camp. Peter was extremely blunt in thus dealing with Simon, but he made his point.

(c) Being wrong about religion was

the issue here, and Simon has had considerable company over the years. Interestingly enough, this man became known in early Christian tradition as the father of all heresy. A century after he lived there were heretics actually called "Simonians." His name also was attached to the sin of "simony," meaning the use of money to attain spiritual ends or the use of money to buy and sell ecclesiastical offices and honors.

III. What Simon was so wrong about —and here is the lesson for ourselves— was that he wanted to be in command of God rather than for God to be in command of him.

(a) Simon's temptation was to exploit faith in order to accomplish his own ends rather than to let faith transform him to higher ends. He was looking for something to enhance himself and dazzle his friends. He probably was one whose prayers were self-centered instead of the surrender of self. Simon itched to control the forces greater than mankind rather than allow his life to become a channel for those forces. His error was in hanging on when he should have let go. God, not man, is meant to be Lord.

(b) Simon's heresy remains widespread. Its manifestations are varied, but the results are the same.

(1) There are many adherents to a popularized form of Christianity which seeks only to soothe its followers while never spurring them to active commitment.

(2) There are found "joiners," people who unite with churches in order to get something from them in a totally selfish sense.

(3) Simon's heresy is revealed in prayers which seek to bargain with God for some specific result.

(4) All of these manifestations of being wrong about Christianity go back to the question of who is in charge: God or man? Is religion self-serving or God-serving?

IV. When anyone is wrong like this, when issues are misjudged, the problem in most cases is that of not having gone far enough or deeply enough into the matter at hand.

(a) When an individual assumes that he alone is the master of his fate, the captain of his soul, he betrays the shallowness of his thinking. Simon the magician looked at things too superficially, and so he erred. People who use Christianity only as a palliative or tranquilizer err as well, as do those who try to use religion for purely selfish gain. No in-depth probing or searching has occurred in such people's experience, and so they end up in the wrong.

(b) That is why Jesus' words have a special meaning when he said to the fishermen who were to become his disciples, "Launch out into the deep." That instruction was given when Jesus wanted to win the allegiance of Peter, James, and John. Following it, these men made a record catch of fish. They also thereupon committed themselves to Jesus' service.

(c) Nowadays we read about that incident and apply its further meaning to ourselves. That we might not err in the things of faith, we also launch out into the deep. We go farther than at first seems necessary. We even take additional risks in order to achieve the best result. Jesus' call to "launch out into the deep" has become a symbol of what is meant to happen to our souls. It becomes our way of acknowledging Jesus' authority over life and faith.—John H. Townsend.

## Illustrations

ON BEING CENSORIOUS. Whenever we judge others, we borrow trouble. Judgment is a two-edged sword. Every judgment is a self-judgment. Every criticism, however sincerely made, is a criticism of oneself. Nothing reveals a man's character more completely than his judgment of other people's manners and customs. We are sure that we would not live as they do and that we would not act as they act. Of course, we could not. Why should we? Indeed, how could we? If we lived as they live and acted as they act, we would not be ourselves. We would be what others are. We come from different backgrounds; we are influenced by different circumstances; we have our own likes and dislikes. This is as it ought to be. But to be thoughtlessly critical of others, to be censorious of their manners and customs, is a form of blindness to our own shortcomings. To be disdainful of the customs of others is arrogant; to ridicule them is impertinent. It is a mark of good breeding, or better still of true gentleness, to be understanding rather than critical, forbearing rather than censorious. We ought never to judge others until we have looked at ourselves.—Arnold H. Lowe.

HEAD AND BODY. No full-length photographs of Lincoln were available for some time after he became famous; only head portraits. To satisfy the demands, an enterprising engraver made one up. He put the head of Lincoln on the body of John C. Calhoun. There was irony in this. For Calhoun was the prime mover of the secession which was broken by Lincoln.

## Sermon Suggestions

THREE TEMPTATIONS. Scripture: Matt. 4:1–11. (1) The temptation to turn stones into bread or to use material means: to raise an army and overthrow Rome by military might. (2) The temptation to cast himself from the temple or to escape from responsibility: to ask God to work a miracle and overthrow Rome by divine interference. (3) The temptation to win the kingdoms of this world by bowing before Satan or a policy of compromise: to make a deal with Rome. —John A. Redhead, Jr.

THE HUMAN PREDICAMENT AND THE DIVINE PROMISE. (1) The ultimate problem. (See Rom. 3:23.) (2) The undeniable guilt. (See Jas. 2:10.) (3) The universal remedy. (See Isa. 1:18; II Cor. 5:21.)—C. Reuben Anderson.

## Worship Aids

CALL TO WORSHIP. "Ye shall know the truth, and the truth shall make you free. God is a Spirit: and they that worship him must worship him in spirit and in truth." John 8:32; 4:24.

INVOCATION. O God, whose name is great, whose goodness is inexhaustible, who art worshiped and served by all the hosts of heaven: touch our hearts, search out our consciences, and cast out of us every evil thought and base desire; all envy, wrath, and remembrance of injuries; and every motion of flesh and spirit that is contrary to thy holy will.

OFFERTORY SENTENCE. "This is the thing which the Lord commanded, saying, Take ye from among you an offering unto the Lord: whosoever is of a willing heart, let him bring it, an offering of the Lord." Exod. 35:4–5.

OFFERTORY PRAYER. Dear Lord and Savior of us all, may we become obedient to thy will both in the dedication of our tithes and of our talents.

AN AFFIRMATION OF FAITH. I believe in the love of God through Jesus Christ.
I believe in the cross of Calvary as the ground plan of the universe.
I believe in the transcendental meaning and hope of life.
I believe that the true good of life lies in the unseen where Christ sitteth at the right hand of God.
I believe that the real values of life are the good, the true, and the beautiful.
I believe in the salvability and immortality of every man and in the infinite value of every living soul.
I believe in the practicability of the kingdom of God and in the freedom to choose it and to work for it.
I believe in the sacramental quality of my day's work and that I may see and serve God in it.
I believe in a grace that can overcome my selfishness and pride and that will enable me to overcome temptation and upon which I need never call in vain.

I believe in love as the final law of life.

And in this faith by the help of God I mean to live this day and all my days. —Richard Roberts.

## EVENING SERVICE

**Topic: What Is a Christian?**
TEXT: Jas. 2:7.

I. *He puts Christ central.* A Christian sees in Jesus the perfect revelation of the nature and character of God. The Christian takes the New Testament as his guide to understanding of the life, teaching, and real meaning of Jesus Christ. What Jesus said about God; the way he trusted God; the way he sought to do the perfect will of God; the way Jesus held God first in all his considerations become the Christian's standard for his own knowledge of the nature and character of God and his goal for his own relationship to God.

II. *He loves.* The Christian, like Jesus, loves God with all his heart and soul and mind and strength and then, following further the example of Jesus, seeks to love his neighbor as himself.

III. *He trusts.* The Christian trusts in Christ so implicitly that he entrusts to him his very life, daring to believe that this way will lead to a quality of living which is eternally right and satisfying.

IV. *He obeys and follows.* The Christian obeys and follows Christ, not asking, "Why should I take the narrow road when the wide road is more attractive?" but asking only for strength to travel the way Jesus has gone before, believing that Christ will lead his loyal followers to the Castle Splendid.

V. *He serves.* The Christian continually strives to make applications of the social philosophy of Jesus in terms of feeding the hungry, giving wholesome drink to the thirsty, clothing the naked, visiting the sick, showing hospitality to strangers, and giving help to all who are downtrodden and oppressed. Why? Because he takes seriously the words of Jesus. (See Matt. 25:40.) While this way seems to some to be the way of foolishness, the Christian dares to follow it because he has accepted the promise of Jesus that whosoever loses his life for the sake of others shall find it, while those who are continually trying to hold onto life for selfish purposes shall lose it. (See Matt. 16:26.)

VI. *He is optimist.* The true Christian reveals by his joyous optimism in the face of difficult situations that he had laid hold upon a basic philosophy of life which keeps him steady and courageous when other people are pessimistic, afraid, and discouraged. By his optimism in the face of frightening conditions in his own community, in his own family, or in his own personal life, and by the way he maintains fidelity to Christ in the face of great crises, he wins his right to be called a Christian.

VII. *He is confident.* A Christian has absolute confidence that this mortal life is only the beginning of a life that shall endless be. Christians show their real colors not only by the way they carry out their relationships with God and with one another in all matters pertaining to life but also by the way they handle that great issue called "death." (See Rev. 21:3-4.)—Homer J. R. Elford.

## SUNDAY: MARCH SIXTH

### MORNING SERVICE

**Topic: Good News for the Unsuccessful (Lent)**
SCRIPTURE: Luke 5:1-11.

I. Most of us are indoctrinated to think that the sacred cannot be found in the ordinary. We see religious experience as something spooky. But that isn't what the gospels teach us. Jesus meets us right where we are. This is incarnation for us, not to turn away from our humanness, our problems, or our lack of success, in order to seek him somewhere else, but to meet him here and now, moving out of the shallows and into the depths, taking the risk of living rather than avoiding the possibility of failure.

II. Jesus does not wait until we are perfect, until we have scrubbed ourselves clean of human concerns. He does not meet us at the end of the rainbow nor is he the reward for good conduct. The truth of the gospel is that he is with us, and we live in him even as we try to take life seriously in the immediate matters that confront us. He even meets us frequently where we have been unsuccessful, at the point of our failures.

(a) Do we realize what good news this is? Do we understand what this means? We do not have to leave part of us behind. Indeed we dare not because it may be in that unsuccessful part that he is drawing near.

(b) Does this say something to us? All of us have a tendency to make things look smooth and successful, to mask our trembling, frightened feelings of change and unsuccess. We fail to realize the damage we do to the gospel and to Christ's incarnation when an unreal, unspoken demand for perfectionism is laid over the good news. In the local church it does two things. It isolates each Christian, making him live his quiet desperation without the aid of others. But worse, the veneer of perfectionism is so thin that outsiders can see through it, often concluding that in actual practice even Christians themselves do not trust the goodness of Christ.

III. The gospel lesson shows that Jesus' meeting with the fishermen at the point of failure and the huge catch of fish which followed did not produce immediate celebration. In fact it had the opposite effect upon Simon who dramatically cried out, "Depart from me, O Lord, for I am a sinful man."

(a) I wish we knew how Peter said those words. It could make a difference in their meaning. We usually assume he said them as a further confession, saying in effect, "I am not only an unsuccessful fisherman; I am an unsuccessful person." Because Christ met him in his immediate vocational failure, he is drawn inevitably into the depths of his need.

(b) Or did Peter say these words wistfully, defensively, already sensing that this Jesus wanted more from him? Is he perceptive enough to see that this relatively superficial encounter is not the end of the pilgrimage? Is he trying to beg off from a deeper call, like Moses and Jeremiah and a host of others before him? "Lord, you don't want me! You've never seen a bigger loser. I can't really perform! Depart from me!"

(1) But Jesus doesn't depart. He does not even say: "Yes, you are a sinner as well as an unsuccessful person. But you've confessed now. That ought to do you a lot of good. Come back after you've reformed, and we'll talk about this again."

(2) Jesus does something infinitely more marvelous. He says, "Don't be afraid." He seems to be saying: "Don't run yourself down. I've got great hope for you. You, who weren't successful catching fish, I'm going to have you out catching men! Yes, you will fail again and again. But someday with Paul you will say, 'When I am weak, then I am strong.' For I can work even through your unsuccessful moments lived and faced honestly."—Vernon L. Dethmers in *The Church Herald*.

## Illustrations

CORRESPONDENCE. The Spartans were noted for their courage. In the days when Philip of Macedon was taking over the Greeks, conquering them city by city and binding all 365 of them into the Hellenic League, there took place between Philip and the Spartans correspondence composed of two letters. Philip's letter announced that if he ever set foot on their territory he would not leave one stone upon another in all Sparta. The Spartan reply has the diplomatic distinction of being the shortest on record. It contained the single word "If."—John M. Jensen.

LETTER FROM GOD. The biblical revelation of God is in essence the fact that God knows your name. And that at the very moment of your birth, and even before, when you were only a thought in your father's mind or a seed in your mother's womb, God knew your name and wrote you a letter. In part he says: 'John (Jane), there is nobody else like you. Nobody with your genes. Nobody with your past or potential experience. Nobody who will have your parents, your friends, or your influences. You are the one and only you that I made, and I want to tell you who you are." Your letter from God is like the one he wrote to Jeremiah, "Before I formed you in the womb I knew you" (Jer. 1:5). But it is tragic that so many people never read the letter that God wrote to them before they were born.—Bruce Larson in *The One and Only You.*

## Sermon Suggestions

CHRISTIAN GREATNESS. (1) He acquires it who does not seek it. (2) He alone has it who never aspired to it. (3) He has earned it who knows that he has neither the ability to earn it nor the price to pay for it. (4) He who has it can never recognize it in himself; he sees it only in others. (5) He who has it will inevitably be recognized by others as possessing it. (6) Only he has it who knows his own smallness and lowliness. (7) Its essence is found in the spirit of humility.

YOU CAN HOPE AGAIN. Scripture: Col. 1:9–14. (1) We can hope again because of redemption. (See vv. 13–14.) (2) We can hope again because of a relationship. (See v. 12.) (3) We can hope again because of resources. (See v. 13.)—C. Neil Strait.

## Worship Aids

CALL TO WORSHIP. "I will praise thee with my whole heart. I will worship toward thy holy temple, and praise thy name for thy lovingkindness." Ps. 138: 1–2.

INVOCATION. Almighty and everlasting God, who givest to all who desire it the spirit of grace and supplication, deliver us, O Lord, from all coldness of heart, from all indifferent wandering of the mind, that we may fix our affection upon thee and upon thy service. Fill us with holy, peaceful, and beautiful thoughts, that with steadfast minds and kindled affection we may worship thee in spirit and in truth.

OFFERTORY SENTENCE. "Of every man that giveth willingly with his heart ye shall take my offering (saith the Lord)." Exod. 25:2.

OFFERTORY PRAYER. Awaken us to the claims of thy holy will, O God, and stir us with a passion for thy kingdom, that we may respond at this time with our gifts and also with our lives.

PRAYER. It is not thy gift we crave but thee. It is when we lose sight of thee that we have fretful days and sleepless nights; when we forget that thou art our strength and our song that we become anxious for the morrow.

We thank thee for the privilege of living in these momentous days when an old age is dying and a new one is struggling to be born; when the things that can be shaken are being shaken that the things that cannot be shaken may remain; that, in a day when many things in which men put their trust have failed, thy mercies have not failed. We thank thee for the constancy of the earth and the fertility of the soil, the unbroken promise that while the earth remaineth seedtime and harvest shall not cease; for the tasks through which we can minister to others and forget ourselves; for health when we have it and for what we may learn from illness; for happiness when it is ours and for insights born of sorrow; for the victories we are able to win over temptation and for the fact that temptation comes, for only as we strive against evil do we grow strong; above all, for him in whose face we see the light of the knowledge of thy glory. We thank thee that his radiant life has touched our own.

Strengthen our faith that we may know that we are not alone in a troubled world; that we may look for the coming of a better world; that, taking firm hold on thee, we may strive to overcome the evil in the world and in ourselves, to do with our might what our hands find to do, to follow more closely in the footsteps of our Lord, upheld by the promise that our labor is not in vain.

It is not thy gifts we crave but thee. Yet do we ask the gifts of thy grace which are requisite for us all: forgiveness and cleansing for our sins, light for our darkness, courage for life's battle, and endurance for life's pain. "Steer thou the vessel of our life toward thee, thou tranquil haven of all storm-tossed souls."—Frank Halliday Ferris.

## EVENING SERVICE

**Topic: A Sense of Soul**
TEXT: Matt. 10:28.

I. "Soul" is a way of speaking about one's inner life. We think of soul as something which exists within us. It is easy to forget that we have an internal territory that is just as extensive as the external territory through which we move daily. It is sometimes said that there are very few frontiers remaining to be explored. When we think of frontiers as being unmapped geographical areas that is very true, but there is a very real sense in which every individual is always faced with the task of exploring his internal frontier—that man-

ner in which he thinks and feels and chooses to relate.

II. "Soul" is a way of speaking about the source of our resiliency. Any form of revitalization or renewal which we experience ultimately has its roots within us. We may be moved, as many are, by the sound of great symphonic music, and we are moved as the music stirs something deep within us. The same dynamic is true of all the trappings and symbols of our religious faith; they stand for the great truths that emerge from within the human spirit. And so when we speak of someone who has a real sense of soul, we are speaking about someone who has cultivated an inner source of sustenance and vitality.

III. "Soul" can be seen as that part of us which participates in the life-giving spirit of God. There is holy ground within human personality, and our task is to discover and cultivate that holy ground within ourselves and other people.

(a) It is easy for us to become frustrated in that pursuit because so much of our living is predicated on the principle of instant gratification. For most of us in middle America what we want is usually within our grasp. But that isn't true with the religious moment. God will not come to us on a demand schedule. (See Isa. 40:31.)

(b) Perhaps "waiting on the Lord" is no more than clearing our internal decks of the confusion and clutter from the day so that we might be able to hear that still small voice. But whatever it might mean, I know that in time we will have the firm feeling that God has heard us and that he has given us his peace.—Robert A. Noblett.

## SUNDAY: MARCH THIRTEENTH

### MORNING SERVICE

**Topic: The Church is Precious (Lent)**
SCRIPTURE: Eph. 3:7–20.

I. The church is precious because it recalls, interprets, celebrates, and communicates "the greatest story ever told." At the heart of our faith is a great story.

This is the resounding theme of the biblical drama. No other religion has it, nor does any other religion have a story to match it. And it is not set in a never-never land of fantasy. It is a part of our human adventure.

(a) "We've a story to tell to the nations." It is the story of God's creation of the world; his fashioning of us in his image to share his planetary enterprise; his continuation and completion of his purpose. The center of it all is the birth of one who is called Jesus or Liberator, Emmanuel or God-with-us. He is the assurance that God is with us and for us and that nothing can ever separate us from his love in Jesus Christ. He is also assurance of the marvelous grace of God which makes it possible for us to be cleansed of our fouled-up lives and made clean for a new start. No wonder the angels sang at the event. One of our theologians has said that the church is in the broadcasting business; it trumpets to the world that God has let loose a great liberating movement in history and through Jesus Christ and that he invites all to join his movement and find life in its power and purpose.

(b) Many talk about the renewal of the church these days; they propose all sorts of programs. But renewal does not come through programs. It comes only as Christians and churches sense afresh the newness, glory, and grandeur of the gospel or good news of what God has done and is doing and will do through Jesus Christ, his unspeakable gift to us humans. This alone will give the heart cause to rejoice. This alone will give motivation to a church or a Christian in days like these. The celebration of the gospel is the first priority of the church.

II. The church is precious because it invites all who will to find fullness of personal life in commitment and obedience to Jesus Christ as Lord and Savior. Paul puts it beautifully when he writes that anyone who is committed to Christ becomes a new being; the old is finished and gone. "All this is done by God who through Christ changed us from enemies into friends" (GNFMN).

(a) Jesus came to give us life filled to the top, pressed down, and running over. He came to save us from all this false living that never really satisfies and that is like a house built on unsolid sand.

(b) A great need of our time is an improvement in the quality of life. On every hand we find a disintegration and even a vulgarization of life. The church

is in the business of inviting persons to participate in the life that is in Christ and to grow up and mature in it so that it may take on all the grand dimensions of humanity that God intends.

(c) Life may be remade, renewed, and redeemed. This is the message of the church. And this message ought to be proclaimed not only with pious words but also in and through the lives of those who share in the joy and peace and power and purpose of Christ.

III. The church is precious because it is the new humanity which God has inaugurated through Jesus who is the man for others. He is more than a personal Savior and Lord; he is the center of a community. He is a corporate person. Where two or three are gathered together in his name, there he is in the midst of them to form them into a new relationship. He is the source of our new humanity. And he has attracted persons of all nations, cultures, classes, and colors together into the pilot community God desires the world to become.

(a) Jesus commanded his disciples on the last night of his life to love one another as he loved them. And they were to love as he loved the Father. It is an outgoing concern that is meant. And when we share ourselves in this way we receive from those with whom we share in rich measure. Only those who love can really know and appreciate love. Love is not sentimental mushiness; it is strong goodwill.

(b) Ephesians has been called the letter about the church. The author writes that those who once were outsiders now are insiders and those who were strangers are now members of the commonwealth of God. Christians have a sense of belonging to the community that counts and is at the heart of God's saving purpose. Belonging to church is more than joining an organization; it is incorporation into a community that is at the center of history. "Once you were, now you are!" Every Christian ought to think highly of membership in the one, holy, catholic, apostolic church of the loving God.

(c) This involves belonging to the

church of all ages, to the communion of saints of all times. It means belonging not only to our denomination but also to all churches which are centered in Jesus Christ as Lord and Savior. It means participating in the worldwide purpose of God's mission to bring all things together under the lordship of Jesus Christ.—E. G. Homrighausen.

## Illustrations

WEAKNESS AND STRENGTH.    G. K. Chesterton said that the church would last forever because it was founded on a weak man, meaning Peter, and for that reason it is indestructible. I believe it will last forever but not for that reason but because the weak man has now acknowledged Christ and Christ has made him strong. Chesterton had a partial truth. Christ chooses to build his church on weak men who confess him and who thus discover in him power beyond that of men.—W. Kenneth Goodson.

CHOICE.    You can't go tramping around from one church to another and fulfill your obligation. You've got to settle on one parish and throw your life into it and build it up. Who would want to go to a picnic all the time and eat out of other people's baskets?—Carl Sandburg.

## Sermon Suggestions

THEOLOGY AND MATURE BELIEF.    (1) What do you believe about the nature and destiny of man? (2) What do you believe about the mission and message of Jesus Christ? (3) What do you believe about the power of prayer in your life? (4) What do you believe about the meaning of human destiny? (5) What do you believe to be the purpose of your life here on earth? (6) What do the words incarnation, atonement, redemption, salvation, revelation, and immortality mean to you?—Charles L. Copenhaver.

WHY WAS THE BIBLE WRITTEN?    (1) To bring men to repentance of sins. (See Jer. 26:2.) (2) To bear witness of the Christ. (See Luke 24:44.) (3) To lead men to Christ. (See John 20:31.) (4) To provide a base for fellowship in God's truth. (See I John 1:3.)—Ard Hoven.

## Worship Aids

CALL TO WORSHIP.    "Having therefore, brethren, boldness to enter into the holiest by the blood of Jesus, by a new and living way, which he hath consecrated for us, let us draw near with a true heart in full assurance of faith." Heb. 10:19–20, 22.

INVOCATION.    O God, in glory exalted and in mercy ever blessed, we magnify thee, we praise thee, we give thanks unto thee for thy bountiful providence, for all the blessings of this present life, and all the hopes of a better life to come. Let the memory of thy goodness, we beseech thee, fill our hearts with joy and thankfulness.

OFFERTORY SENTENCE.    "God is not unrighteous to forget your work and labor of love, which ye have showed toward his name, in that ye have ministered to the saints, and to minister." Heb. 6:10.

OFFERTORY PRAYER.    O Lord, upon whose constant giving we depend every day, teach us how to spend and be spent for others that we may gain the true good things of life by losing every selfish trait.

PRAYER.    Wilt thou look upon thy people, our heavenly Father, with eyes of loving compassion. Wilt thou accept our humble prayers of love as we turn to thee in gratitude and devotion. Wilt thou meet us at the point of our deepest need and our highest aspiration as we open our hearts to thee in faith. May thy grace be our present possession and may we know in our heart of hearts that we truly belong to thee and that all is well for time and eternity.

We thank thee for thy wonderful graciousness toward us in days past, for the way thy providence has been over and above and around us, and beneath us the everlasting arms in every experience of this our life. We thank thee that we can turn to thee now as simply as a man turns to his friend to share with thee the thoughts of our hearts, the needs of our spirit, and the happiness that we enjoy in thy strengthening presence. We are grateful for the thought of a future that is filled with hope and promise and strength because we shall be with thee forever and thou wilt never forsake us. For the wonder of a life that is filled with vitality and strength, with confidence and enthusiasm, with meaning and power because of thy touch upon it and thy presence in it, we give thee our thanksgiving.

Wilt thou bless our fellowship together. Grant that we may look upon one another with eyes of understanding and love and appreciation because of our bond in Christ. And wilt thou truly bless the tie that binds our hearts in Christian love. We thank thee for the privilege of far horizons, of extending this wonderful fellowship in Christ to other lands and, indeed, to all about this earth. For the common prayer of joyous thanksgiving, faith, and praise that binds this whole world by gold chains about thy feet, for this glorious experience of a world fellowship in Christ, we give thee our grateful thanks.

Bless us now as we worship thee from the depths of our hearts. Send us on our way rejoicing through the days of this week as we walk with strong, confident, and sturdy steps because we are with thee. These mercies we ask in our Savior's name, even Christ our Redeemer.—Lowell M. Atkinson.

## EVENING SERVICE

Topic: **Foundations for Two Houses** (Lent)

Scripture: Matt. 7:24–27.

I. All are building a home, a career, a reputation, a character—"the one thing which he can take with him, which he must take with him into the other world. And the choice which he has is not between building and not building but between building well and building foolishly" (Alfred Plummer).

II. All have a choice of foundations. There are innumerable philosophies of life which one may choose, never more than today. But Jesus narrows the choice drastically. A person who hears his words must choose whether to build his or her life on these words or upon some other base.

III. All foundations will be tried by the storms of life. On every life sooner or later the rains descend, the winds beat, and the floods rise, but for one the house of life falls in ruin, while for another it stands strong and secure, and the difference lies not in the intensity of the storm but in the power to withstand. Jesus' words apply to the ordinary storms of life, all of those things which try people's characters and reveal the quality of their lives, but undoubtedly Jesus was thinking of the final scene when each person shall meet the supreme test.

IV. Jesus' teaching affords the only secure foundation for time and eternity. Jesus' words afford security, but they afford security only as one hears and obeys. The phrase "these words of mine" refers particularly to the sermon on the mount. Whoever hears "these words" and does not obey them will be like a foolish man who built his house upon the sand. So the sermon on the mount ends with a warning to individuals but also, we may believe, to nations.—Ernest Trice Thompson.

## SUNDAY: MARCH TWENTIETH

### MORNING SERVICE

Topic: **Forgiveness in a Look** (Lent)
Scripture: Luke 22:54–62.

The searing memory of a rooster's

call could have rendered the big fisherman a spiritual cripple for life, except for one thing. Jesus forgave him. And the healing balm of that forgiveness made possible a different pattern for his life than for Judas Iscariot who ended it all on a homemade gallows. In the days which followed that "forgiving look," Peter discovered certain truths which influenced the shape of his apostolic ministry.

I. Peter learned that God's forgiveness brings with it a *new fellowship.* (a) In the New Testament the word for forgiveness usually paints a picture of "sending away" our sins, but allied with that is the idea of the restoration of the original relationship with God which had been destroyed by the sin.

(b) Look at it in terms of relationships in your own family. Suppose someone you love has hurt you deeply. Your relationship has been injured by the hurt you are carrying. Finally you "kiss and make up." You are able to say "I forgive you" and really mean it. The result is that the sin is "carried away." It is erased from the blackboard of memory. Fellowship with your loved one has been restored.

(c) In a way that's what happened to Peter. With a glance Jesus managed to communicate to Peter that he forgave him. Once more Peter was able to look Jesus in the eye and even to see his own reflection without cringing before the crippling self-image of a coward. His relationship with Christ had been restored.

II. Peter learned that forgiveness brings with it a *new freedom.* (a) Acts 5 records a magnificent story of Peter's confrontation with the religious leaders of his day. Forbidden to preach any longer in the name of Jesus whom "the establishment" had crucified, Peter continued to proclaim the "good news" without fear of compromise. The authorities raged: "Did we not firmly command you that you should not teach in this name? But behold you have filled Jerusalem with your doctrine." Peter and his fellow disciples replied simply, "We must obey God rather than men." (See vv. 28–29.)

(b) The Lord's forgiveness brought a freedom for responsive action which represented a complete reversal of Peter's earlier reaction to danger. There was no cringing in terror now. Aware of the danger but free from signs of fear, Peter challenged the whole decaying religious order in the name of Christ.

III Peter discovered a *new fact.* (a) If we are to be forgiven we must forgive others. Jesus clearly states that unless we ourselves forgive others we have no hope of being forgiven in God. In the Lord's Prayer he teaches his disciples to pray, "Forgive us our debts, as we forgive our debtors."

(b) This saying of Jesus is vividly reinforced in his discussion with Peter about forgiveness. Peter asked him: "Lord, how often shall my brother sin against me, and I forgive him? As many as seven times?" Peter likely felt somewhat generous after making that suggestion. But Jesus forced him into some spiritual higher mathematics. "I do not say to you seven times, but seventy times seven" (Matt. 18:21–22). How many are seventy times seven? Peter soon learned that he had a lot of forgiving to do.—Clarence L. Reaser.

## Illustrations

VULNERABLE. To love at all is to be vulnerable. Love anything, and your heart will certainly be wrung and possibly broken. If you want to make sure of keeping it intact, you must give your heart to no one, not even to an animal. Wrap it carefully with hobbies and little luxuries; avoid all entanglements; lock it up safe in the casket or coffin of your selfishness. But in that casket—safe, dark, motionless, airless—it will change. It will not be broken; it will become unbreakable, impenetrable, irredeemable. The alternative to tragedy, or at least to the risk of tragedy, is damnation. The only place outside heaven where you can be perfectly safe from all the dangers of love is hell.—C. S. Lewis in *The Four Loves.*

REJECTED PARDON. During the days of President Andrew Jackson, a man named George Wilson was sentenced to death for shooting a man who saw him robbing the mails. Before his execution, however, President Jackson sent him a pardon. Then a strange thing happened.

Wilson refused to accept the pardon. Now what was going to be done? Should he be turned loose when he refused to accept the pardon or be executed? The matter went to the courts and finally to the Supreme Court. Chief Justice John Marshall wrote a famous opinion which still stands: "A pardon is a slip of paper, the value of which is determined by the acceptance of the person to be pardoned. If it is refused, it is no pardon. George Wilson must be hanged." In due time he was—all because he refused to accept a pardon from the president of his country. Our God offers us a pardon. Unless we accept it by faith we are not pardoned, and we shall die in and because of our sins.—John E. Brokhoff.

## Sermon Suggestions

NEVER RESENTFUL, ALWAYS FORGIVING. Text: Rom. 12:14–21 (NEB). (1) Jesus replaced the common rule of reciprocity with the spirit of love that is never resentful but always eager to forgive. (2) Forgiveness is not so much an act as an attitude or spirit that determines all of one's actions and relationships. (3) God's forgiveness of us is an expression of his nature and character, will and purpose, love and mercy. If we do not have a forgiving spirit it is impossible for God to forgive us because we are unwilling to accept the transformation that his forgiveness always brings. (4) Forgiveness does not mean ignoring what has been done but rather that goodwill destroys the barrier wrong has erected. (5) Forgiveness has the power of transforming enemies into friends, a spirit every follower of Christ is called upon to demonstrate.—Nenien C. McPherson, Jr.

BEYOND BITTERNESS. Text: Gen. 50:20. (1) Joseph's faith in a God who is real. (2) Joseph's faith in a God who is present. (3) Joseph's faith in a God who cares. (4) Joseph's faith in a God who is able.—James McGraw.

## Worship Aids

CALL TO WORSHIP. "Worthy is the Lamb that was slain to receive power, and riches, and wisdom, and strength, and honor, and glory, and blessing." Rev. 5:12.

INVOCATION. Almighty and everlasting God, in whom we live and move and have our being, who hast created us for thyself so that we can find rest only in thee: grant unto us purity of heart and strength of purpose so that no selfish passion may hinder us from knowing thy will and no weakness sway us from doing it and that in thy light we may see light clearly and in thy service find perfect freedom.

OFFERTORY SENTENCE. "Walk in love, as Christ also hath loved us, and hath given himself for us as an offering and sacrifice to God." Eph. 5:2.

OFFERTORY PRAYER. O heavenly Father, we pray that thy blessings, which are as countless as the stars, may be so used as to bring light and love to thy children everywhere.

PRAYER. Infinite Father, in the stillness of this moment let the hush of your presence fall upon us that we in adoration may become aware that we cannot renew ourselves but can only be renewed by you; that we cannot forgive ourselves but can only accept your forgiveness; that we cannot love one another as we ought but must allow you to love others through us.

Our thanks rise like mists in the morning sun as we reflect on the gifts we have received. Truly the earth is the Lord's and the fullness thereof. From the mystery of your creativeness we have been given life with emotion and intellect, the capacity to experience, to love, and to learn. As the past stretches behind us to the void before creation, so the future looms ahead with endless possibilities as it is lived in the context of your will. For this fact we are eternally thankful.

O Lord, hear our prayer for growth. Lead us beyond the hypnotic awareness that we only find life when we lose life to Christ. Strengthen us as modern-day disciples of Jesus Christ that we not only will be loyal churchmen and women but also will live for Christ in the workaday world. We have come to this service with a variety of needs and problems, conflicts and desires. Direct us into the pathway of Christian fulfillment where we receive answers that bring an unfolding of life's myriad possibilities.

So challenge each of us in this time of worship that we place Christ at the center of our lives, heeding his call to take up our cross and follow him.—Carroll Emerson Word, Jr.

## EVENING SERVICE

**Topic: Life's Crowning Experience**
Text: Gen. 28:16.

I. *God meets us in the most unexpected places.* (a) You can hardly imagine a more unlikely place for God to meet Jacob than that barren hilltop as he slept, lonely and sick at heart, beneath the stars. Yet that is where God met him, and it is in similar places and in comparable situations that God has spoken to men and women across the years.

(b) When the sun shines and we have our health and strength, our natural vigor, we are often too full of ourselves for God to break in. But when the sun goes down and the winds of fortune change and our strength declines, we awake to the recognition of our need and to the awareness of our weakness, and then our extremity becomes God's opportunity.

(c) Our extremity is God's opportunity! Far from dreading the barren rock and the wilderness place we should accept them in faith for, in the providence of God, they may lead us, as they led Jacob, into life's crowning experience.

II. *God deals with us in the most unexpected way.* (a) Was that not true for Jacob? He fled from before the fury of his brother Esau, knowing that that anger was fully justified. He fled knowing that he had deceived his poor old father. And he fled knowing that he had

done evil in the sight of God. No wonder Jacob was afraid when he found that God was in that place. He deserved God's judgment and wrath, but God dealt with him in a most unexpected way—not in wrath but in mercy and not in judgment but in grace.

(b) There is hope for us all for Jesus Christ is able to save from the uttermost to the uttermost all that come unto God by him.

III. *God blesses us at the most unexpected times.* (a) After some twenty years in Syria Jacob returned to the land of Canaan and settled at a place called Shechem. He did not intend what happened there, but it happened nonetheless. Dinah, Jacob's daughter, went out, as young people will, looking for companionship. She found it but not in the way she should have. She was assaulted. Whose fault was it? The boy's? Dinah's? Jacob's? Jacob's conscience knew full well. What had he done to teach his daughter about the God of her fathers? What had he done to fortify her against temptation? Who but himself had brought her to where the temptation was? Despite God's goodness to him he had drifted away from the practice of religion and had failed to be an example to his children. He had neglected to instruct them in the way they should go. Filled with regret and remorse, Jacob said to his household: "Put away the foreign gods that are among you, and purify yourselves, and change your garments; then let us arise and go up to Bethel, that I may make there an altar to the God who answered me in the day of my distress and has been with me wherever I have gone" (Gen. 35:2–3).

(b) To Jacob's surprise God blessed him. "And God said to him: 'I am God Almighty: be fruitful and multiply; a nation and a company of nations shall come from you, and kings shall spring from you. The land which I gave to Abraham and Isaac I will give to you, and I will give the land to your descendants after you'" (Gen. 35:11–12).

(c) Is there no Bethel in your life and mine? Did you never make a vow of allegiance and loyalty and faithfulness to God when your soul was softened with sorrow or stirred with the goodness of God or challenged by some word from the Almighty? What happened to the vow? Did you keep it? Then know this.

Somewhere there is a stone which once you set up as Jacob did at Bethel, and when you go back to it and keep your vow, God will bless you again.—S. Robert Weaver.

## SUNDAY: MARCH TWENTY-SEVENTH

### MORNING SERVICE

**Topic: Troubled by the Cross (Passion Sunday)**

TEXT: I Cor. 1:23.

I. Messiah and Christ both mean the "anointed king." The titles have to do with the ancient Jewish expectation that a messiah or Christ would someday restore the dynasty of King David, drive out the foreign rulers from Palestine, and finally establish a reign of peace and justice throughout the earth.

(a) When Peter said to Jesus, "You are the Christ," it was this kind of political savior which he had in mind. But Jesus told Peter that his expectations were wrong. Jesus said that the Son of Man would be rejected by the leaders of Israel, be killed, and after three days rise again.

(b) Peter didn't want to hear any of that nonsense. He was sure that Jesus was the long-awaited King of Israel. He didn't want to hear anything about suffering or death. But Jesus replied to Peter: "Get thee behind me, Satan, for you are not on the side of God, but of men."

(c) Jesus was saying to Peter in a very strong and forceful way that man's religious hopes and God's plan of salvation were not the same thing. What men would hope for God would undo. Peter wanted salvation without a struggle. He wanted a messiah that made everything "all right." What Peter wanted was a Christ without a cross.

II. Jesus was simply not that kind of easy savior. (a) Since the earliest days of Christianity, Christians have always had to deal with this paradox of a crucified messiah. A savior who suffers is, after all, very difficult to explain or comprehend. Many have found the crucifixion to be puzzling; others have found it an obstacle to the faith.

(b) The cross is a constant reminder to Christians that Jesus the Messiah had to suffer and die. Most Christians don't like to think about the suffering and death of Christ very often.

(c) It's easier to talk about those aspects of Christianity that are joyous, triumphant, hopeful, challenging, and optimistic. Yet how important it is that Jesus refused to be the kind of messiah that people expected him to be. He refused to solve all their political problems; he refused to fulfill all their religious expectations; he refused to be a second King David. Instead he humbled himself, taking the form of a servant, even unto death.

(d) Peter couldn't believe his ears when Jesus told him that the Son of Man would be rejected and killed. "Oh, no, Lord," Peter must have said, "that doesn't make any sense. You're the Christ, the Messiah, God's anointed King!" But Jesus replied to Peter: "Get thee behind me, Satan, for you are not on the side of God, but of men."

III. Peter's Christianity was too small. (a) And it would still be too small today. It would, for example, be a small Christianity that could preach Christ without the cross. It would be a small Christianity that could hold up before us the hope of eternal life but say nothing about suffering, evil, sin, and death. It would be a small Christianity that could promise joy and peace and triumph but say nothing about the sufferings of Christ in the world.

(b) I'm speaking of the kind of religion which only says "yes" to our human aspirations, "yes" to our ambitions, "yes" to our politics, to our nationalism, or to our private morality. It's very easy for that kind of religion to flourish. The kind that only rubber-stamps our basically self-centered ideologies. Of course, this kind of religion would have little in common with the biblical faith, being completely devoid of prophetic judgment or the cross of Christ.

(c) Karl Barth wrote that the cross of Christ is God's way of saying "no" to the hope for a political messiah who could solve all our problems, "no" to the mistaken belief that the will of God and man's highest religious hopes are the same thing. Barth maintained that every aspect of human culture, including institutional Christianity, is always subject to the sin of human selfishness.

(d) God's Christianity will always stand in judgment of man's Christianity. That is what happened when Jesus rebuked Peter. Jesus was saying "no" to a faith which was too small.

IV. It's very easy for us all to become seduced by a faith which is too small.

(a) These days, as in the days of Peter, the true faith of Christ has to compete with man-made substitutes, many of which look like the real thing. This second-rate Christianity which people fabricate can appear very attractive. It can guarantee us peace of mind. Or it can convince us that our politics and morality are identical to God's will. Or it can promise to fill our souls with ecstasy and bliss. But somehow all these painless and easy substitutes for the faith fall far short of the religion of Christ.

(b) At its heart the religion of Christ must always contain the cross. This means that at the center of faith is the conviction that suffering, evil, and death are real and powerful forces, that they should not be underestimated, and that Christ himself had to contend with those forces, even submit to them, before he could help us to overcome them.

(c) The cross is a reminder that being a Christian in this world is not always easy and that in some ways I have to be willing to take up my own cross if I would follow Jesus.—Andrew Fiddler.

## Illustration

RECONCILIATION.    A Japanese minister was serving at Christ Church in Cambridge, Massachusetts, in 1943. That was a war year, and many military personnel attended Christ Church. Dr. Kitagawa, the minister, said that on one particular Sunday a young Marine stopped to speak with him as the worship service concluded. The sermon of the morning had dealt with the God-given unity of mankind seen in the light of Jesus' teaching. This Marine said to Dr. Kitagawa: "Father, I too believe what you said in your sermon is absolutely true. I'm glad that I was in the church this morning to hear you preach that particular message." He paused momentarily and then continued: "I was training as a violinist, but that's all finished, for in the South Pacific my right wrist was permanently injured by shrapnel. When I was discharged, I vowed to kill the first Japanese I met. You know, Father, you're that Japanese!" Having said that, he extended his injured hand to Dr. Kitagawa and left the church.—John H. Townsend.

## Sermon Suggestions

WORDS BEFORE THE CROSS.    (1) Word of the covetous. (See John 19:24.) (2) Word of the thoughtless. (See Matt. 27:40.) (3) Word of religious prejudice. (See Matt. 27:42–43.) (4) Word of spiritual blindness. (See Luke 23:37.) (5) Word of heartless cruelty. (See Mark 15:36.) (6) Words of recklessness and penitence. (See Luke 23:39–42.)—E. Paul Hovey.

THE ANATOMY OF COURAGE.    Text: Luke 9:15. (1) The courage of competition. (2) The courage of conflict. (3) The courage of conscience. (4) The courage of the cross.—J. Wallace Hamilton.

## Worship Aids

CALL TO WORSHIP.    "The cup of blessing which we bless, is it not the communion of the blood of Christ? The bread which we break, is it not the communion of the body of Christ? For we being many are one bread, and one body: for we are all partakers of that one bread." I Cor. 10:16–17.

INVOCATION. Our heavenly Father, we thy humble children invoke thy blessing upon us in this hour of worship. We adore thee, whose nature is compassion, whose presence is joy, whose Word is truth, whose spirit is goodness, whose holiness is beauty, whose will is peace, whose service is perfect freedom, and in knowledge of whom standeth our eternal life. Unto thee be all honor and all glory.

OFFERTORY SENTENCE. "For ye know the grace of our Lord Jesus Christ, that though he was rich, yet for your sakes he became poor, that ye through his poverty might be rich." II Cor. 8:9.

OFFERTORY PRAYER. O Father of our Lord Jesus Christ, we dedicate these offerings to the fellowship of him, whom to know aright is life eternal.

PRAYER. Heavenly Father, as we renew the observance of the passion and death of your Son, help us to know ourselves to be forgiven by you and to discover our own willingness to forgive others who have somehow wronged us. The relationships between human beings are so often fraught with misunderstanding, suspicion, competition, and greed that we find it difficult to forgive or to believe that others truly forgive us. This human experience dilutes our ability to receive your forgiveness or even to know our need for that forgiveness. We tend to be self-confident, assured, and unfeeling toward others. Help us to begin to open ourselves with feeling so that both the joys and the hurts that others experience may be a part of our own experience.

We know that to open ourselves to others means taking the risk of being hurt; it means exposing our own tenderness for all the world to touch. We are reluctant to take such a risk. Teach us to act in imitation of Jesus who exposed himself to Judas, taking the risk of betrayal; to Peter, taking the risk of denial; to Thomas and the other disciples, taking the risk of doubt, uncertainty, and misunderstanding. Yet by taking that risk and trusting in you, he was able to convey to all generations the great love you have for all your children.

Forgiveness teaches us also the strength of the bond of brotherhood for which you have created us. So enable us to honor that brotherhood that the pains of the disenfranchised, the unemployed, the victims of discrimination and hatred and war, and the sick and the lonely may become our pains, and may become the motivating force to guide us into meaningful action on behalf of all your children who suffer anywhere in the world. May our focus now on the suffering of Christ lead us to the triumph of the resurrection; and our concern for the pain of others lead us to the triumph of hope and opportunity and of good for all.

Renew us, we pray, by your forgiving, loving Spirit, revealed in Christ, in whose name we pray.—Madison L. Sheely.

## EVENING SERVICE

**Topic: Can I Possibly Pray for My Enemies?**

SCRIPTURE: Matt. 5:43–48.

I. *Facing my part in the problem.* (a) When we include prayer for our enemies in our prayer life certain things begin to happen. We begin to face our responsibility for any misunderstandings that have arisen. Granted that the problem may be the other person's fault, we always have to check our own feelings and conduct to see how we could have handled it better. Reforming other people is not our job but facing our own anger is.

(b) If we really believe in sin, we realize that in most situations where relationships are strained we are culprit as well as victim. Praying helps us keep our perspective so that we don't let our spirits marinate in self-pity or bitterness.

(c) Throughout this command to pray for those who persecute us, Jesus assumes that the hostility begins with the enemies. But we have to be sure it ends there and is not returned in kind. This is not easy when we are geared to retaliate. Praying may not cure our vindictiveness, but it will give us a good start on our way to recovery.

II. *Seeing my enemy as a person.* (a) Praying for our enemies will help us to see our enemies as persons. In our anxiety, resentment, and anger we are apt to see people who don't like us as threats to our security, objects to be feared or avoided. In our disappointment over their opposition we are sorely tempted to dehumanize them.

(b) We tend to look at them through narrowed eyes and not to see them whole. We see only the aspects of their conduct that we resent. We reduce them to their worst symptoms and judge their whole character by a few of their actions.

(c) Praying for those who treat us wrongly reminds us that they are still persons. Nothing that they have done, are now doing, or will do allows us to view them as less than persons. God made them, and nothing in their attitudes or conduct can nullify that.

(d) The real danger in having enemies is not what they may do to us. The real threat is what we will do to ourselves as we allow harsh, bitter, and angry responses to develop. Our greatest temptation is to react to the actions of others so that we allow their attitudes toward us to shape our attitudes. In other words

we are ever in jeopardy of losing our freedom, of harboring feelings we don't approve of, and of becoming what we don't want to be. Christ's stern command to pray for our enemies is actually a word of grace to protect us from ourselves.

III. *Helping to heal, not hurt.* (a) Can I possibly pray for my enemies? Yes, I can because Christ has told me to. And he knows best. And when I pray for them I do so in the hope that I can heal wounds, not aggravate them.

(b) Life at best can be a kind of friendly sparring and at worst it becomes a knockdown, drag-out fight. Our natural tendency is to trade punch for punch. You insult me, and I insult you in return. You snub me, and I ignore you. You blame me, and I'll toss the blame right back at you. Toe to toe we stand and slug it out. Praying for those who trouble us helps to break this cycle of vindictiveness. As we absorb hostility we help to dissipate its strength. If we return it we are fuel to its fire, and it usually comes back all the hotter.

(c) "Blessed are the peacemakers" Christ told his followers (Matt. 5:9). Praying for our enemies can be our finest contribution to making peace with them.

IV. *Following my Father's example.* To pray for my enemies especially leads me to follow God's own example. (See Matt. 5:44–47.) God treats well even those whose will and ways are set against his. One way to show that we belong to him is to do the same. Grace is his way of life, and he calls us to live as he lives. (See Matt. 5:48.)—David A. Hubbard.

## SUNDAY: APRIL THIRD

### MORNING SERVICE

**Topic: Jesus Christ: King or Criminal? (Palm Sunday)**

SCRIPTURE: Luke 23:1–49.

What a week of incongruous events! Christ is welcomed as a king but put to

death as a criminal. Christ is crucified as a criminal between two criminals by soldiers whose job it was to crucify criminals, and yet the inscription on his cross labels him a king. Many observing the events of these days must have wondered, "What about this Jesus of Nazareth, was he a king or a criminal?"

I. The world received, then rejected its king. (a) On Palm Sunday Jesus entered as a king. Jesus entered the city riding on a donkey. The donkey has had a lot of bad press in our culture. He has been billed as one of the most lowly and humble of the beasts of burden, a liability to one's reputation. It was not so in the time of our Lord. This surefooted, loyal, and gentle beast was quite likely to be stabled in royal places. It was quite common for a king to be welcomed in a city of his rule riding a donkey. It was a mark of dignity and rank. While the horse showed intention of military and political conquest, the donkey was an emblem of peace and goodwill in which the king would be attentive to the needs of his subjects.

(b) On Good Friday Jesus was crucified as a criminal. They rejected his kingship which did not bring military conquest and power but challenged the religious leaders of the people. They accused him of crimes and tried him as a criminal. They put him to death as an enemy of the state and a hazard to society. They nailed him to a cross between two notorious bandits to be sure there was no mistake about their judgment.

II. The world needs a king. (a) It needs a king who is different from worldly kings. It does not need a king who is criminal in the treatment of his subjects, who is a tyrant lording his power over others, or who is a political manipulator whose reign is contingent upon the monetary power he wields.

(b) It needs a king who can keep things together when the world seems to be coming apart at the seams. People need something to hold on to when it appears they are losing their grip on life.

III. God gave the world a king. His name is Jesus Christ. (a) He is lord over all. His authority is of the Father, God our heavenly Father. His rule is here in this disintegrating world of ours. His mission is to redeem rebels and to reform those who have turned their backs on God. His power is over sin, that insidious disease that creeps into human hearts and destroys them. His promise is life to the dying, eternal life with him. He came in peace to give his subjects rest. He gave his life so that we might live.

(b) He is king even though nailed to a cross above that hill outside of the city gate. They raised God's Son to his final victory over sin and Satan himself. The kind of king God sent could be nailed down to a cross and still conquer. He could do that because he was God's Son who had come to be our king, to die for our sins, and to give us the victory of eternal life.

(c) How will we welcome him? Every heart has its throne to exalt him and its Golgotha to crucify him. We need him as king. We need him to rule in our hearts and in our world. We need to welcome him as king and lord.— Walter J. Warneck, Jr.

## Illustrations

WHERE WERE YOU? Martin Niemoeller told a group in Chicago that in the teaching of German schools today the twelve years of Nazi rule are a blank page. History books say nothing about the atrocities and the terror of those years, and teachers omit reference to Hitler and the strange aberrations of the period of his raucous rule. The reason, said Dr. Niemoeller, is quite simple. Teachers are afraid their students might ask, "Where were you?" That question is a haunting one. It may very well be asked of us in the years to come if we care more for survival than for ultimate values, more for security than for freedom, and more for comfort than for the ideals that undergird our heritage.— Harold Blake Walker.

GOD'S PLANS. We have neither reason nor right to allow ourselves to suppose that God's plans can suffer ultimate defeat. It is a species of doubt to which the incarnation, the greatest fact in history, gives flat and emphatic denial. Delay is nothing but a salutary discipline for us men of the moment. Reverses stimulate courage and give occasion to furbish ideals and simplify motives. Bondage, the defeat of a generation, and treachery within do not mean victory for the enemy where God's cause is concerned. God's plans are indestructible, and his purpose cannot be deflected, for he is almighty and is the master of all force.—Charles H. Brent.

## Sermon Suggestions

THE UNSHAKEN KINGDOM.    Text: Heb. 12:28 (NEB). (1) The kingdom is unshaken because it involves not a quantity of living but a quality of life. (2) The kingdom is unshaken because it is not static but possesses creative power. (3) The kingdom is unshaken because it belongs not to time but to eternity.— Donald Macleod.

FROM NIGHT TO DAY.    Scripture: Matt. 26:20–30. (1) The gloom of Gethsemane. (2) The dark night of the cross. (3) The silence of the tomb. (4) The glory of the resurrection.

## Worship Aids

CALL TO WORSHIP.    "The kingdoms of this world are become the kingdom of our Lord, and of his Christ; and he shall reign for ever and ever." Rev. 11:15.

INVOCATION.    Our Father, thou who wast received amid the shouts of an earlier day, open our hearts and journey into our inward parts. Help us to lay aside all prejudices, forsake all sins, and overcome all biddings that might bar thy entrance. Let thy entrance into our hearts be triumphant. Conquer our fears, silence our unbelief, quicken our faith. Lead us, through thy spirit, to spiritual victory and conquest.

OFFERTORY SENTENCE.    "Give unto the Lord, O ye kindreds of the people, give unto the Lord glory and strength. Give unto the Lord the glory due unto his name: bring an offering, and come into his courts." Ps. 96:7–8.

OFFERTORY PRAYER.    As thy faithful disciples blessed thy coming, O Christ, and spread their garments in the way, covering it with palm branches, may we be ready to lay at thy feet all that we have and are, and to bless thee, O thou who comest in the name of the Lord.

PRAYER.    Father of light, we bless thee for the brave men and women who have gone before us, by whose example we have been enheartened and from whose sacrificial living we have profited. We bless thee for the duties of life, its loyalties and obligations, its responsibilities and tasks, from which if thou wilt sustain us in faithful stewardship, satisfying meaning and purpose shall flow into our living. We bless thee for the love of our friends, the beauty of our homes, the entrustment of children, and for every window of affection and goodwill through which light falls upon our lives.

Especially we remember with the gratitude of those who have been redeemed the life of him who for our sakes died on Calvary. We confess our infidelity to him, we who like ancient Jerusalem have often welcomed him with protestations of loyalty and ere the week ended have crucified him. Amid the waywardness of a violent world that has denied his faith and forsaken his way we turn afresh to him. To whom else can we go; he has the words of eternal life. Grant us a fresh vision of his way of living, a resolute decision to let him be our Master, and a new willingness daily to take up our cross and follow him.

In the light of his life and teaching, his death and victory, quicken our consciences that we may feel the sin and shame of man's inhumanity to man. Inspire us with insight and courage that we may combat private greed, social injustice, intolerance and bigotry, the ills of poverty, the misuses of power, and whatever else works enmity between man and man, class and class, race and race, nation and nation. O Christ our Lord, who didst bring to thy first disciples, frightened and dismayed by thy crucifixion, such victorious assurance of thy living presence and power, we need thee now. Say to us once more, "In the world you have tribulation; but be of good cheer, I have overcome the world." —Harry Emerson Fosdick.

## EVENING SERVICE

**Topic: Your King Is Coming!**
TEXT: Matt. 21:5.

I. Your King is different from the run-of-the-mill king. (a) Whereas most come determined to rule, he comes to serve. Whereas most spend their time building their egos with the perquisites of office, he comes with a totally disarming humility. Whereas most kings ride white stallions or majestic Boeing 707s, Jesus rides a donkey. He knew what he was doing. He picked his vehicle of transportation. The horse stands for war. The people wanted a leader who would set them free from the yoke of Rome. He rode a donkey, a symbol of meekness and of peace. How different are palm branches from the click of crossed swords or the deafening blast of a twenty-one-gun salute.

(b) Most kings set themselves up for a hero's death. They picture the heads of all nations standing in silent tribute in the Notre Dame of their imagination as the world pays tribute to their contributions. Jesus prepares for the cross. An ignominious kind of death, marked by the insulting inscription, "King of the Jews." His fellow kings did not fly in from around the world to pay him honor. For your King is a different kind of king.

II. Your King knows precisely who he was and who he is. (a) Jesus knew he was the Messiah. He dressed for the occasion, preparing himself for the kind of entrance described by Isaiah and Zechariah. Those prophets declared that the Messiah would come. Different from the average king, this one would be humble, making his entry on a donkey.

(b) Jesus willingly forced the issue. He deliberately evoked the kind of response he got in Jerusalem that day. This was entirely opposite to his past performance. His whole style of life and ministry was one of shying away

from publicity. He avoided large crowds when he could. He refused to take the dominant power-oriented stance of his contemporary leaders. On this given day he put on the symbols of the Old Testament prophetic utterances. He declared in no uncertain terms by his posture and bearing, "I am the King." He even picked his day.

(c) There was only one problem. He picked his day not so much to gain the adulation of the crowd, which he knew was fickle, but to force the issue for his whole reason for being here on earth. His triumphant entry into Jerusalem was designed to seal his doom. It was the catalytic agent which would stir the anger, the jealousy, of the religious establishment to a frenzy, setting the stage for the greatest event in all human history.

(d) This King comes to you and me with a compassion for souls and bodies. Only hours after his triumphal entry into Jerusalem he wept. He said: "O Jerusalem, Jerusalem, killing the prophets and stoning those who are sent to you! How often would I have gathered your children together as a hen gathers her brood under her wings, and you would not!" (Matt. 23:37). He healed broken bodies as the blind and lame felt free to approach him the day after his triumphal entry, which so quickly turned into the day of his crucifixion. He didn't keep them waiting.

(e) Your King comes sounding a note of judgment along with his compassion. He's not trying to buy your favor. He's not going to give away everything, denying his own righteousness. He tells you what you need instead of what you want. He tells you that the wages of sin is death. He tells you that someday you will stand before God your Maker, accountable for all you've done in this life.

(f) Your King comes purging phony religion. He steps into the temple. He sees the greed, the commercialism, the cold formality, and the exploitation of the masses. This one who never neglected formal worship himself, who celebrated all of the feasts, who memorized the scriptures, and who learned the law, showed his dedication to overturning a religion which exploits people. There's nothing your King likes less than sterile religion. He shouts his declaration, "I am come that you might have life and have it more abundantly!" He comes to tear the veil in two which separates you by ritualistic, cold religion from the inner sanctuary of the holiest of holies.

(g) Your King comes frustrating his foes. That day Jesus knew the dynamics of Jerusalem. He knew that many people would flock to him. At the same time he could see past the throngs into the second-story windows where the shadowy forms of his opponents condescendingly looked down upon the crowds. Your King is a threatening figure. His righteousness makes no accommodation. He refuses to compromise to maintain his power. He will not barter for position or prestige. He is willing to infuriate his foes, no matter what the cost.

(h) Your King is willing to accept fickle people. (1) He knows that no idol is more quickly forgotten than the contemporary pop star. That's just about what he was for those few hours as he made his triumphal entry. He stirred the hopes of the people for political deliverance. His messianic claims were transparent to many. Some expected the military overthrow of Rome. He came to win a much bigger victory over Satan and death.

(2 He wants you with all your doubts, inconsistencies, question marks. You, the vacillating one. He knows you're fickle. He understands. He wants to help you become steadfast in your commitment.

III. Your King is coming! His approach demands your response. Either you are with him or not. There is no neutral ground. Today we have sung our hosannas, which literally mean "saved now!" Do we mean this? Are we serious? Have we come because it is the nice thing to do? Or are we here because we mean business?—John A. Huffman, Jr.

## SUNDAY: APRIL TENTH

### MORNING SERVICE

**Topic: The Difference Easter Makes (Easter)**

SCRIPTURE: I Cor. 15:20-28, 51-57.

The Christian church was founded upon the firm belief that Christ was raised from the dead. It is difficult to explain the vitality and the rapid expansion of the early church apart from the resurrection. With many alleged "miracles" happening in the ancient world, why did this event hold a group of followers so closely? Why was the faith of these disciples more convincing than that of other teachers? What was the appeal?

I. Christ's resurrection was representative of what God intended for all man. Surely God revealed his love in the cross. How much more was that love revealed in the resurrection! Paul described the resurrected Christ as the "first fruits of them that slept." The first fruits probably referred to the first sheaf of the harvest which would be offered at the temple. It was given with the confidence that there was more harvest to come. Raymond Brown suggested that the resurrection of Christ "is the pledge and assurance of our own." It was God's way of telling those in Christ that what they are is too important to be eternally forgotten.

II. The resurrection of Christ was an authentication of Christ's victorious life.

(a) In his life and ministry Christ constantly battled the forces of evil. Many of his successes were described as victories over the demons. If sin is viewed as misdirection, we see in the life of Jesus a life fully committed to God. Here is one who struggled with temptations constantly but who overcame. For once in this world's history a man knew who he was, why he was here, and with his heavenly Father as his centering force he moved out in freedom and authority.

(b) He defeated sin and evil, but could he defeat death? The answer of the resurrection is "yes." Christ struggled with death. Although he prayed for some other route in the Garden of Gethsemane, he agreed to the final battle. But death could not contain him.

(c) He had given his followers a foretaste of this victory when he raised Lazarus from the grave. But of course Lazarus died again. Not so our Lord. He continues to live in triumph over death.

III. This leads to a third reason why the resurrection held such power over the lives of the early Christians. Because they were convinced that Christ lives, they never believed themselves to be beyond his presence and care. He was a constant source of help and a ready line to the resources of their heavenly Father. Since he lived they too believed that thy could lead victorious lives and that God would seal this victory by raising them from the dead.

IV. They saw themselves as part of a divine plan whereby all the enemies of Christ would be destroyed.

(a) God intended from the beginning that men should live in peace and harmony with him. Death is a constant reminder that this peace is violated. As Paul said, "The sting of death is sin and the strength of sin is the law." The law points out our sin. (See Rom. 7:7-25.) Sin brings death. Christ fulfilled the law to conquer sin. When death finally is conquered, the last symbol of enemy force will be destroyed.

(b) For the early Christian, death was overcome not by avoiding it but by being faithful to the Commander-in-Chief who would raise them to life in the end. Those who had not died would still participate in this glorious time of celebration, for their bodies would be changed, enabling them to participate in the new order. Whether dead or alive, they were "in Christ."

(c) Death for the Christian is no longer a penalty but a final challenge to be conquered. The sure reward is eternal life.—Robert V. Forehand in *Religious Herald*.

## Illustrations

CHRISTIAN HOPE. The difference between the Christian hope of resurrection and the mythological hope is that the Christian hope sends a man back to his life on earth in a wholly new way, which is even more sharply defined than it is in the Old Testament.—Dietrich Bonhoeffer.

AUTOPSY. In a church in South America there is a painting of an operating room. It cannot be a very old picture because the doctors are dressed in suits which indicate the late 1890s. It is a very strange painting. The patient on the operating table is a crucifix, a dead Christ on a cross on the table. The painting might be called "An Autopsy on a Dead Christ." And thereby hangs the tale. Too many churches miss the great Easter fact. Too many people miss the great Easter fact. "He is not here" was the core of that fact. Had he been there, there might have been a possibility of an autopsy on a dead Christ.—J. Manning Potts.

## Sermon Suggestions

THE EASTER SURPRISE. Text: Matt. 28:2. (1) How many times we find that the stone has been rolled away? (2) How many times the things we thought were dead and buried we find to be up, about, and alive? (3) How often when we feel that we have lost Christ we find him alive and in our midst?

THE POWER OF THE RESURRECTION. Text: I Cor. 15:1-2. (1) A decisive power: "received." (2) A redemptive power: "by which also ye are saved." (3) A constructive power: "wherein ye stand."—Stephen F. Olford.

## Worship Aids

CALL TO WORSHIP. "Blessed be the

God and Father of our Lord Jesus Christ, which according to his abundant mercy hath begotten us again unto a lively hope by the resurrection of Jesus Christ from the dead, to an inheritance incorruptible, and undefiled, and that fadeth not away, reserved in heaven for you." I Pet. 1:3-4.

INVOCATION.    Praise be to thee, O Father, who didst raise up thy Son from the dead and give him glory, that our faith and hope might be in thee. Praise be to thee, O Lord Almighty, Jesus Christ, the resurrection and the life, who as on this day by thy glorious resurrection didst bring life and immortality to light. Praise be to thee, O Holy Spirit, who dost send abroad the love of Christ in our hearts and makest us to rejoice in the hope of glory. All praise and thanks, dominion and power be unto thee, O holy and blessed Trinity, now and forevermore.

OFFERTORY SENTENCE.    "Greater love hath no man than this, that a man lay down his life for his friends." John 15:13.

OFFERTORY PRAYER.    Eternal God, give us a vision of thy glory that no sacrifice may seem too great, and strengthen us in every step we take from selfishness to generosity.

PRAYER.    Eternal God, thou before whose face the generations rise and pass away, we praise thee for our creation, preservation, and all the blessings of this life. Most of all on this holy day we bless thee for the saving confidence that thy purposes are not limited to this world but that they continue into the life beyond.

We do not pray for the mere extension of our lives, year after year. What we pray for is that richness of life which makes the heart sing. To all who do not know something of such a life, let thy grace abound. Upon all who have merely begun to grasp the meaning of such a life, let thy guiding hand be known. We now bless thee for our Lord, for the things he taught and

the way he lived. We bless thee for the resurrection through which thou didst seal the eternal value of that kind of living.

As on this day we feel eternity near, wilt thou be close to those who have lost loved ones. Give them the assurance that because of Easter they and their loved ones are yet bound in the golden cords of thy love. We pray also for our homes. Guide each one in the way it needs most. Enable them to be redemptive centers of thy Holy Spirit. We pray too for our church that it might increasingly function as the body of Christ and that we might keep close to our Lord and then to the many human needs in our midst.

Upon every individual here let thy guiding hand be very real. Thou dost know our deepest needs. And we affirm that as we are close to thee we may find hope. O God, enable us to know from the depths of our souls that because he lives we too shall live in freedom and in joy.—Warren Arthur Nyberg.

## EVENING SERVICE

Topic: Day of Discovery
    TEXT: Matt. 28:5-6, 10.
    Whether the discovery was made at an empty tomb or in a wayside inn or in an upper room, whether by weeping women at sunrise or by frightened men at sunset, no discovery in all history ever made a greater difference to humanity than the discovery that Christ who had been crucified on a cross and buried in a borrowed tomb had now risen from the grave and was alive forever.

I. That discovery compelled worship. (a) As the women left the sepulchre that early morning hour Jesus met them, saying, "All hail." And the scripture says, "They came and held him by the feet, and worshiped him" (Matt. 28:9.) And then later, when the men saw him, Matthew reports that "they worshipped him" (Matt. 28:17).

(b) Songs and sermons by the thousands today will extol Jesus as a good man, a great teacher, a beautiful ideal, a way-shower, and a noble person who died in a great cause. But if that is all Jesus was, we would not be celebrating Easter. For without the resurrection there would be no Easter.

(c) The reason millions can stand before Christ's tomb outside Jerusalem and worship is because no one is in it. Christ is not there. He is risen! And it is a risen Christ that compels worship. Other great and good men who have died can be admired. But Jesus Christ can be worshiped not because he is a dead superstar but because he is the living Lord.

II. The discovery of Jesus as risen Lord *dispelled fear.* (a) Jesus said to the women who were worshiping him, "Be not afraid." And his first words to the assembled disciples were "Fear not."

(b) What a message for all the fear-filled, fear-ridden, fear-hindered people today! For if God allowed Jesus to be crucified on Friday but raised him from the dead on Sunday, then those who trust in God can live with the abiding assurance that Easter Sunday will always follow their good—or bad—Fridays and that no one need fear the future for a risen Christ is dramatic proof that there can never be permanent disaster to those whose faith is in God.

III. The discovery that Christ was truly risen *impelled the disciples to witness* to that glorious fact.

(a) Jesus said to the worshiping women, "Go tell thy brethren" (Matt. 28:10). And Peter and John said, "We cannot but speak the things which we have seen and heard" (Acts 4:20).

(b) It is not ecclesiastical pressure, or denominational pride, or intellectual grasp, or promotional know-how that ultimately motivates Christian witnessing but the discovery that Jesus is truly alive.

(c) There were no morning headlines in Jerusalem that day, no late-breaking news bulletins on the radio, no evening TV newscast, but the news did get out. And Easter is a news announcement. It is not a theological argument; it is not a promotional gimmick; it is not a philosophical postulate or a psychological formula or a denominational come-on. It is news—good news! And no church and no preacher and no country has a corner on it.

(d) Today, even as on that first Easter, those who have made the great discovery that Christ is truly risen and have allowed him to become their Lord and Savior will be sharing that good news. —William Fisher.

## SUNDAY: APRIL SEVENTEENTH

### MORNING SERVICE

**Topic: When Faith Comes the Hard Way**

SCRIPTURE: John 20:24–29.

I. If faith comes hard to you, dare to expose your doubt with honesty and humility.

(a) Thomas was honest with his doubt. His frankness might upset the other disciples, but at least they had to admire his integrity. He wanted adequate, rational supports for his faith. However, many times that is not enough. No mere mating of intelligence with facts can add up to faith. The heart always has reasons which the head can never understand.

(b) Add humility to your honesty. You need not be ashamed to doubt. Yet do not become proud of it! Such an attitude can be a dangerous trap. Some people express doubt to try to shock other people. Some people express doubt as a means of attracting attention. Some may express doubt as a cover-up for deep moral problems in their lives. A man sincere in his doubts will not be very happy about it.

II. When faith comes the hard way, be willing to submit to certain disciplines.

(a) Let us begin with the discipline of suspended judgment. The total meaning of life does not come all in one package. Faith, like some other things, may come to you on the installment plan.

(b) Another discipline that we need is that of prayer. Prayer can mellow the hard crust of human spirit. Nothing is ever quite the same when it is put into the framework of prayer. If faith comes hard to you, do not give up. Present your case to God in fervent prayer.

(c) A third discipline to guide in the quest for faith is to maintain personal fellowship with those who believe. If a fire is going out, the best way to rekindle it is to gather the dying embers together. It is a mistake for one who is faltering in his faith or who has been struggling with his problem of believing to cut himself off from the fellowship of those who do believe. This is one of the many strengths of the public worship of God. In such a service we are at least in an atmosphere of faith. We need to hear songs of praises to offset the pangs of our own inner loneliness. Thomas missed something by not being with the others on that first Easter evening.

III. The most important consideration is this: Let Christ do with you as he will.

(a) Faith at its best is simple trust in a person. It is a response of one life to another life. In our thinking today it means a response of your life and mine to Jesus Christ. He does not answer all our questions, but to see him in the grandeur of his stainless character and to respond to the depth of his costly love is to find that he himself is the answer.

(b) Thomas had now joined his fellow disciples again in the familiar upper room. Jesus came again and said, "Thomas, look at the nail-prints, touch if you must . . . but be not faithless but believing." Faith had to come the hard way. But it came! And he said to Jesus, "My Lord and my God!"—A. Hayden Hollingsworth, Jr.

## Illustrations

HORSES AND FOOTMEN. The thought came to me that there was no God, no Christ, no heaven, and no hell, that all my prayers were but a farce, and that I might as well have whistled to the winds or spoken to the howling waves. I went to the very verge of the dreary realms of unbelief. I went to the very bottom of the sea of infidelity. I doubted everything until at last the devil defeated himself by making me doubt my own existence. I thought I was an idea floating in the nothingness of vacuity; then, startled with the thought and feeling that I was substantial flesh and blood after all, I saw that God was, and Christ was, and heaven was, and hell was, and that all these things were absolute truths. The very extravagance of the doubt proved its absurdity. When I arose faith took the helm; from that moment I doubted not. Faith steered me back; I cast my anchor on Calvary; I lifted my eyes to God; and here I am alive and out of hell. Now whenever I hear the skeptic's stale attacks upon the Word of God, I smile within myself and think: "Why, you simpleton! How can you urge such trifling objections?" We who have contended with horses are not wearied by the footmen.—Charles H. Spurgeon.

SILENT WATCHERS. Norman Vincent Peale told of a newspaper reporter who was sent to cover the Easter sunrise service held each year on the rim of the Grand Canyon. It was below freezing; and as he stood there shivering he wished he were back in bed. The sun rose and poured into the canyon. The reporter said: "I forgot all about being cold. Then came a flood of radiance, torrents of light plunging down the canyon walls, making them blaze with color. Watching the shadows vanish I had the conviction that the darkness that had filled the great gorge was an illusion, that only the light was real, and that we silent watchers on the canyon rim were somehow a part of the light."

## Sermon Suggestions

AFTER EASTER. (1) Easter is over. We can end it with a period. Another Easter has come and gone, and that's that. (2)

Easter is over! End it with an exclamation point. Easter was a day of triumphant worship in our church and was an occasion for celebration not soon forgotten. (3) Easter is over? End it with a question mark. Cannot Christ's living presence touch all of our days with new hope, flooding our hearts with new peace and transforming even death into victory?—Eugene W. Ebert.

CHRISTIAN LIVING. In Colossians the apostle Paul writes about three things. (1) A change of life. (See Col. 2:12.) (2) A change of clothes. (See Col. 3:10, 12.) (3) A change of master. (See Col. 3:11.)—Charles F. Tame.

## Worship Aids

CALL TO WORSHIP. "Be strong and of a good courage, fear not; for the Lord thy God, he it is that doth go with thee; he will not fail thee, nor forsake thee." Deut. 31.6.

INVOCATION. Almighty God, who of thy great mercy hast gathered us into thy visible church: grant that we may not swerve from the purity of thy worship, but may so honor thee both in spirit and in outward form that thy name may be glorified in us and that our fellowship may be with all thy saints in earth and in heaven.

OFFERTORY SENTENCE. "If any man will come after me (saith Jesus), let him deny himself, and take up his cross daily, and follow me." Luke 9:23.

OFFERTORY PRAYER. O God, who hast given us thy Son to be an example and a help to our weakness in following the path that leadeth unto life, grant us so to be his disciples that we may walk in his footsteps.

PRAYER. O Lord our God, we thank thee that thou hast created an orderly universe in which we can depend upon the coming of spring: the reawakening of the seemingly lifelessness of winter, the evidence of which we see now in the budding of the shrubs and the coming forth of the tulips and narcissi.

We thank thee too that in thy plan for us as thy children there is an orderliness in our lives that thou wouldst have us follow: an orderliness set before us by thy Son, our Lord Jesus Christ. It assures us that, where the seeds of faith are sown, there will follow trust, confidence, and obedience; where the seeds of hope are sown, there will follow encouragement, anticipation, and dedication; where the seeds of love are sown, there will follow harmony, cooperation, and goodwill. Blessed art thou, O God, for thou hast made it so.

There are those among us today who have special need of thy help to overcome a temptation, to make a decision, to stop a quarrel at home, to be comforted in sorrow, illness, or pain, to make prayer more meaningful, or to make life more worthwhile. May the living presence of Jesus Christ enter into each heart that is seeking help for these or other needs. Thou, who art great and merciful, loving and kind, surely wilt minister to our needs as we sincerely pray about them.

There are many troubled spots in our world today that are sparked by turmoil, tyranny, or freedom-seeking drives. As these forces grow strong, may there rise up leaders intelligent enough to cope with the problems, wise enough to seek proper counsel, and faithful enough to know thy will in matters of state.

May we too be intelligent, wise, and faithful in order to be as leaven to work within our homes, our community, our nation, and our world to raise the level of each until it becomes more of what thy kingdom on earth should be.

To this end we would dedicate ourselves in these moments and commend body, mind, and spirit to thy love, thy care, and thy guidance.—Donald A. Wenstrom.

## EVENING SERVICE

Topic: God's Outstretched Arm
TEXT: Deut. 7:18–19.
The time has come for the Children

of Israel to cross over into the Promised Land. Try to visualize that scene in the land of Egypt. Their lives were made bitter by reason of their bondage, and their hearts were not there in Egypt at all but back in the land of their fathers. And to make it worse they were powerless to escape. They were slaves in the land of Egypt. Then God in his wondrous power and his great mercy stretched out his arm—holding back the forces of Pharaoh—and brought them out. It is a beautiful picture of God's dealings with Israel, and if you will look at the end of that outstretched arm you will find three things that suggest God's gracious dealings with us as well.

I. At the end of that outstretched arm there is *an open hand.* How good God has been to us. His gifts are beyond our numbering and his ways past finding out. The open hand provides for our needs, a hand that guides and leads us, and a hand that watches in tenderness over us. God deals with us in love.

II. God deals with us in judgment. At the end of God's outstretched arm there is an open hand, and at the end of that open hand there is *a pointing finger.*

(a) God's judgment is a part of God's dealings with us, and it is a necessary part. It is necessary if God is to be true to himself as a God of holiness, and it is necessary if this world is to be a cosmos and not a chaos. Even parents find it necessary to discipline their children. Even human magistrates find it necessary to give sentences to those who appear before them. How much more imperative is it that the Judge of all the earth should both support the right and do right.

(b) It is a salutary part of his dealing with us. It is for our good and for his glory! Where would David have been if God had not sent Nathan to him? Where would Saul have been if Christ had not accosted him on the Damascus road? And where would you and I have been if God had not arrested us and turned us from our evil ways?

III. He deals with us in grace. At the end of God's outstretched arm there is an open hand and at the end of that open hand there is a pointing finger, and on that pointing finger there is *a ring.*

(a) That is not wishful thinking but the clear teaching of the scriptures. Thus in Ephesians Paul writes that God chose us in Christ before the foundation of the world. Chose us not because we were worthy—for then we did not even exist —but chose us in the wonder of his grace, his unmerited love and favor.

(b) He not only chose us but made us accepted in the beloved. He gave his Son to be our Savior. He has given himself to us. There is a ring on his finger, a symbol of the new covenant which we have with him.—S. Robert Weaver.

## SUNDAY: APRIL TWENTY-FOURTH

### MORNING SERVICE

Topic: God and the Day's Work
TEXT: I Cor. 10:31.

What we do from Monday until Friday, the way in which we do it, and the motivation behind it affect not only our own lives but the lives of many others. Our Christian faith should make a difference both as regards our choice of a daily occupation and what we hope to achieve by means of it. The preacher is not alone in having a divine call. We are all called to glorify God wherever we are employed. Almost without exception we can serve and glorify God more fully and effectively where we work than anywhere else.

I. *The choice of work* for a Christian is very important. If he is to serve God in and through his job he must select his job carefully and prayerfully. At once we are up against a difficulty, not just the difficulty of finding a way of making a living that does not conflict with one's Christian profession but also the fact that for great numbers of young people the choice is limited.

(a) We preachers talk about Christian vocation in terms of leadership, and our minds run to the ministry, missionary work, social service, and the professions, particularly teaching and medicine. Yet the business of keeping the world going involves a vast amount of labor of a different kind. The life of the world could not go on if everybody chose or were at liberty to choose the job which appealed to him most or a job of uplifting character.

(b) What we ought to stress more is not leadership but the obligation for the Christian of doing work, often ordinary and unexciting, which is essential to the good estate of the nation and the world. We place too little value on the obscure but necessary jobs which, if they are not well done, leave the whole of society impoverished. A Christian finds his vocation in doing as well and cheerfully as he can the very best work that is available to him.

II. The way in which work is done, whatever the work, needs to be emphasized.

(a) What matters most of all is the motivation. Is it the pay check? Is it a place at the top of the ladder—status, kudos, one's name in the headlines? Is work a necessary drudgery to be undergone for the sake of what it yields, something to be got through, the hours as short as possible, the wages as high as possible, in order to do something else at the end of the day and in years of retirement? Or is it something done for more than bread-and-butter reasons, as a contribution to the common good and therefore a service rendered to God?

(b) What gives dignity to work is the reason for which it is performed. It is pathetic to see people wearing themselves out with exacting toil and all the time conveying the impression of being so utterly immersed in their occupation as to have quite forgotten what it is for, its ultimate purpose and meaning. Along that road a man becomes hard, unspiritual, and soulless.

(c) Paul's injunction to the Corinthians, "Whatever you do, do all to the glory of God," embodies a permanent truth concerning the Christian attitude toward work. Like the rest of mankind, a Christian must work to earn his daily bread and maintain his family. But he works also from a higher motive and under different pressures than those of fear, insecurity, and greed. He works both for the good of men and the glory of God, and in doing so he finds a satisfaction not to be derived from earthly rewards or diminished by earthly hardships. About work so motivated Jesus says that the final verdict will be: "Well done, good and faithful servant, enter thou into the joy of thy Lord."—Robert J. McCracken.

## Illustrations

OURS BY RIGHT.   No man can rob us of the experiences by which we have gained wisdom; of the strength that comes from a sense of self-respect; of the truth that we have proved for ourselves; of the inspiration of great friendship; of the courage that comes from knowing we are right; of the joy that comes from self-mastery; of the peace that comes from having a clear conscience.—Roy L. Smith.

THREE RESPONSES.   Duty is never worthily done until it is performed by a man who so loves it that he would gladly do more if he could. Some men say of their duties: "I must"; some men say, "I ought"; some men say, "I want to and let me at it." These are the three tones of life. One man is the slave of his necessities; one, the grim moralist doing his duty; one, the man of an abounding sense of privilege in life, who feels all blessings large with God's favor, all trials meaningful with purpose, all duty a glorious prerogative.—Harry Emerson Fosdick.

## Sermon Suggestions

THE POWER OF PURPOSE.   Text: Neh. 6:3. (1) The power of purpose lifts us above the common fear of criticism. (2) The power of purpose lifts us above futility and the scattering of our powers in aimless, pointless existence. (3) The power of purpose lifts us above discouragement.—J. Wallace Hamilton.

BORN TO LIVE AND BORED TO DEATH. Text: Eccl. 12:1, 13. Four things will save us from being bored to death and live the life for which we were born. (1) A transforming experience that puts God rather than ourselves at the center of our lives. (2) An appreciation of the beautiful things created by God and by people who have loved him. (3) Wholehearted dedication to the work to which God has called us, knowing that we are partners with him in subduing the earth and in redeeming all mankind. (4) An unselfish devotion to the needs and interests of our fellowman.—Frank H. Epp.

## Worship Aids

CALL TO WORSHIP. "Wait on the Lord: be of good courage, and he shall strengthen thine heart: wait, I say, on the Lord." Ps. 27:14.

INVOCATION. Almighty and merciful God, who hast created us for thy service and glory: we confess in thy holy presence that we have broken thy commandments and sinned against thee. We have offended by our deeds, by our thoughts, and by the sinful impulses and desires of our hearts. In the greatness of thy love, shed abroad in us a holy sorrow for all our transgressions and make our wills obedient to thy perfect love revealed in Christ Jesus our Lord and Savior.

OFFERTORY SENTENCE. "Remember the words of the Lord Jesus, how he said, It is more blessed to give than to receive."—Acts 20:35.

OFFERTORY PRAYER. Dear God, help us to become unobstructed channels that thy love may flow through us to others and our gifts may be used for the proclamation to all men of thy saving goodness.

PRAYER. Heavenly Father, who hast invited us to call upon thee in the day of trouble and hast promised to hear us, we come to thee with all the cares and trials of our life, all our fears and anxieties, and ask thee to give us the calm and confidence, the strength and courage, the hope and certainty we need to live successfully at a time like this. All we like sheep have gone astray; we have transgressed thy commandments; we have rejected thy guidance; we have forgotten thy love. Forgive us for Jesus' sake. Teach us to pray day by day, naturally and meaningfully, quietly and confidently, and not to wait for emergencies before we turn to thee. Fill our hearts with the assurance that no matter what life may do to us, we are living in thy hands. Then when the time comes that we must leave this earth, may we do it as the Savior did, with the prayer, "Father, into thy hands I commend my spirit."—Armin C. Oldsen.

## EVENING SERVICE

Topic: Fools You Are—Thank God!
TEXT: I Cor. 4:10.

I. Your faith is considered foolish because the world considers Christianity nonsense. In a way it is "nonesense" because not one of your senses can be used to prove the truthfulness of your faith.

(a) Which of your senses prove that "in the beginning God created the heavens and the earth" (Gen. 1:1), that "there is no other God but one" (I Cor. 8:4), that "Christ died for our sins" (I Cor. 15:8), or that "he that believeth and is baptized shall be saved" (Mark 16:16)? How do you prove with your sense that "the Lord is my shepherd" (Ps. 23:1), that "he shall give his angels charge over thee" (Ps. 91:11), or that "I am with you always, even unto the end of the world" (Matt. 28:20)?

(b) Therefore the world considers you a fool for believing in religious "nonsense." You become "a fool for Christ" because "the natural man receiveth not the things of the Spirit of God, for they are foolishness unto him" (I Cor. 2:14).

(c) What fools you are, they say, to

believe in a God no one has seen and to believe that a despised Jew who was born in a barn among some cows and crucified on a cross among some crooks is "King of kings and Lord of lords," the Son of God himself! What fools to believe that stories and letters written by fish merchants and tax collectors, vagabonds and farmers are the inspired Word of God and contain "the power of God unto salvation."

II. Can't a God who can bring a green plant with a red flower from a black seed in the brown ground and who can put such power into an invisible atom that when it is split it can blow islands from the sea and mountains from the face of the earth, also put his saving power into the water of baptism, the elements of communion, and the gospel of Jesus Christ? Sure he can and, though this "preaching of the cross is to them that perish foolishness, to us who are saved it is the power of God" (I Cor. 1:18). Fools for this faith? Thank God "by grace are you saved through faith" (Eph. 2:5).

III. How often we thank God for your "foolish faithfulness." (a) You could have cheated and made the grade. You could have kept that money you found, and no one would have known. You could have fallen for the fun of being "one of the boys" or sold yourself for the popularity of being the "it" girl. But thank God you considered your body "the temple of the Holy Spirit" (I Cor. 6:19) and refused to compromise your character by becoming a spineless jellyfish or a mass of moral pulp.

(b) Thank God your foolish faithfulness makes you "love your enemies, bless them that curse you, do good to them that hate you" (Matt. 5:14). Thank God the love of Christ constrains you to pledge your body and soul for time and eternity to your God and Lord and "be faithful unto death" (Rev. 2:10).

(c) Your "foolish faithfulness" may send you into a fiery furnace like Shadrach, Meshach, and Abednego or into a lions' den like Daniel. It may ostracize you as it did Luther, make you a vagabond like Paul, or finally force you to die a martyr's death like Stephen, but at the end of the road you'll see Jesus and hear him say, "Well done thou good and faithful servant . . . enter into the joy of thy Lord" (Matt. 25:21). Into a fool's paradise? Yes, a fool's paradise, for a "fool for Christ." Thank God!—Oscar L. Sylwester.

# SUNDAY: MAY FIRST

## MORNING SERVICE

**Topic: Counting the Cost of Christian Marriage (National Family Week)**

TEXTS: Mark 10:8; Luke 14:28.

I. Christian marriage is *an unconditional commitment.* (a) There is nothing ambiguous about the words "till death us do part" in the traditional vows. When a man and a woman make that vow together, they are unconditionally committing themselves to a shared life for a lifetime. They are declaring that in their marriage "the two shall become one" and that the two shall continue to be one. Christian marriage is not a contract with an escape clause; Christian marriage is a commitment without conditions.

(b) The explicit intention with which a young couple enter marriage is the key to the whole tone and quality of their life together and determines how they handle the challenges, trials, and uncertainties of married life. A marriage built on the assumption that it is a contract with an escape clause is one thing; a quite different thing is a marriage founded on the conviction that it is a life together for a lifetime. "The two shall become one," and the price is unconditional commitment.

II. Christian marriage is *founded in realistic love.* (a) Today there is a menacing air of unrealism about so much popular thinking about love and its place in marriage. Young people often have curious notions of "real love." These notions owe much to movies, popular songs, and sentimental literature. They tend to lead to the dangerous illusion that imperfect persons can somehow make a perfect marriage, providing that certain standard emotional conditions prevail. Much of our popular culture encourages young people in the quaint belief that, when a young man and a young woman experience that shattering complexity of emotions and sentiments known as "being in love with each other," it is only necessary for them to have the knot tied to ensure that forever afterward everything will be simply wonderful. But perfect marriage, marriage without stress, strain, and problems, is a figment of an excessively romantic imagination.

(b) Love does change in marriage. And when it does, one of two things happens. In some marriages the love on which they are founded becomes rather flabby and there is little else to keep the relationship strong. Many marriages founder because they run out of emotional steam. The other thing that can happen is that love, although losing some of its intensity and excitement, becomes deeper and stronger. But this happens only when it is an outgoing love, not a selfish, ingrown love.

III. Christian marriage *requires spiritual discipline for its maintenance.* (a) Christian marriage is sustained by the practices of the Christian faith. And this involves much more than starting off with a church wedding and all the trimmings; it involves active participation in the life of the church and the taking of a religion seriously in the whole of life.

(b) Young people entering marriage should keep in mind that there are in the practices of religion resources that make for stability and happiness in marriage. But faith cannot be used as a mere gimmick in marriage. Faith is not a magic cure-all for marriage distress which can be used as a wonder drug when the going becomes a bit rough.

Religion cannot be used casually as first aid for the minor injuries and abrasions of marriage. Faith is not very helpful if it is neglected until a marriage is falling apart, although I do know of a number of tottering marriages that were helped back to a fair degree of stability by recourse to the neglected devotions and disciplines of religion.

(c) The kind of faith that makes for stability and happiness in marriage is the kind that is woven into life's whole fabric. There are resources in religion that help develop and nurture those qualities of character and personality that make for successful marriage. But religion must be a matter of continuing concern and not merely a casual, once-in-awhile gesture.

(d) A Christian marriage entails a Christian commitment which is founded in authentic love and sustained and kept lively by the devotions and disciplines of the Christian religion within the worshiping fellowship of the church.—J. A. Davidson.

## Illustrations

TAUT SAIL. The best marriages, like the best lives, were both happy and unhappy. There is even a kind of necessary tension, a certain tautness between the partners that gave the marriage strength, and like the tautness of a full sail, you went forward on it.—Anne Morrow Lindbergh.

WARNING SIGNALS OF A SICK MARRIAGE. (1) When common courtesies are abandoned. (2) When couples begin to think in terms of "I" instead of "we." (3) When they stop complimenting each other. (4) When stubborn silence replaces common-sense communication. (5) When they stop praying together. (6) When they fail to sense and meet the needs of each other. (7) When they fail to express love.—Lindsay Curtis.

## Sermon Suggestions

CHRISTIAN MARRIAGE. Text: Ruth 1:16. (1) A shared life: "whither thou goest I will go." (2) A shared home: "where thou lodgest I will lodge." (3) A shared possession: "thy people shall be my people." (4) A shared faith: "thy God shall be my God."—Bryan Green.

PARENTHOOD AS A MINISTRY. (1) To walk with innocence, simplicity, and beauty. (2) To protect, to instruct, to guide, and to share the joys and the fleeting sorrows of the young. (3) To introduce the young to the Bible, the hymnbook, and to Christ. (4) To open to the young the wonders of the world without and the world within. (5) To observe the unfolding of their powers and to know that in all this marvelous process and growth one has an indispensable and beneficent part to play.—Robert J. McCracken.

## Worship Aids

CALL TO WORSHIP. "I will bless the Lord at all times: his praise shall continually be in my mouth. O magnify the Lord with me, and let us exalt his name together." Ps. 34:1, 3.

INVOCATION. Our Father, we give thanks for Jesus Christ our Savior. Help us to receive the fullness of thy salvation. Grant us grace to live joyful, obedient, and triumphant lives as thy children in this thy world. May the spirit of peace reign within our hearts and invade the nations of the world.

OFFERTORY SERVICE. "And whatsoever ye do in word and deed, do all in the name of the Lord Jesus, giving thanks to God and the Father by him." Col. 3:17.

OFFERTORY PRAYER. Our Father, we thank thee that thou art so generous to us. All that we have is a gift from thee. Help us to serve one another so that we may reflect thy spirit and goodness.

PRAYER. We thank thee, our God, for all who point to our mistakes in love and correct our errors in charity, so that we are encouraged by their admonition and inspired by their reproof. For noble hearts who have given us the benefit of the doubt and the opportunity to make good our failings, we bow in gratitude before thee. In the midst of our trials there were those who bade us take heart, and in the days of our misery there were those who helped us feel that thou didst love us still. We remember them and rejoice in the encouragement they brought. Help us to praise thee by seizing the opportunity to bring cheer to the despairing, companionship to the lonely, understanding to the perplexed, and hope to the downtrodden. Let thy mercies rest on all who are weary and faint in the pursuit of righteousness. And grant unto all who have stumbled or fallen in the path that leads to thee friends of the generous eye who will lift them up and help them walk once more.—Marion C. Allen.

## EVENING SERVICE

### Topic: The Meaning of Life
TEXT: Ps. 8:4.

I. The dimension of meaning can be discovered in the word *relatedness*.

(a) Meaning is interwoven in our relationships with other human beings, with God, and with the physical world in which we are placed.

(b) Relationships can be poisoned, can be tinged with hatred, and can be pinched with hurt. And a great void, a vacuum, develops within one. Sartre was right in saying that "hell is other people," but he was only half right because heaven is also other people. A depth of understanding, a sharing of hopes, and a camaraderie of purposes are also possible.

(c) The meaning of life is discovered when we enter the web of obligation and responsibility which is life and see in it a symbol of giving and receiving.

II. The dimension of meaning can be discovered in the word *acceptance*.

(a) Søren Kierkegaard declared that man is the only creature who refuses to accept what he is. Instead of accepting ourselves as man, we alternate between playing God and behaving like an animal.

(b) The meaning of life begins to break in on us when we accept the burden of having to make choices rather than running from them, when we accept the fact of the limitations upon our knowledge and powers rather than pretending to be all-powerful, and when we accept the pain of being hurt and the responsibility for hurting others rather than trying to avoid the one or making excuses for the other.

III. The dimension of meaning is discovered in the word *creativity*. (a)

The divine intent for man is to become a partner with God in completing creation. God's purpose is not just to save man from his sin; it is also to include man in a dynamic, continuing creativity. The spirit of God works in man to create, not to destroy; to open new windows to beauty, not to deface the universe; to expand man's horizons and his appreciation for goodness and truth, not to cripple or to shrivel man's sensibilities.

(b) The meaning to life comes to a man as he participates with God in this creative process.—Robert Lloyd Shirer.

## SUNDAY: MAY EIGHTH

### MORNING WORSHIP

**Topic: Love Is Not Touchy! (Mother's Day)**

TEXT. I Cor. 13:5 (PHILLIPS).

The word the apostle uses here that is translated "love" is the Greek word *agape*. Agape-love is not weak or soft or sentimental but is undiscourageable goodwill. Booker T. Washington, committed to such a love, was able to say and practice, "I will allow no man to drag me so low as to make me hate him." To hate someone who hates you is to conform; to love this someone is to introduce a transforming power that redeems the relationship.

I. Love is not touchy for it brings to life's relationships *a great imagination*. As the J. B. Phillips translation renders one of Paul's statements on the subject: "Love looks for ways of being constructive." The way to get rid of your enemies is not to destroy them but to make them your friends. Genuine love is imaginative. It returns good for evil. It prays for those who slight you or irritate you. It turns the other cheek. It goes a second mile.

II. Love does not look for limitations but for opportunities. In other words it is *not conditional*. Jesus said, "If you love those who love you, what is the good of a love that does only that?"

How often our attitude is: If you are my kind of people, I will love you. If you hold my political philosophy, I will love you. If you are a Protestant, I will love you. We say to our children, "If you obey me, I will love you." Or "If you get your hair cut to my length, I will love you." But love, agape-love, is without precondition. It is not touchy. It does not say, "I will love you if you love me." Rather it says, "I love you, and I will go on loving you, no matter what your attitude toward me may be."

III. To love with a love that is not touchy, we find our *example and inspiration in Christ*. It seems to be our nature to want definitions. God does not give definitions of what it means to love, but he points to a person. As the apostle Paul writes in his letter to the Philippians: "Let your bearing towards one another arise out of your life with Christ" (Phil. 2:5, NEB). Concerning the example that we find in Christ, the apostle Peter writes: "Who when he was reviled, reviled not again; when he suffered, he did not threaten, but committed himself to the One who judges righteously" (I Pet. 2:23). Once having been to the cross, who can ever forget the magnanimity of the spirit that prayed, "Father, forgive them, for they know not what they do"?

IV. Our text is rendered differently

by various translations: "Love is not irritable or resentful" is the way the RSV puts it. The NEB translates it: "Love is not quick to take offense." William Barclay translates it: "Love never flies into a temper." But the translation which we have used is by J. B. Phillips: "Love is not touchy." All of these translations are of no avail unless there is one more translation—the translation into deed in the relationships of our every day. "By this shall all men know that you are my disciples," Jesus said, "that you love one another." And then he added the kind of love with which we are to love: "Love one another as I have loved you." *His* love is never touchy.—John Thompson in *The Clergy Journal.*

## Illustrations

HUNGRY MOTHER.    In Victor Hugo's novel, *Ninety-Three,* the heroine is a mother. After the French Revolution the fields are devastated. Not a garden has been left growing; everything has been ravaged to the very roots of the grass. A French captain and a private in the army are walking across a field when they see something stirring in a clump of bushes. The captain orders the soldier to see what it is. He walks cautiously to the clump of bushes and carefully runs his bayonet into them. Out walks a woman and two starved little children. The soldier leads them to the captain who takes a long loaf of bread from his knapsack and hands it to the mother. She grabs it, breaks it into two pieces, and hands one piece to each child. The soldier says to the captain, "Sir, it must be that the woman is not hungry." But the captain replies simply, "No, soldier, it is because she is a mother."—Homer J. R. Elford.

STARTING AT HOME.    If you want to reform society don't mount a soapbox. Go home and make it a little society patterned on the great ideal you believe in. If you want law and order and wise government, make your home a place of order, respect, and reverence for God and for authority. If you want a Christian world, start with Christlike attitudes and relations in the home.— David R. Piper.

## Sermon Suggestions

MARY WAS THERE.    Text: John 2:1. (1) Mary was there with her submissive faith. (See Luke 1:31–37.) (2) Mary was there in her worship of God. (See Luke 1:46–49.) (3) Mary was there with an ability to raise her son. (See Luke 2:52.) (4) Mary was there in her sensitivity to the needs of others. (See John 2:3.) (5) Mary was there at the crucifixion. (See John 19:25–26.) (6) Mary was there at the birth of the church. (See Acts 1:14.) —Walter L. Dosch.

FAMILY IDEALS.    Text: Ps. 133:1. (1) See eye to eye. (2) Talk heart to heart. (3) Walk hand in hand. (4) Kneel side by side.

## Worship Aids

CALL TO WORSHIP.    "Whatsoever things are true, whatsoever things are honest, whatsoever things are just, whatsoever things are pure, whatsoever things are lovely, whatsoever things are of good report; if there be any virtue, and if there be any praise, think on these things." Phil. 4:8.

INVOCATION.    O God, our Father, creator of the universe and giver of all good things: we thank thee for our home on earth and for the joy of loving. We praise thee for thy love in Jesus Christ, who came to set things right, who died rejected on the cross, and who rose triumphant from the dead. Because he lives, we live to praise thee, Father, Son, and Holy Spirit, our God forever.

OFFERTORY SENTENCE.    "As every man hath received the gift, even so minister the same one to another, as good stewards of the manifold grace of God." I Pet. 4:10.

OFFERTORY PRAYER.    As we bring our offering today we thank thee, O God, for the happiness of our earthly life, for peaceful homes and healthful days, for our powers of mind and body, for faithful friends, and for the joy of loving and being loved. We pray that these blessings may come to abound throughout all the world and to all people.

PRAYER. We worship thee with gratitude in our hearts. Even in the midst of anxieties and perplexities, we thank thee for thy trustworthiness. Make us aware of all thy gifts to us each day and the love and concern of others for us, especially the love of our mothers who cradled us, that follows us through the years. Many times, O God, our gratitude has been slow to be expressed and often too late. Help us to respond eagerly and quickly to thine every blessing with gratitude and service.

None of us is justified in thy sight; none of us enters thy sanctuary with clean hands and a pure heart. Search us and forgive us, O God, for we need a new and a fresh start. So often we have been swift to criticize the mistakes and failings of others; help us to face our own. Deliver us from our own blindness by thy grace and mercy. Thou hast the power; we do not.

O thou, who hast been and art the light of the world, shine on the paths of our lives. Hallow the names of our loved ones—the children and youth, the wives and husbands, the fathers and mothers, and all loved ones who are with us for the rest of our lives. We pray for them as for our own souls, for without them our lives are incomplete. Speak to each one of us that word that heals and strengthens, that word of power and promise.—Herman N. Beimfohr.

## EVENING SERVICE

### Topic: The Family of God
SCRIPTURE: Eph. 4:1–6, 11–16.

I. The family meets the basic hunger for significant, meaningful, and purposeful human relationships and also provides the opportunity for such depth of sharing and involvement between persons—husband and wife, parents and children—as no other organization or institution can offer. Thus the family as an institution guarantees that helpless young members of society receive the love essential for human survival.

II. We in the church need to remember that our whole Christian enterprise depends not on individual Christians but on families of them. As with the race of men, there is no continuation of the church without the family. It has been well proved that the church doesn't teach Christianity very effectively except through Christian families. That is why the church is laying emphasis upon family worship and encouraging families to come to church for worship and study together. But do not think for one moment because we have assembled our church family in one big room that we have fulfilled our obligation of family worship. Without adequate Christian nurture and training in the homes, explaining why we worship as we do and how we worship and experience the love of our heavenly Father in our hearts and expressing that love to others, we won't do much of a job, no matter what our church program is. You and I would not be here today if our parents had not done their homework.

III. Not only is the church dependent on families for the teaching and training of its children, but it is also dependent on the home as a laboratory in which parents and children learn how to live together in love. How are the members of a family, whose life is one long rivalry and hectic quarrel, going to be able to form in love the intimate beloved family of the church? They can't. They won't. They will hate, fight, quarrel, divide, and break up in the church as well as in the home. So if love, loyalty, concern, and commitment are to be expressed in the church family, they must first of all come from our homes.

IV. There is still another way in which the church and also society is dependent upon the family. Christianity offers a pattern of the good life, of right living or Christlike living to the community, the nation, and the world. Here is the unique opportunity and worthy contribution the Christian family can make to the world. But what hope is there that we can teach the nations to live together in the bond of peace and in any unity of spirit if we, the family of the church, cannot do it? And how can the church be a family if our constituent families are breaking up?

V. It is out of Christian homes, where God is revered, worshiped, and obeyed, that there will be produced people who can make the church what it ought to be, a true family of God. And it is from such a church alone that there will go out into the community Christians capable of helping to establish the brotherhood of all men.—George Hunter Hall.

## SUNDAY: MAY FIFTEENTH

### MORNING SERVICE

Topic: A Life Worth Living
    TEXTS: John 10:14; I Pet. 2:21.
    I. Life is worth living when a person encounters the resurrected Christ.

(a) Eleven frightened disciples were transformed into the nucleus of the Christian church when they encountered the risen Christ. Doubts about themselves and uncertainty about the future were transformed into unconquerable courage and determination. Early Christians were intrepid witnesses to the risen Christ. Consumed with a passion to tell about their liberating encounter, they chose to face lions rather than deny their Lord. Encountering Christ brought a new sense of purpose to their living.

(b) The Galilean always confronts you where you live. Wherever you go, whatever you do, he is there. You can never excuse yourself, saying: "Look how I've been mistreated. My parents were too strict or too permissive. They were neurotic or alcoholic, perhaps both. My formal education was limited. I have two strikes against me. How can anyone expect me to rise above these limitations?"

(c) God's answer to the human predicament is resurrection—transforming old life into new possibilities. We are called out of our tombs of selfishness and anxiety. Encountering Christ we discover our past forgiven, our present accepted, and our future open. Freed from anxieties about the past, we sense new possibilities for meaningful living in the present and future. Individuals and groups in our troubled world can be gripped by the power of this good news and transformed by its hope.

II. Life is worth living when we incarnate the spirit of the Christ we encounter.

(a) "The best way to send an idea," observed J. Robert Oppenheimer, "is to wrap it up in a person."

(1) Amos incarnated his beliefs about justice by entering a marketplace with a plumb line and a proclamation.

(2) Hosea named his children symbolically to remind the nation of God's faithfulness in spite of people's faithlessness.

(3) Jeremiah carried a yoke through the streets to encourage his nation to submit to Nebuchadnezzar as God's instrument.

(4) Mahatma Gandhi wrapped his convictions about freedom in a wizened body and won unparalleled diplomatic and military victory in India.

(5) Martin Luther King, Jr., and his colleagues demonstrated their Christian faith through disciplined, nonviolent actions.

(6) History's definitive incarnation is Jesus the Christ dying on a cross to reveal the suffering love which eternally is in the heart of God. That incarnation is both our example and our inspiration.

(b) Today's texts point to the centrality of Christ as the Christian community's example.

(1) Peter suggests that Jesus' suffering, death, and resurrection are models for incarnating God's concern for persons and structures. John uses pastoral imagery to illustrate the way of a servant of God. The authentic shepherd knows and fulfills his responsibilities. He genuinely cares for persons and seeks to minister to their deepest needs.

(2) Both passages are reminders that a person's identity—who am I?—is tied inseparably with responsibility—what am I to do? Identity and responsibility are two sides of the same coin. Who we are is rooted in whose we are. Whose we are defines how we invest ourselves.

(3) We find life is worth living as we are instrumental in bringing together the brokenness of human lives. Theologians describe this process as reconciliation. God reconciles persons through Christ; we are the instruments to help make it happen.

(c) Today's struggle for deliverance from the threat of meaninglessness can be satisfied. The search for a life worth living may lead through agonies and ecstasies, but it will lead to new faith and hope if we encounter the resurrected Christ and incarnate his spirit of reconciling love in society. Jesus Christ, the good shepherd, offers life infinitely worth receiving and sharing.—William H. Likins in *Selected Sermons*.

## Illustrations

ENDANGERED LEGACY. Yosemite National Park is known the world over for its revelation of God's creative power. But an accident has happened to Yosemite and to the giant sequoia there, and that accident is modern man. Yosemite is known as the slum of the national parks. Natural features which took millions of years of God's planned evolution to come into being are facing mutilation and distortion, and the big trees which are older than Christian history are dying because in less than a century man has changed the conditions which have encouraged their growth. Will our children's children and their children's children be able to view the natural wonders and thrill at the power of God? The warning is written in the National Park leaflet: "Take care, there are enough visitors to the Mariposa Grove to love it to death."—Albert H. Babcock.

REVERENCE. One of Scotland's foremost writers was walking one day near a mountain in Skye. He came near a hut in which lived an old man he had known many years. Seeing him with head bowed and bonnet in his hand, he waited awhile, then quietly walked up to where the old man sat. "I did not speak to you, Sandy," the writer said, "because I thought you might be at your prayers." "Well, not exactly," the old man said, "but I tell you what I was doing. Every morning for forty years I have taken off my bonnet here to the beauty of the world."—Katherine Bevis.

## Sermon Suggestions

THE POWER OF SIN. Text: Jas. 1:15. (1) Power to deceive. (2) Power to betray. (3) Power to separate. (4) Power to enslave. (5) Power to propagate. (6) Power to deaden.—John R. Mott.

WALKING WITH GOD. Text: Gen. 5:24. (1) A joyful walk. (See Ps. 16:11.) (2) A holy walk. (See Heb. 12:14.) (3) A daily walk. (See Luke 1:75.) (4) A rewarding walk. (See Gen. 5:24.)—Robert L. Chason.

## Worship Aids

CALL TO WORSHIP. "Make a joyful noise unto the Lord, all ye lands. Serve the Lord with gladness: come before his presence with singing. Enter into his gates with thanksgiving, and into his courts with praise: be thankful unto him, and bless his name." Ps. 100:1–2, 4

INVOCATION. Heavenly Father, we are grateful for this beautiful world thou hast created for us; for the singing birds, the radiant flowers, the blue sky, the soft breeze; for the dark night which gives way to a bright dawn; for the good earth which, when tilled by the plow, shoots forth the wheat, the corn, the beans that our hungry bodies may be fed; for the trees which will fruit and a thousand gifts which come from thy bountiful hand. Help us to share this wealth, this treasure, with all who are in need.

OFFERTORY SENTENCE. "Every one of us shall give account of himself to God." Rom. 14:12.

OFFERTORY PRAYER. Our Father, help us who claim to be Christians to bring forth fruit consistent with our profession of faith. May these tithes and offerings be so used that others may hear the glad story of thy redeeming love.

PRAYER. Almighty God, our heavenly Father, we call to remembrance thy lovingkindness and thy tender mercies, and with grateful hearts we thank thee:

For the gift of thy Son, our Lord Jesus Christ, for the story of his life and the inspiration of his example, for all the teaching of thy Holy Word;

For work we are enabled to do, for truth we are learning, for whatever of good there has been in our past lives, and for all hopes and desires that lead us on to better things;

For the beauty and the bounty of the world, for summer and winter, for seedtime and harvest, for all gifts of loveliness and use which each season brings;

For all comfort and joy of life, for our homes, our friends, and all our home blessings, for the love of our companions, for the help and counsel of those who are wiser than ourselves;

For all desire and power to help others, for the tasks and trials by which we are trained to patience, self-knowledge, and self-conquest, for everything that has brought us nearer to thyself and drawn us into truer fellowship with thee.—John Hunter.

## EVENING SERVICE

### Topic: A Message to Polluters from the Bible (Rural Life Sunday)
SCRIPTURE: Gen. 1.

What does the Bible say about ecology?

I. Individual responsibility. (See Rom. 14:12, Ezek. 18:20.) We cannot view this crisis without assessing our personal duty. We are all polluters. We all consume resources and produce waste. We often are negligent in both processes and condone negligence on the part of others.

II. That the earth, as created, was good. (See Gen. 1:31.) Ps. 19:1–6, Ps. 104, and Rom. 1:20 imply strongly that it is still good, although perhaps not as glorious as it once was (Rom. 8:19–22).

III. That the earth and its creatures belong to God. (See Ps. 24:1; Ps. 50: 10–13; Matt. 10:29; Ps. 104:31.) If God is aware of the death of one sparrow, what about the extinction of entire species?

IV. That God is concerned with how we act toward his creation. Gen. 1:28 gives us responsibility for God's creation. Think of it! Incidentally the Gen. 1:28 command to "be fruitful and multiply" appears to be one of the few we have obeyed. Just as we are responsible for our own immortal soul, we are responsible for God's handiwork. The Pentateuch has many statements directing the Jews in matters of this type. For instance they were to be careful in depositing body wastes (Deut. 23:12–13), and they were to let the land lie fallow every seventh year (Lev. 25:2–4).

V. That the cause of the crisis is sin. Some have argued that Christianity is responsible.

(a) Selfishness is responsible. (See Luke 16:13.) Many have greedily wasted a precious resource, belonging not to them but to God, for a quick profit. God teaches that land—and by implication what is on and in it—is a trust for future generations (Num. 36:5–9; Lev. 25:13–17).

(b) Laziness and ignorance are responsible. It is easier to throw a can out a car window than to take it to a trash barrel. We have encouraged an expansion in consumption but we were too lazy to think of or incapable of deducing the now obvious consequences.

(c) Waste is responsible. Probably the Bible says little about waste because people in biblical times couldn't afford to waste much.

VI. Certainty of punishment. (a) After the fall man's relation to his environment was changed for the worse (Gen. 3:17–19). After the Israelites did not allow their land to lie fallow as they had been commanded, the land was left fallow for them when they were placed in captivity (II Chron. 36:21).

(b) Rev. 6 and 8 mention disease, famine, fire, destruction of plants and fish, poisoned water, and the light darkened (by smog?). Perhaps these things will be the final result of the ecology crisis and man's other errors.

(c) Many scientists predict ultimate doom. So does God's Word. But it also predicts a new creation, a heavenly city (Rev. 21 and 22). Let us carefully tend the present creation and at the same time look forward with a reverent mixture of fear and hope, mingled with shame, to the new one.—Martin LaBar in *Christianity Today*.

## SUNDAY: MAY TWENTY-SECOND

### MORNING SERVICE

**Topic: What Sort of Man Is This?**
Scripture: Phil. 2:5–11 (neb).

I. What were the qualities that our Lord displayed? (a) He had a keen sense of humor. He is often presented as being so churchy and stuffy that he didn't even know what a smile was, but I believe he had a sense of humor. Can we imagine him keeping a straight face as he gives a group of Pharisees some practical advice, "Don't try and remove a speck of sawdust from your brother's eye while you have a two-by-four in your own"?

(b) He was a man of fairness. He comes to the defense of his disciples when they are falsely accused but never hesitates to reprimand them severely when he detects some genuine failing in them such as a lack of faith (Mark 4:40) or the attempt to turn him from his chosen path of obedience to God's will (Matt. 16:23).

(c) He was courteous. When he had need of a colt for his entry into Jerusalem he instructed his disciples to explain for whom the colt was being taken and that it would be returned immediately.

(d) He was thoughtful. Jesus would often interrupt an activity which seemed very important in order to heal someone most people would ignore. On his way to Jericho he stopped a massive throng of people in order to deal with a single man who needed his healing touch. Amid the intense drama of his seizure in the Garden of Gethsemane he restored the detached ear of Malchus, one of those who had come to arrest him and take him to the cross. Later in the midst of his own interrogation he took a moment to turn and look at Peter as the rooster crowed after his denial.

(e) He was appreciative. He was quick to observe steps of faith in the lives of others, and when individuals made a new step of faith Jesus was right there noticing, encouraging, and making them feel as though he felt the step they had just made was important.

(f) He was tactful. Jesus knew how to get his point across. He knew how to be honest without being brutally honest. When the scribes and Pharisees brought a prostitute to him he could have lectured to her in front of them. But he was tactful. After he had dispersed the crowd, he didn't bother to tell her what she already knew; instead he forgave her of her sins and told her to "sin no more." She knew he knew that she had been doing wrong, and she realized how wrong it was. He didn't want to hurt her any more than she was already hurt. His concern was to help people.

(g) He was consistent. He talked much about prayer, for example, and also made it central in his own life. The strength with which he met everyday living came from intimate conversation with his Father in heaven, and prayer was the means by which they talked.

(h) Jesus had common sense. He was able to determine what was important and what was not. Although he never hesitated to rebuke his opponents, he never made the mistake of giving needless offense. He would avoid useless conflict by leaving a particular city or region rather than sticking around simply to "prove a point." Common sense carried over into his teaching practices as well. He was not a grandstander who was looking for attention. Bravado had no place in his being.

II. There were also some things which were not present in the life of Jesus.

(a) Self-pity was absent. He never bemoaned the fact that he had no place to lay his head while the foxes had holes and the birds had nests. For him the only important thing was to be in the center of his Father's will; obedience was his watchword. While things frequently got tough it was all seen as God's will for him, and so he accepted it as that. Furthermore he was too busy helping and caring about others to spend so much time on himself that he had time to feel sorry for himself.

(b) Neither was he vindictive. Even though he was frequently mistreated, he refused to retaliate. He showed that it is possible to turn the other cheek, and he did it often. The twelve legions of angels were never called. He was unwilling to call down fire on an inhospitable village as James and John wanted him to. And maybe the single best example is Jesus hanging on the cross and crying out to his Father, "Please forgive them, for they don't know what they are doing."

(c) He had no craving for fame. His mission in life was to faithfully serve his Father in heaven, whatever that might mean, and not to win a popularity contest.

III. Three basic traits of his character should be noted. (a) The first is his humility. (1) Jesus said, "I am gentle and lowly in heart" (Matt. 11:29). To us this seems to be an odd designation. It was no less so in his day, for these words asserted an asset that the pagan world regarded as weak and despicable. No Greek writer used the word before the Christian era nor, apart from the influence of Christian writers, after. That should tell us something.

(2) Jesus had a very special relationship with his Father, and yet this did not inflate his ego. He bent down in the midst of the senseless prattering and bickering of his disciples to wash their feet. He did it to teach them humility. (See Mark 10:43–45.) Jesus was humility in action.

(b) Compassion was another trait. The real reason behind all of his miracles was compassion or concerned love and consideration. Jesus knew when people needed him. His help was offered to both the sick and the sinful, and his help was always the result of the compassion he felt for them. We can't explain that kind of love. We surely don't understand it, but we can accept it.

(c) He was at times indignant. Indignation is "anger or scorn resulting from injustice or meanness." There are things in our world that demand a show of "righteous indignation." Jesus could not stand the inexcusable sin of turning his Father's house into a marketplace. He was also indignant with his disciples when they attempted to shield him from contact with the little children. Why? Because he knew their worth, and he did not want anyone to be forcibly separated from him, especially the little children.

IV. The phrase, "Have the same attitude that Christ Jesus had," reminds every Christian of his duty to others. This is not a mere suggestion. The Greek verb is the imperative; it means, "Do it!"

(a) If people clearly see the Master in

us, they will go to great lengths to follow him or be unhappy and at odds with themselves because of their unwillingness. If they don't see the "attitude of Christ" in us, they probably won't think he is really worth following.

(b) How devoted a follower of Christ do we want to be? Do we really want him to be seen through us—in every word and in every activity every day? Jesus left the proclamation of the gospel in the hands of people just like us. This gospel is not a philosophy of life, a ritual, or something else of that nature. Our gospel is Jesus Christ. And one of his primary concerns in the last moments of his earthly life was for those followers whose responsibility it would be to demonstrate "the attitude of Christ" in their own lives and in a world that is not always accepting.—Carl C. Green.

## Illustration

HIS RETURN. E. Stanley Jones wrote about his visit to the Mosque of Saint Sophia, an amazing bit of architecture once a Christian church and now a Mohammedan center in Istanbul, the city that was once Constantinople. All Christian symbols in Saint Sophia have been wiped out and Arabic lettering put in their place. As Jones stood there he looked up over the altar at the dome. He said that his heart stood still. He grabbed the arm of his friend and cried: "Look! He's coming back!" Jones said the coatings of paint of the centuries were wearing thin, and coming through those daubs of paint was the original artist's picture of the ascending Christ. "Oh," said Jones, "you can't wipe him out. He's coming back."—John H. Townsend.

## Sermon Suggestions

WAIT, WATCH, AND WORK. (1) Wait upon the Lord, and his Spirit shall come upon you. (See Luke 24:49.) (2) Be on the watch, and see evidences of God's presence about you. (See Matt. 24:42.) (3) Work as laborers in his service, giving of what you are and have, and the power of the Christian religion shall be with you.—John H. Townsend.

REWARDS OF THE HARVEST. Text: Luke 10:2–3. (1) The reward of deliverance from the prison of self. (2) The reward of a challenge worthy of our best. (3) The reward of doing what we know will last. (4) The reward of knowing we have spent our lives for the best.—Everett W. Palmer.

## Worship Aids

CALL TO WORSHIP. "God hath exalted him, and given him a name which is above every name: that at the name of Jesus every knee should bow, of things in heaven, and things in earth, and things under the earth; and that every tongue should confess that Jesus Christ is Lord, to the glory of God the Father." Phil. 2:9–11.

INVOCATION. Almighty and everlasting God, whom the heaven of heavens cannot contain, much less the temples which our hands have built, but who art ever nigh unto the humble and the contrite: grant thy Holy Spirit, we beseech thee, to us who are here assembled; that cleansed and illumined by thy grace, we may worthily show forth thy praise, meekly learn thy word, render due thanks for thy mercies, and obtain a gracious answer to our prayers.

OFFERTORY SENTENCE. "Every man hath his proper gift of God, one after this manner, and another after that." I Cor. 7:7.

OFFERTORY PRAYER. Almighty God whose loving hand hath given us all that we possess: grant us grace that we may honor thee with our substance, and remembering the account which we must one day give, may be faithful stewards of thy bounty.

PRAYER. O God, for whom no morn arises and no evening sets but who art revealed to us in the tender light of the dawn and the shadowy mystery of the night, we bow before thee with grateful and reverent hearts. In all things beautiful we see the infinite artistry of thy love, but we would be sensitive and aware. We would have hearts that thrill to spring's first "flutes and drums" and miss not the hidden splendor of simple things. Grant unto us the wonder of childlike hearts, and may we never fail to rejoice in the love of parents, the faithfulness of friends, and the quiet heroism of the many who suffer. Enlarge our sympathies and help us to respond to all human anguish and all human need. May we never forget those anywhere to whom life seems a bitter battle. So far as may be, let us bow beneath their burdens and share their pain. Let us see life through the eyes of Jesus and feel life with his great heart.—Roy A. Burkhart.

## EVENING SERVICE

**Topic: The Meaning of the Ascension for Today** (Ascension Sunday)
SCRIPTURE: Luke 24:50–53.
I. The ascension points us to the "spiritualizing of religion," to use James S. Stewart's word. Prior to the ascension the disciples depended upon his presence. Even after the resurrection they still waited for his unexpected visits. But with the ascension all of this became not the visible but the invisible

presence. Now the Holy Spirit could make God real to anyone at any time. Sight has given way to faith. "Blessed is he who believed but has not seen." Faith finds its supreme opportunity because of the ascension.

II. The ascension is directly related to the whole doctrine of our Lord's high priestly life in heaven. While the language that speaks of Jesus sitting at the right hand of God refers to honor and dignity and not to locality, there is an underlying truth it is meant to convey that is of utmost importance. Indeed it is the "consistent belief of the New Testament that Jesus ascended to make intercession for us." (See Rom. 8:34; Heb. 7:25.) Jesus thus ascended not to end his work for us but to continue it. So we do not conceive of a Christ at rest but of one whose activity for us is uninterrupted even now. This is "good news" indeed.

III. The ascension points us to a pledge of the heavenly life. We usually associate that with Easter, but in fact the resurrection stopped short of the life eternal. It could have ended in Christ vanishing from the disciples or even to die again. The ascension, however, points to the life beyond. Thus James Denny could say, "The ascension is the proof that manhood is destined for heaven and not for the grave."—Kenneth R. Callis.

# SUNDAY: MAY TWENTY-NINTH

## MORNING SERVICE

**Topic: Promise of the Spirit** (Pentecost)
SCRIPTURE: John 16:4–15.
I. *Promise of help.* (See vv. 4–7.) (a) Walking with Jesus must have been an exciting experience. Christians today sometimes express the wish to have been present when Jesus healed the blind man, raised Lazarus from the dead, or cast demons from the Gadarene.
(b) The disciples cherished these mo-

ments and their relationship with the Master. The news that Jesus would leave them was distressing (John 16:6). How could they carry on without him? Perhaps these men felt like quitting.
(c) As always the sovereign wisdom of God had devised a plan to provide for the needs of these disenheartened men. They would not be left alone. Jesus did say "I go" but he hastened to add, "I will send."
(d) The Father knows the inadequacy of the human spirit. So he provided the

Holy Spirit to dwell in the believer, filling up the void (John 14:16, 17). Jesus described the Spirit's main function by calling him "the Comforter" (16:7). Thus all believers are guaranteed the presence of a divine helpmeet who is prepared to provide assistance in living the Christian life. The apostle Paul offers one example of the kind of assistance we can expect from the Holy Spirit (Rom. 8:26).

II. *Promise of power.* (See vv. 8–11.) (a) Have you ever told anyone he was doing something wrong, there was a better way of life than he was experiencing, or that he would be held accountable for his actions? If so you are fully aware that these are among the most difficult of all tasks. Yet the Christian is continually called upon to suggest these things among his fellow human beings.

(b) A believer who faithfully proclaims the gospel (Mark 16:15) will find himself deeply involved in these difficult duties: telling others they have sinned, there is a better way of living, and that all must face a judgment of their lives. Even the casual observer can recognize that most people will not respond favorably to such news.

(c) The Christian need only present the gospel; the Holy Spirit will do the convincing. Our logic or persuasive ability cannot get this job done. Only the Spirit's power, working on the heart of man, can accomplish the task of conversion. He alone convinces men of what they are, what they can be, and where they are going.

(d) That anyone today would believe the message given by a crucified Jew almost two thousand years ago is truly amazing. That we would change our entire lifestyles because of such conviction is almost unbelievable. What better demonstration of the Holy Spirit's power to reprove could we find?

III. *Promise of guidance.* (See vv. 12–15.) (a) Jesus spent approximately three years training the apostles. Nevertheless there was much more they needed to know if they were to be effective servants. With Jesus departing the twelve needed continuous teaching. The Master provided that through the Holy Spirit.

(b) One might think the Holy Spirit would emphasize his own ministry. Not so. Jesus plainly states the goal of the Spirit's work: "He shall glorify me [Jesus]." The assistance given by the indwelling Spirit, the power of the Spirit as displayed in conversion, and the guidance of the Spirit as he leads to truth—all are done to elevate the name of Jesus.

(c) Later the apostle John shares the promise of guidance with all believers (I John 2:27). And that guidance will not vary from what the apostles received. Its goal will be to glorify Christ. We can be sure that those who use the Holy Spirit to glorify self or even the Holy Spirit are misusing the Holy Spirit.

(d) Concerned Christians will seek the Spirit's guidance daily. They will guard against making their own ideas sound like guidance from the Holy Spirit. When the Word of God, circumstances, and our inner motivation are in complete agreement we are probably safe to assume the Holy Spirit is guiding.— Jerry M. Paul in *The Lookout.*

## Illustrations

THE CHRISTIAN LIFE. In periods of theological uncertainty a description of the Christian life may be the only way to restore order and perspective. Prior to the creation of theological systems, Christianity can only be described as a life. And when the intellectual framework of an age is called into question, that may be the form theology must take again.—Paul Hessert.

WORLDLINESS. The church is becoming so much like the world that it no longer has the power to change the world. Instead of the church making the world more Christian, the world is making the church more worldly.— Gerald Ensley.

## Sermon Suggestions

THE HOLY SPIRIT AND CHRISTIAN GROWTH.

Text: John 14:26. (1) The Holy Spirit helps us grow in knowledge. (See John 16:13.) (2) The Holy Spirit helps us grow into spiritual maturity. (See Col. 1:27–28.) (3) The Holy Spirit helps us grow in holiness. (See Rom. 8:26.) (4) The Holy Spirit helps us walk in the way of the divine law of conduct. (See Gal. 5:16.)—Ard Hoven.

LIVING UNDER PRESSURE. Scripture: Luke 14:15–24. (1) The pressure of time. (See Ps. 90:12; Mark 6:30–32; Eph. 5:15.) (2) The pressure of task. (3) The pressure of temptation. (See Luke 4:1–13; I Cor. 10:13; Jas. 1:13–14.) (4) The pressure of tension. (See Rom. 7:15–25; 12:2; Eph. 6:10–18.)—Emil Kontz.

## Worship Aids

CALL TO WORSHIP. "Blessed is the man that trusteth in the Lord, and whose hope the Lord is." Jer. 17:7.

INVOCATION. Almighty God, regard, we beseech thee, thy church, set amid the perplexities of a changing order and face to face with new tasks. Fill us afresh with the spirit of Pentecost that we may bear witness boldly to the coming of thy kingdom and hasten the time when the knowledge of thyself shall encircle the earth as the waters cover the sea.

OFFERTORY SENTENCE. "Seek ye first the kingdom of God, and his righteousness, and all these things shall be added unto you." Matt. 6:33.

OFFERTORY PRAYER. O thou source of all light, open our blind eyes to see the beauty of the world as thy gift, and grant us the will and the wisdom to do our part in bringing thy light into dark places.

PRAYER. O God, our Father in heaven, we give thee thanks for this opportunity to come together in this holy place as Christian people and to draw nigh unto thee in spirit and in truth. Our Father, we thank thee for Jesus Christ, thy Son our Lord, the one who hast shown us that thou art indeed the God of great love and compassion; we thank thee for him who is our way to thee, who gives us life that is abundant and beyond death, and who is the truth that frees us from that which is false and hateful and unloving.

O God, we are a Christian church, a part of the church created by our Lord Jesus Christ that now extends throughout this world, in every land, among every people. We pray that as a church we may be always faithful and trusting and obedient to thee.

Our Father, we are different in so many ways. We are all individuals with our own particular backgrounds and our own peculiar needs. And yet, our Father, we recognize how much alike we are in so many ways. We know that we are all sinners, that we have fallen short of the mark thou hast set for us, and that we have been selfish, proud, lazy, and disobedient. We have been fearful when we should have been confident and trusting. We have felt utterly alone and been filled with despair when we should have rejoiced in the still small voice that comes from thee to those who will listen with their whole heart.

We are all alike in our great need of thee. We need to know of thy love for us, the love of the Father for his wayward children; we need thy forgiveness; we need thy companionship and strength as we walk and travel through this earthly life. We need thee, O God, to give us purpose, to give us direction, to take us out of our confusion, to make some deep sense out of our days, and to give us understanding and hope, even in those times of trouble and sorrow and death. And, O God, we are all so much alike, because we need each other in so many ways.—Gordon H. Reif.

## EVENING SERVICE

### Topic: The Holy Spirit and Peter's Hang-Ups

SCRIPTURE: Acts 10.

"Hang-up" is a modern slang phrase that is used to refer to a mental or emotional attitude that becomes an impediment to a person's living life to its fullest. The text is a story of the overcoming of hang-ups. In the events surrounding the encounter of the apostle Peter and the Roman centurion Cornelius, one sees the Holy Spirit busily removing some hang-ups that seriously impeded Peter in his role as an apostle and threatened to divert the church from its course of becoming the "body of Christ" for all men.

I. One of the hang-ups that fell through the power of the Holy Spirit was the hang-up of institutional religion.

(a) Christianity had clothed itself in the institutions of Judiasm. The synagogue, the moral and cultic law, and especially the institution of circumcision were held very sacred by Christianity as a sect of Judaism. But in this circumstance the Holy Spirit placed Peter, who was always considered a conservative by New Testament writers, in a situation in which he had to get past the hang-up of loyalty to these institutions. Here were uncircumcised men whose witness was so strong that he could not deny them entry into the fellowship of the church—the first non-Jews that did not become Jews before being baptized into the Christian faith.

(b) Sometimes today's church has to overcome the hang-ups of the institution's preoccupation with the number on roll, attendance, finances, conferences, boards, etc., in order to be free to be the church.

II. A second hang-up that fell in Peter's life and in the life of the church in the encounter of the apostle and Cornelius was the hang-up of the sacred versus the secular.

(a) This was a prominent idea in Judaism as may be seen in the reference to the "clean" and the "unclean" in Peter's vision (vv. 10–15). In the Judaism of Jesus' day there had developed a sharp division between that which was holy and the rest of life. Thus everyday life was far removed from what was holy by the walls of the temple and a special day in which the circumstances of normal life were suspended so that man would not contaminate his worship.

(b) In Matt. 25 Jesus clearly tells us that our true "religious" worship is in service to "the least of his brothers." Our worship in our churches can be profane if in it we hoard the presence of God in the confines of that time and place and negate his presence in his world and among its people. On the other hand the lowliest talk and even our play become holy when done in awareness of his presence and in the love of his children.

III. Peter and the early church had to get rid of the hang-up of the differences between men.

(a) As an offspring of Judaism the church inherited the idea that Jews were a superior race as the chosen people of God. This was not a tenet of their scripture but a development of man's vanity that crystallized into an accepted idea. The Jews shunned gentiles and Samaritans, and even those who received Judaism and were circumcised were relegated to an inferior place among the congregation.

(b) The most obvious revelation of the vision that Peter had at the house of Simon the tanner was that this hang-up must go. In the vision, the Holy Spirit affirmed that God loved the gentile as well as the Jew and that God had bigger plans for the church than to be a racially exclusive society.—Joseph H. Bulington, Jr.

## SUNDAY: JUNE FIFTH

### MORNING SERVICE

Topic: **Understanding Faith**

Faith, Calvin says, is "a steady and certain knowledge of the divine benevolence toward us which, being founded on the truth of the gratuitous promise in Christ, is both revealed to our minds and confirmed to our hearts by the Holy Spirit." There are at least five things in this highly compressed definition that can help us toward a fuller understanding of faith.

I. *Faith is knowledge.* It is not amorphous or blurry. It has a content. In Calvin's case the content is defined as "the divine benevolence," God's graciousness and well-being toward us.

II. *Faith is assured knowledge.* It is "steady and certain." This is the point at which contemporary persons may have great difficulty with Calvin's definition. How can one talk about "steady and certain knowledge" in a time when everything that we know and believe seems to be under attack and foundering? It is important to see clearly what Calvin means by "steady and certain knowledge." He does not mean that believers have no doubts—Calvin has some wonderfully human passages on doubt—or that all things are crystal clear to persons of faith. He means rather that enough is clear so that we can trust God for the rest.

III. *Faith is existential.* (a) The word of course is not Calvin's, but what the word means to us today is what Calvin meant when he said that faith's knowledge was of "the divine benevolence *toward us.*" Existential truth, Kierkegaard said, is truth that is true for me. And Calvin's concern, at least in this regard, is similar to Kierkegaard's.

(b) Calvin displays extraordinarily little interest in God's inner being; the concern is always with God in relation to us: "The apprehension of faith is not confined to our knowing that there is a God but chiefly consists in our understanding what is his disposition towards us. For it is not of so much importance to us to know what he is in himself as what he is willing to be to us. We find therefore that faith is a knowledge of the will of God respecting us."

IV. *Faith is a gift.* (a) This is not merely a psychological insight propounded to protect mortal creatures from prideful assertions that they can create faith themselves or work their way up into God's presence by dutiful striving, important as those protections may be to a Calvinist. Rather the recognition that faith is a gift is one of the consequences of the content of this particular kind of faith.

(b) A benevolent deity is one who engages in self-offering, whose will toward us is good, who desires our well-being, and therefore reaches out to us even before we are aware that there is a God. Calvin adds to the content of what we may already know of such a deity by telling us specifically that faith is "founded on the truth of the gratuitous promise in Christ," i.e., the grace that always is there first. While we can respond we can never initiate; the most we can do is receive a gift.

(c) Calvin tells us that faith is both "revealed . . . and confirmed . . . by the Holy Spirit." Here too the initiative remains with God. Revelation is a gift from God, and God's power enables us to receive it.

V. *Faith is a relationship* involving the whole person. (a) While it is indeed "revealed to our minds," it is also "confirmed to our hearts," i.e., given to the whole person. It is important that Calvin mentions both mind and heart in the same breath. Stress on the mind alone would reduce faith to dry intellectualism; stress on the heart alone would enlarge it to vague sentimentality. The gift to mind and heart confronts us with the giver of the gift and invites us to enter into living relationship with God.

(b) We emphasized that faith is "founded on the truth of the *gratuitous* promise in Christ." But we do not enter into relationship with a "promise." We must therefore inflect the same statement in a different way: Faith is "founded on the truth of the gratuitous promise *in Christ.*" The nature of this particular promise is that it comes to us in personal terms, in a life to which we can make response but more importantly in a person to whom we can relate.— Robert McAfee Brown in *A.D.*

## Illustrations

EXUBERANCE. God created with seemingly mad exuberance. From our human viewpoint there is too much creation altogether—too many stars, too many galaxies, too many billions of light years, too many species of plants, animals, fish, birds, insects, germs, viruses, too many races among humankind, too many languages, too many cultures, too many religions.

It would have been much more sensible to limit the number of all those things to a manageable size. Wouldn't one race, one language, one religion have been enough? At the risk of being somewhat anthropomorphic, one might characterize God as "showing off," creating with reckless abandon, spewing forth diversity in life in senseless superabundance so as to impress us with his powers and ingenuity.

"Perhaps God was drunk," a poet suggested to me. "What," I asked the poet, "could ever inebriate the deity?" "Why, love," she replied. "What else?"—Andrew M. Greely in *The Christian Century*.

THE NARROW GATE. The abundant life —that is the life lived to the full, realized in all dimensions—is to be reached through the narrow gate. Insignificant events may have infinite meaning, inexhaustible possibilities. In contradiction to modern opinion the fullness of life is not achieved by the quantitative accumulation of experiences. This is the tragic fallacy of romanticism at its worst, and it infects the restlessness of modern man. We may be smothered by too many experiences, lost in them, swept away by too much happening. One of the silliest passages in contemporary literature is Thomas Wolfe's lyrical desire "to ride in all the trains, read all the books, and sleep in all the beds." Under such pressures we do not exhaust events; they exhaust us. Vitality is in depth, not in quantity.—Samuel H. Miller.

## Sermon Suggestions

WHAT ARE YOU TALKING ABOUT? Text: I Sam. 23:16. (1) Talk health and not disease. (2) Talk gratitude and not complaint. (3) Talk goodwill and not suspicion. (4) Talk confidence and not despair.—Aaron N. Meckel.

THY KINGDOM COME. Text: Matt. 6:10. (1) A dream. (2) An admission of a possibility. (3) The expression of a willing heart. (4) The dedication of a determined will.—Frank B. Fagerburg.

## Worship Aids

CALL TO WORSHIP. "How beautiful upon the mountains are the feet of him that bringeth good tidings, that publisheth peace; that publisheth salvation; that saith unto Zion, thy God reigneth!" Isa. 52:7.

INVOCATION. Out of our darkness we are come to thee for light; out of our sorrows we are come to thee for joy; out of our doubts we are come to thee for certainty; out of our anxieties we are come to thee for peace; out of our sinning we are come to thee for thy forgiving love. Open thou thine hand this day and satisfy our every need. This we ask for thy love's sake.

OFFERTORY SENTENCE. "Give unto the Lord the glory due unto his name: bring an offering, and come before him." I Chron. 16:29.

OFFERTORY PRAYER. We praise thee, O God, for thy countless blessings and pray that thou wilt accept these gifts of gratitude in Jesus' name.

PRAYER. Almighty God, the source of all that we can have and all that we can hope for: grant that we may be worthy custodians of the earth in which we dwell. Make us creative so that we will not burden others. Make us conservative so that we will not squander what comes our way. Make us perceptive so that we may properly weigh our necessities against the needs of others. Make us generous so that we may give freely of what we have that others can enjoy a portion of our fortune. Remove from us all trust in anything but thee. Strengthen us in the knowledge that thou wilt always provide all that we really need. And finally by thy grace instill in us that perfect desire to be thy servants and ultimately to be with thee in thy heavenly kingdom, who reignest forever and ever, Jesus Christ, our Lord. —*The Pastor's Prayerbook*.

## EVENING SERVICE

**Topic: The Danger of Being Respectable**

SCRIPTURE: Luke 7:36–50.

I. Simon was fascinated with the possibility that Jesus might be a genuine prophet. So single-minded was his interest in this that he neglected the amenities due a guest from a host—the kiss of peace, the washing of feet, and the perfumed ointment for his head. The woman provided all three but in her own earthly way.

II. Luke is obviously driving at how gentiles received Christ where good Jews had failed. But there is more.

(a) We identify with Simon. He was totally turned off by what the woman did and by the fact that Jesus accepted it. If he were a prophet he would have known the kind of woman she was. He could see no further than that. He liked things in good order. He was a good man, a respectable man. There is the problem. It is very easy for a respectable man to forget that he too is a sinner.

(b) It is easy for a respectable man to let his values become distorted. Simon interpreted everything that happened that day in a perverted way. He saw the woman's act as one of arrogance rather than devotion. He saw Jesus' response as one of stupidity rather than compassion. "Do you see this woman?" asked Jesus. Simon could not see the woman because he was so preoccupied with the sort of woman she was.

III. We cannot forget this nameless woman. We remember what she did that day and what it meant to her and to Jesus. And we think to ourselves, "I wish I could express myself like that!" And the word of the Lord comes to us asking, "Why not?"—J. Roger Bourland.

## SUNDAY: JUNE TWELFTH

### MORNING SERVICE

**Topic: Commandments for the Home** (Children's Day.)

TEXT: Prov. 22:6.

I. Establish God's chain of command. The Bible teaches that for a Christian the head of the home is the Lord Jesus Christ. He is the head of the house, the unseen guest at every meal, the silent listener to every conversation.

II. Obey the love commandment. Jesus said, "This is my commandment, That ye love one another, as I have loved you." This love must begin in the home. Where love pervades, it is a little bit of heaven; but where there is no love, the home is a little bit of hell.

III. Show acceptance and appreciation. We accept each other as God accepts us. How long has it been since you praised

your children instead of criticizing them? David prayed for Solomon and daily praised him, and we are to praise our children daily. Praise your wife. I have found that praise goes a lot further than criticism. Everybody needs to be appreciated.

IV. Have respect for authority. Jesus Christ was under the authority of his Father in heaven. He said his meat was "to do the will of him that sent me." He lived for one thing: to fulfill the will of the Father. There is a chain of command, and the ultimate authority is God at the top.

V. Have training and discipline in the home. In many Western countries we have lost our esprit de corps, our discipline in the national life. In many cities schoolteachers are afraid to go into their classrooms. In Proverbs we read,

"Train up a child in the way he should go," not the way he wants to go or would go but the way he should go.

VI. We are not to commit adultery. God has forever put a fence around marriage and has said, "Thus far and no farther." Anyone who breaks the marriage bond in thought, word, or deed has sinned against God and against his mate.

VII. Have a working family. One of the enemies of the home today is a lack of hard work. We need homes where work is assigned and chores are given to the children. Psychologists are beginning to tell us that children, in order to function normally, need work.

VIII. Pray together and read the Bible together. If you have winsome family devotions in your home, you will be amazed at what they do for your family.

IX. Every member of the family who is a Christian ought to be concerned about the others, that all might be saved. Acts tells us that the Philippian jailer asked Paul what he should do to be saved. Paul replied, "Believe on the Lord Jesus Christ, and thou shalt be saved, and thy house." And we read further that the jailer "rejoiced, believing in God with all his house."—Billy Graham.

## Illustration

HOST OF HEROES.        In one year, lying midway between the Battle of Trafalgar and Waterloo, there stole into the world a host of heroes. During that one year, 1809, let's look at the roll of weakly newborn babies that God was going to use to challenge men's ideas of bigness. In that year William E. Gladstone was born in Liverpool, and Alfred Tennyson was born at Somersby, and Oliver Wendell Holmes was born in Massachusetts. On the very selfsame day Charles Darwin made his debut at Shrewsbury and Abe Lincoln drew his first breath in old Kentucky. Frederic Chopin was born at Warsaw and Felix Mendelssohn at Hamburg. Elizabeth Barrett Browning was born at Durham. Now the biggest thing in 1809 wasn't Napoleon the Mighty but the list of babies in the

world's baby ward. A weakness—ah, yes —nothing weaker than a newborn babe, but it was a tiny seed that God was going to use to confound the strong.— W. Kenneth Goodson.

## Sermon Suggestions

GROWING IN LOVE.        (1) Love possessive and possessed: "My beloved is mine and I am his" (S. of S. 2:16). (2) Love possessed and possessive: "I am my beloved's, and my beloved is mine" (S. of S. 6:3). (3) Love content to be possessed and no longer possessive: "I am my beloved's, and his desire is toward me" (S. of S. 7:10).

THE LIFE CHRIST OFFERS.        Text: Phil. 1:21. (1) A faith to live by. (2) A self to live with. (3) A work to live for.— Joseph Fort Newton.

## Worship Aids

CALL TO WORSHIP.        "Both young men, and maidens; old men, and children: let them praise the name of the Lord: for his name alone is excellent; his glory is above the earth and heaven." Ps. 148:12–13.

INVOCATION.        O God of mercy, in this hour in thy house have mercy upon us. O God of light, shine into our hearts. O thou eternal goodness, deliver us from evil. O God of power, be thou our refuge and our strength. O God of love, let love flow through us. O God of life, live within us, now and forevermore.

OFFERTORY SENTENCE.        "Give unto the Lord the glory due unto his name: bring an offering, and come before him: worship the Lord in the beauty of holiness." I Chron. 16:29.

OFFERTORY PRAYER.        O living Christ, help us to know the ecstasy of thine everlasting lordship that we may more perfectly become cheerful givers.

PRAYER FOR CHURCH SCHOOL LEADERS. We have a faith to share with boys and

girls in our church. We would dedicate our hearts and minds to an understanding of their needs and desires. We would teach with patience, knowing that growth and change come slowly. But we would teach with confidence, knowing the power of your truth, O God. We would teach with love, even when they are most unlovely, that they may see in us some small measure of your own great love for all mankind. Such love can only come from you. Fill our hearts with your love and your power that we may share your truth. We would teach, but we must learn from you. Give us open minds and searching hearts, O God our Creator. Disturb us with your presence. Give us a vision of your way for us, and make us restless until we seek and find your truth. We have a faith to share with boys and girls in our church. We dedicate whatever we have of skill, of love, of faith, of mind and heart to the sharing of this faith. Give us the wisdom to share it with understanding, with joy, and with power.
—Chester E. Hodgson.

## EVENING SERVICE

**Topic: Christians as Parents**

SCRIPTURE: II Cor. 6:14–18.

If you would become a Christian, here are some of the things your Christian faith would give you as you try to raise your children.

I. It would give you the ability over a period of time to develop a Christian home. There would be prayer and Bible reading in your home. You would pray, and hopefully you would lead your family in worship. If both you and your spouse were Christians, you would gradually learn to make your mealtimes a time of prayer and Bible reading, and this would have an impact in your children's lives.

II. You would develop the ability to be an example for your children. Parents who worry about their children becoming involved in alcohol and drugs but who drink themselves are being stupid. Christian parents should be smarter. There will be good literature around such a home too. And with all this the children will have a standard of conduct that they can see which will help them evaluate the influences that come into their lives.

III. You would develop a meaningful relationship to the church of the Lord Jesus Christ.

(a) One cannot be a Christian alone. The church is necessary. This means that you would gradually develop a circle of Christian friends. You would benefit from the worship services and the various societies that the church has to offer. And your children would be involved in this with you.

(b) It is a very meaningful experience for your children to observe you worshiping and to observe that there are literally hundreds of other people just like you who worship God too. This can be a powerful influence in their lives. And as the word of Christ's salvation through his death on Calvary's cross comes into their lives, they learn to trust in Jesus too and pray to him.

IV. You would take a new and vital interest in your children's education. A Christian school where Christ is honored and served in every subject has great molding power in the lives of our children. It helps them think in the name of Christ. It gives them the power of judgment that will enable them to make the choices that they will have to make for themselves.—Joel Nederhood.

# SUNDAY: JUNE NINETEENTH

## MORNING SERVICE

**Topic: Faith-functioning Fathers (Father's Day)**

SCRIPTURE: Luke 7:1–10.

Today is Father's Day. As textual material I point to the centurion with the seriously sick slave and to six faith-functioning features in the makeup of this marvelous military man who was the commanding officer for King Herod Antipas in the seaport city of Capernaum.

I. A father needs friends. (a) Who are your father's friends? Children, often unconsciously and sometimes consciously, size up their father by the friends he keeps.

(b) The centurion had a rather large circle of friends. Among them were his slave described by St. Luke as his "dear" friend, the Jewish elders of the city who were his religious friends, his unnamed friends who were with him at his house when Jesus came near, and his fondest friend Jesus. How do we know that Jesus was his friend? The centurion calls him "Lord." That's a friendly religious term for a gentile to employ in speaking of a Jew like Jesus.

(c) All fathers need the right kind of friends to satisfy their own friendship requirements, but they also need friends in order to demonstrate to their own children the value of having developed the right sort of genuine, lifetime friendships.

II. A father needs to love his nation. (a) According to the Jewish leaders, the centurion "loves our nation." A true test of love for your nation is indelibly declared in our nation's Declaration of Independence. It allows you to examine yourself as follows: "Do I hold these truths to be self-evident? That all persons are created equal? That all persons have been endowed by their Creator with several unalienable rights, and among those rights are life, liberty, and the pursuit of happiness?"

(b) The gentile centurion demonstrated his love for his nation by loving the persons of his nation, regardless of their religious affiliation—as with the Jews of the city and as with his own slave.

III. A father needs to have a money-talking, pocketbook-proclaiming appreciation for religion. (a) This centurion was a missionary-minded military man. He was a gentile, but discovering the Jews where he was stationed had no permanent place of worship, he built and then paid for a synagogue so that these Jewish citizens might worship their own God in their own way and in their own kind of church.

(b) Fathers who give skimpily to the Lord and his programs and projects usually breed sons and daughters who are skimps.

IV. A father needs to be unworthily worthy. (a) The first delegation, composed of the Jewish elders, contended, "Jesus, this centurion is worthy to have you heal his slave." The second delegation, composed of friends of the centurion, reported, "Jesus, this centurion claims that he is not worthy to have you come into his house."

(b) The realization that we are not deserving in our own eyes, providing it is an honest appraisal, may aid us in appearing to be more deserving in the eyes of our peers, in the eyes of our family, and especially in the eyes of God. A father would do well to be unworthily worthy in the confines of his own home.

V. A father needs to be a man of authority. (a) The centurion was admittedly "a man of authority." He was serving under a higher authority—King Herod Antipas. He knew how to take orders, and he did not take those orders irresponsibly. The centurion also knew how to give orders authoritatively. "I say to one, 'Go,' and he goes; and to another, 'Come,' and he comes; and to my slave, 'Do this,' and he does it." Yet he seemed to be embarrassed in the presence of one like Jesus whose authority he must have recognized as superior authority.

(b) Billy Graham has often claimed that permissiveness is to blame for many of our nation's ethical problems. "Americans," he proposes, "should begin now with the children. We must come back to the home, the church, and the educational system." There can be no wise fatherhood without judicious authority.

VI. A father needs a faith in the wonder-working power of Jesus Christ.

(a) The crowning contribution of any father to his family is his acknowledgment and his acceptance of the divine power of Jesus Christ. The centurion recognized God in Jesus Christ, and Jesus acknowledged by commenting, "I tell you, not even in Israel have I found such faith." Jesus publicly rated the centurion as having a finer functioning faith than any Jewish churchman, yet his name wasn't even on a church's roll.

(b) A father may grant his children every seemingly worthwhile wish they desire. He may shower them with the finest of toys and boats and cars. He may send them to the most prestigious schools. He may bequeath them big bundles of banknotes. But if he cannot share with them a functioning faith in Jesus Christ as divine Lord and Savior, he has failed them as a Christian father. —Leslie Conrad, Jr.

## Illustration

TRIAL AND TERROR.     When Karl Barth became professor at Goettingen he used to talk wistfully about "getting back to the pastorate," but when the opportunity came he shrank from it. Writing to his friend and collaborator, Eduard Thurneysen, he says: "I am troubled by the memory of how greatly I failed finally as a pastor of Safenwil. The prospect of having to teach children again, of having to take hold of all sorts of practical problems is really fearful to me." Theological debates and lecture rooms filled with interested hearers from all over the world presented no terrors to Barth, but a group of restless kids in a confirmation class was a sore trial.— W. B. J. Martin in *The Presbyterian Outlook.*

## Sermon Suggestions

MARKS OF A CHRISTIAN.     Text: I Cor. 11:1. (1) Spiritual vision, insight into life's meaning that goes beyond the things that can be detected by the senses of the flesh. (2) Reverence and a sense of awe and wonder in the presence of the mysterious, the unknown, and the sublime. (3) Dynamic faith and a response in gratitude for what God has done for us in Christ. (4) A life controlled by the spirit of intelligent love.

WHAT THE YEARS HAVE TAUGHT ME. Text: Neh. 2:18. (1) There is a guiding hand. (2) The Christian life must be affirmative. (3) People are greater than they know. (4) We must take a long view and see life in its entirety and not in fractions. (5) The future of the world is in the hands of good people. (6) Patience is a gift of grace. (7) To inquire in God's temple is to find his truth sure and steadfast, his promises trustworthy, his spirit illuminating, his life satisfying, his service rewarding, his redemption strengthening, and his Son my Redeemer, my Lord, and my Master. —Hugh Ivan Evans.

## Worship Aids

CALL TO WORSHIP.     "Come unto me, all ye that labor and are heavy laden, and I will give you rest. Take my yoke upon you, and learn of me; for I am meek and lowly in heart: and ye shall find rest unto your souls." Matt. 11:28–29.

INVOCATION.     Almighty God, who hast given us minds to know thee, hearts to love thee, and voices to show forth thy praise, we would not know thee if thou hadst not already found us: so assist us again to know thee with pure minds, to love thee with warm hearts, and to praise thee with a clear voice, world without end.

OFFERTORY SENTENCE.     "He that hath a bountiful eye shall be blessed; for he giveth of his bread to the poor." Prov. 22:9.

OFFERTORY PRAYER.     Cleanse and accept these our gifts, O God, and may they be used according to thy will to redeem, restore, and renew the ministries within thy kingdom.

COMMENCEMENT PRAYER.     Mighty and merciful God, maker and master of the world and its peoples, who grants to all of the human family times and spaces to be filled by learning and caring, by growth and friendship, we gather now to give witness to the filling of those spaces and to celebrate the rich rewards of one span of time together here. Be present, we pray, as we raise before you all that has gone before this day and all that is to follow.

Receive our thanks for the living and learning that have enriched the days of all who gather here—of parent and child, teacher and student, of friend with friend.

Receive our prayers that the new stage on life's way here beginning may be enlightened and enlivened by the light and life found here, strengthened and supported by the bonds of sharing woven here, received and welcomed on the sure foundation of ability and achievement acknowledged in this ceremony so rightly known as commencement.

Be present, O Lord our God, to hear our words, to know our thoughts, and to bless this new beginning.—James E. McPherson.

## EVENING SERVICE

### Topic: All In the Family

SCRIPTURE: Eph. 5:15–20 (PHILLIPS).

Paul speaks to the family about the supportive role each member is to perform if the total body is to function adequately. Phillips' paraphrased version begins, "Live life, then," and he specifically mentions seven considerations on how life is to be lived.

I. "Live life, then, with a due sense of responsibility, not as men who do not know the meaning and purpose of life but as those who do." Irresponsibility can be the death of healthy relationships.

(a) When we are irresponsible with the feelings of others, we create mental anguish, soul-crying, hurt, bitterness, and lack of self-appreciation in them. We must learn the sensitivities of others and steer clear of the damaging words that sting and burn. Irresponsibility

also surfaces in the general upkeep of a house both inside and out.

(b) When people are careless in the distribution of their possessions, when people fail to pick up after themselves, when people fail to consider others' time, energy, and needs, then the result can only be hard feelings and resentment.

II. "Live life, then . . . Make the best use of your time, despite all the difficulties of these days." If life is time and time is life, we've got to find more time for each other in our families. We've got to do this "despite all the difficulties of these days."

III. "Live life, then . . . firmly grasp what you know to be the will of God." We can't afford to omit from our lives those conscious reminders of God. Worship, Bible study, prayer, the quiet time, and good books—these we must have.

IV. "Live life, then . . . Don't get your stimulus from wine . . . but let the Spirit stimulate your souls." It's popular, so socially acceptable to drink the cocktail, the nightcap, the morale booster, the bracer. Problem drinking is America's worst drug problem and a great enemy of the home. People who are drinking more and more of Christ's Spirit are drinking less and less of the spirits. Better to be liberated by the cup of the Lord than captured by the bottle.

V. "Live life, then . . . express your joy." Learn how to laugh with each other. Put levity into life. Learn how to laugh at yourself. Learn how to say, "I love you"—sincerely. Give gifts, give love, and give praise.

VI. "Live life, then . . . Thank God for everything." That's hard. "Thank you, Lord, for this struggle we're now experiencing. Somehow make us stronger, more loving, and more humble." "Thank you, Lord, for this food." "Thank you, Lord, for teenagers—exasperating, entertaining, irritating, lovable, hatable, but thank you. We would not want to be without them." "Thank you, Lord, for parents—old-fashioned, out of step sometimes, still singing

'Sh-boom' and 'Red Sails in the Sunset.' But they really do love us, want us, and are trying to do what is best for us."

VII. "Live life, then . . , fit in with one another." (a) We find it easier to "fit out" than to "fit in." We sometimes see more that divides us than unites us.

(b) Paul said, "Because of your common reverence for Christ." Christ is the common denominator. People who are committed to him and are consciously trying to live life his way are finding ways of loving instead of hating, of pulling together instead of pulling apart, of fitting in and not fitting out.—Jerry Hayner.

## SUNDAY: JUNE TWENTY-SIXTH

### MORNING SERVICE

Topic: For God's Sake

TEXT: I Cor. 10:31.

Did you ever think of doing something simply for the sake of God? I have heard the expression, "For God's sake, do something!" many times. I have often regarded that as a form of profanity. It need not be if you really mean it. It may be instead an attempt to reach a deeper level of living. This is almost what is meant by the statement "doing the will of God" except it gets beyond the *what* to the *why*, beyond the act to the motive.

I. Look now at some of the characteristics of life *for God's sake!* There are four clearly defined in our scripture.

(a) This kind of life must be *without ostentation*. The flamboyant person who seeks to call attention to himself rather than the God he serves gets what he seeks. He is seen of men, but he cannot please God at one and the same time. Jesus said, "Let your light so shine before men [not on yourself but from yourself], that they may see your good works, and glorify your Father which is in heaven" (Matt. 5:16). But which one of us has not "played to the gallery" to win a point?

(b) The second characteristic of this kind of life is that it is life *without playacting*, without hypocrisy. Not one of us is without his masque, playing at least to some extent our parts, posturing upon the stage of life. The Greek word for playactor was *upercritos,* which we have merely transliterated into our language as "hypocrite."

(c) Life, particularly for the committed Christian, is to be *without purely personal ambition*. Ambition may not be wrong in itself, but it can get out of hand easily. The apostle Paul, looking at life before and after his Christian experience, said, "How changed are my ambitions!" (Phil. 3:7, PHILLIPS.) What he meant was that his personal air castles had melted away and had been replaced by the structure of God's purpose and plan.

(d) Life for God's sake must be lived *without sought publicity*. Deeds, prayers, and met needs are to be a part of life because they are right before God and not so that men shall praise us. The reward we receive is from God, who sees even the most secret act, who knows our innermost thought, and who will reward us in his infinite wisdom from his inexhaustible supply.

II. There are four principles which may well be helpful to us who aspire to live our lives for God's sake.

(a) The first is the principle of *voluntariness*. This principle runs through all committed Christian life. No one can even come close to being a Christian unless he wants to be. "If any man wants to come after me, let him deny himself, take up his cross and follow me" (Matt. 16:24). An intense personal desire precedes any valid Christian experience.

(b) There is the principle of *aloneness*. Basically every decision in the Christian life is a lonely one. Maybe this was what Paul was getting at in Rom. 1:17 when he spoke of "faith from beginning to end." Really in any

Christian decision there is only the person and his God. It was no accident that Moses went to Midian, Paul to Arabia, and even Jesus to the wilderness. Whether you or I go geographically apart or not, we have to drop a curtain between ourselves and this world we live in. The opening must first be only to God. In the valley of decision we can look no way but up.

(c) A third principle is *positiveness*. Our whole faith is active, not passive. The Christian acts rather than waiting to be acted upon. In each of the three duties—almsgiving, praying, and fasting —action is posited. We may refrain from doing wrong all our lives and add up to a big fat zero. Righteousness in itself is an activity, never a state. We may well say, "Do something for God's sake," particularly if we leave out the comma.

(d) A fourth principle is *self-judgment* rather than the judgment of others. Of course no one can keep from judging, but Jesus cautioned his disciples to use the same standard or a harsher one on themselves than they used on others. Instead of being harsh with myself and lenient with others, I find myself rationalizing my mistakes and castigating the mistakes of others. This certainly is not for God's sake. Rather it is for my own satisfaction.—Dotson M. Nelson, Jr.

## Illustrations

HOLLOW RUIN.    Old George C. Boldt built his castle on the St. Lawrence. He engaged the finest architects and artists in the world. He quarried the finest granite and purchased the rarest marble and mosaics and rich tapestries from all around the world to build this castle summer home as a tribute to his wife whom he dearly loved. When two million dollars had been spent and the castle was near completion, the wall of his life just tumbled in—for his beloved died. In one brief hour the castle was transformed. From a scene of great activity it quickly had become a tomb of quiet. Workmen dropped their tools. The place became deserted. Birds and bats came to make their nests in quiet dusty halls. Spiders spun their webs over fireplace and stair. Today the scene of what was planned for gaiety remains a monument to heartache, an uncompleted dream, a hollow, dusty pile of aging stone. Its towers pierce the skies and remaining windows still reflect the glimmer of the sun, but its insides are left empty—the hollow ruin of what might have been.—Charles E. Welsh.

THE GODS WE FASHION.    When Balzac lay dying he thought he was surrounded by his own fictional characters. He longed for a certain doctor from one of the novels he had written. Balzac was sure that this physician, a creation of his own imagination, could cure him. So it is with us many times. We pride ourselves that we have outgrown the need of the Savior Jesus Christ. We pick and choose from many religions such items as appeal to us. We turn away from our childhood faiths and don't bother to find a real and mature faith. Or we make a god of our own in our own image. The trouble is that such a god is no god at all. When the chips are down we call upon him in vain.— Charles M. Crowe.

## Sermon Suggestion

YOUR LIFE IS NOT SECRET.    Text: Jer. 23:24. (1) Our lives are exposed. (2) Men know all about us. (3) God looks into the heart. (See Ps. 44:21; Eccl. 12:14; Luke 12:3–4.)

## Worship Aids

CALL TO WORSHIP.    "It is good for me to draw near to God: I have put my trust in the Lord God. . . . God is the strength of my heart, and my portion for ever." Ps. 73:28, 26.

INVOCATION.    Eternal God, in whom we live and move and have our being, whose face is hidden from us by our sins and whose mercy we forget in the blindness of our hearts: cleanse us, we beseech thee, from all our offenses and deliver us from proud thoughts and vain desires, that with lowliness and meekness we may draw near to thee, confessing our faults, confiding in thy grace, and finding in thee our refuge and our strength.

OFFERTORY SENTENCE. "To do good and to communicate forget not: for with such sacrifices God is well pleased." Heb. 13:16.

OFFERTORY PRAYER. Dear Father, help us to be ever concerned to find thy way for our lives, and may we never be satisfied to give thee our second best in return for thy great gift of love.

VACATION PRAYER. Loving Father, who didst make this earth so fair, open our eyes to see its wonders and our hearts to feel its beauty. In our days of refreshment and recreation, draw us nearer to thee through the things which thou hast made. May the joy of thy sunshine, the quiet of thy forests, the murmur of thy streams, and the steadfast strength of thine everlasting hills teach us the deep secret of thy peace.

Calm our fretful spirits. Deepen the current of our shallow lives. Renew in us faith and courage, physical strength and spiritual vision, that we may know ourselves to be safely held in thy strong hands and may joyfully conform our lives to thy great purposes.

From this life, so near to Nature's heart, may we drink in new strength to help us reach the restless hearts of men. May we go back to the world and its duties, stronger, simpler, and sweeter, and thus become more worthy messengers of him who saw his Father's goodness in the sparrow's flight and his Father's love in the beauty which clothes the lilies of the field.

## EVENING SERVICE

Topic: Christ's Call to Service

TEXT: John 9:4.

It is instructive to observe that the Greek rendering here reads, "We must work the works of him that sent me," an obvious identification of our Lord Jesus with his disciples. He is showing them that association with him in the doing of the work of God is nothing less than divine service. What dignity, liberty, and urgency this brings into our Christian service!

I. *The divine obligation to service.* (a) This divine obligation expresses itself in a lifelong sense of responsibility to God. Service for the Lord Jesus Christ was not only important but imperative. In other words there was a "must" in every aspect of his redemptive work. (See Luke 2:49; John 3:15–16.)

(b) Furthermore the Savior's sense of being sent made him ever aware of his accountability to God. He never spoke or did anything without heaven's permission. We cannot afford to act independently of God for our very oneness in Christ in salvation makes us one with him in service.

II. *The divine objective in service.* In the last analysis the work of God is to bring men and women to believe on the Lord Jesus Christ. We have no idea of God's purpose in Christian service unless our ultimate objective is "warning every man, and teaching every man in all wisdom: that we may present every man perfect" (Col. 1:28). In other words evangelize them, enlist them, and then edify them for Christ and his kingdom. Our spheres of activity may be varied, but the objective is ever the same: the completion of the body of Christ through every member evangelism.

III. *The divine opportunity of service.* A sense of urgency characterized our Lord in everything he said and did. Indeed he taught and demonstrated by his life two important principles in regard to the matter of opportunity.

(a) All time must be redemptively utilized. Jesus worked to a timetable and therefore never wasted a moment.

No one has ever been great or useful in the highest sense who has not regarded time in a similar manner.

(b) All talents must be redemptively exercised. The Lord Jesus gave his all, and so must we.—Stephen F. Olford.

# SUNDAY: JULY THIRD

## MORNING SERVICE

**Topic: Controversy Is Creative**
TEXT: Acts 19:8–9.

I. Controversy can be destructive. (a) I am thinking of controversy that is belligerent, pugnacious, and hostile. I have in mind the kind of controversy that is vicious and vindictive, altogether negative in its characteristics and completely futile in its results.

(1) When controversy is demoralizing to the individual and destructive to the community, it serves no Christian purpose.

(2) When controversy drives a wedge between Christians and causes them to become bitter antagonists, its value is doubtful.

(3) When controversy destroys the working unit of the Christian fellowship, its virtue is suspect.

(4) When controversy possesses the whole thought of a people, draining both thought and feeling of all reserve energies and thus making positive and creative accomplishment impossible, its evil is apparent.

(b) Certainly controversy is not creative when it is reduced to little more than an emotionally charged and overheated argument.

(c) Can we not agree that when controversy become "personalized"—that is when the individuals come "front and center" and overshadow the basic issue —it is wrong? And can we not also agree that when it gets to the level of being harshly judgmental, cruelly vindictive, bitterly retributive on an individual basis, a person-to-person basis, it is wrong?

(d) It is precisely because this so often happens that so many of us will try to avoid controversy—sometimes at almost any cost. This is why we will say of someone, "He is a controversial person!" This is why we make the observation about someone, "I don't know why, but he is always embroiled in some kind of controversy!" This is why there are those whose common response is something like this, "Don't get me involved in that, it's too controversial!"— and we usually mean we simply cannot take the stress and strain of conflict. The conclusion is clear: for most of us controversy is undesirable and something to be avoided if at all possible.

(e) There are countless citations in the Bible where Christians are especially admonished to keep clear of controversy. Here is just one among many. The apostle Paul wrote to Timothy, "Having nothing to do with stupid, senseless controversies; you know that they breed quarrels." It can be said beyond challenge that the whole New Testament, excepting the four gospels, is concerned for the most part with the problem of controversy that had become destructive in the earliest days of the Christian church.

II. Controversy can be creative. (a) Any serious consideration of the history of the Christian religion or any survey of the saga of this nation makes persuasive the fact that all growth is brought about by change, and all change inescapably carries controversy with it.

(b) This nation was born out of controversy and has often reached its peaks of performance in days of deep controversy rather than in days of easier contentment. Controversy is accepted as a fact in our free way of life: it is written into our Constitution with its set of delicate balances, it is the theory behind our insistence upon free press, and it is established as the rationale for our whole system of justice. From the very beginning at the very heart and soul of this nation, controversy is assumed to be a necessity for a vital and free people.

(c) Controversy *can* be creative. Here stands a clear truth. And let us see that this can be documented not only in our national life but also in the historical facets of the Christian religion.

(1) In our Bible there is the record of giant issues in conflict, massive controversies. The God of the Old Testament in controversy with the forces of evil. In the New Testament our Lord Jesus Christ in constant controversy with the wiles of Satan. In the epistles the apostle Paul is in open controversy with the establishments of religion.

(2) The creative accomplishments of Christianity have been born out of the labor pains of controversy—the issue of the free man released from the tryanny of the state, the issue of the abolishment of child labor, and the issue of women's rights—all of these furthered by creative controversy within the Christian church. The apostle Paul standing firm against the pagan religions of the Roman Empire, Luther stubbornly challenging the conscience of the corrupt church of his day, and the German pastors of the Confessional Church defying the edicts of Hitler.

(3) One can be persuaded that the great creative moments of the Christian church in history have been moments when controversy was sharpening the minds and stirring the hearts of the true believers. And one can at least consider the possibility that these troublous and turbulent times for the present-day Christian church may in the view of history be judged to be another moment of creativity, a moment of growth through change, a moment when God uses controversy to serve his purpose.

III. There ought to be a place for open thought and open discussion within the church where honest effort is made to turn the light of the Christian faith on the vital issues of our time.

(a) I believe that moving waters are full of life and health and still waters carry the stuff of stagnation.

(b) I believe in creative controversy—a matching of honest and sincere minds to try to determine Christian truth when good men differ as to what is right.

(c) I believe controversy can be creative when it is carried on with mutual respect, in honesty and good faith, with courtesy and humility.

(d) I believe that controversy, when it is open-minded and good-spirited, can contribute new facts to our common thought, broaden our experience, furnish fresh information and expand our general knowledge. I believe that controversy can be stimulating, exciting, and challenging, and that it can lead to better understanding.—Charles L. Copenhaver.

## Illustrations

ACTS AND PRINCIPLES. Should our fathers and mothers see us simply standing before statues of the past, unheeding of the pressing problems of our day, irresponsive to the call for radical new forms for our day, they would lash out in disappointment and anger and cry, "Shame; you have denied your birthright!" So alive are the principles from which they leaped out to encounter their day that we must do our best to identify and apply those dynamics to our contemporary conditions. Is our heritage the acts or the principles? If it is simply the acts of past generations, then we can settle back and enjoy the liberty they have bought us with so great a price, shoot off our fireworks, and have another beer. But if it is the principles of dynamic response to the cry for liberty, then we like them must follow our God into the arena where he is involved in the affairs of men.—Louis H. Evans, Jr.

TEMPERED FREEDOM. Historical dislocation can bring an enormous sense of freedom of not being bound by the past and of creating oneself at each moment of one's existence. Yet characteristically a philosophy of absolute freedom is usually a philosophy of the absurd; the signs of this freedom are not joy and triumph but nausea and dread; and its possessors are not the creators but the strangers and outsiders of the universe. Few men, young or old, ordinary or extraordinary, can live contentedly, much less joyously, without some relationship other than total freedom. Paradoxically it is comforting and perhaps necessary to feel one's freedom limited.—Kenneth Keniston.

## Sermon Suggestions

WHOSE LAWS IN WHAT ORDER?    Text: Luke 20:25. (1) Caesar is Caesar, and some things belong to him. (2) Caesar is not God, and many things do not belong to him. (3) For God's sake we should render unto Caesar the things that are Caesar's, but for Caesar's, as well as God's sake, we had better render unto God the things that are God's. (4) Our business, our country's business, and every country's business is to be about God's business.—Melvin E. Wheatley, Jr.

CHRISTIANS IN CRISIS.    (1) Keep cool. (2) Keep your perspective. (3) Keep a balanced view. (4) Keep the Christian spirit.

## Worship Aids

CALL TO WORSHIP.    "And we declare unto you glad tidings, how that the promise which was made unto the fathers, God hath fulfilled the same unto us their children." Acts 13:32–33.

INVOCATION.    Almighty God, who in thy providence hath made all ages a preparation for thy kingdom: we beseech thee to make ready our hearts for the brightness of thy glory and the fullness of thy blessing.

OFFERTORY SENTENCE.    "Bring ye all the tithes into the storehouse, saith the Lord, [and I will] open the windows of heaven, and pour you out a blessing." Mal. 3:10.

OFFERTORY PRAYER.    We thank thee, O God, for another anniversary of our nation's independence and pray that this rich gift many be an opportunity to serve one another in love.

PRAYER.    Almighty and eternal God, we thank thee for our country. We are grateful for her hills and valleys, her fertile soil, her trees, her plains and mountains. Especially we thank thee for our fathers, who seeking a new life dared heavy seas to come to these shores. We are grateful that our country was founded in thy name and that our fathers revered thy holy Word. We would not forget thee now. Forgive us when we seek material power and material influence alone. Forgive us if in our prosperity we have condescended to others. Forgive us if we have neglected the admonition of our fathers that we build on thee, the Rock of salvation. We confess our mistakes and humbly ask thy forgiveness.

Make us a great nation, full of truth and righteousness. We have built our nation upon the knowledge that all men are equal in thine eyes. May we love every child of thine. We would be what we profess to be—a nation with liberty and justice for all—a nation taking its direction from thee, the most high God.

O God, prompt thy children to honor thy name. Command the fire of thy truth to fall upon us, burn out the dross of selfishness, and cause us to praise thee in our lives.

Give direction to our leaders. Teach them to express in word and deed the spirit of justice. Teach them so to discharge their duties that other nations may see our true values and honor our decisions. If any of our leaders seek temporal glory, rebuke them. If any look only for the dawn of tomorrow, may they be prompted to look into the long days of the years that the foundations of thy kingdom may be established.

We commend this nation to thy care. May she trust in thee. May she be so dedicated to thy ways that all the world may look upon her and be guided to thee. Let our nation know that she cannot purchase life that shall never end with a price. Only thou canst give that endless life, and thou dost not give it for silver and gold. Thou dost give it in love. May we receive it through dedicated lives. May our nation be great in thy name.—Albert Buckner Coe.

## EVENING SERVICE

### Topic: Help for a Difficult Task

TEXT: Josh. 1:6, 9, 18.

What work has the Lord given you to do? Does it tower menacingly over you? Are you equal to the task? If it is God's will for you to do this work, take heart, be strong, and be courageous. His resources are available to you.

I. *By God's grace we are stimulated by responsibility.* Because Joshua had to lead the children of Israel in the conquest of Canaan, he did it.

(a) We were made for responsibilities. A child gives evidence that he is maturing normally when he gradually assumes more responsibility. To Adam was given the task of subduing the earth. To Eve was given the task of motherhood. A barber who frequently preaches to his captive audience a two-point sermon—work and pray—quoted to a customer a German proverb he heard as a child, "Work makes life sweet."

(b) We are made by responsibilities. A task will test our mettle, challenge hidden powers, and bring the soul to the light. A teacher said to his students, "Sometimes when I am in a distant city and tempted to do something wrong, I think of you, and it keeps me safe."

II. *By God's grace we are supported by his own presence.* Joshua had the assured support of God in his endeavor. Thus his battle had cosmic dimensions.

(a) What we do is of special concern to the God who gave us our task. Nothing escapes his notice. His eye is upon us. He is unceasingly awake to care for us. He "knoweth the way of the righteous" (Ps. 1:6).

(b) God is a power both outside us and within us. He works independently of us.

(c) He works through us. He uses the activity of the human mind, the human tongue, and the human hand. He uses the power of Christian love and of intercessory prayer. Prayer opens the door to the work of God in our lives.

III. *By God's grace we are strengthened by human comradeship.* Other men went with Joshua. They shared his task and outlook, and they gave strength to his endeavor.

(a) God's hand in our lives is strengthened by the help we give to one another. Jesus called twelve "to be with him." He sent out the seventy in his name. This is the business of the church: "We ought to see how each of us may best arouse others to love and active goodness, not straying away from our meeting, as some do, but rather encouraging one another, all the more because you see the Day drawing near" (Heb. 10:24-25, NEB).

(b) Good friends and helpful companions make you think better, pray better, live better, and work better. Charles H. Spurgeon never stood before his congregation to preach without the assurance of the prayers of his deacons.

IV. *By God's grace we are stabilized by obedience.* What Joshua did about God's revealed will would determine his success or failure.

(a) What is obedience? To obey is simply to do what God shows to be his will. Sometimes the directions are explicit in the Bible. At other times the issues must be clarified through prayer. We may need the special counsel of mature Christian friends. Answers to questions about the will of God are really not difficult to find for those who really want to know.

(b) If we are disobedient to God, we may fail. But God will not fail. Though God often accomplishes his pure purpose with the cooperation of human beings, he is not utterly dependent on their help. It is within God's power to make even the wrath of men to praise him. However, God's best work is done through those committed to him. It is up to us as to whether we shall be mere instruments of God or partners of God. —James W. Cox.

# SUNDAY: JULY TENTH

## MORNING SERVICE

**Topic: Peter Speaks to Our Churches**
SCRIPTURE: I Pet. 1:13–16.

I. *Gird up your minds.* (a) Peter was saying, pull yourselves together. He was telling Christians to get ready for hard theological thinking. People of his time got ready for hard work by pulling up their robes and tucking them into their belts. Today we say we "roll up our sleeves" when we tackle a difficult task. This is the image: Christian people should prepare for the tough work of understanding the Christian faith.

(b) This advice the Christian church needs to hear. Many present the Christian faith as an elementary, easily understood thing. Little tracts offer five easy steps to spiritual growth, a simple plan of salvation, a do-it-yourself faith.

(c) Peter was saying that being a Christian does not excuse one from hard theological thinking. We must be able to give a sound reason for our Christian profession; we must wrestle with the meaning of salvation, sin, the Holy Spirit, and eternal life. The popular cry for a simple gospel is not in keeping with the Bible as a whole and is certainly not in keeping with Peter's letter.

II. *Be sober.* (a) In our terms this means keep cool, keep steady. This is a profound need, especially for those who see the Christian faith in overly emotional terms. Peter was urging the importance of keeping calm and steady in hostile circumstances.

(b) "Sober" brings to mind the characteristics of one who does things to excess, appears imbalanced and foolish to others, and is impulsive and often repulsive.

(c) "Drunk with religion" describes religious fanatics who are sure their way is the only way and are unable to make reasonable or forgiving judgments. When Peter told his readers to be sober, he was telling them to be steady, to be thoughtful, and to be forgiving in their Christianity. He knew that there is a vast difference between religious fanaticism and religious enthusiasm. Enthusiasm we desperately need; fanaticism we need to be done with.

III. *Be holy.* (a) When Peter advises his readers to be holy, he does not mean to be self-righteous. He does not mean to be holier-than-thou. The holier-than-thou person probably scares off as many as he reaches. The Christian who is always pointing to his halo is forbidding and often repulsive.

(b) To be holy means literally "to be set apart for a special purpose" or in our language to be God's agent for reconciliation. The ancient Jews looked on themselves as God's chosen race and failed to see that meant special responsibility, not special privilege. More will be expected of us than of those who do not profess Christianity.

(c) Peter is specific. He says to be holy in all our conduct and not just in some things, not just on certain days of the week, and not just in some circumstances. He knew that the best argument for Christianity is found in those who embody it in all conduct.—John Rutland, Jr.

## Illustrations

DANGEROUS FAITH. A young man was converted to Christ in India. Someone asked him how he became interested in Christianity. He said: "Because my family warned me it was dangerous. I wanted to know more about a religion so dynamic that it was dangerous."—Charles M. Crowe.

SUMMER PARABLE. Now it came to

pass that, as the time of vacation drew near, a certain member of the church bethought him of cool streams where fish were found and his children thought of sandy beaches by the sea and his wife thought of the mountains. And this church member spoke and said: "Lo, the hot days come, and my work lieth heavy upon me. Come, let us depart and go where fishes do bite and where the cool winds bring refreshment and the land is beautiful about us." "Thou speakest words of wisdom," said his wife. "Yet three, nay, even four, things must we do ere we go." "Three things I think of but not a fourth," said her husband; "that we ask our neighbors to minister unto our flowers, that we arrange for our grass to be mowed and watered, that we have our mail forwarded; but no other thing cometh to my mind." "The fourth is like unto other three but greater than all," said his spouse, "even this, that thou dig into thy purse and pay the church pledge in order that the good name of the church may be preserved, that the heart of the treasurer be made glad, and that it may be well with thee. For verily I say unto thee, thou hast more money now than thou will have when thou dost return."

## Sermon Suggestions

WHERE CHRIST IS LOST.    Text: Luke 2:46. (1) He is lost when his disciples give primary attention to secondary concerns. (2) He may be lost in liturgy and forms, the very acts which are intended to convey him to his people. (3) He is lost in bad personal relations within the church.—Edward L. R. Elson.

WHAT'S IN YOUR NETS?    Scripture: Luke 5:1–11. (1) Unrewarding labor. (2) Hesitating obedience. (3) Living proof. (4) Overwhelming reverence. (5) Catching men.—Ron Kerr.

## Worship Aids

CALL TO WORSHIP.    "If a man love me, saith Jesus, he will keep my words: and my Father will love him, and we will come unto him, and make our abode with him." John 14:23.

INVOCATION.    Eternal and ever-blessed God, grant this day light to the minds that hunger for the truth and peace to the hearts which yearn for rest. Grant strength to those who have hard tasks to do and power to those who have sore temptations to face. Grant unto us within this place to find the secret of thy presence and to go forth from it in the strength of the Lord.

OFFERTORY SENTENCE.    "If thou draw out thy soul to the hungry, and satisfy the afflicted soul; then shall thy light rise in obscurity, and thy darkness be as the noon day." Isa. 58:10.

OFFERTORY PRAYER.    Our Father, help us to trust thee more fully and to accept our responsibility toward thy work and thy children who are our brethren in Christ.

PRAYER.    God, whom we gather to worship, rejoices that you are here in this company of his people. Before you is a cross, reminding you of God's suffering, serving love for you. Before you is a baptismal font, reminding you of his forgiveness and of his ability to give new lives for old. Before you is a Bible, reminding you of his promises and of his commands and of his past actions for his people. Before you is a table, reminding you of God's own presence with his people in fellowship and love. Come, let us worship God.

O God, who always keeps watch over mankind collectively and who knows us each with our particular joys and sorrows, we worship you, we adore and praise you. Help us each to receive your love and your discipline. Refresh us, one and all, with unexpected—and unmerited—mercies. Startle us, everyone, with new commands for our obedience for this very day, for this very week. Because we know you, through Jesus Christ, as personal, powerful, and purposeful, we are bold to pray to you, together, as

Jesus taught his disciples to pray . . . —David M. Currie.

## EVENING SERVICE

**Topic: No Greater Joy**
TEXT: III John 4.

I. *The greatest joy: "I have no greater joy."* There are always plenty of prophets of pessimism who see nothing but gloom and doom for the church. But John could see, in spite of all, the gospel prevailing. And it did. Not many years later Christianity had covered the entire known world. This beloved apostle had great faith in the power of the gospel; therefore it was his greatest joy to see it conquer.

II. *The greatest news: "to hear."* Like a general hearing of the triumph of his armies in battle, John was glad to hear of eager and earnest saints walking in the light. The sweetest sounds that giants of faith like John, Luther, Wesley, and others longed to hear were shouts of victory from saints marching to Zion.

III. *The greatest relationship: "my children."* We see that sin causes separation. Christianity brings a bond of unity that exceeds all other relationships and earthly ties. John seemed to be telling Gaius the extent of his love for the souls he had brought to Christ and the churches under his care when he referred to them as his children.

IV. *The greatest walk: "walk in truth."* When asked how he conquered the world, Alexander the Great replied, "By not wavering." John's greatest joy was to see his children in Christ going steadily heavenward.

V. *The greatest way: "truth."* Christ had said that he was the truth. The prospect of truth is so wonderful that Christ proclaimed it to be pure joy. So the loving apostle, who was so close to Christ, found the greatest joy in seeing the joy of Christ in the lives of his children.—John D. Hansen in *The Preacher's Magazine.*

# SUNDAY: JULY SEVENTEENTH

## MORNING SERVICE

**Topic: Chance, Fate, or God's Will?**
TEXT: Rom. 8:28.

The Christian faith maintains that there is a God who rules the universe, who is all-power and all-love, and who cares for each of his creatures. Jesus stated that there was not a single sparrow who was forgotten by God; even the hairs on our heads are numbered. The people of biblical times believed that God sat in his heaven, watching over his children on earth; but how should we, who think in terms of solar systems and of galaxies, understand divine providence? What is it that God has "provided"?

I. God has provided for us a physical universe of order and regularity. There are evidently laws, and the elements of nature obey them. We would not want it otherwise, if on that order and regularity we depend; without it no life could exist, no science, no progress, and no civilization.

(a) These forces of nature work evidently without regard for human worth or unworthiness: fire warms the scoundrel as it warms the saint; water stills the thirst of the murderer as well as that of the missionary; cancer strikes the body of the useless playboy as that of the much-needed mother. Jesus saw that clearly when he said, "God lets his sun shine on the good and the evil, and his rain fall on the just and the unjust." We would not want it otherwise, for if the forces of nature would always treat people differently, depending on their goodness, then there would be no order and no dependability.

(b) Ours is a moral universe. Here too are laws that are valid for individuals, families, and nations. A family without a certain amount of loyalty, affection, and cooperation will go to pieces; a society without some measure of justice will not long endure; a nation based primarily upon violence and greed will soon perish.

II. God has provided us with a mind, with reason by which to observe, learn, accept, and obey these laws. What is all scientific and technological advance but the learning of the laws written into the universe? Thus it would be more correct not to speak of inventions but of discoveries.

III. God has given us freedom to make our own choices. He could have created us in such a way that we would follow unerringly and blindly the dictates of our instincts as the animals do. But then we would be hardly more than physical and moral robots, would never learn to decide and to choose, and would never become mature and real persons. Thus God, giving us freedom, took a risk with us that sometimes we might make the wrong choices and the false decisions and have to bear the consequences of them, but this is the price we have to pay for our freedom which lifts us above the level of the animals.

IV. There remain many nagging questions whenever we think of individuals. Someday, perhaps in the not too distant future, we may know the laws of the human body so well that we shall be able to prevent cancer. But what of those millions who died painful, premature deaths before this knowledge came to man? Someday the laws of navigation, of airplane construction, and of radar may be so well known that air crashes will be eliminated. But what of those many that died tragically before that?

(a) The answer must be: We do not know. We must admit that here is a mystery, as there are many more for our limited human minds. We can only say that if we knew all the answers we would be like God. But we are only men.

(1) We are like workers at an immense tapestry of which we know only the very small piece before us, while God, the master artist, sees the whole design. Or as the apostle Paul put it:

"We see in a mirror dimly . . . We know in part."

(2) Is this not one of the reasons why Christianity has always staunchly insisted that death is not the end? That this life of ours here on earth is not the complete story but only chapters one and two and three? And that where we write finis, the end, God writes, "To be continued"?

(b) Yet once in awhile the veil is lifted and we get a glimpse of a deeper, wider, and richer meaning than we usually grasp with our limited vision and understanding.

(c) God at the very time when everything seems to go wrong "provides" for us opportunities for growth and for service that enrich us already here on earth much more than any pleasures could do and that prepare us for the greater life which is to come after this. May this not be what the apostle Paul had in mind when out of a life of incredible hardship and sufferings he could write, "We know that in everything God works for good with those who love him"?—Herbert Gezork.

## Illustrations

LESSONS FROM THE REDWOODS.    First of all, they have a communal life. They are close together. Thousands of them are so close together they protect one another from storm and wind. They huddle together like cattle in a storm. In the second place, one of the distinctive characteristics of redwood trees is that they send their roots both wide and deep into the earth and intertwine them with the roots of all the other trees in the immediate neighborhood. That is the real secret of their strength and longevity. They send their roots to drink strength from the soil but more importantly they intertwine their roots together and thereby form an embattled, common, communal strength. That is why they are the oldest living things on earth. They have learned that no tree lives alone for long. They have learned how to give strength to other trees and

how to get what they need from them.
—John Muir.

COMPENSATION.    Someday an epic will
be written about the law of compensation, the most dramatic thing in nature.
The peacock, with his aristocratic, incomparable display of color, has only a
wretched squawk of a voice. The nightingale, embodiment of glorious, soul-
stirring song, has plumage of dullest
russet and gray. And the albatross, mas-
ter-flyer, walks awkwardly along the
sand, moving as though each step
brought him acute agony.—William
Beebe.

### Sermon Suggestions

TAKING OUR CHANCES.    Text: Eccl.
9:11. (1) Chance is a real factor in life.
(2) The way we face it helps to determine the quality of life. (3) When we
rise to the spiritual level of faith, hope,
and love, we see how God's dealings rise
above the level of luck and chance.—
Ralph W. Sockman.

GOD WILL DO WHAT WE CANNOT.    Scripture: Ps. 139:1–12. (1) We can never be
where God is not. (2) We can never ask
what God cannot do for us. (3) We can
never do what God cannot forgive.

### Worship Aids

CALL TO WORSHIP.    "O come, let us
sing unto the Lord: let us make a joyful noise to the rock of our salvation.
Let us come before his presence with
thanksgiving, and make a joyful noise
unto him with psalms." Ps. 95:1–2.

INVOCATION.    Almighty God, our heavenly Father, who reignest over all things
in thy wisdom, power, and love: we
adore thee for thy glory and majesty,
and we praise thee for thy grace and
truth to us in thy Son our Savior. Grant
us the help of thy Holy Spirit, we beseech thee, that we may worship thee
in spirit and in truth.

OFFERTORY SENTENCE.    "Offer unto God

thanksgiving; and pay thy vows unto
the most High." Ps. 50:14.

OFFERTORY PRAYER.    We give thee
thanks, O Father, that through our
tithes and offerings thou dost give us
an opportunity to illuminate the dim-
ness of the future and to glorify our
present life with the word of him who
is the light of the world.

PRAYER.    Our God, creator of all life,
we bow in worship because you have
made your love for us known through
the life of Christ. We come in thankfulness because you have loved us through
the lives of Christlike people.

We come in quietness and meditation
seeking to understand your love for each
of us. We feel secure when we sense
your knowledge of our lives and our
world. Thank you for knowing us and
accepting us as we are.

Forgive us when we make mistakes.
Give us comfort and direction when we
are troubled or downhearted. Help us
to include others in our thoughts and
action. Keep us from selfishness. Give us
the wisdom and courage to live each day
as your children and as brothers and
sisters to one another.—Gene N. Bran-
son.

## EVENING SERVICE

### Topic: Why Men Worship

John Wesley says that worship consists of four elements: praise, thanksgiving, deprecation (by which he means
penitence), and petition.

I. We stumble over the word "praise"
because we think of it as flattery. Is
God like a conceited man or a vain
woman who demands and basks in continuous adulation? But etymologically
praise comes from the French verb
*priser*, the Latin verb *pretiare*, meaning
*to prize*. This is its first dictionary meaning: to prize, to value, to appraise, and
then to express appreciation. Praise in
worship is appreciation raised to the nth
degree. Appreciation raised to the nth
degree is adoration. Adoration, says
Baron von Hügel, is the end of all re-

ligion. It is the awed, glad, and spontaneous response of the spirit of man to the infinite and eternal Spirit who called him into being and to whom he is akin.

II. The second element in worship is thanksgiving. We may stumble over this too, for some of us do not find it easy to say "thank you."

(a) We do not ordinarily give thanks to one who does something for us. We give him a tip which relieves us of any sense of obligation. We cannot square our account with God by giving him a tip. He is in need of nothing. The silver and the gold are his. The cattle upon a thousand hills are his. The sunset and the dawn belong to him. There is only one thing we can do: say "Thank you, Father."

(b) If the writer of Revelation is correct, thanksgiving is the language of heaven. Unless we begin to learn it here we shall be dumb, inarticulate aliens there. "Bless the Lord, O my soul, and forget not all his benefits." Bless him too for the benefits I do forget, for he bestows not only in our conscious hours but also gives to his beloved in their sleep.

III. The third element in worship is penitence. This too is not easy. Hard for us to say: "It was my fault. I made an error of judgment, a stupid mistake." Harder to say: "I have sinned. I need to be forgiven."

(a) We are deathly afraid of the inferiority feeling. "He has a bad case of inferiority." How would you like that to be said of you? I wonder if there is not something to be said for a feeling of inferiority. When the high-born, high-minded young Isaiah had a vision of God, high and lifted up, he exclaimed: "Woe is me! For I am a man of unclean lips, for my eyes have seen the Lord." That is the spontaneous response of an unspoiled man to a sense of God's presence.

(b) We hear it said, sometimes jauntily, sometimes sadly, that modern man has lost his sense of sin. This is a superficial diagnosis of modern man's spiritual plight. His real trouble is a lost sense of God. When his sense of God returns, his sense of his own unworthiness will return.

IV. The last element is petition. (a) Petition means asking benefits for ourselves. That is selfish, you say, and unworthy. No, according to Jesus, God is interested in our needs and loves to supply them as we human parents love to supply the needs of our children.

(b) Emerson reminds us we must be careful for what we ask lest our prayer be answered. Sometimes we ask for the wrong things. We ask for trifles when God stands ready to give us of his wisdom and his love.

(c) The measure of the prodigal's recovery may be seen in his two requests of his father. The first was "Father, give me my share of your estate." The second was "Father, make me as one of your servants." There are times when we can rightly pray, "Father, give me what I need." But our prayer is on a higher plane when its burden is "Father, make me what I ought to be."—Frank Halliday Ferris.

## SUNDAY: JULY TWENTY-FOURTH

### MORNING SERVICE

Topic: **Weapons Divinely Potent**
  TEXT: Eph. 6:12 (NEB).

I. The first of the weapons of God is *truth*. The Christian begins with the evidence of God's existence both in the creation and in his intervention in human history. This personal God communicates with men and reveals his truth to his creatures. It is this message that we buckle on as we go into battle. We do not launch out in blind faith but are undergirded by the knowledge that God's truth stands, whether we do or not.

II. The second part of the Christian's armor is the breastplate of *righteousness*. The NEB calls it the coat of mail of integrity. Perhaps this is what Jesus called being "pure in heart"—being of unmixed motives, transparent but also possessed by a righteousness not our own, the goodness of the indwelling Christ.

III. The third feature of God's armor is the footwear of the gospel of *peace*. The metaphor implies that an agile soldier needs shoes that speed him on as he carries the message of peace with God. He is a courier of good tidings, urgent in his desire to publish the message, and enthusiastically announcing it as he encounters an expectant world.

IV. The fourth weapon is *faith,* our shield against Satan's missiles. We may expect the Adversary to hurl every kind of difficulty in our path. The subtle temptations of security, the pressures of conformity, the dismay of misfortune, the pain of criticism, the burden of grief, and the pride of our professional dignity—all these flaming arrows and more will be fired at us.

V. The fifth of God's weapons is the helmet of *salvation,* the saving life of Christ within the Christian. The resurrected Christ who indwells him through the agency of the Holy Spirit is the guarantee of salvation, the foretaste of victory. This is what makes the disciple invincible in trouble: Christ in control and we yielded to his use. It is this adventure of surrender to Christ's lordship that provides the ultimate assurance of his saviorhood.

VI. The *Word of God* is the sixth of our weapons. It is alive and active. It cuts more keenly than any two-edged sword, piercing as far as the place where life and spirit, joints and marrow divide. It sifts the purposes and thoughts of the heart.

VII. The last part of God's armor is *prayer*. When all other weapons seem inadequate to cope with the viciousness of our foe, when truth is twisted and integrity ridiculed, when our urgent proclamation of the news of peace with God falls on deaf ears, when our faith in God's promises falters, when some gnawing sin has alienated us from our Savior and his indwelling presence is dimmed, when our involvement in the world has interfered with our study of God's message, and when in short we are backed to the wall there is yet prayer.—David J. Seel in *Christianity Today*.

## Illustrations

BEARER OF DIVINE FIRE.    Emma Calve, the noted French soprano, after beginning a singing career in Brussels, went on to Paris and London and then became a leading member of the Metropolitan Opera Company in New York. At one time she spent a week in Venice, in anguish and suspense, waiting for the arrival of a letter. It came at last with crushing news. It filled her with such despair that it prompted her to go out on the balcony of her hotel and hurl herself in the waters of the canal below and so end it all. But on the balcony she was arrested by the voice of a singing gondolier, toiling at his oar. Hearing that, a new prompting laid hold on her the passionate desire to sing just once more before she died. She hurried from the hotel and entered a barque at the foot of the stone stairs and began drifting down the canal. She sang with a deep passion all the songs she had ever known. She sang as if it were the last time she would ever sing. She put into her singing all her soul and strength and also all her grief and sorrow.

Only after she had sung herself out did she realize that a mass of small boats filled with people had gathered around her gondola. She retreated to the shelter of the hood of her gondola and returned to her hotel. The following morning a bouquet of flowers was delivered to her hotel with this message: "From Paul and Jeanne, who love each other greatly, to whom you have given an unforgettable night! May the blessing of God be upon you who are the bearer of the Fire Divine." Then she turned to prayer and thanked God that she was still alive.—Martin A. Punt.

POWER AVAILABLE. The professor leaned back in his chair and removed his glasses. It was a well-known and well-loved act, and his class, young New Testament scholars, readied pens and listened expectantly. The professor gazed at his seminary students in silence. Then he said, "Gentlemen, there is enough power in this room right now to change the world, if you will have it so."— James Comfort Smith.

## Sermon Suggestions

GETTING THE MOST OUT OF LIFE. Scripture: Rom. 12:1–13. (1) Getting the most out of life demands that we develop a sincere interest in people. (2) Getting the most out of life means to accept the fact that "man partly is and wholly hopes to be" (Robert Browning). (3) Getting the most out of life means practicing faith in a Christlike God, the Father of all men everywhere who frees us from overdependence on things, overconcern with ourselves, and overcontentment with what we have won or achieved.—Nenien C. McPherson, Jr.

LIVING DANGEROUSLY. Text: Luke 6:26. If we are to live nobly we must live dangerously. When do we live dangerously? (1) When convictions supersede mere convention. (2) When the right takes precedence over caution. (3) When we espouse a worthy cause even at the sacrifice of personal advantage and safety.

## Worship Aids

CALL TO WORSHIP. "I will lift up mine eyes unto the hills, from whence cometh my help. My help cometh from the Lord, which made heaven and earth." Ps. 121:1–2.

INVOCATION. Teach us, good Lord, in our days of rest to put our worship and prayer first, and may we never let the services of the church be crowded out of our lives. Keep before us the vision of thy dear Son Jesus Christ, who in his boyhood days worshiped with his family, and may that vision inspire us and all men to unite as members of the church universal in witness, in worship, and in love.

OFFERTORY SENTENCE. "Take heed what ye hear: with what measure ye mete, it shall be measured to you: and unto you that hear shall more be given." Mark 4:24.

OFFERTORY PRAYER. Dear Lord, as we travel the highways of life give us a generous and sympathetic spirit for all people in all circumstances of life.

PRAYER. At times, O God, we wonder about thee, whether thou really knowest all things, whether thou canst see peace coming on earth in the midst of wars and armament races, and whether thou canst tell what we will do tomorrow or a minute from now when we don't even know ourselves. We want desperately to believe that thou hast the whole world in thy hand and that thy eye is on the sparrow and on us, but we are just not sure. Forgive our stubborn lack of faith; take our skepticism and sanctify it.

What gives us trouble, Lord, is our imagination, for we can see the world and ourselves evaporated by a bomb. We can imagine some accident or some madman ending in a moment what thou hast taken eons to make and all that we have come to love. Or we can imagine our lives going on and on in the same old rut, boring us to death from here to eternity. But we would not blank out our imagination, even if we could, for it is all that keeps us dreaming and praying that the world will get better and ourselves along with it.

Sometimes, Lord, we wish we were not so sensitive both to the little hurts that spoil our days and to the ugliness and evil we can't help seeing on every side. Never let us get to the place where we stop feeling pain lest we become so anesthetized we can't even feel joy. Never let us blind ourselves to outrageous wrong lest we fail to see the astonishing beauty of goodness.

And bless us, Lord, with concentration that keeps us from being the prisoner of our alternating moods of hope and despair, of joy and sadness. Let us hope and despair and let us rejoice and weep, but let us do them at the right time and for the right reason and always in the firm knowledge that the final triumph of righteousness is assured and eternal life is ours through Jesus Christ our Lord.—Harry W. Adams.

## EVENING SERVICE

### Topic: All Things for Good
Text: Rom. 8:28.

I. "We *know* that all things work together for good." Here is truth in operation. Here is an axiom which will work in all eventualities of life. It will work anywhere, anytime. Paul is not saying that everything is good. Sin, death, sorrow, sickness, and poverty are not good. Infantile paralysis, cancer, and war are not good, and we are not asked to believe that they are good. Our reason would not allow us to do so. But somehow, as we shall see, for those who love God, all the events of life work together for good. As the flower can grow from mud, as preachers can come from drunkards' homes, as the oyster can produce the pearl, so out of despair and evil, good can come.

II. "We know that *all* things work together for good." Had Paul said "some things" or "a few things work together for good," it would not bother us much because we all recognize that some of the things in life work together for good. But when he said "all things," he was speaking from his own personal experience. Thinking about his life, his persecutions, and his problems, he still said, "It has all worked together for good."

III. "We know that all things *work together* for good." (a) The Greek word is *sunergie*. The ingredients in medicine work together. The pharmacist takes a bit of medicine over here which would not in itself effect a cure and another bit of medicine over there which in itself would not effect a cure and works them together. They then effect th[e] cure.

(b) All things—the sunshine and th[e] darkness, the laughter and the tears, th[e] problems and the heartaches—work to[-] gether for good. The events which ar[e] not good in themselves combine with other events to make it right. Robinson Crusoe said, "How strange a checker board of providence is the life of man."

IV. "All things work together fo[r] *good*." (a) It does not say, "Work to[-] gether for pleasure and laughter." Go[d] does not promise that we shall g[o] through life with unending pleasure. H[e] says that it works together for our good. God does not look for our pleasure an[y] more than the physician does for hi[s] patient. The physician does not give u[s] medicine to make us happy but to effec[t] a cure. Imagine yourself asking about a doctor, "Well, does he make you well?" Someone answers: "No, but he make[s] you laugh. He's a real comic. He tel[ls] you the funniest jokes, and he give[s] you a medicine that tastes like candy." You would not go to such a man. Yo[u] go for a cure for your ultimate good. Sometimes the medicine or treatmen[t] hurts, but you know this is best becaus[e] of the cure that is effected.

(b) God does that which is for ou[r] best interest. All things work togethe[r] for our best interest, for our ultimat[e] good. (See II Cor. 4:17; Jas. 1:4; Heb. 4:11.) But this involves our response t[o] God's leadership.

(c) This is a limited promise. Ther[e] is no promise here for those who hav[e] rejected Christ. People throw thes[e] words around flippantly, "Everythin[g] works out all right." But this is not [a] general promise to humanity. This is [a] specific promise only to Christians. "T[o] them that love God, to them who a[re] called according to his purpose" is wha[t] the Bible says. This whole promise [is] contingent upon our attitude towar[d] God. For the child of God there is th[e] assurance that he will be the victor ove[r] the circumstances of life or under them

(d) This involves life after deat[h] which is why it involves the Christia[n] faith. There will come a time when all things will be proved to have been good for us. "In that day," said Christ, "ye shall ask me nothing." We are going to be satisfied with the good that has been produced, and we shall say at the throne of heaven, "It was good."—Edgar M. Arendall.

## SUNDAY: JULY THIRTY-FIRST

### MORNING SERVICE

Topic: The Splendor of Jesus (The Transfiguration)
SCRIPTURE: Luke 9:28–36.

I. "He was transfigured before them." His face changed. Even his clothes looked different. They were so white that they dazzled them by their brilliance; they were whiter than white. It was as though all the dust and dirt on the roads of Galilee had suddenly disappeared, as though every cloud of suffering, rejection, and death had been blown away and the sky was clear blue. There he was in his original brightness and beauty without a particle of dust to obscure it.

(a) In our analytical minds we are bound to ask, did Jesus really change, or was it his friends who changed? In other words, was this an objective or a subjective experience? My answer is that both changed.

(b) Jesus had come to the point where he accepted suffering as the only way to save his people. And Peter at least had begun to see the same thing, and when he once saw that he was in a position to see his glory. He lost sight of it many times; but for a moment he saw it without a blur, without a particle of dust or doubt.

II. There were two other men talking with Jesus, Moses and Elijah. Moses was the father of the nation; and Elijah, you might say, was the savior of the nation. They were the two great figures in the past, the lawgiver and the prophet; and Jesus was seen talking with them about his future course.

(a) The past is never erased. Sometimes it is buried deep in the subconscious, and you are not even aware that it is there; but when a crisis arises it sometimes comes to the surface. When has a crisis ever arisen in this country in which a leader with great gifts has risen to meet it, we have not thought of him together with Washington and Lincoln, the father and the savior of the nation?

(b) Peter did not know what to say. He was completely dazzled by the whole thing. On this occasion, when he really was completely bewildered, he blurted out to Jesus, "Let us make three shrines, one for Moses, one for Elijah, and one for you." He wanted places where he could keep them. He wanted to keep the precious moment.

(c) What the story says to us at this point is something like this: Glory comes; glory passes by; you cannot keep it; you can only see it and remember it.

III. A cloud overshadowed them almost before Peter had finished the sentence. The brightness didn't last very long. It almost never does. Those moments of vision when we seem to have seen right into the depth of existence and when without any of the distractions of dust and dirt or any of the blurred images of life we see life as it was meant to be, these moments are at best brief and fleeting.

(a) Out of this very cloud a voice spoke. The voice said, "This is my Son; listen to him." It was the same voice, saying essentially the same thing, that spoke to Jesus at his baptism. Now the same brief declaration is being made to his closest friends. Don't think that if you had been there with a tape recorder you would have been able to record any voice. It wasn't that kind of voice. It was God saying in a way that only God can speak to us, "This is my flesh and blood; pay attention to him."

(b) For nearly two thousand years men

have tried to explain Jesus theologically, philosophically, psychologically, even politically. But when the voice of God came out of the cloud and spoke to Jesus' most intimate friends, there was no explanation at all. All the voice said was, "He belongs to me; listen to him." When he says, "If any man will come after me, let him deny himself and take up his cross every day and follow me," listen to him. When he says, "What doth it profit a man if he gain the whole world and lose his own soul?" listen to him.

(c) What would have happened in our world if people had done that simple, single thing? I am not minimizing the necessity of the explanations that men have tried to work out because we have to think about an event so colossally great as Jesus in its relationship to every other event. But what would happen if we occasionally put aside our attempts to explain him and listen to him? It is far more fascinating to figure him out than to follow him.

IV. "And suddenly, when they had looked round about, they saw no man anymore save Jesus only." In the end he rises above all others, incomparable in his solitary glory. That is something you have to see. No one can argue with you about it, and if you think that he is in the same class with some other giant of our race, like Socrates, no one can argue you out of that opinion. You have to see his glory for yourself.

(a) If you ever once heard the voice of Kirsten Flagstad you can say that there is no other. If you have ever read the sonnets of Shakespeare there are no others that can be compared with them. They rise above them all. If you have seen the windows in Chartres you can say, "I see no others save these only."

(b) If you ever see Jesus there is quite literally no one who can stand beside him. This does not in any way diminish the others. This is not to say anything to detract from the glory and the wonder of other human beings who are like stars in the firmament of the human race. This is only to say that when you have once seen his glory there is none other like him.

(c) There is a glory about him which once you see you can never describe, never explain, not if you live to be a thousand. You can only reflect it occasionally, dimly, in your own peculiar way.—Theodore P. Ferris.

## Illustrations

THE INCOMPARABLE CHRIST.    Faith may languish; creeds may be changed; churches may be dissolved. But one cannot imagine the time when Jesus will not be the fair image of perfection. He can never be superseded. He can never be exceeded. Religions may come and go, the passing shapes of an eternal instinct, but Jesus will remain the standard of the conscience and the satisfaction of men's final needs, whom all men seek and in whom all men will yet meet. —John Watson.

HALLMARK.    The greatest libel ever perpetrated against God is the notion that he likes to see men express obedience to him through somber, long-faced, mirthless piety. The Bible teaches that the true hallmark of religion is joy. A careful count reveals that the word "joy" is found in the Bible 164 times, while the verb "rejoice" appears 191 times.—Louis Cassels.

## Sermon Suggestions

THE ATTRACTIVENESS OF CHRIST.    Text: John 7:37. (1) His gentleness with the outcasts and the unlovely. (2) His courage in the face of opposition, betrayal, and death. (3) His impatience with rules and regulations. (4) His inner integrity of spirit. (5) The disturbing, probing presence of love broken on a cross, the haunting notion that here is the clue to ultimate reality and to what's at the center of this baffling existence of ours to give it purpose and meaning.—Edmund Steimle.

CORNERS THAT NEED BRIGHTENING.    Text: Matt. 5:14–16. (1) We are called to brighten the corners of public and private morality. (2) We are called to bring the light of common, ordinary honesty into the dark corners of duplicity. (3) We are called to spread the light of compassion in the dark corners of loneliness and suffering. —Clarence J. Forsberg.

## Worship Aids

CALL TO WORSHIP. "They that wait upon the Lord shall renew their strength: they shall mount up with wings as eagles; they shall run, and not be weary; and they shall walk, and not faint." Isa. 40:31.

INVOCATION. Almighty God, whose chosen dwelling is the heart that longs for thy presence and humbly seeks thy face: deepen within us the sense of shame and sorrow for the wrongs we have done and for the good we have left undone. Strengthen every desire to amend our lives according to thy holy will. Give light to our wills and rest to our souls that we may do those things which are pleasing in thy sight.

OFFERTORY SENTENCE. "The end of the commandment is charity out of a pure heart." I Tim. 1:5.

OFFERTORY PRAYER. Our Father, enable all Christians to know that their lives may be lived with Christ in God and that their gifts are means by which thy love in Christ may reach into the lives of wayward and needy persons everywhere.

PRAYER. O God, in times of doubts and questionings, when our belief is perplexed by new learning, new teaching, and new thought, when our faith is strained by creeds, by doctrines, and by mysteries beyond our understanding, give us the faithfulness of learners and the courage of believers in thee; give us boldness to examine and faith to trust all truth; patience and insight to master difficulties; stability to hold fast our tradition with enlightened interpretation, to admit all fresh truth made known to us, and in times of trouble to grasp new knowledge readily and to combine it loyally and honestly with the old, alike from stubborn rejection of new revelations and from hasty assurance that we are wiser than our fathers. Save us and help us, we humbly beseech thee, O Lord.

## EVENING SERVICE

### Topic: The Transfigured Christ
SCRIPTURE: Mark 9:2–8.

I. *The meaning of the transfiguration* (v. 2). (a) This great event took place six days after Peter's confession at Caesarea Philippi that Jesus was the messiah. The apostles expected Christ to set up his messianic kingdom at Jerusalem immediately. But instead he told them that he was going to Jerusalem to suffer and to die. All their hopes were shattered. And doubts must have plagued their minds as to whether after all he actually was the messiah.

(b) For the inner circle of the three closest to the Master the problem was soon resolved. Jesus took Peter, James, and John "up into an high mountain." Here Jesus was "transfigured before them." The verb is *metamorphoo,* related to the noun *metamorphosis,* which has been taken over into English as a biological and chemical term indicating a change of structure. The verb is used in the parallel passage in Matt. 17:2. Luke describes the transfiguration (9:29) but does not use the term.

(c) To the onlookers—Peter, James, and John—this event was a complete confirmation of the fact that Jesus was really the messiah. They could never doubt again.

II. *The message of the transfiguration* (v. 7). (a) If the sight of Jesus' glistening face and clothing had not been enough to convince the three disciples, the voice from heaven was the final proof. The Father spoke out of the overshadowing cloud: "This is my beloved Son: hear him." This was similar to the declaration made at the baptism (1:11). These are among the strongest statements of the deity of Jesus to be found in the synoptic gospels.

(b) The added admonition, "Hear him," was probably a rebuke to Peter's suggestion about making three booths ("tabernacles"), one each for Christ, Moses, and Elijah (v. 5). Thus he was placing Christ on the same level with Moses (representing "the Law") and Elijah (representing "the Prophets"). But Christ is utterly unique as the Son of God and should never be bracketed in the same breath with the founders of other religions. All of them were merely human; he alone is uniquely divine.

III. *The moral of the transfiguration* (v. 8). (a) As the sound of the voice faded away, suddenly "they saw no man any more, save Jesus only with themselves." The three disciples had been overwhelmed with the vision and the heavenly visitors. Now they were left with "Jesus only."

(b) The value of a vision depends on its permanent results. If the experience of ecstasy or emotion is genuine, it will leave us with a heightened sense of our Lord's presence. The transfiguration must transfigure us!—Ralph Earle in *The Preacher's Magazine.*

# SUNDAY: AUGUST SEVENTH

## MORNING SERVICE

### Topic: The Light of the World
SCRIPTURE: Matt. 5:14–16.

Who could describe or even number the blessings of this "light of the world"?

I. *It is light to see by.* It shows human nature for what it is, not angelic, not demonic, but torn between good and evil, yet precious in God's sight, so precious that he sent his Son for our salvation. In this light we see the world of nature not for a shallow nature-worship but as the handiwork of God. We see our pilgrimage as a journey toward our home.

II. *It is light to work by.* A watchmaker could not do his work without a light to guide his hands and eyes. But what of his motive and spirit? Said Jesus of his gospel, "Walk while you have the light, lest darkness overtake you; he who walks in darkness does not know where he goes." Substitute "work" for "walk" and the warning would be just as true. What happens when we work for cash? Shoddy, mass-production goods, a society in which every man is every man's rival and a world divided into "haves" and "have-nots." Thus we brag about our great technological progress which we dedicate to profit, and suddenly automation becomes a fear of Frankenstein.

III. *It is light to pray by.* (a) Every man believes in God. A man may refuse the name God, perhaps because pious people have filled it with dreary meanings or even have fashioned it in man's own image. But every man still has some name for God: Truth, Beauty, Reality, the Ultimate Concern, the Ground of Being. We can hardly say "limit" without some dim conception of the Unconditioned. So the question is not "Do you believe in God?" but "What kind of God do you believe in?" Christ shows us what kind of God.

(b) The mystery we call God is never resolved in our poor minds but is always revealed by his grace. If there were no mystery there could be no worship. If the terrors of the Eternal and his gentlenesses were completely understood, God would be prisoner of our minds, and we ourselves would become our own grotesque God. Our faith is this: the burning heart of the abyss called God is the love which we see in the cross of Christ. Therefore we pray "in the name of our Lord Jesus Christ."

IV. *It is light to befriend by.* (a) On what strange foundations we try to build the true society. Athletics? But there we have rivalry that easily becomes bad feeling. Music? But the artist is rather notoriously given to a prima donna complex. Education? But a college is marked by jealousies, not only among the students, but among faculty also. Enlightened self-interest? That is a contradiction in terms. Trade? Have not our wars been fought, in partial motive at least, for arable land, oil fields, and mines?

(b) What is the bond of a true society? Is it not the spirit of Christ? Man is that "strange creature who can view his own life." There is in him alone an eternal term by which he is able to say, "Time is swift." So men are joined in that deep ground of life, in the kingdom that came into history with the coming of Christ, in the grace of the beatitudes.

V. *Light may be overcome by darkness or may cease to shine.* (a) There are widening circles of illumination: "house," "a city set on a hill," "world." In each circle there are snuffers which extinguish the light just because our human nature is the battleground for good and evil. The house or home brings threats through carking care, or financial anxiety, or love taken for granted and therefore lost. The city brings threats, for their lurid excitements beckon, or we are persuaded that "business is business," or aimless crowds make us wonder if any life is precious.

(b) Is there not a story of a blind man carrying a light? He himself explained the anomaly: "So people will not stumble over me at night." The phrase brings judgment and remorse, for people do stumble over us when our light goes out. But the better reason for the lamp, even for the blind man, is that other people shall see their way.

(c) The disciple does not shine in his own light or for his own sake. Sometimes a church brags about itself, calling attention to its budget and to its building, but such a claim is a dark inversion. The disciple is a bright presence in the world for men's sake, lest the world become dark, and for God's glory.

(d) The word "glory" does not mean that God is proud or that he makes his men puppet-lightbearers, for God's glory is the love that died on a cross. Only God by his renewing spirit can tend our little lamp of life. Only he can trim the hard wick. Only he can provide the oil for the lamp. So the wise alternate movement of the disciple's life is that shown in the mount of transfiguration: from the mountain of prayer to the valley of need.—George A. Buttrick.

## Illustrations

IN THE PIT. A missionary who had served in China told about one of his converts. The man attended services and apparently listened to the preaching and teaching, yet he resisted the invitation to become a Christian. One morning he arrived at the missionary's home obviously happy and excited.

"I had a dream last night," he said, "and now I understand. I dreamed that I fell into a deep pit and lay there helpless. A Confucian, seeing my plight, leaned over and said, 'Let me give you some advice, my friend. If you get out of your trouble, don't make the same foolish mistake again.'

"Then a Buddhist came, and said, 'If you can manage to climb up so I can reach you, I will help you out.'

"Finally Christ came. Without a moment's hesitation, he climbed down into the pit, gently picked me up, and carried me out. Now I know what the word 'emmanuel' means."—John W. Wade.

CENTRAL MIRACLE. Here is the central miracle of Christianity: Christ. The central miracle is not the resurrection or the virgin birth or any of the other miracles; the central miracle is just this person for he rises in sinless grandeur above life. He is life's sinless exception, therefore a miracle. Now turn from that central miracle toward these lesser miracles and they become credible in the light of his person.—E. Stanley Jones.

## Sermon Suggestions

THE LIGHT OF THE WORLD. Text: John 8:12 (NEB). (1) Jesus Christ: the visible vehicle of the divine presence. (2) Jesus

Christ: the source of guidance for the godly. (3) Jesus Christ: the deliverer from spiritual darkness.—William McLeister 2nd.

FRUIT OF RELIGIOUS EXPERIENCE. (1) Gives a person deeper insight into his own motives. (2) Touches the inner core of the personality, strengthening it and helping it to go on. (3) Creates in a person a stronger love for God and man.

## Worship Aids

CALL TO WORSHIP. "Thou wilt keep him in perfect peace, whose mind is stayed on thee: because he trusteth in thee. Trust ye in the Lord for ever: for in the Lord Jehovah is everlasting strength." Isa 26:3-4.

INVOCATION. Grant, O Lord our God, we beseech thee, that now and every time we come before thee in worship and in prayer we may be vividly aware of thy presence, become conscious of thy power and a sense of thy protection, and finally know in our hearts and minds and souls the wonder and the grace of thy peace.

OFFERTORY SENTENCE. "It is God who is at work within you, giving you the will and the power to achieve his purpose." Phil. 2:13 (PHILLIPS).

OFFERTORY PRAYER. Accept, O Lord, these offerings thy people make unto thee and grant that the cause to which they are devoted may prosper under thy guidance, to the glory of thy name.

PRAYER. Father, you've been very near for many of us this week. We thank you for the spiritual ministry of many of our laymen and laywomen. Thank you for the ways in which you are working in the life of this congregation. Thank you for your presence focused in our worship today.

We praise you for your constant care, for your sufficient grace, and for your unfailing love.

Father, we confess our failure which is sin. We've been preoccupied with self and blind to the needs of others. We've done good things but neglected the best. While Jesus "went about doing good" we've just been going about.

Forgive our indulgence which is harmful, our harmful habits, our overeating, our overwork, and our senseless worry.

Father, we pray for others. We know that "morning never wears to evening but what some heart doth break."

We pray for the brokenhearted: for those disappointed in others, in themselves, and in life's circumstances; for those who have received bad news at school, at work, at home, and from their doctor.

We pray for youth with their great potential and perplexing problems; for adults who carry such heavy responsibilities; for senior adults with their wealth of experience and for whom life is narrowing.

Now give us direction in our perplexities, faith in our doubts, grace for our inadequacies, forgiveness for our sins, purity in our pleasures, and celebration and joy in our worship.—Alton H. McEachern.

## EVENING SERVICE

### Topic: The Book of Life

TEXT: Rev. 20:12.

I invite you to write a book. The book is the book of your life. This book can be started today. God willing, it will be finished years from now.

I. To whom will your book be dedicated? Perhaps I should ask, what will your book be dedicated to? Too many times we dedicate our lives to unworthy ends.

II. Your book of life should be dedicated to just one person. The dedication might read: "To God the father, who has been a constant inspiration to me, who has accompanied me along every step of my journey, who has watched over and protected me through every trial, and who has blessed me beyond my deserving, this book is lovingly and worshipfully dedicated."

III. Next you must write a table of

contents. You must decide on chapter headings. Permit me to suggest three such headings.

(a) Let us entitle the opening chapter "My service to God." Let each one of us strive in every way possible to be of maximum service to him.

(b) Suppose we call chapter two "My service to my fellowmen." Is any person more to be pitied than the person who finds no enjoyment in helping others? How callous and unfeeling a human being must be to see misery and let it go untouched. How hard a human being must be to see suffering and not try to remedy it. How unthinking a person must be to see poverty and think that he can remain rich. The book of life is simply not complete without this chapter dealing with your service to others. God grant that you may make it good reading.

(c) My suggestion for the third chapter would be "My service to myself." I hope you notice carefully the order in which these chapters come: first serve God, then others, and last of all yourself. Hopefully you will find that if you serve God and others before yourself, your own need will diminish greatly. You'll feel a warmth within you that previously you simply have not known.

IV. The book itself remains to be written. In a very real way we have all blank pages before us. The days, weeks, and months ahead will determine what the story sounds like. That story is yours to write as you will. You can do what you please with the book of your life. Will your book be a masterpiece or trash? The answer is up to you. By your deeds, your words, and your thoughts you alone will determine the review your book will receive.—James H. Middleton.

## SUNDAY: AUGUST FOURTEENTH

### MORNING SERVICE

**Topic: Responding to the Gospel**
SCRIPTURE: Acts 17:1-5, 8-13.

I. *At Thessalonica—reception and opposition.* (a) In the largest city of Macedonia on three consecutive sabbaths Paul "reasoned," explained, discussed, argued "with them out of the scriptures." He presented the Christian message, Jesus as the Christ, the Savior of all men, out of its background in the Old Testament. Some Jews, a few more Greeks, and a few of the leading women were persuaded and joined Paul and Silas. However the Jews as a whole were jealous, set the city in an uproar, and attacked the house of Jason, Paul's host. It appeared that the Thessalonians were an easily excitable people.

(b) Patriotic hysteria, when used in defense of personal privilege and profit, is difficult to cope with. When that was fueled by sectarian pride, as in Thessalonica, it created an untenable situation, and the brethren sent Paul and

Silas by night to Beroea. But a spiritual force had been released in the city.

II. *At Beroea—acceptance and interruption.* (a) Beroea was located fifteen miles southwest of Thessalonica. Immediately upon arrival Paul and Silas went to the synagogue of the Jews and found there the Jews more open-minded, eager to listen, inquisitive, and liberal. The message was the same as at Thessalonica. The people in Beroea decided to pursue the course of honest investigation of Paul's message. They tried to give him a fair hearing because they were eager to know what the word of God taught. God revealed himself and his message of redemption to them through Paul. Many Jews believed along with a few Greek men and women of high standing.

(b) But selfishness, sectarian pride, and jealousy, wafted by emotionalism and nationalism, soon blew into Beroea from Thessalonica. Those disgruntled at Thessalonica were determined to stop the outreach of the gospel and hastened to Beroea to continue their attack upon "those that had turned the world upside down." Their accusation was the same: disloyalty to the emperor, a trap that the Jews didn't want to be involved in. However the Christians at Beroea, sensing the situation, sent Paul away before any charges could be brought. Even though his ministry was cut short in Beroea, Paul left the nucleus of a new church in Beroea.

III. *At Athens—respect and indifference.* (a) It seemed that immediately upon his safe arrival in Athens from Beroea that Paul sent back instruction for Silas and Timothy to join him there. It appears however in I Thess. 3:1–3 that they did not join Paul in Athens, but Silas went to Philippi and Timothy to Thessalonica.

(b) So alone in "violet-wreathed" Athens, Paul started to reason and dispute in the synagogue on the sabbath with the Jews and God-fearers. During the weekdays he talked with the gentiles in the marketplace, the Agora, where Socrates had taught. Since Athens was most famous as a city of philosophers, Paul found the philosophers most cynical and derogatory of him. They cynically asked, "What does this babbler"—seed-picker, parasite, bum—"want to say?"

(c) The philosophers were no more cynical of Paul than he was provoked at them and the city as he observed omnipresent idols which crowded the city of Athens. He was embittered that Athens, the city of knowledge, was so given to idol worship. Provoked, he stood up in the midst of Mars Hill, and using the words of an inscription he had seen, "To an Unknown God," he launched out with his message. The message was quite straightforward: God who made all things cannot be contained in manmade temples nor is he to be worshiped through idols. The true God is Father of all, and his Son came to be redeemer of all. His message was also one of repentance.

(d) The reception the gospel received at Athens was twofold: some scoffed while others procrastinated. Someone

rightly said, "Faith in tomorrow instead of Christ is Satan's nurse for man's perdition."

(e) No one can fault Paul for being provoked while in the city for there is an appropriate time to be provoked spiritually. Not even the highest achievements in art and the memorials of human wisdom should ever cloud spiritual reality while paganism reigns. Whenever people are in bondage to sin, devoted to material idols, and blinded by their own superficial wisdom, the Christian should be stirred within.—Herbert C. Gabhart.

## Illustrations

LEVELS OF LIFE.    Paul Tillich called our attention to three levels on which people may live. There is the most superficial level of the autonomous self where one is concerned only about himself. There is a deeper level of the heteronomous self where one realizes that he cannot be a law unto himself, where he is concerned with others, and where sometimes Christian love he puts others above himself. Then there is the deepest self, the theonomous self. It is the self that in faith gives himself to God in love and obedience and that seeks ever to know and understand the revealed word of God—the incarnate word in Christ—and to be sensitive to the promptings of the Spirit of God.—Hampton Adams.

VERBAL SMOKE SCREENS.    We in the church of Jesus Christ often beat around the bush. We indulge in small talk. We even set up verbal smoke screens to evade the real issues. We ought to know that in the church our main concern is to talk *about* God. More than that, to talk *with* God. Even more than that, to wait *upon* God.—Rudolph E. Gruenke.

## Sermon Suggestions

MISSION: THE CHRISTIAN'S CALLING. Text: I Pet. 2:9. Where can we be missionaries in the larger sense of the word? (1) Within the organized church.

(2) Within the family. (3) In daily work. (4) In the nonchurch groups in which we participate. (5) In the political life of our community.

THE NEED FOR MALADJUSTMENT.    Text. Rom. 12:2. (1) Christians must be prepared to be maladjusted to their society. (2) Christians must be prepared to use their minds. (3) Christian obedience is totalitarian.—Murdo Ewen Macdonald.

## Worship Aids

CALL TO WORSHIP.    "O send out thy light and thy truth: let them lead me; let them bring me unto thy holy hill, and to the tabernacles." Ps. 43:3.

INVOCATION.    Almighty God, our eternal Father, with whom a thousand years are as one day and one day as a thousand years: teach us so to number our days that we shall apply our hearts unto wisdom. Teach us to walk in trustful fellowship with thee, our God.

OFFERTORY SENTENCE.    "Seeing ye have purified your souls in obeying the truth through the Spirit unto unfeigned love of the brethren, see that ye love one another with a pure heart fervently." I Pet. 1:22.

OFFERTORY PRAYER.    O Christ, may we walk constantly in thy way and work fervently for those causes which are dear to thee.

PRAYER.    Almighty God, creator of the universe, our Father, ground of our being, help us to understand who you are, what you are like, and how you speak to us today.

From scripture we remember the "burning bush," the "voice from the cloud," and other strange and traumatic manifestations of yourself, and sometimes we have felt cheated because we were not Moses or one of the early disciples or apostles.

Mostly we feel that you do not speak to us at all because we have never heard you speak in the unusual and unreal ways in which we have come to expect you to speak. How do you speak to us today, O God? How are you communicating with us in this modern age in which we live?

Are you speaking to us through the church, especially when we hear a voice or an opinion with which we do not agree?

Are you speaking to us through the poor and dispossessed as they seek to gain power so their voices can be heard?

Are you speaking to us through efforts for peace?

Are you speaking to us through other events and happenings in our day?

How do you speak to us today, O God? Help us to hear your voice.—Lyle V. Newman.

## EVENING SERVICE

### Topic: The Dividends of Belief
TEXT. I John 5:5.

What is meant by believing that Jesus is the Son of God? The answer depends on our own personal experience. Every man comes to his own understanding of the gospel. The apostle Paul said, "The God and Father of our Lord Jesus Christ." One writer, contemplating on this phrase, wrote that God was the response from the unseen which answered to the faith that was in Jesus. Or conversely God was the gracious approach from the unseen that expressed itself in the life and work of Jesus of Nazareth. This approach to the mystery suggests simplicity and humility, and if we ponder it long enough, beauty and strength. This is the belief that overcomes the world. Two dividends issue from such a faith and from wrestling with the faith.

I. *The dividend of courage.* (a) Life has its struggles. That we know and know well. But we are called upon to act responsibly and to promote and preserve that which is beautiful and lovely in our homes, in our church, in our community, and in our world.

(b) To be released from all care and responsibility and to become self-indulgent is not to overcome the world. We smile over the verse of Omar Khayyam who pictures the perfect life as a jug of wine, his love, and a lovely shade tree. That has its place, to be sure; but life which masters the world calls for courage to face the hard tasks, the demanding routines, and the required responsibilities.

(c) George Tyrell, after wrestling with demands on his person made by church and society in his day, wrote in his diary, "Again and again I have been tempted to give up the struggle, but always that strange man on the cross sends me back to my tasks again and again." Who is it that overcomes the world? He who believes that Jesus is the Son of God.

II. *The dividend of confidence.* (a) One of the unfailing supports to individual growth and achievement, whether in children or adults, is the feeling which comes when we have been accepted by our family and friends. It hurts when people think evil of us.

My security depends in part on what my fellows think of me. This idea of accepting a person for what he is—his good qualities and his wants—is essential.

(b) The second dividend I see in the belief of our faith is confidence born of the conviction that we are accepted of God. This despite the fact we are imperfect human beings.

(c) One of the great insights of the Old Testament comes in the verse which commands, "Son of Man, stand on thy feet." That's the dignity commensurate with our being human beings. We are to acknowledge our limitations but also to know that we are accepted. Are our blunders in the home, at work, in the church and country covered with mercy? Until at last we face our death? Is that covered with mercy too? Who is it that overcomes the world but he who believes that Jesus is the Son of God?—William F. B. Rodda.

## SUNDAY: AUGUST TWENTY-FIRST

### MORNING SERVICE

**Topic: Let the Redeemed of the Lord Say So**

Text: Ps. 107:2.

I. "Let the redeemed of the Lord say so" *wherever they go.* (a) In this mobile society in which we live it is increasingly important for Christians to have a faith that will travel—to have a faith relevant enough and vital enough to share no matter where they go.

(b) But not only should the redeemed of the Lord say so in the new neighborhood or community or city to which they move; they should also share their faith, their ethical principles, and their religious priorities wherever they go—whether on a vacation, or to a ball game, or to a friend's home for a social event. Why should the Christian be the only one to clam up, to be apologetic, or be too cowardly to speak up at such places?

(c) A true Christian should always be alert for openings and opportunities to bear witness to his faith whether by word, or attitude, or charitable comment, or kind gesture, as well as by direct and open witness. No Christian should ever allow the climate or atmosphere of which he is a part to be totally non-Christian.

II. "Let the redeemed of the Lord say so" in *whatever experience they face.*

(a) Is Christian faith good only for the happy times? The easy times? The uncomplicated times? Or is it relevant and supportive for the tough times, the times of adversity and reverses and unexplained tragedies?

(b) Do we, as Christians, witness to our faith and the adequacy of God's grace when we lose our job? Or when we see our investments melting away? Or when sickness or bereavement come? Or when our children are proving a disappointment? Or when our highest hopes turn to heartaches?

(c) Do we as the redeemed of the Lord really "say so" by word and attitude? Or by a spirit that says that no permanent disaster can ever come to a person whose faith is in Jesus Christ?

(d) The Christian of course is just as sensitive to pain or sorrow or setbacks as others. But by personalizing and personifying the promises of God, he says to the world or to his corner of it that God's grace is truly sufficient and that through the presence and power of his God he will see it through victoriously.

III. "Let the redeemed of the Lord say so" *in whatever they do.* (a) Let them "say so" at work, at school, at the office, in the store, in the union meeting, at the business luncheon, or in whatever situation their secular employment involves them.

(b) Real Christians are tired of being thought of as strange or kooky or "off their rockers" because they don't indulge in wicked or wasteful habits or amusements or because they actually like to pray and read their Bibles and go to church. And they are asking how they can more effectively penetrate the secular atmosphere around them with a genuine witness to what Christ really means to them.

(c) It is the power of God's Spirit that will enable the redeemed to "say so" in such a way as will bring glory to Christ's name and advancement of his cause. For it is the power of God working within us that enables us to effectively witness to the redemptive work of Christ and to the reality of his love in our lives.—William Fisher.

## Illustrations

CONVERSATION. In a passage in Silone's *Bread and Wine,* two priests are talking. Don Piccirilli says, "The trouble with our time is immodesty of dress, don't you think?" To this Don Benedetto replies slowly, looking Piccirilli right in the eye, "The trouble with our time is insincerity between man and man."

Don Piccirilli quickly changes the subject because he knows the uncomfortable truth of what Benedetto is saying. He begins speaking about the spiritual progress being made in his parish and states as evidence that the number of confessions has increased 40 percent. "Poor Piccirilli," laments Don Benedetto, "you talk of *spiritual* progress but express yourself in calculations and percentages like a bank manager!" We can see the focus of this passage. One man is thinking of externals while the other is driving him back to see the significance at the heart of the universe. —Paul Trudinger.

FAITHFULNESS. A. J. Cronin told of a district nurse he knew when he was in practice as a doctor. For twenty years, singlehanded, she had served a ten-mile district. "I marveled," he said, "at her patience, her fortitude, and her cheerfulness." She was never too tired to rise for an urgent call. Her salary was most inadequate, and late one night, after a particularly strenuous day, I ventured to protest to her: "Nurse, why don't you make them pay you more? God knows you are worth it." "If God knows I'm worth it," she answered, "that's all that matters to me." You see, she was working for God and not for men and realized that God's ultimate standard of judgment is "faithfulness."—Bramwell Tillsley.

## Sermon Suggestions

SPIRITUAL GROWTH. Scripture: Phil. 1:8–11. (1) Spiritual development (v. 8). (2) Spiritual discernment (v. 10). (3) Spiritual discipleship (v. 11).—Ed Irwin.

LIFE IN CHRIST. (1) To grow is to live. (2) To forgive is to live. (3) To suffer is to live. (4) To have convictions is to live. (5) To die is to live.

## Worship Aids

CALL TO WORSHIP. "He that dwelleth in the secret place of the most High shall abide under the shadow of the

Almighty. I will say of the Lord, He is my refuge and my fortress: my God; in him will I trust." Ps. 91:1–2.

INVOCATION.    Our heavenly Father, who by thy love hast made us, and through thy love has kept us, and in thy love wouldst make us perfect: we humbly confess that we have not loved thee with all our heart and soul and mind and strength and that we have not loved one another as Christ hath loved us. Thy life is within our souls, but our selfishness has hindered thee. We have not lived by faith. We have resisted thy spirit. We have neglected thine inspirations. Forgive what we have been; help us to amend what we are; and in thy spirit direct what we shall be; that thou mayest come into the full glory of thy creation in us and in all men.

OFFERTORY SENTENCE.    "Every good gift and every perfect gift is from above, and cometh down from the Father of lights." Jas. 1:17.

OFFERTORY PRAYER.    Our Father, help us this day to remember that we do not live in our own strength but that thou art our help and that from thee cometh even these gifts which we consecrate in Christ's name.

PRAYER.    Eternal God our Father, who dost sustain thy universe, who dost not rest from thy labor, and whose work never ceases, we come to thee recognizing that thou hast placed great tasks upon us and provided us with resources great enough for their consummation. Far too often we shirk the hard tasks of life, fleeing from them as a frightened deer flees from the hounds. We seek the easy way and the light burden, notwithstanding that we know that thou dost never ask of us more than we can bear or accomplish. Thy faith in us is often greater than is ours in ourselves. O God, renew our faith in ourselves by relighting the fires on the altars of our faith in thee. Then send us forth to undertake our life's tasks in the sure knowledge that thou art with and within us, sustaining and strengthening us for whatever work thou wouldst have us do.—Chester E. Hodgson.

# EVENING SERVICE

## Topic: When Grief Is Good
TEXT: II Sam. 12:22–23.

What are the fruits by which we know that grief is good?

I. Good grief identifies one with his humanity. As children of God's creativity we are unique combinations of body, mind, and emotion. Of this fact each needs to be aware. So long as our bodies are frail, which they will always be, and the reach of our minds and ability is limited, as it will always be, there will be seasons of grief, and there are no exceptions. Neither wealth nor rank offers immunity. It was a brokenhearted king who said, "Oh, Absalom, my son, would that I had died instead of you." In the presence of loss, disappointment, or death we are all unkinged.

II. Grief is good when it causes one to discover resources that have always been available but of which he was unaware. When all goes well we skim along the surface with little apparent need for pausing to dig deeply. Then when we are suddenly overwhelmed, grief sends tap roots to new depths from which new resources are drawn. The immediate result is extra power in one's own life. Not infrequently a grief-stricken person says, "I don't think I could." The reason one didn't think she could is because she never had to. All of us have additional resources on deposit that can be drawn when needed.

III. Grief is good when it leads to the discovery of resources beyond oneself that become allies. Again surprised, one says, "I did not know I had so many friends." When the need arises friends respond, and sympathy is experienced as a universal language. What a privilege it is to belong to a church which becomes a larger family at the time of grief. The strength of friends is an immeasurable resource.

IV. Grief is good when it leads to the

discovery of inner resources, the strength of friends, and when it prompts one to take the resource of faith. Faith serves when needed and trusted. When all is "normal" we do not reach to take the hand outstretched to meet our own. It was in the valley of suffering that Job declared, "I know that my redeemer lives." Through grief one discovers God's presence at midday or midnight and knows the strength for the valley.

V. When is grief good? Not when misused nor as a camping site. Grief is good when its purpose and strength are understood, when it helps one identify with his own humanity, when it leads to new resources, when it makes one aware of what is left and what is left undone, and when the lessons of the valley are turned to a larger service. Then those who mourn shall indeed know comfort.—Wesley P. Ford.

## SUNDAY: AUGUST TWENTY-EIGHTH

### MORNING SERVICE

**Topic: Four Pillars of Faith**
TEXT: I Cor. 15:58.

I. *The first pillar is faith in the power of God* and suggests something we are apt to disparage: our dependence on God for life, for strength, hope, light, and peace. In the physical world electric power becomes effective when released through positive and negative wires. In the spiritual world God's power becomes effective when released upon a similar principle—the inflow of his power into the hunger of our souls.

II. *The second pillar of faith is God's Word.* (a) Why? Because it contains God's Word to man regarding the supremacy of spiritual values. Unfortunately we do not always allow God to speak to our hunger and need through the Bible. Too often we do not read it at all, keeping it rather as a fetish on a table or using it as a vehicle of magic.

(b) The Bible becomes a pillar of faith when it is God speaking with disruptive discernment through the hopes and fears of other generations, through the triumphs and heartbreaks of the prophets, and the agony and despair of ordinary people like ourselves.

(c) Whether or not the Bible is God's Word depends on whether or not we are listening as God speaks, on whether or not the world's static drowns out what he is saying, and on whether or not his Word reaches us with its hope, light, strength, and peace.

III. *A third pillar of faith is the church,* that mighty army of believers whom God has called to be a bulwark of righteousness, a witness to the gentiles, an example of servanthood, a fellowship of the saints, and an instrument of reconciliation.

(a) It has been said that people are killing the church and that if in another generation there are people who have faith it will be in spite of the church.

(b) One thing seems certain: if the church is to serve as a pillar of faith for us, it needs first to die, not the death of ease and indifference, of self-esteem and self-sufficiency, but to die the death of Christ, for truth and righteousness' sake, in love and forgiveness.

(c) This does not mean that we must destroy our sanctuaries, for men need a temple in which they can reorientate their lives and join with others in praise and prayer to the unseen God. It does not mean that we must discard our forms and structures for men need discipline of spirit and soul as well as of mind and body. It does mean that we must identify ourselves with the life of men, rich and poor, educated and ignorant, righteous and unrighteous, white and black, red and yellow—without prejudice or pride.

IV. *The fourth pillar of faith is Christ,* the one foundation on which to build the temple of the soul. Men have tried in every way to assail and discredit Christ. One and all, both ancient and modern, have failed. In this time of change, rebellion, heresy, and confusion, every institution, every tenet of faith, and every individual is being tried as silver in the fire. The true test of our faith is not when we are within the watchful eye of parent or peers, friends or foes, superiors or inferiors, but when "in a far country" we live according to the faith once delivered to the saints.— John W. McKelvey.

## Illustration

TOO GOOD TO BE TRUE. Many things are too good to be true. Spring is too good to be true and the blue sky of day and the starry sky of night. Mountains are too good to be true and trees and flowers and birds. Music is too good to be true—Beethoven's *Pastoral Symphony* and Bach's chorals and Handel's "Hallelujah Chorus." Cathedrals are too good to be true and the Parthenon and the Taj Mahal. Great pictures are too good to be true—*The Sistine Madonna* and *The Last Supper* of Leonardo and Millet's *Angelus* and a thousand more. The home is too good to be true and the church and the school and the university—even with all their defects. Poetry is too good to be true and philosophy and science and art and literature. Above all, goodness is too good to be true and faith and hope and love. God himself is too good to be true and Christ and the Spirit of Truth who guides into all truth. Yet all of these things are true and spiritually indestructible. Therefore we will not fear though the earth be removed and though the very mountains tremble with the destructive forces of nature and man. For those who have caught "the heavenly vision" look for a city that hath foundations, whose builder and maker is God, and for a new heaven and a new earth wherein dwelleth righteousness.—John Wright Buckham in *The Meetinghouse*.

## Sermon Suggestions

THE SIN OF PRAYERLESSNESS. Text: I Sam. 12:23. (1) By prayerlessness the cross of Christ is despised. (2) By prayer-

lessness the church of Christ is deprived. (3) By prayerlessness the cause of Christ is defeated.—George B. Duncan.

HOW TO HAVE COURAGE. Text: Deut. 31:6. (1) We must have great convictions upon which to build courage. (2) We may gain courage as we share our experiences with others. (3) We gain courage as we give courage to others.

## Worship Aids

CALL TO WORSHIP. "Let all those that put their trust in thee rejoice: let them ever shout for joy because thou defendest them: let them also that love thy name be joyful in thee." Ps. 5:11.

INVOCATION. Eternal God, in whom we live and move and have our being, whose face is hidden from us by our sins and whose mercy we forget in the blindness of our hearts: cleanse us, we beseech thee, from all our offenses and deliver us from proud thoughts and vain desires, that with lowliness and meekness we may draw near to thee, confessing our faults, confiding in thy grace, and finding in thee our refuge and our strength.

OFFERTORY SENTENCE. "Give unto the Lord the glory due unto his name: bring an offering, and come before him: worship the Lord in the beauty of holiness." I Chron. 16:29.

OFFERTORY PRAYER. Our heavenly Father, may thy kingdom be uppermost in our minds, our hearts, and our loves. Accept our gifts and with them the rededication of all that we are and have to thy greater glory.

PRAYER. O God, who hast put a song in our hearts: we give thee thanks for every voice that praises thee, the author of all things good; for the sunlight which brings life to the world; for everything that grows and lifts its head toward thy light; for the stars in their courses, proclaiming a divine hand in their order; for the kindness of human hearts that cannot be crushed; for the hopes which, though crushed, rise eternally toward better things; for the deep impulses of the soul which set us toward thee. We thank thee that above all the bewilderments of life rises the song of man's unconquerable faith—his assurance that thou art the eternal spirit of good, that thou hast better things in store for thy sons than they can ask or desire, and that through darkness and through light thou art the abiding friend of all the sons of men. Put that song in our hearts this day as we gather in thy house. Give us the spirit of praise and accept the devotion of our hearts to thee and thy purposes.—Morgan Phelps Noyes.

### EVENING SERVICE

**Topic: Christ Above All (Festival of Christ the King)**

SCRIPTURE: Col. 1:15–27.

I. *Christ is the image of the invisible God.* This means, among other things, that God is like Christ. We believe that God is like Christ, with a father's love for all mankind. We are not orphans in an indifferent world but sons and daughters in our Father's house.

II. *Christ is the creator of the world.* He is not one spiritual being among many, as the Gnostics thought, but the creator of all things in heaven and earth including whatever spiritual beings there are. For us this means that the power and the mind and the heart which has created the world is the power and the mind and the heart which we see in Jesus of Nazareth.

III. *Christ is the end of the world.* "As all creation passed out from him, so does it all converge again toward him." It will find its completion, its fulfillment in him. The conditions of existence are so ordered that without

Christ or the spirit within Christ it cannot attain its perfection. The God who controls our destinies, who makes the wrath of man to praise him, and who determines the goal that mankind shall reach is the God who became incarnate in Jesus Christ. However far the world may be from his spirit today, in the end it shall reign supreme because he is both the beginning and the end, the source from which all its forces and energies have been derived, and the goal toward which they inevitably tend.

IV. *Christ is the preserver of the world.* As Paul puts it, "He is before all things and in him all things hold together." Any individual, any social institution, any nation, or any international organization which sets itself against the moral law of the universe, as revealed in Christ, tends to disintegrate, to fall apart. In him and only in him do all things hold together.

V. *Christ is working in the church for the redemption of the world.* We may wonder at first why the church should be mentioned alongside Christ who is the beginning and the end of creation. But the church, Paul reminds us, is his body. The church draws its life, its energy, and its power from him who is its head, but at the same time it is the agency through which Christ is working to reconcile man to God and therefore to one another. As Paul says, "He is the head of the body, the church; he is the beginning [but only the beginning], the first-born [but only the first-born] from the dead, that in everything he might be preeminent. For in him all the fullness of God was pleased to dwell and through him to reconcile to himself all things, whether on earth or in heaven" (Col. 1:18–20, RSV).—Ernest Trice Thompson in *The Presbyterian Outlook.*

## SUNDAY: SEPTEMBER FOURTH

### MORNING SERVICE

**Topic: Work—More than Hateful Necessity (Labor Sunday)**

TEXT: II Tim. 2:15.

I. "Do your best," Paul wrote. (a) Perhaps he remembered the hard labor of making tents, stretching skins and sewing them together when, if he had had his way, he would have been preaching the gospel. Like the rest of us, he had to discipline himself to do the things he would rather not. But, like the good workman he was, he put himself into making tents with the same dedication with which he preached the gospel.

(b) It is an inescapable fact that every job involves doing some things we would rather not. In my job there are the sheer drudgery of filing material for sermons and the painful necessity of endless committee meetings. There is the problem of raising money to make the ministry of the church possible. When I catalogue the things I do that I would rather not, I wonder why I decided to be a minister. On the other hand I've discovered that there is a challenge in doing the things I'd rather not. A committee meeting is a challenge to get something done, and it is a challenge to file the right illustration in the right place. It is a challenge to raise money with which to do the kingdom's work.

(c) I dare say that there is something waiting for you to do that you wish you could avoid that could be an impetus to growth and a means to creative self-discipline. "Do your best," put yourself into whatsoever your hands find to do and do it with all your might. You may be surprised at the way time flies. What is more, you may discover that your job is not half as distasteful as you thought. Maybe you can learn new ways of being more efficient and more effective, so that job dissatisfaction becomes job satisfaction.

II. Paul went on to say: "Do your best to present yourself to God as one approved" (II Tim. 2:15, RSV).

(a) That is to say, do what you do in such fashion that God can approve it. After all, "When you work you fulfill a part of earth's furtherest dream, assigned to you when that dream was born" (Gibran). You have something to contribute to the symphony of God's creation.

(b) God gives us our capacities and powers, but he cannot build a church,

develop a business, create a poem, or fashion the good society without men and women who use their skills and talents in ways he can approve. We need to be reminded, as Henry van Dyke wrote, "Honest toil is holy service, faithful work is praise and prayer."

(c) Work is more than a hateful necessity to which we have been summoned in order to earn a living. It is a vocation to which we have been called, a means by which we use our God-given skills "to fulfill a part of earth's furtherest dream, assigned to you when the dream was born." Not to toil in such fashion that God can approve the way we do what we do is to emasculate the dream.

III. Paul went another step. He urged Timothy to be "a workman who has no need to be ashamed."

(a) The words are a rebuke to all too many of us. We ought to be ashamed of work half done, of carelessness, inertia, and indifference. We ought to be ashamed to waste God's time and company time. We ought to feel guilty about letting our capacities and skills rust and decay. But with little sense of vocation we are content to coast. We need to be reminded however that there is only one way to coast, namely, downhill.

(b) In the thinking of Jesus it is a sin to bury a talent. Wasted human resources are an affront to God. In the Master's parable of the talents the men who multiplied their talents were commended, and the implication of the story is that we were born to expand our powers by using them.

(c) The "workman who has no need to be ashamed" is the man who makes the most of what he's got. At his work he is not the last to arrive or the first to leave. He is forever preparing himself for the next step ahead, seeing that relationship between his job and the whole business of which he is a part. He makes it his business to know more about the functions of his department than anybody else. He is forever seeking ways of accomplishing more in less time.

IV. Paul's final word is his injunction to Timothy to handle the truth rightly.

(a) Paul wanted his young friend to relate the truth to life so that he and his contemporaries would have a valid sense of values related to the purposes of God. Success is not really success without some meaning beyond itself.

(b) Alfred North Whitehead looked at the universe in all its relationships and then proposed what he called the "principle of concretion," the doctrine that everything on earth is related to everything else and nothing happens anywhere without having repercussions everywhere. Our lives, yours and mine, are related either positively or negatively to the ultimate purposes of God, and Gibran was right, "When you work you fulfill a part of earth's furtherest dream, assigned to you when that dream was born."

(c) The dream found its ultimate fruition in Jesus Christ, the watershed of life and history. The work we do and the way we do it have their significance in the way they relate to him. The prayer, "The work of our hands, establish thou it," can be answered only as the work we do is done in his spirit. The meaning of the rancher's toil, the secretary's labor, or the lawyer's work depends on its relationship to the purposes of God revealed in Jesus Christ.— Harold Blake Walker.

### Illustrations

WHAT GOD NEEDS.    Ideally the Minnesota congregation was right when a new sanctuary was being built. A big sign in front announced: "This Church Built by God." But underneath someone used a can of spray paint to add these words: "Plumbing by Swenson." This emphasized a very practical truth. God cannot build a church alone. He needs human talents to create the building where his church meets. The body of Christ has hands and feet and voices that are our own.—William F. Wills in *Family Devotions.*

BEYOND COMPUTERS.    The essential problem of man in a computerized age remains the same as it has always been. That problem is not solely how to be more productive, more comfortable, and more content but how to be more sensitive, more sensible, more proportionate, and more alive. The computer makes possible a phenomenal leap in human proficiency; it demolishes the fences around the practical and even the theoretical intelligence. But the question persists and indeed grows whether the computer will make it easier or harder for human beings to know who they really are, to identify their problems, to respond more fully to beauty, to place adequate value on life, and to make their world safer than it now is. Electronic brains can reduce the profusion of dead ends involved in vital research. But they can't eliminate the foolishness and decay that come from the unexamined life. Nor do they connect to the reality of pain in others, the possibilities of creative growth in himself, the memory of the race, and the rights of the next generation.—Norman Cousins.

### Sermon Suggestions

HOLDING YOUR LIFE IN TRUST.    Text: I Cor. 4:7. Paradoxes describing the central truths upon which the Christian trusteeship of life rests: (1) If you have it you owe it. (2) If you give it you keep it. (3) If you share it you care.—Gene E. Bartlett.

BEING GOOD FOR BAD REASONS.    Text: Matt. 5:20. (1) Be more heartfelt than the scribes and Pharisees who tried to be good in order to keep rules and fit patterns. (2) Be more humble than the scribes and Pharisees who were proud of their righteousness. (3) Be more creative than the scribes and Pharisees who tried to keep the rules but not to improve them. (4) Be more self-forgetting than the scribes and Pharisees who had an eye on the rewards of their efforts.

### Worship Aids

CALL TO WORSHIP.    "We are laborers

together with God: ye are God's husbandry, ye are God's building. Let every man take heed how he buildeth. For other foundation can no man lay than that is laid, which is Jesus Christ." I Cor. 3:9–11.

INVOCATION. Heavenly Father, we come before thee in trembling because we are conscious of our many sins; yet boldly because we know that thou dost love us. Forgive us our sins, and help us to become more worthy of thy goodness and love. May we gain that strength from communion with thee which will enable us to walk humbly and righteously before thee and uprightly before the world, manifesting in life's every experience that faith and courage which befit thy children.

OFFERTORY SENTENCE. "Let the beauty of the Lord our God be upon us; and establish thou the work of our hands upon us; yea, the work of our hands establish thou it." Ps. 90:17.

OFFERTORY PRAYER. God of all good, who hath rewarded our labors, we acknowledge thankfully thy favor and do now dedicate a share of our material gains to the even more satisfying ministries of the spirit.

PRAYER. Father of all mankind we pray that to this church all thy children may ever be welcome. Hither may the little children love to come and young men and maidens to be strengthened for the battle of life. Here may the strong renew their strength and win for their life a noble consecration. And hither may age turn its footsteps to find the rest of God and light at eventide.

Here may the poor and needy find friends. Here may the tempted find succor, the sorrowing find comfort, and the bereaved learn that over their beloved death has no more dominion.

Here may they who fear be encouraged and they who doubt have their better trusts and hopes confirmed.

Here may the careless be awakened to a sense of their folly and guilt and to timely repentance.

Here may the oppressed and striving souls be assured of the mercy that triumphs over sin and receive help to go on their way rejoicing.—*The Pastor's Prayerbook.*

## EVENING SERVICE

### Topic: The Importance of Your Paycheck

SCRIPTURE: I Cor. 9:24–26; II Tim. 4:7–8.

I. Paychecks are important because they put a price tag on the work you do, and it is this price tag which helps to value not just your work but where you rank among your fellow workers in the same vocational field or in the same line of work.

(a) The paycheck involves more than money because the paycheck carries enormous psychological meanings and messages besides the more obvious economic considerations.

(b) A cut in our paycheck hurts. We may feel the loss of the financial income when our paycheck is reduced and we suffer some financial pinch. More important than this economic loss is the psychological pain we feel and suffer. A smaller paycheck means that the value of our work has been diminished. To devalue our work suggests a deflation of our own personal self-esteem as well because our essential identity is wrapped up so closely with our occupation and our daily work.

(c) Paychecks are important not just because of the money they represent but because of the additional psychological meanings and messages which the paycheck communicates to us, to our family, to our friends, to our fellow workers, and to society in general.

II. Our compensation must include more than economic considerations if we are to be fully satisfied as persons.

(a) This explains why there are so many thousands upon thousands of volunteer workers in America. These people give themselves unstintingly to many good causes and never get a dime for their services. But these volunteer workers are not unpaid. They feel themselves well paid because the service they render is valued by those who receive it and is rewarded with public recognition or with personal self-satisfaction. These volunteer workers feel well paid when they see someone in fresh touch with God, when they see lives profoundly changed, and when they see institutions of fear dismantled and possibilities of faith increased. They feel deeply compensated when they sense themselves caught up in something bigger than themselves.

(b) Because our psychological paychecks are important to us, there are some things that people will do and some sacrifices they will make without money and without price. And there are some things that people won't do for money alone.

III. Isn't it amazing how the Bible so often anticipates the emphases and the findings of psychological discovery or philosophical truth?

(a) Studies in industry and business management have described over and over again that the paycheck is important to each worker but especially important in relation to his fellow workers. Why? Because each person needs to have his life validated by others. The Bible tells us that we are made to live in Christian community and that our membership in the body of Christ enables us to suffer with our fellow members or makes it possible for us to rejoice with them.

(b) Psychological studies in the field of business management have taught us that the paycheck is important to workers but that the noneconomic factors may become more important than money itself. The Bible knew this truth about us as persons and as human beings, and we are enjoined and encouraged in the Bible to compensate ourselves by choosing worthy goals which are worth our effort and our sacrifice.
—William F. Keuchner.

## SUNDAY: SEPTEMBER ELEVENTH

### MORNING SERVICE

**Topic: Encouraging Words for Growing Christians**

TEXT: I Thess. 5:2, 9–10.

If you were a new Christian, what would you want most? What is it that you would need? This is the basic question on which Paul's first letter to the Thessalonians was written. They were new Christians. They needed encouragement and strength-giving food, and that is what the letter conveyed.

I. If you are a new Christian one of the first things you want to know, as did the Thessalonians, is, Am I really in?

(a) The apostle Paul answered that to these friends in the last part of the first chapter when he said, "You turned to God from idols"; that is to say they were converted; they turned around from that which hadn't satisfied, that

which they had done in ignorance, and that which wasn't fulfilling. They had found life in God. "Yes," he said, "you are in. You have changed." Their conversion was real.

(b) You may have heard it said in the verse, "I am not ashamed of the gospel of Christ for it is the power of God unto salvation" (Rom. 1:16), that the word "power" comes from a Greek word from which we get our word "dynamite."

(1) That is correct but in this matter is a most unfortunate comparison. *Dynamos,* the basic word in Greek, projects its truest meaning in our language through the word "dynamic." Many of the young people understand this today. They are familiar with words like aerodynamics where the dynamic is not the power that blows a roof off but controlled power that can do creative, worthwhile, and valuable things. Simi-

larly the structural dynamics of the bridgebuilder and the one who erects the great skyscrapers is not the power that destroys but power that puts things together and keeps them together, using gravitational and other forces God has given.

(2) When Paul says, "The gospel came to you in the dynamic of the Holy Spirit," it was a creative force. The Holy Spirit, to be sure, does convict people so that they themselves may literally be torn, but then the Holy Spirit convinces them of the grace of God and regenerates them. That is being "born again" so that one is changed into a child of God. When that has happened you are in.

II. The second thing a new Christian wants to know is, How can I be really assured of my salvation? In Paul's letter of encouragement to the Thessalonians you see the expression "the gospel of God" appearing again and again. That is where assurance is based—the gospel of God.

(a) Gospel means good news. What is the good word from God? Luther stated in his Smaller Catechism that "the gospel is the good news that Jesus is the way to salvation to every one who believes." The good news from God is that he sent his Son into humanity as a perfect man, a man who revealed God, who performed many great works, who truly loved the people and showed what God is like.

(b) His major mission was his great work of redemption. He atoned for men's sins by taking sin into his very being, as Paul related to the Corinthians (II Cor. 5:21). He became a sinner not only by proxy but also by injection, so to speak, of the virus of human sinfulness into his being "in order that we might be the righteousness of God in him."

(c) The gospel is the good news that through the death and resurrection God has given us through Jesus Christ forgiveness not only in the sense that the slate is wiped clean but also a cleansing in the sense that we have been washed, cleansed through and through by the atoning blood of Christ.

III. Follow Paul's encouragement as he meets the third request of a growing Christian: How can I maintain this new life? We are led to the answer in Paul's statement, "We worked night and day, that we might not burden any of you, while we preached to you the gospel of God . . . for you know how, as a father with his children, we exhorted each one of you and encouraged you and charged you to lead a life worthy of God" (I Thess. 2:9–12, RSV).

(a) There are two emphases there. One is teaching. How are you going to maintain the Christian life? How are you to keep growing as a Christian? Be very well acquainted with the Bible. Read it, study it, and ponder it. Become very familiar with the Word of God. If a person will seriously study the Word of God he will come to know God's will. If you do not read the Word of God regularly you will shrivel on the vine. You will be defeated again and again. Follow God's Word. That's where life is.

(b) The other emphasis is the motivation of leading "a life worthy of God." It is a great thing to live so as to please God. That is the perfect rule. There is no way you can falsify when you are seeking to please God because he knows everything. If you are trying to please God you are not trying to gain some ascendance over someone else and you are not trying to build a status or anything of that kind.

(c) How does one live a life worthy of God? You can't possibly do it unless you first believe that God cares for you. Love puts it all together. (See Col. 3:14.) This leads to holy obedience to God, not in the sense of merely following regulations in the fearful sense as a slave but of following God's will because he loves you and you love him.

IV. Young people want to know about death. Young people are close to the reality of the tenuousness of life and of the frightening possibilities of failure "to make it." There is an awesome sobriety about it. They want to know about death and about the future. After death, what then?

(a) What happens when a person dies? To answer one must understand what a human being is. When God was creating man and the physical anatomy was all complete, God breathed his spirit into man and man became a living being, a spirit person similar to God himself. On the basis of that and right on through our studies of humanity we understand that while man is a physical being consisting of flesh, bones, blood, a nervous system, etc., he is most essentially a personality, a spiritual being. The real you, mind and psyche, the one that loves, the you that feels sad or feels glad, is not your body or even your brain. There is something deeper. It is the real self, the personality. Some call it soul, but more correctly it is spirit.

(b) When a body finishes its animated function and the life support system falters that body becomes an untenable house for the spirit-personality and that real self departs from the body. For the Christian this is to experience what Jesus promised the repentant thief on the cross—and it is significant that the teaching was given right at the beginning—"Today you will be with me in paradise." So the real self simply leaves the house of clay and is with God in the presence of Jesus who himself went through mortal death, "the first fruits of those who have fallen asleep [in death]" (I Cor. 15:20, RSV).

(c) Dying from a physical point of view is sometimes not too pleasant because there is pain or struggle. At other times it is beautiful, like closing one's eyes and waking up in heaven. Death then is the real self, the spirit of a person, simply moving out of a habitation that has become untenable because of certain chemical or mechanical deficiencies and "returns to God who gave it." Paul said, "Though our outer nature is wasting away"—the physical body begins to suffer some of the deterioration of age or illness—"our inner nature is being renewed every day" (II Cor. 4:16, RSV). The real you is more fully alive when it leaves this earth scene to be with God than it has ever been before.—Paul P. Fryhling.

## Illustrations

KNOWING GOD. To know the world profoundly in its origins, actualities, possibilities, and promises is to know God and to live in the world with unconditional concern for the realization of its manifold and multiform excellences is to worship him in spirit and in truth.—Philip Phenix.

LASTING GIFT. A child's world is fresh and new and beautiful, full of wonder and excitement. It is our misfortune that for most of us that clear-eyed vision, that true instinct for what is beautiful and awe-inspiring, is dimmed and even lost before we reach adulthood. If I had influence with the good fairy who is supposed to preside over the christening of all children, I should ask that her gift to each child in the world be a sense of wonder so indestructible that it would last throughout life as an unfailing antidote against the boredom and disenchantments of later years, the sterile preoccupation with things that are artificial, and the alienation from the sources of our strength.—Rachel Carson in *The Sense of Wonder*.

## Sermon Suggestions

THE NEXT DEVELOPMENT OF MAN. Text: Ps. 8:3–5. When does a man grow to his fullest stature? (1) When he has a goal worthy of his supreme devotion. (2) When he has a supporting fellowship. (3) When he finds a mission of unselfish love.—Roy A. Burkhart.

CHOOSING BETWEEN RIGHT AND WRONG. Text: Luke 12:57. (1) What does my proposed course of action or my type of response do to my personality? Does it increase my sense of self-respect? Does it make me stand a little taller or make it a little easier for me to live with myself? (2) What does my course of action do to others? (3) Would I want my conduct to become a universal practice? (4)

Is it in harmony with the insights of the great personalities of the Bible and Christian history?—Nenien C. McPherson, Jr.

## Worship Aids

CALL TO WORSHIP. "Lift up your heads in the sanctuary, and bless the Lord. The Lord that made heaven and earth bless thee out of Zion." Ps. 134:2–3.

INVOCATION. Lord God Almighty, holy and eternal Father, who dwellest in the high and lofty place, with him also that is of a humble and contrite spirit: we come before thee, beseeching thee to cleanse us by the grace of thy Holy Spirit, that we may give praise to thee, now and forever.

OFFERTORY SENTENCE. "Give, and it shall be given unto you; good measure, pressed down, and shaken together, and running over." Luke 6:38.

OFFERTORY PRAYER. O God, thou giver of all good gifts, in gratitude we bring our gifts on this day of joyous worship. Refine them, we pray thee, in the mint of thy divine purpose and use them to the end that thy kingdom may come and thy will be done on earth as it is in heaven.

PRAYER. Our gracious heavenly Father, we pause humbly before thee in prayer. Thou hast never failed to meet our daily needs. In gratefulness we turn to thee for thy goodness toward us which is shown in so many ways. In daytime the sun gives us light without failing, and at night we behold the beauty of the moon and the stars.

We come before thee, O Lord, to be reminded that thy truth needs to be brought before all the nations, but before this can happen it needs to find a place within every individual believer.

Thou hast promised us that where "two or three are gathered together in thy name" thou wilt make thy presence felt in their hearts. May we experience thy presence in this sanctuary. Let us not depart from this place without feeling deep in our hearts that thou hast spoken to us. Give us also the right directives through thy Word.

We also come before thee with a prayer to meet our varied needs. We would not ask thee for them for selfish reasons, but let every need met by thee make us stronger in our faith. Once strengthened in faith, give us the desire to apply it for the advancement of thy kingdom in our midst.

And now, our gracious heavenly Father, look with thy compassion upon the sick and heal them, if it be thy will. Bring comfort to the sorrowing where human words fail. Sustain the weak with thy mighty hand where there is no other help available.—John P. Dany.

## EVENING SERVICE

### Topic: Learning to Live

SCRIPTURE: Deut. 6:3–15.

I. *Learning has to do with God.* (See vv. 4–5.) (a) This is not just a pious place to start. It is the fundamental declaration of our faith that God is the most important fact in our existence and that learning to live is to find and to understand the will of God. So "you shall love the Lord your God" with all your faculties; he is to be the center of your thought and action.

(b) To declare that learning has to do with God means much more than slotting God or religion into a school curriculum. It means teaching a God-shaped view of life into which all learning fits as a consistent whole and which begins to equip a young person to deal with the moral decisions that life throws up.

II. *Learning has to do with life.* (See vv. 7–9.) (a) Christian education is not to be thought of as parceling up a little area of life and filling it full of quaint dogmas that must be regurgitated on religious occasions. Nothing could be further from the truth of the Bible. Learning the values of a God-centered world is as wide as the world itself. It is not life-denying but positive and life-affirming. So in these verses the teaching becomes part of the daily round of activity, and if it makes no contribution to life as we get up, move among men, or live in our own home, then it makes no sense at all.

(b) Christians, along with others, have stressed that the whole of man is involved in learning. God is interested in all our life and talents and in the development of individual potential, whether it be mental or manual skill, artistic creative ability, or whatever. Let us not imagine that any academic rat-race view is necessarily Christian. Learning is about the personal worth of a child, his total development, his unfolding individuality, and that's much wider than getting him down to reading, writing, and arithmetic.

III. *Learning has to do with human influences.* (See vv. 6–7.) (a) Learning for the child does not drop down from heaven. It comes through rightly directed human influences. A New Testament illustration of this is Timothy, influenced and led to faith by his mother and his grandmother (II Tim. 1:5), so that Paul can write "from childhood you have been acquainted with the sacred writings" (II Tim. 3:15). The natural human influences in the family had provided his instruction.

(b) Young people need to look at the tremendous need for committed Christian teachers not simply to take religious education out of school hours but by their very presence among staff and pupils to be the natural human influence for the Christian gospel.

(c) This is not an appeal for "Christian indoctrination" methods but a plea for us to recognize the enormous influence of the teaching profession. "Our educational establishment imparts a system of values wrapped up in a package of facts" (Arthur Koestler). A system of values is always there, and they will be humanist values, some other values, or Christian values. As parents or teachers we need not be ashamed of admitting to beliefs, values, attitudes, and a concern to produce mature adults with rational convictions and loyalties.
—John Wesson.

# SUNDAY: SEPTEMBER EIGHTEENTH

## MORNING SERVICE

**Topic: The Meaning of Worship**
TEXT: Ps. 96:3.

"Worship," William Temple said, "is the nourishment of the mind upon God's truth. Worship is the quickening of the conscience by God's holiness. Worship is the cleansing of the imagination by God's beauty. Worship is the response of my life to God's plan for my life." Worship is a many-sided thing, involving the whole personality.

I. "Worship is the nourishment of the mind upon God's truth." (a) That's why the Bible is so important in worship: the objective encounter with the strong words of the prophets, the massive sanity of the sermon on the mount, the words and deeds of the Man of Nazareth.

(b) The only thing that will rescue religion from a mess of subjectivity is the radical encounter with the biblical witness.

II. Worship is "the quickening of the conscience by God's holiness." (a) Conscience, like any other human activity, becomes moribund and sluggish. Not every man who obeys his conscience is obeying something fresh and alert and up-to-date. The older we get, the more used we become to evil, to meanness, and to compromise.

(b) Ever and again a man needs to have his conscience checked, sensitized, and renewed. He needs to turn again and again to that place where conscience is quickened—the holiness of God. And God's holiness is what it says: his wholeness, his passion for wholeness, integrity, oneness of aim and method, ends and means. For ultimately what dulls conscience is lack of wholeness: our unfortunate tendency to live in compartments and to adopt double standards—to have one standard, easy and accommodating, for ourselves; another, exact and demanding, for others; one rule for work, another for worship.

III. "Worship is the cleansing of the imagination by God's beauty." (a) William James said, "Where the will and the imagination are in conflict, the imagination always wins." We double our fists and we screw up our resolution; but when it comes to a showdown what really counts is the purity or impurity of our hidden life, the unconscious that we have fed either with healthy or unhealthy pictures. The cleansing of the imagination is a great feature of worship. What we take away may seem very meager sometimes, but who can gauge the steady percolating influence exerted by good words, healthy sentiments, and exalted visions?

(b) This is one reason why we should be so careful about the hymns we sing— that they don't weaken life by self-pity or selfish individualism but should be strong and objective; why we should use the best music and the loveliest symbols we can command; but above all why the vision of the good life should take precedence over our carping sins.

IV. "Worship is the response of my life to God's plan for my life." Let me say two brief things about our attitude of worship.

(a) The finest worship service in the Bible was where Jacob wrestled with God and God wrestled with him. Every real encounter with truth is a disturbing experience; every real meeting with beauty and goodness seeks to overthrow us, to conquer us. So we should be prepared for disturbance.

(b) We get nothing by being mere spectators. Well, that's an exaggeration! God is good! But the attitude of spectator is the least adequate we can adopt. "A congregation," Kierkegaard said, "is not an audience for whose special benefit minister and choir give a performance." No! The audience is God; he is the only spectator; and the congregation are the actors, with minister and choir, at best prompters, reminding us of our lines.

It would make a lot of difference if we remembered that.—W. B. J. Martin.

## Illustrations

CHURCH ENTRY.    Just after the Russian revolution a friend of Nicolai Berdyaev, the philosopher, was hesitatingly wondering whether to enter the Orthodox Church. "My life is spiritually very poor," he said. "I feel that we should come to the church with a dowry." "No," replied Berdyaev firmly, "you should come into the church naked."— *Forward Day by Day.*

HAPPY WITH GOD.    We all long for heaven where God is, but we have it in our power to be in heaven with him right now—to be happy with him at this very moment. But being happy with him means: loving as he loves, helping as he helps, giving as he gives, serving as he serves, rescuing as he rescues, being with him twenty-four hours a day, and touching him in all his distressing disguises.—Mother Teresa.

## Sermon Suggestions

HOW IS YOUR HEARING?    Texts: Mark 4:2–3, 9 (NEB). (1) The indifferent hearer. (2) The divided-minded hearer. (3) The superficial hearer. (4) The responsive hearer.—William McLeister 2nd.

DENIAL OF GUILT.    Text: Prov. 28:13. (1) Denial of guilt destroys character by eliminating responsibility and therefore freedom. (2) Denial of guilt makes forgiveness impossible by denying that there is a sin to be forgiven. (3) Denial of sin turns people into scandalmongers and gossips because it makes them project their own guilt to others to escape their uneasy consciences. (4) Denial of guilt leads to greater sin by making conscience less reproachful and virtue more distasteful. (5) Denial of guilt leads to despair which develops into a positive fanaticism against religion and morality. —Fulton J. Sheen.

## Worship Aids

CALL TO WORSHIP. "Let us search and try our ways, and turn again to the Lord. Let us lift up our heart with our hands unto God in the heavens." Lam. 3:40–41.

INVOCATION. We turn our minds unto thee, O God, that thou wilt give us deeper insight of thy Son our Lord. We turn our hearts unto thee that thy love may flow through them. We turn our wills unto thee that thou mayst guide us in all that we do and in all that we say.

OFFERTORY SENTENCE. "If there be first a willing mind, it is accepted according to that which a man hath, and not according to that which he hath not." II Cor. 8:12.

OFFERTORY PRAYER. O God, in whose sight a contrite heart is more than whole burnt offerings; help us with these our gifts to dedicate ourselves, body, soul, and spirit, unto thee, which is our reasonable service.

PRAYER. May we have the nerve, Father, to look at who we are, to bring our attention to our own selves, to be here in spirit as well as body, without leaving our outside concerns. May we be able to bring our full concerns here, to face ourselves, to face each other, to face whoever we are in thy sight. May the shams, pretenses, and games which we use to protect ourselves and also to keep us lost be put down. May we become soft-hearted, open-minded, honest, without prejudice, listening, and if it should be that our own name is called while we are here, may we have the courage of Samuel to say, "Here I am; send me." And if not, forgive us.— J. Bruce Evans in *Grant, Father.*

## EVENING SERVICE

**Topic: What Can We Do About Race Relations?**

TEXT: Acts 10:35.

I. We can rejoice and be glad that God has made a colorful world. There are 88 keys on the piano. Play only the white keys, you get some music. Play only the black keys, you get other music. But you have to play both black and white to have harmony and great music. So God has a plan for all the races. The black man doesn't need to be made in the image of the white man or the white man in the image of the black. We all need to learn by the grace of God to reflect our individual images.

II. Equally important is the frank facing of racism in our own hearts. Few people will admit to being outright bigots anymore. We like to protest, I don't have any prejudice! But inside each of us does have areas of deliberate misunderstanding. Sin affects each of us, cuts us off from God, and makes us insecure; so we try to gain a feeling of security by cutting someone else down, perhaps someone of another race. This is a subtle process that infects each of us. The first step in really coming to know the power of Jesus Christ is a genuine honesty that is willing to let God search our hearts and show us in our own lives areas where we need cleansing.

III. We must learn to accept freely the fact that God accepts us as we are when we come to him in faith and let the "blood of Jesus Christ, God's Son, cleanse us from all sin." God can wipe away the strain of prejudice. A lot of so-called race relations have been built on guilt, fear, and manipulation by both sides. This is a poor basis for understanding. Guilt covers over what's inside us and festers into fear and resentment that poisons. Grace, on the other hand, opens us up and produces genuine love.

IV. We can let God show each of us a place where we can build a bridge. This isn't a matter of running helter-skelter in a hundred different directions. It's a matter of quietly letting the Holy Spirit direct each one of us to do what lies within our power. This will mean sharing the Christ who can change men's hearts. It will mean supporting laws that oppose all kinds of discriminations. Laws can't make people love one another, but they can help to prevent flagrant injustice. We can make friends with those of other races.—Leighton Ford.

# SUNDAY: SEPTEMBER TWENTY-FIFTH

## MORNING SERVICE

**Topic: The Fellowship of the Spirit**
SCRIPTURE: Phil. 2:1–5.

There are two complementary truths which we need to understand. The first is that Christian fellowship is a fact that has already been given to us by God. And the second is that Christian fellowship is an ideal that still has to be worked for by us. Here in the same passage Paul speaks of it as both.

I. *The divine gift of fellowship.* (a) In v. 1 Paul repeats the word "if" four times in the Greek: "If there is any encouragement in Christ, if there is any incentive of love, if there is any fellowship of the Spirit [as the Greek is, or 'participation in' the Spirit], if any affection and sympathy" (RSV). This is not because he is casting any doubts upon these things. No, these things are the facts of every Christian believer's experience. They are the basic facts of the Christian fellowship and the foundation upon which the fellowship is built. So he is challenging the Philippian church to live out these facts, as much as to say "if these things are a reality, as indeed they are, then prove it, demonstrate it in your Christian community."

(b) Perhaps there is an allusion here to the trinity. Perhaps there is even an echo of the so-called "grace" that comes at the end of Corinthians. But I think the emphasis is on the words "in Christ" (v. 1). This was Paul's favorite expression for the Christian believer. Every Christian is in Christ, united to him as a limb is united to the body or a branch is united to the tree, and in Christ God has given us everything we need for the living of our Christian life.

(1) In Christ we have encouragement. Jesus Christ is the world's and history's greatest encourager, able to bring encouragement to the most disheartened, disillusioned, dispirited, and dejected person.

(2) In Christ too there is an incentive to love because he first loved us.

(3) In Christ there is the fellowship of the Spirit because in Christ every Christian has received the Holy Spirit. He dwells in the church, he dwells in the individual believer, and the fellowship of the Spirit is this common participation in the Holy Spirit.

(4) In Christ we receive compassion and mercy. God for Christ's sake has had compassion and mercy on us.

(c) Here then is the given basis of the Christian fellowship. And it is this that distinguishes Christian fellowship from every other type of human association.

(1) For there are other human associations and groupings in the community which have some kind of esprit de corps. For instance soldiers enjoy good comradeship in the regiment to which they belong; stamp collectors, music lovers, football fans, even bird watchers can enjoy some kind of getting along with one another through their common interest.

(2) We Christian men and women have got something more than a common interest and more than a common concern. We have got a common possession. We are shareholders in the same spiritual capital. We have this common share in the Holy Spirit, and this is the givenness of the Christian fellowship.

II. *The human outworking of the Christian fellowship.* (a) Although God has given us all these blessings it does not mean to say that we experience Christian fellowship automatically, for we can still deny what we are.

(1) There are a number of hints in

his letter that Paul was disturbed by the lack of fellowship in the Philippian church, and that is why he is urging them to love one another and to live at peace. They are to work out what God has given them.

(2) The basic lesson that Paul teaches them is that the secret of unity is humility, the kind of humility exhibited by Jesus. He goes on to tell them that humility begins in the mind, for the Greek word for humility means literally "lowliness of mind."

(b) There is a great deal in these verses about the mind for it is obvious that how we treat people depends on what we think of them. If we despise somebody in our mind, then we treat him like dirt; if we respect somebody in our mind, we will treat him respectfully. So Paul urges them: "Do nothing from selfishness or conceit, but in humility count (esteem) others better than yourselves" (v. 3).

(c) Many people find this verse very difficult. They ask: "How can I esteem somebody better than myself when I know that he is not better than myself? For example if he is a drunkard and I happen to be sober or if he has got a vile temper and I do not happen to have that particular problem, how then can I esteem him better than myself? Have I got to close my eyes to his faults and pretend that he is better than he really is?"

(d) Surely we must begin by saying it does not mean that, for humility is not a game of blind man's buff nor is it another word for hypocrisy.

(1) It is interesting that the Greek word for "better" does not in itself mean morally better. Literally it means to be "above" or "over" something, and when it is used in a literal context it is used sometimes of a hill rising up over the horizon or of an object projecting out of the earth, and it is used of a tall person who stands head and shoulders above somebody else. So it comes to refer to people whom we sometimes call our "superiors" who may not excel us in ability or in character but

who excel us in their rank or their influence because they are set over us.

(2) We might therefore translate this word as esteeming others "more important" than ourselves. For conceit is an exaggerated view of my own importance, while humility is a recognition of the great importance of other people in the sight of God.

(e) Now this is a revolutionary principle. Our fallen nature says to us, "Treat him as an inferior." The world says, "Treat him as an equal." But Jesus Christ says: "Treat him as your superior. Look up to him. Think of his importance, his great worth as a creature made in the image of God and a sinner for whom Christ died."

(1) It is this principle that brought Jesus to earth and to the cross. For Paul goes on: "although he was in the form of God he did not count equality with God a thing to be grasped" (v. 6) for his own enjoyment. No, he laid aside his glory and privileges.

(2) Jesus was not a hypocrite. He did not pretend that he was anything other than he was. He did not deny his own deity and say he was really nothing at all. But what he did was to recognize the importance and worth of human beings, and that in comparison with his own status and his own glory he was prepared to lay aside his privileges in order to have the privilege of serving those he loved.

(f) So we are called to follow in the footsteps of Christ and to let this mind be in us that was in him; not clinging to our status or even to our status symbols, not despising those who lack our status and its symbols but counting other people more important than ourselves and regarding all our privileges as nothing in comparison with the great privilege of serving other people.—John Stott.

## Illustration

CORPORATE VIRTUE. The destinies of those who inhabit this closely knit planet are now seen to be as inseparable as the destinies of a group of travelers on a spaceship. It follows then that our ethical thinking must be guided by a conception of a virtue that is corporate or even global in its scope, and such a virtue is peace. Traditionally of course the three principal Christian virtues were reckoned to be faith, hope, and love. But these are qualities that we associate more readily with the life of the individual than with the life of society. Even love, the crown of the Christian life, is usually considered as a relation between individuals. If the conditions of our time are demanding that we think in corporate terms, then it is arguable that we should see the crown of the Christian life in the unquestionably corporate virtue of peace.— John Macquarrie.

## Sermon Suggestions

DIGGING WELLS. Text: John 4:13–14. (1) Life means only as much to us as we seek to make it mean to others. (2) It is much better to be a digger of wells than merely a builder of selfish monuments. (3) Until we lose ourselves in the giving of ourselves we can never find ourselves.—Fred R. Chenault.

THE MASTERY OF PASSIONS. Text: II Tim. 2:22. (1) Recognize our passions, have a wholesome respect for their dangerous propensities, and carefully avoid any occasion of overstimulation or loss of control. (2) Positive aims give constructive outlets for dynamic energies. (3) Associate with those who are singleminded in their desire to please God. (4) Surrender our whole selves to God's pure, uncompromised, and loving purpose.—Edward W. Stimson.

## Worship Aids

CALL TO WORSHIP. "They that wait upon the Lord shall renew their strength; they shall mount up with wings as eagles; they shall run, and not be weary; and they shall walk, and not faint." Isa. 40:31.

INVOCATION. As we begin another day, most gracious Father, make us to know that we never drift out of thy love and care. Faces may change, conditions may alter, but thou art never so near to us as when we need thee most.

OFFERTORY SENTENCE. "Go, and sell that thou hast, and give to the poor, and thou shalt have treasure in heaven: and come and follow me." Matt. 19:21.

OFFERTORY PRAYER. O Lord, who hast given us the privilege of life, help us to magnify eternal values and to show forth by our loves and our tithes the Christ, whom to know aright is life eternal.

PRAYER. Thy beauty, O God, is upon us; autumn splendor everywhere! Days lucid with vision or dim with mist, haze, and smothered sunshine; nights wistful with summer memories. The trees are touched with ripe, mellow colors, and the leaves begin to fall and flutter away, as frail as the generations of men. The birds are going south, following a viewless path, like the homing instinct in the soul of man.

Lord, we thank thee for beauty: in its soft enchantment matter and spirit join, time and eternity blend. Let our thankfulness be the flower of thoughtfulness and our prayer the fruit of joy. Who does not hear an autumn anthem singing low in his heart! Help us, O God, to make the life of man as lovely as the world in which he lives and the brotherliness of humanity equal to the beauty of nature.

Thou hast made our life a summer sowing, an autumn harvest, and a great white winter; too short for hate and only long enough for the love that lifts the load we all must bear. Oh, teach us to toil while we may and do somewhat of good before our spirits take their flight on wings homeward bound—doves at thy window.—Joseph Fort Newton.

## EVENING SERVICE

## Topic: The Promise of Plenty

SCRIPTURE: Ps: 81:10–16.

I. *The spiritual capacity which God demands.* (a) The God who made us knows that there is nothing outside of himself which can ultimately satisfy the deepest desires of the human heart. Someone has put it: "There is a vast capacity for God within the human personality and therefore a vast emptiness without him." For this reason God demands a spiritual capacity from each one of us for his glory and for his eternal good.

(b) This spiritual capacity suggests two things. (1) A spiritual openness. A person who never opens his mouth will never be fed and will ultimately die. In similar fashion a Christian who never opens his mouth to God in desire, prayer, and faith will suffer spiritually. Our spiritual capacities can only grow as we observe his clear command, "Open your mouth wide, and I will fill it" (v. 10). God has a promise of plenty for us, but even heaven's best is utterly wasted if we are not prepared to open our mouths.

(2) This spiritual capacity suggests a spiritual eagerness—"open your mouth wide." There is a difference between opening your mouth and opening it widely.

II. *The spiritual sufficiency which God directs.* (a) God's purpose of sufficiency is what we might term the blessing of triumphant living. (See vv. 13–15.) God had never intended that his people should be the victims of the world, the flesh, and the devil but rather victors in every situation of life. Paul exclaims, "We are more than conquerors through him that loved us" (Rom. 8:37) and "Thanks be unto God, which always causeth us to triumph in Christ" (II Cor. 2:14). The whole purpose of God's redemptive plan is that we might know what it is to triumph daily—in the home, in the church, and in the world. Jesus came to this world to demonstrate that as a man, dependent upon the indwelling Spirit, he could live a triumphant life. Then he died to make this life available to all who would believe. Now his purpose is that this quality of life should be reproduced in us and through us as we trust and obey.

(b) There is also the blessing of abundant living: "I would feed you with the finest of the wheat, and with honey from the rock I would satisfy you" (v. 16). The reference is to that quality in the grain of wheat which is the very staff of life. But with the wheat there is also the honey out of "the rock." In Palestine, as well as in other eastern countries, honey at its best is found in the clefts of the rocks where it is protected from the elements and purified by the bees themselves. Like wheat, honey is one of the most nourishing foods known to man. It not only strengthens but also sweetens life.

III. *The spiritual delinquency which God deplores.* (a) The question arises as to what the psalmist means by this spiritual delinquency. In simple terms it involves the failure to hear God's word: "But my people did not listen to my voice; Israel would have none of me" (v. 11). Unfortunately, as in the days of old, so in modern times, people refuse to hear the word of God. We turn to the philosophies of men and investigate the most recent speculations of science but fail to hear the word of God. We tell ourselves that there are no absolutes, that the commandments of Jehovah are only relative, and that the Bible has no message for our age. The fact that Jesus Christ has broken into history and has uttered God's final word leaves us unimpressed and unaffected.

(b) This failure to hear God's word is inevitably followed by the failure to heed God's will: "O that my people would listen to me, that Israel would walk in my ways!" (v. 13). It is one thing to hear God's word and to be orthodox in our respect for the authority of divine truth, but it is quite another matter to translate that word into obedience to God's will. Perhaps the greatest danger in evangelical circles is that of knowledge without obedience and belief without behavior. To understand and not to obey is to merit God's judgment.

—Stephen F. Olford.

# SUNDAY: OCTOBER SECOND

## MORNING SERVICE

**Topic: Love and Need (World Communion Sunday)**

SCRIPTURE: Isa. 55:1–5; Matt. 14:13–21.

Who or what shall separate us from the love of Christ? St. Paul is confident that nothing is able to do that. But are we that confident? Today's gospel illustrates how great and powerful this love of God is. The Lord who feeds can also strengthen our faith in God's sustaining love for us.

I. The need was great. (a) St. Matthew sets the size of the crowd at considerably more than five thousand. Will the task prove too big for our Lord? What problems today seem equally big, equally impossible of solution?

(b) It was a lonely place. There was no help to be seen on the horizon. What is more, danger was close at hand. John the Baptist had just been beheaded. But even in such a hopeless situation there is still reason to hope in God. Those people in the gospel had gathered in a lonely place, but they were not alone for he who feeds and sustains the world was with them.

(c) The day was over. The hour was late, and the darkness of night was coming on. Had the time for helping already passed? No, our Lord knew what he would and could do.

II. The power of God was as great as the need. (a) The people "need not go away." Those who abide with Christ need not fear that the concerns of temporal life will take them from him. This story illustrates what our Lord had preached in the sermon on the mount (Matt. 6:25–33). There is but one source for all life's blessings, and in Christ Jesus we have access to that source.

(b) "He ordered the crowd to sit down." This large crowd sitting down, looking toward and waiting on the Lord, gives us a picture of the church. God's people bring what they can—even as little as five loaves and two fish—and then they leave the rest to God. When we have done what we can with our problems, we too must learn to sit down and wait to see what God will do.

(c) The leftover pieces were gathered. This bread is longer lasting than the manna in the wilderness. This reminds us that the bread which God gives is more than earthly. The prophet in the first lesson was also speaking of the true bread of life when he spoke of God's "everlasting covenant" and his "steadfast, sure love." The most nourishing food of all is revealed in Christ. In the Eucharist we are partakers of this true bread.—Richard G. Herbel.

## Illustrations

IN HIS NAME. During Holy Week of 1945, American Forces were penetrating deeply into Germany. As the senior chaplain of an Army Corps, it fell to my duty to announce to the German officials in conquered territory what our religious policies would be, and also, as far as possible, to arrange for proper celebration of Easter by the troops of our command. The arrangements for the use of German churches were made in conference with church leaders and other officials. For this purpose there had been assigned to me as interpreter an old man who was a professor of etymology and an expert linguist.

When the tense conferences were past and all others had departed, the old man lingered awhile and we exchanged a few warmhearted, Christian expressions. When we were about to part, the old man put forward his hand—then drew it back quickly because he realized that fraternization, even a handshake, was not permitted in those days of heavy combat. Somewhat uncomfortable I stood at attention perhaps too formal even for Germans.

After a silence the old man bowed courteously and said: "Well, after all, we have arranged to celebrate the resurrection, and, friend or enemy, our Lord promised, 'Where two or three are gathered in my name, there am I in the midst.' And he has been here."— Edward L. R. Elson.

UNPARDONABLE SINS. There are three unpardonable sins today: to be flippant or superficial in the analysis of the world situation; to live and act as though halfhearted measures would avail; and to lack the moral courage to rise to this historic occasion.—Charles Malik.

## Sermon Suggestions

THE DIVINE ENCOUNTER. Text: II Cor. 5:17. (1) A new person in Christ is one who is finding new beginnings. (2) A new person in Christ is one who is finding a new sense of values. (3) A new person in Christ is one who is finding new motives for living.—F. Philip Rice.

THE MEANING OF COMMUNION. (1) A feast of obedience. (See I Cor. 11:24.) (2) A feast of thanksgiving. (See Matt. 26:27.) (3) A feast of remembrance. (See I Cor. 11:24.) (4) A feast of testimony. (See I Cor. 11:26.) (5) A feast of communion. (See I Cor. 10:16–17.) (6) A feast of anticipation. (I Cor. 11:26.) (7) A feast of consecration. (See Luke 22:20.) —David J. Tarrant.

## Worship Aids

CALL TO WORSHIP. "Now in Christ Jesus ye who sometimes were far off are made nigh by the blood of Christ. For he is of our peace, who hath made both one, and hath broken down the middle wall of partition between us. Now therefore ye are no more strangers and foreigners, but fellow citizens with the saints and of the household of God." Eph. 2:13–14, 19.

INVOCATION. O heavenly Father, who hast given us a true faith and a sure hope: help us to live as those who believe and trust in the communion of saints, the forgiveness of sins, and the resurrection to life everlasting; and strengthen this faith and hope in us all the days of our life.

OFFERTORY SENTENCE. "As we have therefore opportunity, let us do good unto all men, especially unto them who are of the household of faith." Gal. 6:10.

OFFERTORY PRAYER. O thou who art the Father of all, may we live as thy children and brothers of all whom thou hast made to dwell upon the face of the earth that thy kindness may be born in our hearts.

PRAYER. Eternal God, we bow in your presence to express gratitude to you because we may join Christians all about the world in fellowship, prayer, and sharing. As we share what we have in order to alleviate suffering and build a better world we follow in the way of the Lord. Keep us aware that you continually share him with us and that in his suffering and death he gave himself to us. Help us to an awareness that worship involves the total self, all that we have, all that we are, and all that we may become. Teach us that we truly worship you in fellowship one with another, those who are here gathered and those persons everywhere. May we and everyone be blessed, uplifted, helped, and dedicated. As we receive the symbols of sacrifice and love may we have a vision of a world that is one where peace and harmony reign. Then grant, O Lord, that we shall have the will to make our vision into a reality. —Chester E. Hodgson.

## EVENING SERVICE

**Topic: Paul's Appeal for Christian Unity**

SCRIPTURE: Phil. 2:1–18; 3.

Paul declares that God gave Christ a

name above all names; at the name of Jesus every knee should bow and every tongue confess Jesus Christ as Lord.

(1) The occasion which prompted Paul's confession of faith was the disturbance in the church at Philippi. The unity of the church was upset by factions and vainness (2:3), by murmuring and disputing (2:14), and by two other classes of people.

(2) One group was the Judaizers who taught that salvation depended not only on faith in Christ but also in the keeping of the circumcision rite of Judaism. The other group which Paul called "dogs" and "evil-workers" was a group who paraded under the guise of Christian liberty but lived like pagans. The unity of the church was threatened.

(3) Paul makes a threefold appeal for Christian unity.

I. Paul appeals for unity on the basis of their Christian experience. They share in the love of God, the tender mercies and compassion of God and in the fellowship of the Spirit of God. Therefore Paul continues, be of the same mind, the same love, and the same sentiment (2:1–2).

II. Paul points to the example of Christ. He gives a threefold interpretation of the meaning of the incarnation of Christ.

(a) In his preexistent state Christ was in essence God. In his relationship with God, Christ was equal with God, but he did not esteem (prize) this relationship with God to the extent that it prevented him from becoming human in order to redeem man. He chose not to hold onto this position but laid it aside.

(b) In his humiliation Christ took upon himself the likeness of man, and "having been thus found in the fashion as a man, he humbled himself and became obedient to God even so far as to suffer the ignominious death of the cross."

(c) God however exalted him above all creatures. At the name of Jesus every knee will bow; every tongue will confess Christ as Lord and God will be glorified.

III. Paul uses his own life as a model.

(a) He had a fortunate birth and a noble religious heritage. He was successful, ambitious, and righteous, but Paul, following the example of Christ chose not to hold onto these advantages but forsook them for Christ.

(b) Paul realized that in comparison with the nature, humiliation, and exaltation of Christ he not yet had obtained that perfection. But Paul declares his intention "to press on toward the goal unto the prize of the high calling of God in Christ" (3:12–16).—William C. Corley in *The Christian Index*.

# SUNDAY: OCTOBER NINTH

## MORNING SERVICE

### Topic: What Humility Can Do

TEXT: Jas. 4:6.

I. Humility is a right assessment of what God is and has done and what we ourselves are and have done.

(a) It is neither a boasting of our attainments beyond the facts nor a denial of our ability where we are talented. To be humble we do not have to belittle ourselves or hold a lower view of ourselves than the truth warrants. We have to recognize this truth about ourselves and live in the light of it.

(b) The humble man will recognize his own gifts. One person has organizing ability, another can speak fluently and persuasively, one can do a good repair, another can play a musical instrument well, yet another can say a kind word. It is not humility to deny we have the ability that God has given us.

(c) The humble man will willingly admit his own limitations. If he has no ear for music he will not insist on his singing in the church choir. If he useless in organizing he will not seek to be in charge of the church projects that call for this type of ability.

(d) The humble man will recognize the source of his gifts. The Lord has given him the talent to speak well. He will know that innate ability is a reason for thanksgiving to God, not for making idle boasts. He has succeeded in business. He will then recall, as the Lord pointed out to Israel, that it is God who gives the ability to get wealth. He will know that God gives talents in trust. They are then not ours to do with as we like but to be used for his glory in the service of other people. As they are given in trust, the giver can at any time recall them.

(e) The humble man will reject the feeling that he is superior in every way to any single person or to men generally. He will recognize that he is not the only person who has gifts. Because he is not able to do a repair job well, he will not despise that man who can. He is a musician but cannot organize, yet he will still respect the superintendent who cannot sing but is a tremendous asset in the Sunday school. He will also appreciate his minister's ability to give a first-class, relevant sermon.

II. The greatest of men was the humblest. (a) Jesus Christ, outstanding in all branches of his activity, never boasted of his miracles. He acknowledged God his Father as the source of his power. In Jesus' day rabbis received personal praise from their disciples. Jesus' superb teaching was not his own, he said. He sought neither position nor personal honor for himself but urged men to honor his Father. Though he was the Lord of glory, Jesus served men, even the obscure and poor, to the extent of dying for them. He was prepared to accept the position where he owned no place to sleep.

(b) Jesus never set himself to establish a reputation. He never sought to defend himself by taking vengeance against those who falsely accused him. Without ever losing his dignity in doing it, Jesus accepted attention from prostitutes and invited himself for a meal in a despised tax official's home.

(c) As Calvary was drawing near, the disciples argued about which of them was the greatest. Jesus then poured water into a basin, took a towel, and began to wash the disciples' feet. This was a task men did for themselves. In wealthy circles it was done by a slave. Here was humility in action. Most striking of all, the amazing event of his coming down from heaven to the humiliation of dying by crucifixion on earth was the finest example of any person's humility.

III. As humility was the hallmark of Jesus Christ it will also characterize his true followers. Humility is evidence of spiritual maturity.

(a) Humility enables a man to increase his knowledge and his effectiveness because he is willing to learn from insignificant informers.

(b) Humility makes God's presence more real and essential for successful prayer. We can talk more easily to one we know is close to us. As it is the almighty God's presence that we feel so near to us, we have a greater appreciation of his gifts. We can talk freely to him and ask more urgently for his help.—Gordon Chilvers in *The War Cry*.

## Illustrations

SENSITIVITY OF JESUS. He felt the sparrowness of the sparrow, the leprosy of the leper, the blindness of the blind, the crippleness of the cripple, and the frenzy of the mad. He had become joy, sorrow, hope, anguish, to the joyful, the sorrowful, the hopeful, and the anguished.—Howard Thurman.

SPIRIT OF THE AGE. A piece of peculiarly bad advice is constantly given to modern writers, especially to modern theologians: that they should adapt themselves to the spirit of the age. If there is one thing that has made shipwreck of mankind from the beginning it has been the spirit of the age, which always means exaggerating still further something that is grossly exaggerated already.—G. K. Chesterton.

## Sermon Suggestions

THE PSALMIST'S GOD. Text: Ps. 46:1. (1) A personal God: "God is *our* refuge and strength." (2) A protecting God: "God is our *refuge*." (3) A providing God: "God is our . . . *strength*."—C. Neil Strait.

IN AND OUT. Text: John 10:9. (1) We must learn the principle of alternation between the going into the shelter of the Christian faith and out to the exposure of it. (2) We must alternate between going into the restraints of religion and going out to the liberties of it. (3) We must go into the close-up views of the sheepfold and go out to the long vistas of the pasture, the intimate and the personal aspects of religion alternating with the general and the social.—Ralph W. Sockman.

## Worship Aids

CALL TO WORSHIP. "Sing unto the Lord, sing psalms unto him. Glory ye in his holy name: let the heart of them rejoice that seek the Lord." Ps. 105:2–3.

INVOCATION. O God, who makes thyself known both in the stillness and in the flurry of life: come to us as we seek to come to thee, in this place of prayer. In music, word, and song lift our hearts to thee, and so purify our thoughts and strengthen our resolves that we shall go forth into the world of tomorrow, confident that thou art with us.

OFFERTORY SENTENCE. "Every man shall give as he is able, according to the blessing of the Lord thy God which he hath given thee." Deut. 16:17.

OFFERTORY PRAYER. O Lord Jesus Christ, who hast taught us that to whomsoever much is given, of him shall much be required: grant that we, whose lot is cast in this Christian heritage, may strive more earnestly, by our prayers and tithes, by sympathy and study, to hasten the coming of thy kingdom among all peoples of the earth, that as we have entered into the labors of others, so others may enter into ours, to thy honor and glory.

PRAYER. All glory, thanks, and praise to thee, O Lord our God and Savior, for those who take up their cross and follow bravely after thee. For those who tread the way of sorrow in the calm of faith. For those who battle for the right in thy strength. For those who bear physical pain with sweet and sanctifying grace. For those who endure petty slights forgivingly. For those who rise above still greater wrongs. For those who continue their duties conscientiously whether so recognized or not. For those who by thy heavenly wisdom are enabled to teach the way of life. For those who tend thy flock with diligent care. For those who love others unselfishly in thee. All glory be to thee, O Lord most high.

## EVENING SERVICE

### Topic: Anchors That Will Hold

TEXT: Acts 27:29.

The apostle Paul suggests four anchors that can steady our lives in these perilous days. In a world where the outward pressures seem to grow every day there are inward braces that will hold.

I. *The anchor of courage.* Paul writes to the church at Corinth that "we are always of good courage."

(a) Any successful life must be lived with courage, bravery, and daring. "Nothing ventured, nothing gained." If we have not the courage to live an adventuresome life for Christ's sake, then we will not live much of a life for Christ.

(b) It takes courage to spend our lives making a better world for others. The easy thing to do with our life is to simply go along with everybody else, for this takes no courage. The easy thing is to be a "yes man" and to please those in authority, for this takes no courage. The easy thing to do is to close our eyes to injustices and to blame all our troubles on outside agitators, for this takes no courage.

II. *The anchor of faith in the Christ-like God.* (a) What you believe will determine the way that you behave. "As a man thinks, so he is." When people all around you are losing courage in the face of life's hurricanes, the Christian will put his trust in his God.

(b) If you believe that you don't need God, then you will live your life in such a way that it reflects only your own desires and only your own wants. If you believe that you are a robot on this earth and that God has wound you up until you simply one day run down, then you will resign yourself to automatic living and a deadly routine.

III. *The anchor of faith in the future.* (a) Paul reminded his frightened fellow passengers on that ship bound for Rome that he believed "that it shall be as God has told me." The Christian assumes that God is faithful and that with God the "best is yet to be." There is no room for pessimism in the Christian faith. The "good old days" are ahead of us, not behind us.

(b) Have you faith in the future? Or do you think that the future looks hopeless? How do you view the future?

(c) Faith in God gives us courage in the present and a faith in the future so that we know God is with us no matter what trouble and sorrow come our way.

IV. *The anchor of patience.* Scripture says that "all things are possible to him that believes," and I believe that but not all at once.

(a) Paul says that "they let out four anchors and prayed for the day to come." We often must do what we can and then wait patiently for the day to come, for the sun to rise.

(b) We Americans are very impatient people who want action. We demand instant coffee, instant tea, minute rice, instant cereal, and instant potatoes. We seem to have placed a premium on quick action. The trouble comes when we settle for a minute steak when we could have had sirloin. We are like the man who prayed, "O Lord, give me patience, and give it to me right now."

(c) Someone has said that "looking for God is like the oldest game in the world, hide-and-seek. God hides and we seek. But we get tired first, give up the game, and go home." We lose patience. Certainly this is the way that some of us feel, for God does reveal himself when and where and how he pleases, and we who would follow him must learn patience and not "give up the game."— C. Thomas Hilton.

# SUNDAY: OCTOBER SIXTEENTH

## MORNING SERVICE

**Topic: The Spiritual Man (Laity Sunday)**

TEXT: 1 Cor. 2:15–16 (RSV).

I. The first mark of a genuine spiritual person is a deep and penetrating realization of the spirit of God dwelling within, dominating his spirit.

(a) The spiritual person knows that he is a child of God by his spiritual rebirth in Christ which enables him to say, "I am his and he is mine," that this personal relationship is the all-important thing in life, and that anything which helps in making and keeping this relationship right and healthy, warm and active, growing and glowing is more important than anything else in the world.

(b) The spiritual man has a deep consciousness of the spirit of God abiding within, shepherding him and his spirit is in tune with the Infinite.

II. The spiritual man has spiritual discernment, insight into the meaning and purpose of life, and gives supreme devotion to spiritual values.

(a) The spiritual man is able to judge the value of everything. He discerns between the things which are temporal and spiritual, the things essential and the nonessential, and the things that perish and the imperishable. He chooses the things of real and lasting worth.

(b) Spirituality is not simply otherworldliness. Let no one be so anxious for heaven that he despises the good things of this world which our heavenly Father has intended for us to enjoy. After all, heaven is where God is, and God may be enjoyed in the here and now as well as in the hereafter. To be spiritual is to see the hand of God everywhere and to appreciate the good, the true, and the beautiful.

III. The spiritual man knows and speaks the truth of God. (a) The spiritual man should have a good knowledge of the Word of God, for it is the revelation of God's truth, telling of God's wise plan and mighty acts to bring us into the joy and glory of his great salvation. The spiritual man should be able to give reason for the blessed hope that is within him. It is not necessary that he know all that is to be known about the Bible, for that is a lifelong process and then some, but he ought to be a student of the Word and compare scripture with scripture.

(b) The spiritual man ought to be able to communicate spiritual truth and to give spiritual advice and help others. He will have a healthy appetite for the Word of God and will tell the good news of God's love to other hungry and thirsty souls. He will not hesitate to pray with them and for them. He will not be ashamed to speak frankly and helpfully with other men about Christ and his church. It is still true that a good word spoken for Christ by earnest laymen, even though their speech is halting and untrained, is much more effective than when the minister does it. This world will be won to Christ not by the eloquence of erudite ministers but by the simple testimony of laymen witnessing for Christ in the common life.

IV. The spiritual man should apply the Word of God to his own life and be consistent in his walk and conversation.

(a) This certainly is the kind of men every age needs: straight, honest, truthtelling, trustworthy, fair and square in their dealings, having a system of ethics that is strict and demands irreproachable conduct. If spirituality does not result in upright living, it is worthless.

(b) A man may look as pious as a saint and may make all kinds of high pretenses, but if his word is not as good as his bond, if he cannot be trusted in a business deal, if he is not "all wool and a yard wide," if he is not pure in heart, clean in thought, and wholesome in speech, then his spirituality is "sounding brass and tinkling cymbal."

V. The spiritual man has a keen sense of partnership or stewardship with Christ in the greatest goal in the world— the kingdom of God.

(a) The living Christ is engaged in the work of evangelism, liberating the souls of men and women, children and youth, from sin and death and granting unto them new life, abundant life, eternal life.

(b) This is all-inclusive, all-embracing, tremendously difficult, fraught with hard fighting, with defeats and setbacks, with challenges that penetrate to the very core of our beings and to the outer rim of our world, but by the grace of God the spiritual man is out to win, to fight on to victory, and to win the whole person and the whole world for Christ, and the humblest person may consider himself a partner with Christ in this mighty mission.

VI. The spiritual man is characterized by loving service rendered to his fellowmen in the spirit of Christ. Genuine spirituality expresses itself in daily, loving service, speaking kind words, doing helpful deeds, and filling up the hours of the day with healing goodness. "He went about doing good" is the never-to-be-forgotten biographical sketch of Jesus of Nazareth. And because he lived that way, he and his followers have changed the face of the world and the heart of mankind.—George Hunter Hall.

## Illustrations

THOSE IN BETWEEN. Francis of Assisi

was twenty-five when he founded the Franciscan order. Xavier was twenty-eight when he teamed up with Ignatius Loyola to organize the Jesuits. Luther was thirty-three when he nailed his theses to the door at Wittenberg. Calvin was twenty-seven when he completed the first edition of his *Institutes*. Whitefield was a successful evangelist at twenty-five. Wesley began his real life's work at thirty-five. Spurgeon was twenty-seven when his congregation built for him the great Metropolitan Tabernacle in London. Billy Sunday left home plate for the pulpit at thirty-three. Billy Graham was thirty-one at the time of his now-famous Los Angeles crusade.—*Christianity Today*.

WOMAN POWER. If you want to understand Barak, look to Deborah; if you want to understand Timothy, look to Lois and Eunice, his grandmother and mother; if you want to understand Augustine, look to Monica, his mother; if you want to understand Martin Luther, look to Katherine von Bora, his wife; if you want to understand George Whitefield, look to Lady Huntingdon, his patroness; if you want to understand John Wesley, look to Susannah, his mother; if you want to understand Timothy Dwight, look to his mother, Mary, daughter of Jonathan Edwards; if you want to understand David Livingstone, look to Mary Moffat, his wife; if you want to understand Rembrandt, look to Cornelia, his mother; if you want to understand Søren Kierkegaard, look to Regine Olsen, his fiancée; if you want to understand Adoniram Judson, look to his successive wives, Ann Hasseltine and Sarah Boardman; if you want to understand Dwight L. Moody, look to Emma Revell, his wife; if you want to understand William Booth, look to Catherine, his wife.—*Decision*.

## Sermon Suggestions

WHEN IS ONE A MAJORITY? Text: II Kings 6:17. (1) The unseen is always mightier than the seen. (2) Right ultimately wins and man with God cannot be defeated. (3) The whole universe works with the man who works with God.—Fred R. Chenault.

EVERYTHING UNDER CONTROL? Text: I Cor. 9:25. (1) Self-control means self-mastery. (2) Self-control means self-discipline. (3) Self-control means self-denial. (4) Self-control means to be God controlled.—John R. Brokhoff.

## Worship Aids

CALL TO WORSHIP. "Bless the Lord, O my soul: and all that is with me, bless his holy name." Ps. 103:1.

INVOCATION. Eternal God, who committest unto us the swift and solemn trust of life, since we know not what a day may bring forth but only that the hour for serving thee is always present, may we wake to the instant claims of thy holy will, not waiting for tomorrow, but yielding today. Consecrate with thy presence the way our feet may go, and the humblest work will shine and the roughest places be made plain.

OFFERTORY SENTENCE. "Whatsoever ye would that men should do to you, do ye even so to them; for this is the law and the prophets." Matt. 7:12.

OFFERTORY PRAYER. Almighty God, may we trust more and more in thy kind providence, and may our submission to thy will be revealed in the deep devotion expressed through these gifts we offer in Christ's name.

A LITANY OF THE DISCIPLES' WAY.
We are disciples of Christ and called by his name. Let us draw near unto him who is the living way.
*Help us, O Master, to walk in thy way.*
For our weakness and failures, grant us true repentance; and that we may turn from self to thee.
*Help us, O Master, to walk in thy way.*
Through each day's plans and choices, grant us vision and courage to follow thee.
*Help us, O Master, to walk in thy way.*

In joy and in sorrow, in victory or in defeat, in all times and occasions, be thou our confidence and strength as we pray in thy name.

*Help us, O Master, to walk in thy way.*

Stir us to go forth and serve thee, thou who art one with all sufferers, the perplexed, and all who need.

*Help us, O Master, to walk in thy way.*

In thy house and at thine altar, in fellowship with thy people, grant us through worship new power to do thy will.

*Help us, O Master, to walk in thy way.*
—*Forward Day by Day.*

## EVENING SERVICE

**Topic: Why Go to Church?**

TEXT: Heb. 10:25.

I. God's word commands us to go to church: "Neglect not the assembling of ourselves together." And here is the mood: "I was glad when they said unto me, let us go into the house of the Lord." To neglect worship is to become ineffective, muted, and impotent disciples. Our Lord went to church—a sordid, vulgar, and quarrelsome village church. He worshiped alongside imperfect people with imperfect usages. "Straightway on the sabbath day he entered into the synagogue," Mark 1:21 records. We have the command of God and the example of Christ as our guide.

II. God has made us so that we are not whole without him. "Thou hast made us for thyself and our hearts are restless until they rest in thee," wrote St. Augustine. The norm for the Christian's life is the way of faith. By bowing before God and by opening our lives to his energies, his wisdom, and his holiness, we become whole. We are spiritual beings, and we can be satisfied only by the supernatural power of God.

III. We must worship in this age if we are to be adequate for its demands. There is indeed no substitute for the worship of God in meeting the challenge of this age.

IV. Worshiping together makes an impact upon the world which cannot be made by an individual witness. In worship we not only draw strength from the knowledge of God's power but in true worship we also offer ourselves to God as channels of power. When we worship together we make a collective witness of believers in Christ which the world needs.

V. Corporate worship is one way to keep our own lives aglow. If we neglect worship and attempt to live our lives alone or in a vacuum, the fire of our faith is soon extinguished. From the psalmist comes the cry, "As the hart panteth after the waterbrooks, so panteth my soul after thee, O God." This consuming desire of the spirit is why we are here in church today. We just have to have God. We need a word from God's book and the overture of love from Jesus Christ which reaches through to us in God's house. We want and need to have our souls flooded with the love of God in Christ.—Edward L. R. Elson.

# SUNDAY: OCTOBER TWENTY-THIRD

## MORNING SERVICE

**Topic: God Requires Goodness**

TEXT: Mic. 6:8.

I. Micah leaves no question that goodness is dictated as a virtue of character for any person desiring to do God's will. He maintains that goodness belongs to and with the Godlike person. To be Godlike is to be good. If we are at all interested in leading the spirit-filled life, we will find it only when we have embraced goodness.

(a) Man has learned across the centuries in God's world that it is better to be good than to be bad. Few would debate the fact that in the long run goodness, morality, and truth are the masters of evil, immorality, and falsehood. Yet many persons are bone-tired of trying to be good anymore. They often wish they were good. They bemoan their lack of goodness.

(b) We need to be good because more than just our own individual lives are involved. We influence others one way or the other. If goodness is gained through its attractiveness, then we may be the someone through whom another person gains goodness without the super-human effort involved in trying to be good.

II. There are two kinds of good persons: those who achieve virtue by volition and those who have a spontaneously overflowing goodness which fills life with joy.

(a) Few of us have escaped the imposition of laws, discipline, or force designed to make us good. Some of us are good because we are strong-willed enough to discipline ourselves into the good life. Too often goodness is like that of the Pharisee who pointed out to God in his prayer that he was not like other men: "I fast regularly as required by the law, I give my tithe to the temple, and I keep the commandments." For the Pharisee that equated his life with God's goodness. He was obsessed with keeping the letter of the law.

(b) We are attracted by the person who finds goodness to be the spontaneous response to God's love and goodness. Life is not repressed and persimmon sour. It is joyous and a delight to behold. It is a natural goodness which becomes attractive to the beholder. He comes closer that he might touch the hem of the garment of this good person, and thereby perchance to find transmitted to his life those joyous qualities of Godlike goodness.

III. Goodness lives because of the contagion of character in human society. By the same token, badness, ill, and evil thrive on contagion. There is a contagiousness about character in the human scene that we often forget. "I want to do my thing," we say. And that's socially acceptable as a principle so long as doing my thing does not influence you for evil or become a stumbling block in your path toward God's good-ness in your life. One needs to be good for goodness' sake to be sure, but one needs to be good also for the sake of those for whom he can help make goodness vital and alive or repellent and dead.

(a) This calls us to see the importance of standing under the influence of the highest and best we know that we may catch our share of this joyous, spontaneous goodness. There is a persuasiveness about goodness that moves into our lives from the influence of a good person. It is like the tide of the Atlantic; nothing that one can do can really stop it.

(b) This is the genius of the Christian faith and experience. We stand under the influence of the highest and best that humanity has ever known—Jesus of Nazareth. In his presence we cannot be cheap or evil or dishonest or immoral. There is something commanding about him. There is a moral imperative in his very presence. Yet it does not repel us because it is a spontaneous and joyous kind of goodness which God has showed us in Jesus.

(c) If we are to be good we had better seek to live in the divine-human companionship with God which he has made real for us in Jesus.

(1) Jesus can attract you into goodness. He can lure you into Christian love. Only in this fashion can your life be transformed from evil to good, from bad temper to goodwill, and from sin to true piety.

(2) To know Christ is to know God and to experience his love and his goodness in our lives. It is to be attracted by his goodness, allured by his love, and transformed by this divine-human companionship.—Hoover Rupert.

## Illustrations

ALIENATION. Hell is where no one has anything in common with anybody else except the fact that they all hate one another, cannot get away from one another and from themselves.—Thomas Merton.

VALIDITY. It is possible to be religious in the sense of having the assurance of personal salvation and yet be blind or insensitive to the vast areas of human suffering. While it is true that life is never adequate without reverence, it is true at the same time that no experience is valid unless it leads to acts of justice and mercy.—Elton Trueblood.

## Sermon Suggestions

THE WAY ISN'T EASY! Text: John 14:6. (1) Loving unlovable people. (See Matt. 5:43–46.) (2) Forgiving unpardonable people. (See Matt. 5:23–24.) (3) Returning good for evil. (See Matt. 5:44, 47.) (4) Serving the unworthy and the ungrateful. (See Matt. 5:44, 47.) (5) Cross-bearing without complaint. (See Luke 9:23)—Chester E. Swor.

PERSPECTIVES OF PRAYER. (1) Adoration: the humble recognition that God is Lord of life. (2) Thanksgiving: the joyous acceptance of God's varied gifts in gratitude and with responsibility. (3) Confession: the open admission of our sins to a merciful and understanding God. (4) Intercession: the concerns we express for the needs of others. (5) Supplication: the sincere sharing of our needs with God. (6) Reflective thought: the meditating on God and listening to God. (7) Oblation: the offering of ourselves to God to be his servants in his world.—*Inquiry: A Search for Faith.*

## Worship Aids

CALL TO WORSHIP. "Lord, who shall abide in thy tabernacle? Who shall dwell in thy holy hill? He that walketh uprightly, and worketh righteousness, and speaketh the truth in his heart." Ps. 15:1–2.

INVOCATION. Blot out, we humbly beseech thee, O Lord, our past transgression; forgive our negligence and ignorance; help us to amend our mistakes and to repair our misunderstanding; and so uplift our hearts in new love and dedication that we may be unburdened from the grief and shame of past faithlessness and go forth to serve thee with renewed courage and devotion.

OFFERTORY SENTENCE. "Every man according as he purposeth in his heart, so let him give; not grudgingly, or of necessity: for God loveth a cheerful giver." II Cor. 9:7.

OFFERTORY PRAYER. Open our eyes that we may see thy goodness, O Father; our hearts that we may be grateful for thy mercies; our lips that we may show forth thy praise; and our hands that we may give these offerings according to thy wish and desire.

PRAYER. O God, we do not always feel you near; in fact sometimes you seem so far away. Sometimes we are overwhelmed by your greatness, and sometimes we wonder if you are at all. As Moses found you on a mountain and Jesus found you in a garden, may we find you in this "set-apart" place today.

Give us the courage to deal with ourselves; we would rather examine someone else for his sin is ever before us. When our uncertainties and fears come rushing out of us as vengeance on some other sinner, forgive us. When we are unfairly and unjustly treated by one youth or one elderly person, help us not to make those individuals into large groups and thus condemn youth or age.

Forgive us for hiding behind personal religion when the community needed our support, and forgive us for hiding behind the community when we were unwilling to deal with our personal faith. Help us not to feel joyful in worship if that means we are overlooking our brother's anguish.

Today we pray for peace, for we are so aware that peace is something our world cannot give, but it can certainly take away. Today may each one of us see more clearly a purpose for his life.

Spirit of God, help us to experience joy today. Forgive us that we settle so quickly for cheap thrills. Give us a willingness to live our whole lives as Jesus Christ seemed to do.—Earl F. Lindsay.

## EVENING WORSHIP

**Topic: For Those Who Need Help**
TEXT: Col. 2:2.
I. *Discouraged people need help*, and Jesus can help them. (a) Paul prays "that your hearts may be encouraged," that is comforted, cheered, and strengthened. Why does he pray the prayer for the Colossians? Because among them were discouraged people. Discouraged people need help. Are you under some weight or discouragement? Jesus cares about that.

(b) We are so prone to keep returning to the scene of the crime and of going back. We've got to keep going, discouragement or no discouragement. Paul prays "that your hearts may be encouraged."

II. *Desolate people need help,* and Jesus helps desolate people. (a) Paul goes on to pray "that their hearts will be encouraged, being knitted together in love." Isn't that a beautiful expression? That which has become unraveled will be knitted together in love, wielded together, firmly bound, and united together in love.

(b) A human being who feels desolate, who feels desperately lonely, and who feels isolated and abandoned is a person who needs help. There are so many lonely people in our world. They are all around us in this city. Human beings were not made for solitude in this sense. We need one another. We need the support of a community, a knitting together in the love of Jesus.

(c) This is why the writer to the Hebrews is concerned about those who forsake the assembling of themselves together, as the manner of some is, especially in view of the fact that the day is approaching. It is dangerous for a person not to feel knitted together in a fabric of Christian fellowship.—David L. Larsen.

## SUNDAY: OCTOBER THIRTIETH

### MORNING SERVICE

**Topic: Disguised Opportunities (Reformation Sunday)**
TEXT: I Cor. 16:9.
Opposition and opportunity often go hand in hand. Just as the denial of our momentary wishes may be the concealed blessing of God, so the frustrations of circumstance and event can prove to be disguised opportunities. The church in a day of many adversaries, conscious, intentional, and otherwise, must be able to recognize that opposition and opportunity often go hand in hand. The only real tragedy would be to let the difficulties obliterate the opportunity.

I. Paul writes some specific instructions and personal details. (a) The Christians at Corinth are to share in the great churchwide offering for their brethren at Jerusalem on a regular basis, putting aside, week by week, the material evidence of their benevolence. Paul was quite obviously concerned about more than their money; it was their continuing concern and involvement he sought to encourage. He goes on to tell them of his plans, assuring them that he is aware of the necessity of a visit.

(b) The opportunities in Ephesus from which he writes are great and growing. He describes them as a great and effectual door that is opened to him. Nonetheless there are many adversaries; there is much opposition. Things do not always go the way that Paul desires, but he has learned through the years of experience that what he sometimes considers hindrances and stumbling blocks can prove to be the very opportunities that God is providing. Far from opposition making Paul all the more eager to flee from Ephesus, it seemed to be making him all the more eager to remain. It is as though he considered the adversaries, the opposition, as itself an essential part of the opportunity.

(c) This is much different from a man who loses heart when things do not go exactly as he would wish or plan. There is no sense in Paul of wringing of the hands or a bitterness that the way has not been cleared of obstacles and that the effect of his preaching and teaching is not immediate change. Through many trials Paul has learned the secret of disguised opportunities.

(d) All of you must have experienced at some time that feeling of the thwarting of your hopes and dreams when the door seemed to be shut in your face, only to recognize later when doors are closed all around it is to direct your attention to the one that is open, the one that is best for you. It is more than merely the overcoming of handicaps. It is the realization that life consists of our reaction to and our use of what happens to us. The secret is in learning to recognize the disguised opportunities.

II. The chance for fruitful fulfillment grows most often out of our reaction to seemingly adverse circumstances.

(a) Opposition can make us take an appraising look at our position again. It can lead us to consider what is of abiding value, what can be lost without all being lost, and what is unshakable and enduring. Perhaps it can also lead us to change.

(b) The history of the Christian church has exemplified this many times. (1) Had there been no heresy there would have been no clear statement of creed and doctrine, and the faith of the church would have been that much weaker. It was the very existence of the adversaries that caused the fathers of the church at last to sit down and through much debate to say, "This is what we believe; this is what we mean." The very existence of heresy was disguised opportunity.

(2) It was abundantly clear again at the time of the Reformation. It is becoming increasingly evident and urgently so today. Blessings concealed and opportunities disguised are the gift of God. It is learning to recognize them and then to use them that is important.

III. Who were those adversaries of whom Paul spoke that yet seemed to him to open a great and effectual door? Some

of them we can discover from the account of his missions and ministry in the Acts of the Apostles and others from the letters which he wrote to the young churches of the Christian faith.

(a) There were the Jews of the Dispersion. They believed that this man was a traitor of the worst sort, having grown up and been trained in their faith; in his young manhood zealous in combating what they considered the heresy of the Christian way; now he had turned to the enemy. They cast him out and were often instrumental in causing his imprisonment, stoning, or at the very least, scourging, as a disturber of the peace.

(b) There were the Jewish Christians. They believed that men should come to the Christian way only through all the exercises and disciplines, the regulations and ritual of the ancient Jewish faith. To them it seemed that Paul was opening the gates far too wide, for in their view how could men be Christians if they were not first Jews? Sadly their opposition was almost as strong as that of the Jews themselves.

(c) There were the gentiles who saw their own gods being degraded and dethroned; and besides that, their business interests were quite likely to suffer. This was particularly noticeable in the town of Ephesus for here was situated the great shrine to the goddess Diana. Wherever you find a religious shrine, lurking in its shadow will be a multitude of shops and booths selling relics, trinkets, or mementos for the superstitious-minded. So is it now; so was it then.

IV. We would do well to recognize that there is still much opposition, and one of our tasks is to recognize the disguised opportunity which it affords.

(a) There are the unchurched. Amid all the statistics of ecclesiastical conceit it remains true that for vast multitudes the church has so merged into the landscape that it just does not exist. These are not actively hostile but largely quite indifferent and apathetic. Among them are those who, if they think about it at all, consider the Christian faith quite irrelevant to the issues and concerns of the day.

(b) I would count as adversaries those who feel that the old-line, old-time religion is being attacked when we try to apply it and express it for the issues and concerns of our time.

(c) There are those whose economic interests put them on the side of the opposition. Not least in strength in this camp are those wealthy laymen who say, "Let the Church keep silence on all matters political, social, and economic." One must be allowed to wonder what it is they fear.

(d) The opportunity is in the very obvious need. Often the lack and the confusion are disguised as opposition. How then did Paul turn difficulty into opportunity? His answer is, "Let everything be done in love." Vague? Not at all. Demanding? Yes, of the very utmost that is in us.—J. Ernest Somerville.

### Illustrations

PROPHETS TRUE AND FALSE.    The false prophet extols first-century Christianity and God's mighty deeds in the Reformation; the true prophet expects God to deliver us—as we repent and reform— from our present national corruption and from atomic catastrophe. The false prophet glories in past ages; the true, in God's new age.—Nels F. S. Ferré.

THRUST.    The impact of Christianity on the society of the Roman Empire was powerful for the elevation of the status of women, the care of the poor, the abolition of slavery. The Reformation may be said to have had an even greater political, economic, and social influence. Many ideas that are being talked about today, such as the equality of all persons, the rights of the individual, and the responsibility of people to "do their own thing," are secularized visions of the teaching of Luther, Calvin, and their followers. Many of the social and political reforms of the nineteenth century likewise sprang directly out of the Evangelical Revival, leading to action to protect exploited workers, to free Negro slaves, and to help the poor and downtrodden.—W. Stanford Reid.

### Sermon Suggestions

THE RECURRING REFORMATION.    Text: Acts 3:19. (1) Salvation is God's gift. (See Eph. 2:14.) (2) The Bible is God's word. (3) The church is God's people. (See Eph. 5:25. (4) Society is God's world.— Emil Kontz.

GOD'S GOOD NEWS FOR MAN'S BAD NEWS. Text: Hos. 6:1–3. (1) Good news of healing. (2) Good news of new life. (3) Good news of refreshment.—John R. Brokhoff.

### Worship Aids

CALL TO WORSHIP.    "Great is the Lord, and greatly to be praised; and his greatness is unsearchable. One generation shall praise thy works to another, and shall declare thy mighty works." Ps. 145:3–4.

INVOCATION.    Most gracious Father, who withholdest no good thing from thy children and in thy providence hast brought us to this day of rest and of the renewal of the soul: we give thee humble and hearty thanks for the world which thou hast prepared and furnished for our dwelling place, for the steadfast righteousness which suffers no evil thing to gain the mastery, for the lives and examples of those who were strangers and pilgrims and found a better inheritance in peace of soul and joy in the Holy Spirit, and above all for the life, teaching, and sacrifice of thy Son our Savior Jesus Christ.

OFFERTORY SENTENCE.    "Lay up for yourselves treasures in heaven: for where your treasure is, there will your heart be also." Matt. 6:20–21.

OFFERTORY PRAYER.    We pray thee, O God, to give us sight to see the Christ, the insight to choose him, the steadfastness to follow him, and the stewardship of loyalty represented in these gifts offered in his name.

PRAYER. Almighty God our Father, who by thy Son Jesus Christ didst reach out to us hands of love, we are met this day to reach out to thee hands of faith that our hands and thine may be clasped together. Help us in these moments to know verily that we are thy people and thou art our God. Impart to us such light upon the dark problems of our lives that we may be able in all things to be brought into closer touch with thy victorious power. Bury all past errors and failures in thy forgiveness as we frankly confess them to thee, and make all future days better by the blessed grace of obedience.

On this Reformation Sunday we thank thee for the great heroes of Protestantism who broke the shackles of fear and churchly dictatorship from the human spirit and taught us once more the great lesson of St. Paul that each of us is brought to God by his own faith and his own humble prayers. We bless thy name that our forefathers won for themselves and for us the right to worship according to the dictates of conscience and not according to the dictates of church and state. Make us worthy of this great privilege, that freedom to worship may not be an occasion to neglect the things of the spirit but an occasion for each of us to come to thee with greater faithfulness and that freedom in this nation and the world may have as its support a loyal and godly people worthy to be free.

Hear us, O Lord, as we pray for all free churches in the world that they may be true to their heritage; for all authoritarian churches that they may be true to the Christ who is the head of all churches; for all leaders of men and all nations seeking peace that they may be brought face to face with the God of peace in whose service alone true peace and freedom are to be found.—Nathanael M. Guptill.

## EVENING SERVICE

### Topic: Why Belong to the Church?
TEXT: Eph. 4:4–5.

I. There is no such thing as solitary Christianity. Archibald M. Hunter has said, "The New Testament knows nothing of unattached Christians." Cyprian said, "He cannot have God for his father who has not the church for his mother."

II. We need the church to call us to nobler living. God has created us with immense potentialities which can make possible full and rich lives. But even though God has given us the capacity for greatness, too often we choose to live mediocre lives. We need the church to remind us unfailingly that we are children of God, created in his image, and meant for the best.

III. We need the church to help us put the rest of life into perspective. The church should not be an escape from the real world, but neither should it merely echo the confusion and frenzy of the workaday world. The church, and especially its worship, reminds us that there is more to life than running up escalators and meeting deadlines. The church gives us a perspective from which to face all issues and problems that come our way.—Lovett Hayes Weems, Jr.

## SUNDAY: NOVEMBER SIXTH

### MORNING SERVICE

### Topic: Clean Hands But Dirty Hearts (World Temperance Sunday)
TEXT: Matt. 15:20.

I am sure that many little boys who are allergic to soap and water will say "amen" to v. 20. They usually prefer to avoid the washbowl on their way to the table. But Jesus is speaking of a far deeper matter than eating with dirty hands. He is talking about those people who appear so proper and righteous outwardly but who are so filthy and unrighteous inwardly. And in so doing he sounds a note of warning to each of us.

I. Jesus says by inference that we should be more careful about what we put into our hearts and minds than about what we put into our stomachs.

(a) Our nation has food and drug laws to protect our stomachs, but it has scarcely any laws to protect our hearts and minds. Even the United States Supreme Court dodged the issue of pornography by leaving it to every locality to define such for itself. At the request of a district attorney I examined some of the pornographic literature seized in raids. No filth comparable to it ever went into a garbage can or sewer!

(b) Which means that in the absence of legal protection you must be your own guardian in this regard. Unless reduced to the lowest level of poverty no sane person will eat out of a garbage can. Yet how glibly multitudes feed their hearts and minds upon far filthier garbage. By law movies are rated in semblance of effort to protect the young and immature. But, parents, if a movie is too filthy for your children to see it is too filthy for you to see. The same rule applies to reading the trash that travels under the guise of respectability as literature.

(c) Our bodies are so made that such garbage is not discharged. It festers in the mind. It pollutes the heart. And from the heart flows the nauseous result. Now I believe in laws to forbid such filth in order to protect the weak and immature. But do not point the primary accusing finger at legal bodies or even at the producers of such pernicious garbage which preys upon the lowest level in human nature. Point that finger at yourself if you patronize such. The only language that the morally depraved producers understand is the profit motive. If the box office and balance sheet show that they are losing money on such, they will stop it themselves. Thus the patrons are as guilty before God as the producers and purveyors.

II. Jesus directly says that we should give more attention to our inner than to our outer condition or appearance.

(a) It naturally follows that if you can choose between having clean hands or dirty hearts, you should give primary attention to having a clean heart. Your greatest problem is not ceremonial uncleanness but uncleanness of the heart. The ancient custom of ceremonial washings may seem not to apply to you and me. But it says much when the principle is put in the modern context.

(b) Just think of the meticulous care you give to your body and the neglect you give to your spirit. Since the biblical figure is set in the religious context, let us for the moment bypass our relationships in business and social life to focus upon our spiritual life. It will be seen however that even this reflects itself in the broader areas of human concourse.

(c) Let us think about going to church on Sunday. In preparation you go to the barbershop or beauty salon so that your hair may be properly groomed. Though you may bathe every day, the "Saturday night" bath is proverbial. On Sunday morning you anoint your body with sweet-smelling perfumes. You clothe it in your Sunday best. Then you adorn the whole with jewels and other accessories. In a sense you go to church with "clean hands." But what about your heart, your spirit? So many people carry along the "evil thoughts" of inordinate pride and prejudice—racial, social, and economic. What about "false witness" or gossip and "blasphemies" or insulting speech to one churchgoer about another?

(d) With such an attitude and practice as you sing praises to God are you not doing what Jas. 3:9–11 says about the tongue which expresses an evil spirit? In short you cannot in truth worship God with clean hands and dirty hearts.

III. These dirty hearts besmirch every other area of life. (a) You have not committed "murder." But Jesus shows in the sermon on the mount that the root of overt murder is a wrong attitude in your heart toward others. Likewise about "adulteries, fornications" or any kind of sexual impurity. Lust in the heart after another person is defined by Jesus as making one guilty of sexual evil. That is, if you have given the consent of your will—prevented only by lack of opportunity or fear of the consequences—you have already committed adultery in your heart.

(b) What about "thefts"? Do you charge more than a fair profit for your goods? Then you are stealing from your customers. Do you pay less than a fair day's wage for a day's work? Or give less than a full day's work for a full day's pay? Then you are stealing from your employees or employer. The examples of such could be multiplied almost beyond measure.

(c) The point is that whether in the church building, home, or marketplace you should stand before God with clean hearts. There is nothing wrong with "clean hands" so long as we also have "clean hearts." Your hands cannot really be clean, whether in worship or work, unless your heart is clean. Someone said, "The head has not heard until the heart has listened." And by the same token we can say that the hands are not clean until the heart is clean.

(d) The Bible says, "Keep your heart with all diligence, for out of it are the issues of life." A few years ago many efforts were made at heart transplants but mostly with disappointing results. However, even if medical science should perfect this surgical procedure, it still would be to transplant into a body a heart which functions physically. However it will be a heart still enslaved to the sinful passions so common to man. Only Jesus can take your old heart and make it a new one.—Herschel H. Hobbs.

## Illustrations

WAYWARD. A wandering microbe destroys health and hope. A wandering hurricane destroys a city and with that city many a human dream. A wander-

ing temptation catches the spirit off guard.—George A. Buttrick.

CHOOSING A LIFESTYLE. A lifestyle is a vehicle through which we express ourselves. It is a way of telling the world which particular subcult or subcults we belong to. The real reason why lifestyles are so significant—and increasingly so as society diversifies—is that, above all else, the choice of a lifestyle model to emulate is a crucial strategy in our private war against the crowding pressures of overchoice.

How we choose a lifestyle, and what it means to us, therefore, looms as one of the central issues of the psychology of tomorrow. For the selection of a lifestyle, whether consciously done or not, powerfully shapes the individual's future. It does this by imposing order, a set of principles or criteria on the choices he makes in daily life.—Alvin Toffler in *Future Shock*.

## Sermon Suggestions

FOOL'S GOLD. Scripture: Isa. 51:7–9, 11–16. (1) Gambling corrupts sportsmanship. (2) Gambling confuses the human necessity and virtue of taking a risk for a worthy end with that of taking a risk merely in the hope of getting something for nothing. (3) Gambling weakens the two imperative virtues of industry and thrift. (4) Gambling is a repudiation of intelligence and a return to primitivism. (5) Gambling denies brotherhood and is a return to the behavior of the jungle in which one preys upon another. (6) Gambling under the auspices of a church or charity prostitutes them by making a vice appear as a virtue.—Everett W. Palmer.

WHEN CHRISTIANS SAY NO. Text: Rom. 12:2. (1) Say no, but be consistent. (2) Say no, but be positive. (3) Say no, but be redemptive.—Frank H. Epp.

## Worship Aids

CALL TO WORSHIP. "Delight thyself also in the Lord; and he shall give thee the desires of thine heart. Commit thy way unto the Lord; trust also in him; and he shall bring it to pass." Ps. 37: 4–5.

INVOCATION. Most holy and gracious God, who turnest the shadow of night into morning: satisfy us early with thy mercy that we may rejoice and be glad all the day. Lift the light of thy countenance upon us, calm every troubled thought, and guide our feet into the way of peace. Perfect thy strength in our weakness and help us to worship thee in the spirit of Jesus Christ our Lord.

OFFERTORY SENTENCE. "If ye then, being evil, know how to give good gifts unto your children: how much more shall your heavenly Father give the Holy Spirit to them that ask him?" Luke 11:13.

OFFERTORY PRAYER. Our Father, forgive our indifference and neglect and help us to hear thy call to partnership with thee in making a new heaven and new earth.

PRAYER. O God, our heavenly Father, we thy children come now to thy feet with our supplications. We cannot live without thy blessing. Life is too hard for us and duty is too large. We get discouraged and our feeble hands hang down. We come to thee with our weakness, asking thee for strength. Help us always to be of good cheer. Let us not be disheartened by difficulties. Let us never doubt thy love or any of thy promises. Give us grace to be encouragers of others, never discouragers. Let us not go about with sadness or fear among men, but may we be a benediction to everyone we meet, always making life easier, never harder, for those who come within our influence. Help us to be as Christ to others that they may see something of his love in our lives and learn to love him in us. We beseech thee to hear us, to receive our prayer, and to forgive our sins for Jesus Christ's sake.—James Russell Miller.

## EVENING SERVICE

## Topic: Do You Want to Be Healed?

TEXT: John 5:6.

This question addressed to a man who was sick seems abrupt and almost cruel. Here was a person who had been sick for many years and who was unable to get into the pool where he could be healed because there was no man to help him. But Jesus raises the question as to how sincere he is and how much he wants health.

I. This man apparently had fallen into the pit of self-pity. He went through the motions of seeking healing, but really he preferred it the way it was. Being excused from all active participation in life had its rewards. He could enjoy the shade in the summertime when other men were doing their work, and he could talk with his friends and cronies. He was not the first nor the last man to use sickness as an excuse for denying all responsibility. If you follow the story through to the end, you will discover that he was not a very admirable character.

II. Jesus came to him as he comes to all men to penetrate their pretenses. We cover ourselves with a veneer of hypocrisy, and we pretend to be what we are not. Jesus might ask America today if we want to be healed. We talk about peace and education, freedom and concern for the world. But if you look at our budget you discover that we spend a hundred to one for comfort and dissipation. Jesus spoke his hard word to the good people of his time, and he would do the same to us. The Pharisee, he said, did not really want piety but notoriety. The priest did not want to serve; he wanted privilege. Does the Christian church want to be healed? Or does it prefer its sick condition of mediocrity and safety?

III. The truth is that it takes a great deal of courage to be healed by Jesus. For physical health is not an end in itself. Methuselah was not a great success because the Bible says he lived nine hundred and sixty-nine years. Meaningless leisure is a threat to our society and a condition in which our morals deteriorate and our tastes cheapen. To be healed by Jesus means to be concerned about all the world and to be committed to a great purpose. It means to discipline our lives for spiritual achievements, and it means the end of comfort as a goal. He may be putting the question a different way to us and asking "Do you have the courage to be healed?"

IV. Actually the great truth in this story is that men have to be healed from within. Dangers, great as they are on the outside, are not the real ones facing us either as a nation or as a church or as persons. Life begins to make real sense when we understand that we carry with us the enemy we have to defeat. When the great physician cures our fears and suspicions, we are able to wage our battle with faith and assurance. The first question is always the same, "Do you want to be healed?"—Gerald Kennedy.

# SUNDAY: NOVEMBER THIRTEENTH

## MORNING SERVICE

**Topic: Witnessing for Christ**

SCRIPTURE: Isa. 19:19–22; Acts 1:1–8.

How do we make our witness? How do we raise another person's consciousness of Jesus Christ to the level that a decision about God is brought to focus?

I. Our witness for Christ to another will be deeply personal rather than propositional.

(a) To the extent that we may feel free to talk to another about our faith, we shall center more upon who Christ is to us than some plan of salvation we may have memorized. The reality we point to is the personality of Christ in whom we believe and not a set of proper statements that describe him. We witness not to propositions but to Christ.

(b) Our task is simply to express to another who Jesus is and what he means to us. It is important that we be able to tell another person something of the character of Jesus. The one whom we call Lord was a person who lived out on this earth a certain style of life and had some specific things to say about God and our relating to God in life and work.

(c) We need to express why Jesus is important to us. The need is not to give an all-encompassing expression, for that is impossible. But we need to convey the feeling that this one makes a difference in our lives.

(1) I might tell someone that for me Jesus is the window through which I see what is really real in the world. Here in Jesus I see an unbounded love that accepts me as I am and encourages me to love as I am loved. I could speak of those times in my own life when my faith in God was so dim that it hung only by the thread of Jesus' faith in God, and I couldn't believe Jesus was wrong.

(2) Another person would express what Christ means personally in quite different terms. We are not theologians trying to say something definitive but believers who want to point another person to Christ.

II. If we are faithful to the way Jesus dealt with others, we will need to say that our witness in some way conveys the message that when you take Jesus Christ seriously you are going to have to change your ways.

(a) We need to make it clear that for us a decision about Christ involves decisions in how we think, the way we feel, and what we shall actually do.

(b) When the rich young ruler came to Jesus to ask him about eternal life, Jesus did not just say, "Believe in me." He said, "Sell all that you have and distribute to the poor . . . and come follow me" (Luke 18:22). In this story in which the ruler turned away sorrowfully we see that we don't always get a "yes" answer, but that does not mean we should make the cost of discipleship any cheaper. That is not our choice to make.

(c) Questions of economics, vocation, prejudice, human relations, and family living—all of these and more—become personal burning issues when you meet Christ. We shall witness to others about the reverberations that a Christ-commitment makes in every aspect of one's life.

III. Fundamental to our whole witness is the embodiment of Christ's spirit in our own lives.

(a) We can never separate a witness of words from a witness of deeds. It has been said that when the Christian gospel first went into India the criticism passed through three stages. First people said, "It is not true"; then, "It is not new"; and finally, "It is not you." They could only believe in the good news of Christ's love when they experienced that Christlike love in those who taught and preached it. There is no substitute for witnessing to Christ by being a person who cares for persons the way Christ cares.

(b) We may feel awkward talking to another about what Christ means to us. We may find it difficult to confront someone with the decision that Christ calls forth from that person's life. But there are persons we can befriend. There are ones known to us who need our love even as they need to know Christ. In our caring we may be building a bridge from one heart to another over which Christ can walk.

IV. Jesus sees us as ones who have his Holy Spirit and who are his witnesses. The problem is not that we do not witness to Christ but that we do not do it as fully as we would like. It is not that we lack the Holy Spirit but that we do not utilize the power God makes available to us.

(a) To be a witness for Christ is not easy. It requires us to open ourselves to another in a personal way that leaves us vulnerable. We may be seen only as meddlers and busybodies. We may be rejected. We hesitate to take the risk.

(b) At just this point we find particular meaning in Jesus' words about our having the power of the Holy Spirit.

God's empowering presence is with you to help you in the making of your witness. The need is to recognize that presence and rely upon that power.

(c) Is there not someone known to you who needs your witness to Christ? Do not procrastinate, but trust in God's power to help you move toward that person with loving care. Your witness can make all the difference in the world to that person.—Colbert S. Cartwright.

## Illustrations

RELEVANCE. The world of money, the earning of it, the spending of it, and the saving of it, covers by far the largest area of man's total life, endeavor, time, and recreation. The fabric of society is built around it directly or indirectly. Therefore to profess on the one hand that the Christian life covers the whole of life and on the other hand to pretend that the largest area of human interest can be excluded from the obligations of Christian discipleship is the best possible way to make nonsense out of Christianity and to render Christ utterly irrelevant to the realities of man's world. —Campbell Ferenbach in *Preaching Stewardship.*

A TITHE? There is value in the old Jewish principle of the tithe, the tenth part of income freely given up for God's service. We are not Jews and we are not under the law, and therefore the tithe must never become a matter of legal exaction. And in the modern world the calculation of the tithe is much more difficult than in earlier and simpler times. The state may take anything up to a third of a man's income; much of this money will be spent on purposes such as education and the care of health which used to be the church's sphere and were entirely supported by the charitable gifts of the faithful. On what basis is the heavily taxed citizen of the present day to calculate his tithe? Various answers are possible; any true answer must heed the first principle of the claim of God on human possessions and the glad recognition of this by the believer, shown in setting aside a part of his possessions for God's work.— Stephen Neill.

## Sermon Suggestions

MAKING FAITH REAL IN OUR DAY.   Scripture: Luke 14:25–33. (1) The stewardship of our lives. (2) The stewardship of our time. (3) The stewardship of our abilities. (4) The stewardship of our treasure.—Murray B. Jose.

TRUE REPENTANCE.      (1) Change of mind. (See Matt. 21:28–29.) (2) Contrition or godly sorrow for sin. (See Ps. 38:18.) (3) Confession of sin. (See Luke 15:18.) (4) Forsaking of sin. (See Isa. 55:7.) (5) A turning to God. (See Acts 26:18.)— *Christianity Today.*

## Worship Aids

CALL TO WORSHIP.      "The Lord is exalted; for he dwelleth on high: he hath filled Zion with judgment and righteousness. And wisdom and knowledge shall be the stability of thy times, and strength of salvation: the fear of the Lord is his treasure." Isa. 33:5–6.

INVOCATION.      O thou who art the light of the minds that know thee, the life of the souls that love thee, and the strength of the wills that serve thee, help us so to know thee that we may truly love thee and so to love thee that we may fully serve thee, whom to serve is perfect freedom.

OFFERTORY SENTENCE.      "Upon the first day of the week let every one of you lay by him in store, as God hath prospered him." I Cor. 16:2.

OFFERTORY PRAYER.      Our Father, open our eyes, we pray, to the glorious opportunities of sharing with others our blessed experiences of fellowship with one another and with thee.

LITANY.      O God, we thank you for assigning us the significant role of stewards in your kingdom.

*Help us to be good stewards of all you have placed in our care.*

We thank you for a daily allotment of time without which we could do nothing.

*Help us to use all our hours in ways that are in line with your will.*

We thank you for the ability to do and to learn to do literally millions of marvelous tasks.

*Help us to develop and use our varied skills in accord with the counsels of Christ.*

We thank you for money and for all to which it serves as a key.

*Grant that all our earning and spending, all our investing and giving, may be acceptable in your sight.*

We thank you for all the resources with which the world has been supplied.

*Grant that we may so use the soil, the air, the water—all of nature's bounty— that future generations may not be robbed by our irresponsibility.*

We thank you for the gifts of freedom and influence.

*Help us to use whatever freedom and influence we have for worthy objectives and purposes.*

We thank you for healthy bodies and sound minds.

*Grant that we may shun all habits and practices that unnecessarily reduce our physical or mental well-being.*

We thank you for the priceless privilege of children.

*May we never betray so great a trust.*

We thank you for the glorious gospel of Christ.

*Help us to live according to the light Jesus has given us, and guide us in sharing this light with others.*—William C. Sanford.

## EVENING SERVICE

### Topic: Zacchaeus: Man of Property
SCRIPTURE: Luke 19:1–10.

On his way to Jerusalem for the last time Christ passed through Jericho. Among the masses of curious spectators was a well-known and well-to-do man named Zacchaeus, about whom we shall note four things.

I. *His character*. Zacchaeus was a Jew by nationality and a publican in position. He had a passion for money. He thought more of money than he did his nation, the respect of his fellowmen, his soul, or God. He was an extortionist, levying the taxes to the limit, paying Rome her demands, and adding the balance to his personal savings.

II. *His condition*. (a) Zacchaeus was small in stature. He was a social outcast. Sitting in his booth one day, he observed a crowd of people down the street. Being curious he inquired as to what it meant and was informed that Jesus Christ had come to town.

(b) Zacchaeus resolved that he would go to see Christ Jesus, which desire was most commendable. However it was not at all easy for him to accomplish his purpose because of the multitude surrounding the Savior and his own smallness of stature. Undaunted by these handicaps, he went on ahead of the crowd and climbed the famous sycamore tree. That was a very undignified thing for a public official to do, but Zacchaeus was out for something far better than dignity, namely to see Christ.

III. *His call*. When the Savior arrived at the tree which Zacchaeus had ascended, he looked up at him and said, "Zacchaeus, make haste, and come down; for today I must abide at thy house." The Master knew his name, nature, position, and thoughts, so the call was quite personal. This call startled him. It proved to be effective for "he made haste and came down."

IV. *His conversion*. Zacchaeus' conviction of sin, unfeigned repentance, reception of Christ, confession of him, restitution of possessions, joy of heart, and reformation of life were excellent evidences of his genuine conversion.—H. C. Chiles.

## SUNDAY: NOVEMBER TWENTIETH

### MORNING SERVICE

Topic: **Thanksgiving in a Time of Trouble** (Thanksgiving Sunday)
Scripture: Phil. 1:3–14.

I. Times like ours call forth greatness from our lives. It is a time to be great. Let us thank God for the possibility of greatness.

(a) A man may be a perfect garrison soldier, but it is the battle that demands courage. A pilot may be efficient in routine flights, but it is the bombing mission that calls for calmness under stress. A skipper may have conducted many peaceful voyages, but it is the voyage through storm that tests his ability to command a difficult situation.

(b) A time of trouble like ours demands greatness from all of us. We are called to live beyond ourselves, to seek more than our private gain, and to give ourselves to the common good. Our time demands of us magnanimity, justice, and openness to change without undue fear.

(c) We are called to understand the nature of the disorders of our time and to treat the illness rather than the symptoms. We are asked to champion the causes of the weak, oppressed, and underprivileged. We are spurred to put human values above economic ones. We must emphasize justice along with law and order. If we cannot speak of justice, we have no right to speak of law and order. For law and order must be grounded in justice.

(d) The discharging of our responsibility to our time demands courage, risk, sacrifice, and sometimes insecurity. There can be no real greatness without these. Times like ours do not result automatically in greatness. They may have the opposite effect. Our time can plunge us into despair, make us cynical, and turn us to violence. Or they can make us reactionary and turn us to the past like stone faces while our world sweeps past us.

II. We should thank God for a chance

at a better world. (a) We can't go back to the world we have known. We can't turn the clock back. The movement of history is forward, and it is irreversible. However the stuff of history is malleable and its movement can be guided. Signs of hope appear. It is for us to see that the realities to which the signs point come to pass.

(b) There is a rising tide of hope and expectance in our world. Only a few years ago large segments of our world's population believed they could have nothing better than their fathers had had. History was a revolving door. History was not really going anywhere. That which was will be again, and there is nothing new under the sun. But all of that has changed now. Men everywhere know that they live life better than their fathers did. Rather than history going round and round it moves forward at accelerated speed, although its goals are not always clearly defined.

(c) The time is near when no child need cry himself to sleep at night because of hunger, no person need shiver in a threadbare garment, and no man need sleep without a roof over his head. Modern education battles with success the problem of illiteracy. Medical science increasingly brings its blessings to men everywhere. There is a rising expectancy concerning physical, economic, medical, and cultural values.

(d) There is a rising expectancy for human values. Never before have such words as freedom, dignity, and equality had such magical power on such a worldwide basis as now. The hearts of men everywhere leap at their sound. We speak of the new nations that have appeared at such a phenomenal rate since World War II. Never before in history have so many men been made so free in such a brief period of time to determine their destiny.

(e) We are nearer the day when we shall be willing to accept people as persons. When that day comes, what reason we shall have for thanksgiving!

III. We should thank God that he is with us in our time of trouble. (a) In studying the Bible you must have discovered that the great revelations of God have come in times of trouble. It is true that God is in the still small voice, but it is also true that, amid the shrieking cries of the wind, God tells us his name and, against the face of dark and threatening skies, he shows us his face.

(1) The great event of the Old Testament was the Exodus. There was nothing quiet and unperturbed about that. It was a traumatic event. Oppressed people who had been slaves were delivered and given a freedom they didn't know how to handle. But it was in that event that the hand of God was seen more clearly than anywhere else.

(2) G. Ernest Wright has reminded us that all the prophets of the Old Testament were called in times of crisis. They saw God's judgment in the upheavals of history and heard his voice amid the storm of unsettled times. They saw God's mercy healing the brokenness of men who were often caught in the injustices and dislocations of history.

(3) In the New Testament Jesus came to his disciples only once at sea, and that was through storm. They saw him upon the troubled waves and believed him to be a phantom, but through the howling winds they heard his voice saying, "It is I; be not afraid." And so through storm he tells us who he is.

(b) In the cross of Jesus Christ, God made his supreme revelation of himself. Fear, hatred, prejudice, and bigotry broke around that cross like a fierce storm. Here you see how deceptive respectable men can be and how sinful good men can be. It was the power structures of respectability that put Jesus to death rather than hoodlums and gangsters. But within the lurid shadows of that cross you see the absorbing, healing, and forgiving love of God more clearly than anywhere else.

(c) It is a good time to catch a fresh vision of God and to understand his ways among men in our time. He is with us in the storm. He is with us judging us, forgiving us, healing us, reconciling us, and calling us to the task of making a better world.—Chevis F. Horne.

## Illustrations

CALL TO THANKSGIVING. On this day let our people, as befits Christian citizens of this land, gather in their appointed places of worship to offer heartfelt thanks to God in the name of Jesus Christ our Redeemer and our Lord.

Let us gratefully remember all of his dealings with us which manifest his great love for us and for those also in which love is hidden from our eyes; for friendship and duty; for good hopes and precious memories; for the joys that cheer us and the trials that teach us to trust in him.

Let us gratefully remember all the tokens of his mercy; his protection round about us; his guiding hand upon us.

Let us gratefully remember his unbounded favor unto our land; his gifts of liberty and order; unity and peace; peaceful times and fruitful season.

Above all let us gratefully remember that in his inestimable love he redeemed the world by our Lord Jesus Christ and gave to all mankind the means of grace and the hope of glory.

Let us, therefore, as we give thanks unto almighty God for all his benefits toward us, also beseech him to give us that due sense of all his mercies, that our hearts may be unfeignedly thankful and that we may show forth our praise not only with our lips but also in our lives.

May he grant unto us, along with his continued gifts and magnanimous mercies, hearts to love him and wills to serve our fellowmen. And may we delight in all things to do his blessed will and seek to walk before him in holiness and righteousness all our days.
—Herman L. Turner.

THE SOURCE. A mandarin's daughter from China came to the United States years ago to study in one of our women's colleges and specialized in English literature. One day she went to her professor and said: "I am puzzled. Every time I read a great classic of the English speech I find ideas and ideals that seem to be common property and are different from anything in my land. There must be a reason. What is the source?" And the professor said: "Do you know the Bible?" "No," she replied, "I never read it." "Well," he answered, "if you are ever going to understand you will have to know the Bible."—Harry Emerson Fosdick.

MAGNET SWEEP. If one should give me a dish of sand and tell me there were particles of iron in it, I might look for them with my eyes, and search for them with my clumsy fingers, and be unable to detect them; but let me take a magnet and sweep through it, and how it would draw to itself the almost invisible particles by the mere power of attraction. The unthankful heart, like my finger in the sand, discovers no mercies; but let the thankful heart sweep through the day, and as the magnet finds the iron, so it will find, in every hour, some heavenly blessings; only the iron in God's sand is gold.—Henry Ward Beecher.

## Sermon Suggestions

WHY THANKSGIVING DAY? (1) Because it is part of our religious heritage as recorded in the Bible and perpetuated by our religious customs. (2) Because we feel a great thirst which can be quenched only as we drink freely from the fountain of our national heritage. (3) Because it is the mark of people of character to want to express an inner feeling of gratitude for all of the gifts of life.—Homer J. R. Elford.

HOW TO READ THE BIBLE. Text: Acts 8:31. (1) Believingly. (2) Prayerfully. (3) Carefully. (4) Systematically. (5) Obediently.—George Sweeting.

## Worship Aids

CALL TO WORSHIP. "O come, let us sing unto the Lord: let us make a joyful noise to the rock of our salvation. Let us come before his presence with thanksgiving, and make a joyful noise unto him with psalms." Ps. 95:1-2.

INVOCATION.    Creator and giver of every good and perfect gift, thy harvest of blessings has bountifully fallen upon us, giving our lives fulfillment and satisfaction. We have come to give thee our heart's thanksgiving. As thou art like a river eternally, lavishly, and unceasingly pouring goodness upon us, transform us into streams that share with thee and our fellowman. Give us souls like waterfalls outflowing with love divine. Inspire us to live thanksgiving lives as we serve thee.—Harold A. Schultz.

OFFERTORY SENTENCE.    "Thou crownest the year with thy goodness. . . . Samuel took a stone, and set it between Mizpeh and Shen, saying, Hitherto hath the Lord helped us." Ps. 65:11; I Sam. 7:12.

OFFERTORY PRAYER.    Our Father, may we who have seen thy providential hand in all the experiences of our lives seek to possess such greatness of mind and spirit that we shall be enabled to offer these gifts with an unselfish joyfulness.

PRAYER.    O God our Father, we thank thee for the gifts which thou hast given to us and to all mankind.

We thank thee for all the nobility which thou hast put into the hearts of men. We thank thee that thou hast made us able to toil until we pass the breaking point and do not break. We thank thee that thou hast made us able to love until even self is forgotten. We thank thee that thou hast made men able and willing to sacrifice even life itself for those whom they hold dear. We thank thee that thou hast made us such that somehow we cannot sin in peace, such that goodness always haunts us and sin ever brings its remorse.

We thank thee for the skill which thou hast put into the minds of men. We thank thee that thou hast made men able to find ways of defeating disease and easing pain. We thank thee that thou hast enabled men to conquer distance and to bring the ends of the earth close to each other.

We thank thee for the visions and the ideals which thou hast placed in the souls of men. We thank thee for those who had the vision of freedom for all mankind; for those who to this day dream, and plan, and labor for a world at peace; for those who campaign and toil for a country and a world where men will live in good homes and work under just conditions; for those who work and pray for a world in which all men shall know thee and love thee from the least even unto the greatest.

We thank thee for the blessings which we enjoy every day. We thank thee for the friends in whose comradeship we delight. We thank thee for the work whereby we earn a living and for the strength to do it. We thank thee for homes where we have comfort, peace, and joy. We thank thee for loved ones without whom life could never be the same.

Above all else we thank thee for Jesus Christ, thy greatest and thy best gift to men, in whom thou hast given us thyself and all thy love.

Accept this our sacrifice of thanksgiving and of praise, for thy love's sake.—William Barclay.

## EVENING SERVICE

**Topic: Thanksgiving in Three Tenses**
TEXT: I Cor. 15:57.

Paul is looking in three directions as he sings this hymn of gratitude: the past in which God has visited him with the gift of new life, the present in which the stings of adversity are fashioning a character for him, and into the future of that victory which the gospel promises to him. We all live in these three tenses.

I. Paul looks backward and thanks God that something unspeakably great has happened to him.

(a) Paul has lived through a moral revolution which retrieved him from a life of failure and made him over again into a man. You will agree that a man like that has something to be grateful for. Not for the little lifts along the way but for the lift out of failure into present victory.

(b) I doubt if we can celebrate a Christian thanksgiving without looking upon the cross of Christ and being awed and inspired by its redemptive presence in our lives. The reason Thanksgiving Day has so often generated into a mere national fetish is that men can look upon Jesus Christ and his cross without an inward sense of humility and shame. It is the lives through which God has and is doing something real which feel the greatest need of thanksgiving. The unregenerate heart cannot sing. The spiritual pigmy feels no need of thanksgiving. This nation of people will have to bow their knees in penitence before they can rise to sing hallelujahs of gratitude.

II. Note the second altitude from which Paul sings out his hymn of thanksgiving. With a great price had he been bought. Now Paul thanks God that he may share in God's plan of redemptive suffering.

(a) This isn't thanking God for good luck. It's thanking him for the purgatorial fires of adversity and hard knocks which alone can fashion true character. Paul is no fair-weather saint. Despised for his Christian faith. Hurt and stoned by the very ones he tries to help. Thrust into prison stenches. In various shipwrecks on the sea. About to be beheaded by some bloody Caesar at Rome for the peerless purity of his life and heroic quality of his faith. And for this Paul thanks God!

(b) We are to thank God for a faith which gladly accepts adversity and turns it into redemptive power. The souls that have been finely tempered by hardships are the most grateful.

III. Paul thanks God for the deathlessness of his faith. (a) This verse is part of that great dissertation on the resurrection. "O death, where is thy sting; O grave, where is thy victory; the sting of death is sin, and the strength of sin is the law; but thanks be to God who giveth us the victory through our Lord Jesus Christ!" Here is posited the victory of life over death, the crowning conquest of spirit over matter, the victory of Christ over the world. And Paul thanks God for that!

(b) God not only wrests these lives of ours out of their sinful selfishness, but he does so for a purpose. We are not here to glean a character by heroically battling with the slings and arrows of outrageous fortune but also are doing so for a purpose. We go to battle with those forces which make for war and wholesale suffering in the world today in the confidence that the ultimate victory is not in the hands of men but grounded in the heart of eternal God.

(c) I thank God for a faith which thrills me with new life in Jesus Christ, for a faith which enables me to bear my share of hardships as a loyal soldier of Jesus Christ, and above all for a faith which enables me to look into the future with a risen Christ.—Aaron N. Meckel.

## SUNDAY: NOVEMBER TWENTY-SEVENTH

### MORNING SERVICE

**Topic: What the Church Might Mean to You (Advent)**

SCRIPTURE: I Pet. 1:1–15.

I. We find little meaning in church experiences unless we sense that the church means something different. It offers something to people that no other religious movement does.

(a) Many Christians have fallen prey to a sort of unhealthy eclecticism which concludes that one religion is as good as another. But the truth is we have had something revealed to us, we have had a call placed upon us, and we must understand what the offer is, what the claim is, and what the call is as it has come to us from God. We must understand that Jesus Christ is uniquely different from every other religious leader who ever lived.

(b) When we ask about the fruits of his coming, we sense that we are freed from the condemnation of personal failure, while many of the religions of the world simply offer good advice at this point. His death means the free gift of God's forgiveness to sinful people who know they sin against creation and their fellowmen.

(c) Such a gift was offered to men historically through the Christian church. The church gave us the Holy Bible which contains the account of this love. To all who believe, peace and joy flow into the human heart to relieve it from guilt and from the pain of sin and wrongdoing against God and against others. It is an act of trust on our part as we receive this.

(d) This act of redemptive love which we receive to be forgiven and put in love and charity with our neighbors creates a fellowship that is distinctly different.

(1) When I enter into it there is something I receive consciously which is the difference between existence and living. I feel that I am near the center of reality, the ground of our being, as Paul Tillich says. I am moving with the grandest design for a human life which is love in every relationship.

(2) As one forgiven by love I am moved to forgive in love. As one receiving the patience of God I am moved to be patient with others. As one receiving a rightness from God which I do not deserve I am moved out of gratitude to live a life that is right.

(3) This adds stability and strength to my life. It helps me to know who I am, why I live, and where I am going.

II. To be a Christian, to appreciate the church, and to receive what it has to offer is to recognize that the church means something dangerous for us.

(a) It has meant this to those who have been forced to suffer for their faith. This something different means that some things we hold dear might be endangered. We will not be put in prison for worshiping as we freely choose in our time, but the danger comes in that the things we hold dear may be in contrast to the will and purpose of Jesus Christ, and we shall have to give them up. Many aspects of your social standing, your circle of friends, your time, your income, and your sense of values may be endangered if you take seriously the role of the Christian church in your life, the message it proclaims, and the Christ it represents.

(b) Christianity is unique in that it calls us to sacrifice. Yet some of us wonder why the church means so little to us. It is because we have sacrificed so little in its behalf. We sing an old gospel song, "On a hill far away stood an old rugged cross." The truth of the matter is that the farther away that cross is the better we like it because that cross means self-denial. Jesus calls us to bear it as he did and to die to our sins in order that we may live again and bring others to life. We sing about the cross, but we don't bear it. We are not willing at times to bear even the simple discipline of going to Sunday school, worshiping God in his church, or of committing ourselves to being a teacher or leader in his church. And yet we wonder why we receive so little from the church. The church means that we will have to give up some things if we are going to find fulfillment in its life.

III. The church should mean something dynamic. (a) That is a word that is greatly overused today, but I couldn't find a better one because a dynamo receives energy, stores it, and then gives it out. A Christian receives the very energy of God into his life and soul as he worships, studies, prays, and has fellowship with other like-minded people. This sustains him. Then it sends him out in service to others who need a Savior.

(b) The church of Jesus Christ offers unto such people the peace that passes all understanding which they can only receive by faith in Christ. In truth we must be as the children of Israel who during forty years of wilderness wandering were the recipients of manna from heaven. This dynamic power is something we cannot manufacture, but it can be received by an unfaltering trust.

(c) For too many of us Christianity and the church have been a sort of side show, not the main event. The side show is closed, and yet we play at the matter of keeping our names on the church rolls. It is important to see that it is one thing to belong to the church and quite another to be in it all the way. And unless we are in it all the way, having received the forgiving grace of God through Jesus for ourselves, unless we sense that we are really a part of this fellowship of prayer, worship, and service, and unless we have become a sacrificial part of this living organism of God, then the church will not be for us what it ought to be.—Thomas A. Whiting.

## Illustrations

CONVICTION.     The security patterns of our fond imagination do not hold up in the face of the gospel. The Greeks had a word for this kind of freedom from emotion. It was the word "apathy" or undisturbedness. This is not what Christ offers to any man. Indeed the opposite: "In the world you have tribulation; but be of good cheer, I have overcome the world." Christ offers instead the promise to make life new. Regeneration always involves a revolution. He offers to forgive sin and raise us to eternal life, and penitence always sends us through pain. But all the time he offers to be with us. "And his name shall be called Emmanuel because he is God with us." The conviction of these things makes a vital difference: God is in the midst of his creation; he does care what happens now and forever; our lives were made not for the endurance of any human failure or the destiny of any human evil but for eternity.—Robert E. Luccock.

DANCING FOR JOY.     Christians are blissful people who can rejoice at heart and sing praises, stamp and dance and leap for joy. That is well pleasing to God and doth our heart good when we trust in God and find in him our pride and our joyfulness. Such a gift should only kindle a fire and a light in our heart so that we should never cease dancing and leaping for joy.—Martin Luther.

## Sermon Suggestions

WHAT MAKES A CHURCH GREAT?     (1) Not soft seats and subdued lights but strong and courageous leadership. (2) Not the sweet tones of the organ but sweet personalities that somehow reflect Jesus. (3) Not tall towers having chimes and bells but a lofty vision of its people. (4) Not big budgets but big hearts. (5) Not the amount of finance received but the amount of service rendered. (6) Not a large membership but God's presence and direction and power. (7) Not what it has done in the past but what it is doing now and in the future.

THE CHURCH'S THREE SHIPS.     (1) Worship. (2) Fellowship. (3) Stewardship.

## Worship Aids

CALL TO WORSHIP.     "Arise, shine; for thy light is come, and the glory of the Lord is risen upon thee. Lift up thine eyes round about and see." Isa. 60:1, 4.

INVOCATION.     O Lord of light, in this hour of worship in thy house make pure our hearts, and we shall see thee; reveal thyself to us, and we shall love thee. Strengthen our wills, and we shall choose the good from the evil, and day by day manifest in the world the glory and power of thy blessed gospel, which thou hast made known to us through thy Son Jesus Christ.

OFFERTORY SENTENCE.     "I will freely sacrifice unto thee: I will praise thy name, O Lord; for it is good." Ps. 54:6.

OFFERTORY PRAYER.     Our Father, help us to love thee so well that we shall have all thy kingdom interests and all thy children at heart.

PRAYER. God of might and mercy, in thee we seek the peace that man can neither give nor take away and the life that counts even losses as gains if they be suffered for thy sake. We see thee in the far-flung stars of night and the goodly sun by day; we seek thee where the mountains touch the sky and the rich earth brings forth thy bounty. We see thee in the life of man with man, in the common toil of every day, and in the holy comradeship of family and friends, in the love that leaps the battle lines of human strife and binds us even to those whose wills we must oppose. We see thee in the one whom thou didst send to show thy life to man and who spoke the word the whole world heard, even Jesus Christ thy Son.

Grant then, O God, that what we see in everything around us we may in truth believe and love. Spare us the anguish of searching the world for what lies at our feet. Grant us thy blessing, and then, having peace ourselves, vouchsafe that we may be free for the tasks to which thou dost summon us. Remove the thought of gain from the service we offer thy kingdom. Give us victory if victory will serve thee best, or bring us to the end of hope if by despair thou canst more surely accomplish thy will. Establish us in some place where the needs of men cry out for strength beyond themselves, and there let thy light so shine through us that, seeing thee, men may also love thee, and loving thee, come at last home to thy peace.— William Croft Wilson.

### EVENING SERVICE

Topic: How Shall We Pray for Others?
TEXT: II Thess. 1:11 (TEV).
I. *Pray humbly.* We should not be too sure we know what another person or group needs. We must be sure that our desires are in harmony with God's purposes.

II. *Pray in the spirit of Christ.* This is what we mean when we say, "We ask it in Christ's name" or "Through Jesus Christ our Lord." This means to pray in fellowship with Christ in love and obedience. We trust Christ, and we love one another as Christ commanded. By praying in Christ's name, through Christ, we come to God not as strangers but as those wonderfully connected to him through Christ.

III. *Pray specifically and persistently.* Pray for persons by name. Pray for their actual needs as you know them. Pray persistently and patiently, expecting the very best to happen to and in and through the person for whom you pray. You may pray for anything if you pray Christ's prayer, "Thy will be done."

IV. *Make your prayers for others large enough.* Include as many as you can. When I visit someone in a hospital and offer a brief prayer for the person, I try to do more. As I pass the many rooms of other patients I say a silent prayer that they too may be open for God's spiritual healing. I pray for the surgeons, the doctors, and the nurses, if only in a short "arrow prayer." John Calvin said that medicine is a gift from God. Paul Tournier has written, "Every doctor, Christian or not, is a collaborator with God."

V. *Whenever possible pray with others.* The power of united prayer cannot be measured. This is why worship of God in our churches is essential. Jesus prays for us. He said to Peter, "Peter, the devil has sought to capture you, but I have prayed for you, that your faith fail not."—Abridged from *The Best of David A. MacLennan.*

## SUNDAY: DECEMBER FOURTH

### MORNING SERVICE

Topic: Name Above All Names (Advent)

TEXT: Isa. 9:6.
I. *Lord!* (a) It signifies authority, supreme authority. It was the title given to Roman emperors. More than

that in the Old Testament it is the title given to God. Yet when we cross from the Old Testament to the New we find it taken and applied to the lowly Galilean. Born of humble parents, brought up in the despised town of Nazareth, working at a carpenter's bench till he was thirty, then for three years a homeless itinerant preacher, owning no more than the clothes he wore, he was accorded the same title as was accorded Caesar, as is ascribed to God.

(b) Why? Because there was that in him which men would fain call Master. A peasant's dress and a workman's lot could not disguise his nobility. By the irresistible royalty of his person he drew men to himself. Right down the centuries it has been the same. From generation to generation his influence has been magnetic. North and South, East and West, his authority has been acknowledged. It would be impressive to know how many people around the world when this day is done have gathered in his name.

II. *Jesus!* (a) It is the name he was given at his birth, an honored and heroic name in Israel with prophetic significance as well as historical associations: "You shall call his name Jesus for he will save his people from their sins."

(b) We speak of the Jesus of history and we have in mind the man: his body human, growing as other bodies do, nourished by food, susceptible to hunger and thirst, to weariness and temptation, to suffering and death; his mind human, his intellect having the same faculties and working by the same laws as ours, for he asked questions to elicit information, he felt and expressed surprise, he learned obedience by the things which he suffered.

(c) Jesus was human, "very man of very man," and yet he was unique in his humanity, the one and only perfect and truly human being that has lived on earth. When Pilate brought him out to the crowd and said, "Behold the Man," he meant only, "Behold the man whom you insist on crucifying." But Pilate's words in retrospect have a wider, profounder meaning. People have realized that they signified more than Pilate knew. Behold *the* Man!

(d) In Jesus we see humanity at its holiest, highest, and best. This also has been the verdict of the centuries. To this day people, even while they shrug their shoulders at the impossibility of it, acknowledge that if we were all like Jesus our problems would be solved. What is this but to acknowledge that to be like him is to be in perfect harmony with the purpose of God?

III. *Christ!* (a) To catch the full import of the title perhaps one has to be a devout Jew. For the devout Jew, messiah is the name above every name, the name at which every knee bows. The messiah is the anointed one, the representative of God on earth, his mission to bring in the day of brotherhood and the end of the night of wrong, to inaugurate the kingdom of God on earth—a kingdom moral, not nationalistic; spiritual, not materialistic; social, not individualistic; universal, not local.

(b) Every leader who has risen head and shoulders above his contemporaries has been absorbed by one master thought. In the case of Napoleon it was the domination of Europe. In the case of Buddha it was the reincarnation of life. In the case of Socrates it was the immortality of the soul. In the case of Jesus it was the rule of God in the hearts of men and in the life of the world. And he saw himself as the agent of that rule, as the one commissioned by God to usher it in and make it universal. To believe on Jesus as the Christ is to believe that he is the one divinely appointed to make God's sovereignty over men real and to be the world's Savior.—Robert J. McCracken.

### Illustration

HUMAN FACE OF GOD.   I believe that Christianity has given the name of Christ to what we might call the voice of God to man; and I like to think of the word "Christ" as meaning what we might call the human face of God. The veil of reality has been broken as though some being had come toward us out of the darkness; and we can say to the universe not "It is there" but "Thou art there, and thou carest for me."— William Ernest Hocking.

## Sermon Suggestions

JEHOVAH AND HIS REDEEMED PEOPLE. (1) Jehovah Jireh: the Lord will provide (Gen. 22:14). (2) Jehovah Rapha: the Lord thy healer (Exod. 15:26). (3) Jehovah Nissi: the Lord our banner (Exod. 17:8). (4) Jehovah Shalom: the Lord our peace (Judg. 6:24). (5) Jehovah Raah: the Lord my shepherd (Ps. 23:1). (6) Jehovah Tsidkenu: the Lord our righteousness (Jer. 26:6). (7) Jehovah Shammah: the Lord is here (Ezek. 48:35).

WHY DID JESUS LEAVE HEAVEN?    Text: Luke 19:10. (1) To bring light. (See John 12:46.) (2) To judge willful blindness. (See John 9:39.) (3) To kindle a fire. (See Luke 12:49.) (4) To cause division. (See Matt. 10:34; Luke 12:51.) (5) To enthrone truth. (See John 8:37.) (6) To bestow life. (See John 10:10.) (7) To seek and to save. (See Luke 19:10.)

## Worship Aids

CALL TO WORSHIP.    "O Zion, that bringeth good tidings, get thee up into the high mountain; O Jerusalem, that bringeth good tidings, lift up thy voice with strength; lift it up, be not afraid: say unto the cities of Judah, Behold your God!" Isa. 40:9.

INVOCATION.    O Lord God, who hast left unto us thy holy word to be a lamp unto our feet and a light unto our path: give unto us all thy Holy Spirit, we humbly pray thee, that out of the same Word we may learn what is thy blessed will, and frame our lives in all holy obedience to the same, to thine honor and glory and the increase of our faith.

OFFERTORY SENTENCE.    "Verily, verily, I say unto you, he that believeth on me, the works that I do shall he do also; and greater works than these shall he do. And whatsoever ye shall ask in my name, that will I do, that the Father may be glorified in the Son." John 14:12–13.

OFFERTORY PRAYER.    Our Father, take us with all of our failures and develop us after thine own heart. Give us more of the mind of the Master, more of his spirit of compassion, and more of his sacrificial and loving heart.

PRAYER.    Almighty God, prepare us, we pray, for the hours when we shall celebrate the birth of thy Son. The world is so much with us, and its allurements are so steadily before us. We long to save this Christmas for thy purposes, but so frequently our good intentions have lost their way in the forests of dinners and parties, in the jungles of buying and wrapping. So we beseech thee to loose us from the bondage of our long-established habits and in this time of the Advent to fix our minds on him whose coming we proclaim.

Let these be days of judgment, days when we remember thy creation of the world and thy decision that it was good, days when our hearts encircle all its distant reaches and comprehend the cruelty which man has worked upon his brother man, and days when we understand our own responsibility for the wickedness that brings thee pain. Grant that our heads may not rest easy on pillows bought with greed or injustice, and be thou the end of any peace that has no better source than ignorance, indifference, or such enchantment with our own concerns that we have no leisure for the agonies around us. Deny us success when we try to forget that men are starving—now, that men are homeless—now, that men are persecuted—now; and if we hail the coming of thy Son, let it not be without the awareness that inasmuch as we have not done the deeds of righteousness to one of the least of thy creatures, we have not done them unto thy Son.

But vouchsafe that these may also be days of joy, days when we recall that the Word became flesh when flesh had no right to expect it, days when we recognize anew that thou dost love thy people less because of their merits than in spite of their unworthiness, days when we find in the life and death of Jesus the evidence of thine unflagging toil for our redemption. If thou didst care enough for the world to give thine only begotten Son that whosoever believed on him might have abundant life, protect us from the insolence of despising what thou dost love. If the earth is thine and its people are thy creatures, save us from the folly of believing that thou hast lost control of thy creation. If thou hast kept thy favor for the righteous and laid in a manger thy gift above all other gifts, deliver us from the fear that the horses of history no longer respond to thy reins.

Make us ready for Christmas, God. By peace or by strife, by joy or by anguish, by life or by death, prepare us for the holy day of incarnation, and when thou art praised for the birth of thy Son, may it be by men and women born again in him whose birth they sing.—Roy Pearson.

## EVENING SERVICE

Topic: The Backroad to Christmas (Advent)

SCRIPTURE: Mal. 7:1-7.

The main road leads up and down Main Street and through the round of social, civic, and church functions. The backroad is different; it is not geographical but spiritual.

I. The backroad goes all the way back to our most primitive ancestors. These remote ancestors struggled to relate to each other and to reach out and make contact with each other. Slowly they began to make things and draw pictures and to leave traces of life in the dwellings and crude implements which they constructed for themselves. The earth contains the remains of man's attempt to fashion a meaningful life. Primitive man was frightened and insecure, flailing about, looking for some way to resolve his inner restlessness.

II. The backroad winds down into Egypt, picking up at a most unlikely group of Hebrew slaves. Off they went into the desert, wandering for forty years until finally they stumbled into what they called the promised land.

III. Another thousand years and the road leads through a small town in Nazareth of Galilee and winds the 70-odd miles down into Bethlehem of Judea. It is an obscure road. The birth in the stable didn't cause a ripple in the powerful Roman Empire.

IV. The backroad to Christmas runs through the life of a man who came into the world to give men a taste of the eternal. A man who spoke for God, and whose words still do so. A man whose terrible meekness so shook the world that beginning with the day of his humble and obscure birth mankind went back and divided history into B.C. and A.D.

V. The road winds into your life and mine because in each of us there is that empty place which only God can fill. Sometimes we know that emptiness through pain and loss or through some kind of personal crisis. The backroad to Christmas runs through the places in your life where you hurt the most and where great questions cry out to be answered.—I. Carroll Starling, Jr.

## SUNDAY: DECEMBER ELEVENTH

### MORNING SERVICE

Topic: Weeds and Flowers in the Christmas Garden (Advent)

TEXT: Matt. 13:30.

As Christians we have a bad conscience over what has happened to Christmas. We feel guilty because we have allowed the church's festival of our Savior's birth to slip out of the church's hands and become a general folk festival shot through with secular customs that have no relation to our Savior's birth. In fact the sacred and secular are so mixed together that we can no longer distinguish one from the other. It's like a lovely flower garden which has become a jungle of weeds that not only hide the flowers but threaten to choke them out of existence. Those weeds are not the pleasant customs of Christmas that simply detract attention from Jesus; they are the basic attitudes and philosophies of life which are hostile to the spirit of Jesus and which Jesus himself expressly condemned.

I. *Weeds.* (a) One weed is *materialism.* I am not talking about our pleasant custom of exchanging gifts. I am talking about the obsession with material things that takes hold of us at Christmas as the obsession with horse-racing takes hold of a compulsive gambler. Jesus said that a man's life does not consist in the abundance of his possessions. It certainly does at Christmas. And such possessions! Such abundance!

(b) Another weed in the Christmas garden is *self-indulgence.* It's astonishing how many decent folk, who manage to live soberly for 51 weeks of the year, feel that they can make Christmas week the excuse for an annual binge. That's all the more ironic when we recall that Christmas itself was originally invented as a counterattraction to an annual binge. For the first 380 years of its life the church got along very nicely without celebrating Christmas at all. Then its leaders noticed that every December, when the great pagan festivals rolled around, many converts in the Roman Empire regretted that they were missing out on the fun, and some slipped back into their old ways. Pondering what they could do about it, the church decided to sponsor their own party, a birthday party.

(c) Another weed in the garden is the sheer *idolatry* of Christmas. The purpose of Christmas or any other religious festival is to keep alive and dramatize and communicate a spiritual truth—in this case the truth that God sent his Son into the world to live and die for the world's salvation. For many people that remains the essential meaning of Christmas. They enjoy the pleasant secular customs which have grown up around the season, but they do not allow those customs to come between them and the truth the season celebrates. Others come nowhere near that truth. They celebrate Christmas, but they never get beyond Christmas. They worship the festival but not the Lord of the festival, and that is a form of idolatry. We are acutely aware that Christmas, as celebrated in our society, may obstruct rather than communicate spiritual truth, and some of us feel guilty for allowing that to happen.

II. *Flowers.* (a) *Beauty* is a flower in the Christmas garden. Whatever some people have done with Christmas, it remains the loveliest season of the year and therefore of incalculable benefit to man's morale. Transformation happens to the world at Christmas; its drabness gives way to loveliness and its darkness becomes a fairyland of light. In homes, offices, shops, and streets people feel warm and happy and relaxed. For some people Christmas is the only season for the year that puts any color into their grim, gray lives, and we should be infinitely poorer without it.

(b) *The joy of children* is a flower in the Christmas garden, and anyone who would deprive them of it was never a child himself. Was Christmas ever so wonderful for you as when your children were small and you saw it through their innocent eyes? Will you ever forget the excitement, the mystery, and the magic of Christmas Eve when they left milk and cookies beside the fireplace? Will you ever forget the gleam in their eyes when they came downstairs on Christmas morning and found those victuals gone? Not a lot of it had to do with Jesus, or maybe it did.

(c) *Friendship* is a flower in the Christmas garden. It is a precious flower these days when so many things drive people apart. Family life is not what it used to be. Our homes have become dormitories from which we are always running away. We don't have much time for our friends either. In our mobile society, where we are always traveling, commuting, and moving, we tend not to make lasting friendships anymore. We tend not to relate to people. Comes Christmas however and they might just drop in on their next-door neighbors. Comes Christmas and they might send cards or letters or even make phone calls to people who thought they were dead. Comes Christmas and the children and grandchildren will be home, and the whole family will sit down to a relaxed meal. Comes Christmas and even some hostile hearts are reconciled. Comes Christmas and we become human again.

(d) *Generosity* is a flower in the Christmas garden. God bless Christmas for what it does to people, even the most miserable people, for its warm, gentle spirit that thaws out frozen hearts, instilling in them a new softness, a new patience, a new kindness, and a new generosity. God bless Christmas for the refreshing breeze of love that blows through a world stifling in the stagnant atmosphere of hate, quickening our hope that peace and goodwill among men may not be such an impossible dream.

III. "Let both grow together until the harvest." (a) I think that's what Jesus is saying to us in our Christmas guilt. He is telling us not to have a bad conscience over what has happened because we ourselves enjoy the secular pleasures of the season. He is the last person in the world to take the fun out of Christmas. He came into the world to put fun into our lives and to give us some reasons for goodness and gladness and love and laughter. As for the weeds in the Christmas garden, he tells us not to destroy them, or we may destroy some of the flowers as well.

(b) We may even destroy the most precious flower of all. That flower is the childlike humility of people once a year before a mystery that they cannot understand; the suspicion that this world isn't everything but that beyond it is a power that once invaded this world and acted for our good. I am not altogether sure that any of the Christmas flowers will survive if we try to separate them from the weeds. We had better leave them alone and let both grow together until God's harvest.— Leonard Griffith.

### Illustration

THE CENTRAL EVENT.    There is one thing to which all of us have grown accustomed. In fact we hardly give it a thought—the central event of Christmas. Notice, will you, just how I put that. I said, "The central event." For of course to millions of us Christmas means family reunions and turkey and presents and a tree lit up and loaded, and for some of us it means snow, and for others in Australia and elsewhere, heat. To some of us there may be passing allusions on the Christmas cards to "peace on earth and goodwill among men," but it amounts to little. And the angels and all that which form part of the decorations mean little more than Father Christmas and the reindeer. But all these are the trappings—good trappings, good fun—but trappings nonetheless! I am talking about the central event of Christmas, and it is this which so easily gets forgotten, which so easily we get accustomed to, and about which we get blasé.— F. Donald Coggan.

### Sermon Suggestions

HOW TO SUCCEED IN LIFE.    Text: John 3:30. Three characteristics of John the Baptist made him effective. (1) He knew who he was. (2) He knew what he was to do. (3) He had the courage to do it.—Walter L. Dosch.

THREE ROADS TO BETHLEHEM.    (1) The road of necessity taken by Joseph and Mary. (2) The road of curiosity taken by the shepherds. (3) The road of commitment taken by the wise men.— Clarence J. Forsberg.

## Worship Aids

CALL TO WORSHIP. "Ho, every one that thirsteth, come ye to the waters. Incline your ear, and come unto me: hear, and your soul shall live; and I will make an everlasting covenant with you, even the sure mercies of David." Isa. 55:1, 3.

INVOCATION. O desire of nations, long-expected Christ, when wilt thou appear among us in thy glory? Thy coming in humility brought great gladness and peace to those who waited for the kingdom, but even today how few of all mankind know that thou hast come, and fewer still have learned to walk in thy ways. Something more than this was promised, and something more has kept the advent hope living in the hearts of men. Yet the centuries pass, and men ask, "Where are the signs of his coming?" Yet we feel thou art at hand. Hope still is strong. By thy grace wilt thou quicken this hope in all our hearts. May we be prepared to welcome thy coming, O Christ. Cleanse our hearts. Strengthen our faith. Give us new confidence as we worship together in thy house this day.

OFFERTORY SENTENCE. "Prepare ye the way of the Lord, make straight in the desert a highway for our God." Isa. 40:3.

OFFERTORY PRAYER. May we find it to be a joyful experience, O Lord, to offer these gifts in the name of Jesus. Grant unto us the wisdom of the men of old who found a token in a star, worshiped the child as a newborn king, and made offerings at his feet.

PRAYER Our Father, who didst so love the world that thou gavest thy Son Jesus Christ to save it, we are grateful beyond words for thy gifts which are beyond measure. For the good earth with its bounties, for health of body and mind, for the love of family and friends and for the blessings of freedom and security—for all these we give thee hearty and profound thanks. Amid the confusing calls of the world may we hear thy still small voice speaking to us of love and beauty and goodness. Help us to think of the good until we love it and hope for the best until we bring it into being. Warm our hearts with the glory of the Christmas season. Kindle in us a deeper affection for those near to us and a more determined goodwill toward our neighbors in all lands.— Ralph W. Sockman.

## EVENING SERVICE

Topic: **Whatever Happened to the Wise Men?** (Advent)
SCRIPTURE: Matt. 2:1–12.

I. The wise men were not in a hurry. They did not come with flashing lights or screaming sirens but rather, led by a star, quietly and with steady pace. They knew the star belonged to the centuries. In contrast to the star-led gait we jump with quickened pace from event to event, as each in turn is heralded as the greatest of all. Lacking the discipline of those traveling by the stars we are pushed by passing events that consume our energies. Whatever happened to the wise men that we should be so pushed from event to event without the steadying balance of the centuries?

II. The wise men did not come to get; they came to observe, to learn, and to give. Falsely we identify wisdom with clever bargaining for self-advantage. Imagine the wise men in a modern setting. Aware of the uniqueness of the new babe and that the parents were poor, they might have made a deal. "Let us be his managers, and we'll give you ten percent." Twentieth-century wise guys! But that's not the way it was. The wise men came to learn and to bring their gifts. They had not come to make a million.

III. Wisdom does not await a majority. It does not have to be on the day's winning side. Wisdom knows that today real winners will not be determined for at least another century. The wise men traveled independently by the light of a star and went back a different way. In contrast we are anxious to get aboard the popularity train. Succumbing too readily to the herd level, we become both the victim and the perpetrators of subpar conduct.

IV. The wise men stayed to worship. Aware that they did not have all the answers, they waited reverently to learn. A wise man knows his need to learn and to grow. He also knows that he has never fully reached his God-given potential including his moral potential. Christians see God as revealed by Jesus Christ and in worshiping him offer themselves to be motivated in his image and to have their priorities reordered in his likeness. It is not enough that we increase our comforts and our goods. More than comfort we need compassion and goals more than goods. To this end the major business of life, whether expressed in a church or in business or in government, is to glorify God. This is the end and aim of life's process.

V. The wise men went back a different way. A different way? That's what worship is about. Isn't it time to recognize that our ways have not been good enough? Do we want more of the same? Surely the world needs a different way. Maybe we can be wise enough to take our clues from a distant star that has held steady through the centuries.— Wesley P. Ford.

## SUNDAY: DECEMBER EIGHTEENTH

### MORNING SERVICE

Topic: The Real Reason for Christmas (Advent)

SCRIPTURE: John 1:1–14 (NEB).

I. The real reason for Christmas, the basic justification for its celebration by Christians, is pointed to in a verse of the opening poem of John's Gospel, "The Word became flesh; he came to dwell among us."

(a) In this context "Word" designates the active reality of God, and the verse declares the great central idea of the New Testament, that God himself came into human life and history in a unique and decisive way in the person of Jesus. And in the final analysis that is what Christmas is all about.

(b) This idea which declares that Jesus was both human and divine is what later Christian thinkers came to call the doctrine of the incarnation. This is a puzzling doctrine, an awkward doctrine, a doctrine that can keep some who are drawn toward Christian faith from committing themselves to it.

(1) The word "incarnation" means literally "infleshment." Christian thinkers through the centuries have never been able to come up with a satisfactory explanation of it. And that provides pretty cold comfort for those who are puzzled by it. Why then should we bother about the doctrine? Is it really necessary? Is it useful in our religion?

(2) Christian doctrines have grown out of the faith-experience of Christians, not out of the speculations of deep thinkers who had nothing better to do. Doctrines are simply guides and guards of faith, and if they are doing their job, stimulants of it. The doctrine of the incarnation is the church's continuing meditation on its experience of God's expression of himself in and through Jesus Christ.

II. Despite the rigorous thinking of theologians the incarnation remains a mystery. There is no standard explanation of it which can claim to be orthodox. Mysteries make us uncomfortable. We demand—in the last chapter or in a scene just before the final commercial —definite answers. When we cannot have such answers we suspect that whole thing is really not worth bothering about. Because of that we are in danger of missing the point when we come to the mystery that is the incarnation.

(a) The incarnation is not the kind of mystery which simply awaits the arrival of a theological Sherlock Holmes or a philosophical Perry Mason to sort it out with a few bold strokes of logic and astonishing flashes of intuition. The incarnation is and will remain a mystery because we do not have the intellectual equipment to probe the depth of wonder in God's coming for our redemption in the person of Jesus. As Arnold Toynbee put it, Christ is "as accessible to the human heart as he is incomprehensible to the human understanding."

(b) When you are confronted by the mystery which is the incarnation there are two things you can do. You can say, "This is a mystery for which there seems no satisfactory intellectual solution; therefore it is probably utter nonsense and should be ignored." Or you can try to go back from the mystery, back from the inadequacies of the doctrine, back to the experience which precedes the doctrine.

III. The doctrine of the incarnation is not a puzzle to be solved. It is rather a continuing meditation on our experience of God in Jesus Christ.

(a) The whole New Testament witnesses to the experience of the earliest Christians that "the Word became flesh; he came to dwell among us." It was left for later generations to attempt the explanations and to develop the doctrine. And despite all the ambiguities in its thinking on the incarnation, the church has persisted in its proclamation that Jesus Christ is both human and divine and that in him God did come in a uniquely redeeming way into history.

(b) Through the centuries Christians have not found justification for their belief in the incarnation in intellectual speculation. They have found it in the practices of faith—in prayer and in worship; as they have read the Bible and particularly when they have let their minds become saturated with the gospel story; as they have come to the Lord's Table. One of the fundamental meanings of the sacrament of the Lord's Supper is that in it we express, in symbol and symbolic action, the experience we have of God in Christ which words cannot adequately express.

(c) More than a century ago Frederick W. Robertson found himself greatly disturbed by the doctrine of the incarnation. The sheer mystery of it made him uncomfortable. The loose ends of its theology distressed him. The inadequacies of all doctrinal statements of it challenged his faith. Then he found his way, and he wrote out this resolution for himself: "To try to fix attention on Christ rather than on the doctrine of Christ." That would seem to establish the right priority on the incarnation.—J. A. Davidson.

## Illustrations

SOLUTION. In my own view the doctrine of the incarnation of God in the man Christ Jesus is the one possible solution for the tragedy of a world that has lost itself.—A. A. Bowman.

CHRISTMAS PERSPECTIVE. A prophetic day looking not so much backward as forward. It belongs to an order of life not yet attained, to a religion not yet realized, to a coming but distant time which all prophets have foreseen when all men will be ruled by "the angels of our higher nature," and justice will reign, and pity and joy will walk the common ways of life.—Joseph Fort Newton.

## Sermon Suggestions

THE TWO GOSPELS OF CHRISTMAS. Text: John 1:10–12. (1) The Bethlehem gospel about Joseph and Mary, the shepherds and the wise men, and the baby—a gospel of a few days and soon forgotten (2) The gospel of the love of God coming in his Son and of the length to which that love is capable of going—a gospel that never can be forgotten.— Charles H. Buck, Jr.

GOOD TIDINGS OF GREAT JOY. Text Luke 2:10. (1) The joy of creation. (2 The joy of redemption. (3) The joy o fulfillment.

**Worship Aids**

CALL TO WORSHIP. "Lo, the star, which they saw in the east, went before them, till it came and stood over where the young child was. When they saw the star, they rejoiced with exceeding great joy." Matt. 2:9–10.

INVOCATION. O God of the infant Jesus, God of the man Christ Jesus, God of his cross and resurrection, how can we thank thee enough for coming into our human life as a baby born in Bethlehem long ago, to grow into manhood and to bring us salvation into life eternal? May we lift our celebration of this glorious event out of all that is unworthy, that Christ himself may be born in our hearts anew and in the hearts of thy children everywhere.—David A. MacLennan.

OFFERTORY SENTENCE. "And they came, every one whose heart stirred him up, and every one whom his spirit made willing, and they brought the Lord's offering to the work of the tabernacle of the congregation, and for all his service." Exod. 35:21.

OFFERTORY PRAYER. Our Lord Jesus Christ, whose birthday has become a season of benevolence and giving, bless these our gifts which we offer in thankfulness for thyself, God's unspeakably precious gift.

PRAYER. We thank you for Jesus, your Son, the babe whom you sent to live among men as a messenger of your good news.

We thank you that he grew to be a man, preaching and demonstrating your love and concern for men, teaching your will, and healing the sick. We thank you that from your Son's life there has grown a ministry that has taken the teachings, the acts, and the spirit of the babe who became the Christ out to some in all nations and the races on earth.

But we know, our Father, that the purpose for which you sent Jesus to minister to men is far from being accomplished. While many men and women through long generations have worshiped you and have to some degree followed in Jesus' footsteps—and these have brought the good life and health of your creation to millions—there are still more who have not heard and yet greater numbers who have not heeded the message.

This day we ask that your spirit—the spirit that was in Jesus—may again be born in each one of us, and that we may communicate "to the uttermost parts" of earth as your messengers of peace, goodwill, proclaiming your continued love and concern for all.—W. W. Reid.

## EVENING WORSHIP

**Topic: Take the Young Child**

TEXT: Matt. 2:13.

I. "Taking the young child" meant *safety*. (a) Taking Christ into our lives is the safest thing any of us can do. Many people have become shipwrecked because they dared to face the storms of life without Christ.

(b) With Christ we are able to face any situation, whatever it may be. He provides sufficient grace for any crisis. He is able to lead us safely through the difficult times in life which every individual faces sooner or later. Christ is our safety when we are attacked on every side by Satan himself. He is our rock of ages and our fortress in the time of storm.

II. "Taking the young child" meant *preparing for the future*. (a) On this occasion God was concerned about the future of his Son, and he gave instructions accordingly. God is also concerned about the future of mankind and has made provision for our future abode in heaven.

(b) To prepare for that future, people must take Christ as their personal Savior and Lord. Many people today are busily engaged and seemingly are more concerned about their present status than they are their future status. While we cannot ignore today and its obligations, neither can we ignore our preparation for the future. Too many people act as though they are going to live on this earth forever, but this is not the case.

(c) Eternity awaits all of us, and how very wise is that person who prepares for the future by taking Christ into his life and into his life's plans. Some individuals are afraid of what lies ahead; the fear of the future torments many people. When we have Christ in our lives and when we live for him, the future is bright. We need not fear what it holds for us.

III. "Taking the young child" meant *fulfilling an obligation.* (a) The care of Christ as a child was entrusted to Joseph and Mary. They had a parental obligation to him, and it was their duty to obey the instructions of the angel.

(b) Is it not true that when we take Christ into our lives we too assume obligation? It is our obligation to be Christlike in our actions, conversation, and attitudes. We must strive to be like him.

(c) We also have an obligation to share him with others. To be acquainted with Christ—to have him within our hearts—and then not to want others to know him as we know him is selfish, to say the least. People all around us—in our neighborhoods, on the job, on the street, or elsewhere—are hungry to hear the message we have to tell. And we have an obligation to tell the message of salvation to those who are lost.—O. W. Polen in *Church of God Evangel.*

## SUNDAY: DECEMBER TWENTY-FIFTH

### MORNING SERVICE

**Topic: Are You Going Home for Christmas?** (Advent)

TEXT: Luke 2:3.

It is a simple, sentimental question, no doubt meant to suggest that people seem to belong home for the holidays, but I want to borrow it for our meditation and take a larger look at what we are and what we are doing this Christmas. Are you going home?

I. This is one place where you are irreplaceable. There is only one of you there. The only place where no one else can take your place is in your home. There are a multitude of other areas where you are important, even some where you could be essential, but only in your own home are you absolutely irreplaceable.

(a) In our modern whirl, in all the world of misplaced values and conflict, as we do our part as the script requires, there isn't much room to be an individual any longer. The world squeezes us into its own mold, and makes us what we never wanted to become. But it's different in your own home. Here you are irreplaceable.

(b) We know what it is to be together as a family and nothing else matters to us now. This applies to all of us. So you are home from college, or you are in high school, or in junior high, or you work, or you don't. There is one irreplaceable part for you to play this Christmas. You are the only father to your children; you are the only husband to your wife; you are the only wife to your husband; you are the only children your parents will ever have, whatever your age. The only irreplaceable part we play is in the personal relationships of our lives—the only neighbor, the only son, the only daughter.

II. There is a second way I want to use the word "home." (a) It is more difficult, perhaps impossible, to define exactly, but we might describe it as something of the nature of the simplicity of Eden before we were driven out to fend for ourselves. What do you call it? It may be the easy simplicity of youth, the enthusiasm for whatever it was that kept your buoyant hopes alive and well. It may be that expectation of the spirit, the honest longing to be involved in something meaningful and worthwhile. It may be the idealism we admire, then compromise, then lose.

(b) Home is the place where you used to dream, to use the great, wide world as your own great stage where you could walk the part of any goal you chose. It was the time when things were simple—before the world got complicated and we got complicated with it.

(c) When did you lose it? Once it was a lovely garden, serene and quiet. Once it was peace. Now look at it: the flowers all trampled down, overgrown with weeds, and all the songbirds flown away. Once it was peace; now it is the great turmoil and hurt and death and argument and disappointments and loneliness and sadness and hate.

(d) And the theme returns again: Are you going home for Christmas or will you stay over there where you are, wedded to the compromises we all have to make? There is the compromise between the possible and the actual—between what we want to do and what we have to do. There is the compromise between the extraordinary dreams and the ordinary routine of our everyday worlds. There is the compromise between what we are and what we long to be.

(e) "Blessed are the homesick," wrote Thielicke, "for they shall come home." Come home to stay where you can kick off your shoes and sit down and be yourself again, where you don't have to pretend, where that discrepancy between what you long to be and what you actually are doesn't matter, and where you can be honest with yourself and honest with your God.

III. There is a last sense in which we will use the word "home." It is the sense that God is at home in the world.

(a) We will be careful not to say too much, but there is a sense in which we can say, as the Christian gospel has always believed, that God came home at Christmas. Through Christ, God makes us at one with the universe itself and with all of life that is in it.

(b) It's all right now—the one who runs the whole place chose to come. He chose to come—he invited himself into the whole human predicament, right smack down in the middle of it all, where pressures mount and tempers rise, where people hate and disappoint and are hopelessly muddled and lose the meaning of it all and spin forever around on the merry-go-rounds of human existence. God came there. He came to experience it all.

(c) The Christmas carol says it plainly: "Love came down at Christmas." Love itself came down—the embodiment of all that love can be; the example and the experience are one. The experiment is over; in Christ, God came home at Christmas.

(d) Through Christ, God understands what it is that you and I are up against. He knows what it is like to live, to be caught up in mixed motives and emotional tangles. He knows what you mean when your soul wonders why it is this way, why it isn't all it's cracked up to be. He knows when you are caught in the thought of what you did or are going to do, of what happened or will happen. He knows the great, awful discrepancy between where you wanted to go and where you are. He knows the disappointments that love must endure.
—Richard M. Cromie.

## Illustrations

BORN THROUGH LOVE. Even if Christ were to be born a thousand times in a thousand stables, laid in a thousand mangers and in a thousand Bethlehems, unless he is born in our own hearts through our responsive love, we do not have the faith of the incarnation, we do not know what Christianity is.—Joseph Fletcher.

QUESTION. A schoolteacher in England supervised the construction of a manger scene in the corner of her classroom. Her children were thrilled to set up the model barn and cover its floor with real straw and then arrange the clay figures of Mary and Joseph and the shepherds and the wise men and the animals, all facing a little crib in which lay a tiny doll representing the baby Jesus. One little fellow could not tear himself away from the corner of the classroom. He kept looking at the manger scene with a puzzled expression on his face. Finally the teacher noticed him and asked: "Is anything bothering you? Do you have a question to ask? Is there anything you'd like to know?" His eyes still glued to the manger scene, the boy said slowly, "What I'd like to know is—where does God fit in?"

## Sermon Suggestion

THE GOOD NEWS OF CHRISTMAS. Scripture: Luke 2:1–20. (1) A message of authority. (See Heb. 1:1–2.) (2) A message of great joy. (See Matt. 1:23; I Tim. 2:5.) (3) A message to all people. (See Mark 16:15; John 3:16.) (4) A message of salvation. (See Matt. 1:21; John 3:17.) (5) A message of peace. (See Isa. 9:6; John 14:27.)—Paul R. Bauman.

## Worship Aids

CALL TO WORSHIP. "Behold, I bring you good tidings of great joy, which shall be to all people. For unto you is born this day in the city of David a Savior, which is Christ the Lord. Glory to God in the highest, and on earth peace, good will toward men." Luke 2:10–11, 14.

INVOCATION. Our loving, giving Father, who planned for us the amazing miracle of thy Son who came to earth to show us what thy love is like, send thy light into our hearts this Christmas. Burn away any selfishness and prejudice, any unkind or unloving thought. Make us clean and new. Turn our eyes toward tasks thou hast for us, even as Jesus grew into young manhood and turned to tasks thou didst have for him. As we prepare our hearts and minds for Christmas, may the Christmas spirit, the spirit of Christ be with us every moment of our lives. And, our Father, may "peace on earth, good will toward men" come into living reality through us.— Chester E. Hodgson.

OFFERTORY SENTENCE. "When they were come into the house, they saw the young child with Mary his mother, and fell down, and worshiped him. And they presented unto him gifts: gold, and frankincense, and myrrh." Matt. 2:11.

OFFERTORY PRAYER. O God, who didst give to us the gift of thy Son, stir us with such love toward thee that we may gladly share whatever thou hast entrusted to us for the relief of the world's sorrow and the coming of thy kingdom.

PRAYER. O Father of infinite love, whom even the heavens could not contain, our hearts beat fast with joy as we behold thee burst forth into the world in the birth of thy Son at Bethlehem. Reveal thyself to us in all thy glorious majesty and holiness as we kneel in wonder beside the manger.

In the setting of a sinful and needy world, O God, may we envision new vistas of heavenly grace and divine righteousness. Deliver us from the fell clutch of materialism which threatens to engulf us. In our grim struggles for meaning and survival, may we not drift to the gods of this earth who perish but place our trust in thee who art everlasting.

Kneeling here in adoration, may we rise to nobler heights of Christian living in love, goodness, and power. Through the incarnated Christ, challenge us, we beseech thee, to follow his unselfish example of service in the home, at work, and at play. May the Christ be born anew in us, O Lord, not only to save our own lives from destruction but also that others might be saved through us.—A. F. McClung.

## EVENING SERVICE

### Topic: One Gift That Is Often Unclaimed

TEXT: John 3:16.

I. The first Christmas gift was not the gold, frankincense, and myrrh of the Magi. Their gifts were accepted, and their counterparts today are readily claimed. Rather the first Christmas gift, the one most often unclaimed, was the gift which God offered to mankind.

(a) The biblical writer foresaw the fact that the gift might not always be accepted, and he wrote, "He came . . . but his own people did not receive him. Some, however, did receive him and believed in him; so he gave them the right to become God's children" (John 1:11).

(b) Because they accepted and received the gift many changes have taken place in the lives of people. These changes are not in the realm of fantasy. Many of the memorable events of history and in the lives of creative individuals cannot be explained other than by their acceptance of the gift of the Christ.

II. There are those gifts which make us more selfish. Some gifts are not fully unwrapped before the new owner exclaims, "That's mine and you can't play with it." But the gift has the strange, mystic effect of generating the spirit of sharing and generosity, of kindness and concern within the one who has accepted him. Thus it becomes a tragedy when the gift of God at Christmas time goes unclaimed.

III. Evidence that the gift remains unclaimed exists in universal, national, community, and family circles. For those who fail to claim the gift, the Christ, simply do not possess within themselves the power to overcome the concern of self which is dominant in each of us. Full acceptance of the Christmas gift of God provides the means by which we can with God's help be more than conquerors over the trials and conflicts which can destroy life within ourselves and others.—E. Paul Hovey.

# SECTION XI. A Little Treasury of Illustrations

TRIVIAL TRIUMPH.    An instrument developed by an engineer in the Bell Laboratories was a box containing a mechanism which, when turned on, caused the lid to open. A hand came out, reached down, turned the switch off, and then settled back into the box. Its only function was to turn itself off. Granted, there are probably some folks whom you would like to see operate as that gismo does, but its triumph was pretty trivial compared to what it might have done with the same mechanical power.—Hoover Rupert.

STORY OF COURAGE.    Harper Lee in her novel, *To Kill a Mockingbird,* describes a sick woman named Mrs. Dubose. She had taken morphine as a pain killer. As the last months of her life drew nigh, she had become a morphine addict. She could have taken the drug to the end, being relatively free from pain. But she set her mind to breaking the addiction before she died. So she endured the terrible agony of not having the drug, and by the time of her death she had freed herself from addiction. And the father sent his son to read to Mrs. Dubose to help her pass the hours away. Why? The father explains: "I wanted you to see something about her—I wanted you to see what real courage is, instead of getting the idea that courage is a man with a gun in his hand. It's when you know you're licked before you begin but you begin anyway and you see it through no matter what. You rarely win, but sometimes you do. Mrs. Dubose won, all ninety-eight pounds of her. According to her views, she died beholden to nothing and nobody. She was the bravest person I ever knew."—Robert C. Brubaker.

TAKE ME BACK.    An eight-year-old girl did something which not only left her feeling guilty but alienated and separated her from her mother. In spite of her mother's words of assurance, the child became increasingly hostile and angry. She found a new dress that her mother planned to wear to a party that evening and with a pair of scissors mutilated it in a mad attempt to hurt her mother. When she discovered what the child had done, the mother fell on the bed and began to cry. After a little while the eight year old stood beside the bed and whispered, "Mother." There was no reply. She said it again. "Mother, Mother." And then still louder, "Mother, please!" And the mother answered, "Please, what?" And the child cried, "Please take me back, take me back."—Robert E. Goodrich, Jr.

RENOUNCING THE DEVIL.    Bishop Dana Dawson was called to one of the churches to receive a group of young people into the church. He asked the old question, "Will you renounce the devil and all his works?" The young lad in front of Dawson just looked at him. Dawson leaned over and whispered, "Say I will, if you will," The lad in a loud voice exclaimed, "I will if you will!"

CENTRAL COMMITMENT. The one who follows Christ belongs to two "cities." He is in the world but must not be of the world. He is a stranger, a pilgrim. He is also a citizen of a different kingdom. He has another master; his allegiance is to a new order from which he derives his ways of thinking, feeling, and judging. His heart and thought and ties are elsewhere. He therefore cannot give ultimate allegiance to the world and its way of operating. His first duty is to be faithful to the Lord. The central life commitment for a Christian must be to the lordship of Jesus Christ.— Mark Hatfield.

FACE IN THE DARK. A little boy, told to take some milk bottles out onto the steps one night, protested because of the darkness. "I'm scared to go way out there by myself," he whined. "Now it's time you stopped being frightened by the dark," his mother answered. "Just remember that God is out there with you." To which the tearful son objected, "Yes, Mother, that's all right, but I want somebody with me who's got a face."—Marion C. Allen.

FELLOW CHRISTIANS. Early in 1945 as the United States forces pushed deep into Okinawa, they came across a village unlike any they had ever seen. Here at Shimabuku they were met and welcomed by two old men who invited the troops in as "fellow Christians." Correspondent Clarence W. Hall described the scene: "We'd seen other Okinawan villages, uniformly down at the heels and despairing; by contrast this one shone like a diamond in a dung heap. Everywhere we were greeted by smiles and dignified bows. Proudly the old men showed us their spotless homes, their terraced fields, fertile and neat, their storehouses and granaries, their prized sugar mill."

Searching for an answer as to why this one village was so different from all the rest, Hall uncovered an incredible story. Some 30 years before, an American missionary on his way to Japan had paused at Shimabuku and stayed only long enough to make two converts and leave them a Japanese Bible. These new converts, with only instructions to read the Bible and live by it, began sharing their faith with neighbors. Before long the whole town had accepted Christ and for 30 years had been following the Bible completely.

The correspondent was so moved by this experience that he later requisitioned a jeep and investigated the town more fully. He attended the primitive but deeply spiritual service and came away even more impressed. After the shattering war Hall wondered what had happened to the tiny hamlet. Fifteen years later he went back there to find that while "civilization" had swallowed Okinawa, the spiritual influence of Shimabuku remained. In *Reader's Digest* he wrote, "Physically surrounded, it remains spiritually remote from the honky-tonks. Its life is still centered on the Bible. Most important in keeping it so is the lovely church the villagers have built with their own hands. It includes a separate Sunday school building and a social hall for young people and has a lively seven-day-a-week program that makes Christianity the core of Shimabuku's society."—Charles R. Hembree.

HIDE 'N SEEK. Dick Van Dyke tells about a mother who was trying to tell her three-year-old daughter about God's presence. "God is everywhere," she told her. "You can't see him, but he can see you." The little girl grinned and then said, "Let's guess where he's hiding."

RATIONALE. A man was ill and had to have surgery, so he asked for the best surgeon in town and the highest priced. The surgery was successful, and the doctor submitted his bill for $3,000. "But," said the man, "that is too much. I can't pay that." The doctor reduced it to $2,000, and the man still complained it was too high. Finally the doctor suggested $500, and the man said he didn't have that much money. Exasperated, the surgeon asked: "Listen, you know of my reputation and the high fees I receive. Why did you insist that I be the surgeon if you didn't have the money to pay?" The man replied, "Well, when it comes to my health, money is no object."—C. A. McClain, Jr.

HOW TO BE A SAINT.    When Anatole France was a little boy, he often wished to be very good. He read a big book about men who were called "saints"— holy men. He thought about the different things they did, and he decided he would copy them and become a saint like them. One saint had given away all the things that he had to the poor people, so Anatole one morning opened his nursery window and started throwing out his toys on to the street below. Sometimes he just missed startled people who wondered where the toys were coming from. Anatole's mother shut the window when she found out what was happening!

The story of Simeon the Stylite interested the little boy because this strange saint in the fifth century lived for 30 years on top of a pillar about 60 feet high. Anatole thought he would try this. He couldn't find a pillar, but he climbed onto a chair which he had put on top of the kitchen table. He was going to spend the rest of his life there, praying! The cook and the rest of the family didn't think this was such a good idea, and the poor little boy had to give up his plans. He wrote later: "I soon understood that it is a very difficult thing to be a saint while living with your own family! I saw why Simeon the Stylite and the other holy men had gone to live far away on their own."

Anatole's adventures make us smile, but he was trying to be good. Do we want to begin at home in showing others that we love Jesus and follow him? Remember that the light that shines farthest always shines brightest at home. —Ronald Armstrong.

WHAT JESUS MEANS TO ME.    Christ Jesus has prompted me in times of perplexity, helped me in hazards, guided me in glooms, directed me when doubts came, strengthened me and given me victory under the assaults of temptation, comforted me in times of sore bereavements, and gladly saved me from my sins.

To me he has been heaven's bread in times of spiritual hunger, heaven's water in times of spiritual thirst, heaven's light in times of spiritual darkness, heaven's comfort in times of bitter sorrow, heaven's shelter in times of mental and spiritual storms, heaven's justification for human condemnation, and heaven's salvation for human damnation.

Today Jesus, the outstanding miracle of all ages, is the solvent for all problems of any sort. Jesus is literature's loftiest ideal, philosophy's highest personality, criticism's supremest problem, theology's fundamental doctrine, and spiritual religion's cardinal necessity.— Robert G. Lee.

PREACHER SMITH.    Near that far-famed town known as Deadwood, in the Black Hills of South Dakota, are several monuments to famous and infamous people. Climb up the mountain south of Deadwood and you may visit the grave of Deadwood Dick. Nearby rest the remains of Calamity Jane, who had a reputation for her ability to drink more whiskey, play better poker, draw faster, shoot straighter, and cuss with more resounding eloquence than most men of her time.

Up another mountain to the north you will find a memorial to Theodore Roosevelt, who went out there a sickly youth and grew to become quite a man. Then toward the northeast, on the old stage to Spearfish, is another monument. It celebrates the memory of a pioneer minister of the gospel known as "Preacher Smith." It represents him striding along with a Bible in his hand and stands at the place where 100 years ago he was ambushed, killed, and scalped by the Indians.

"Preacher Smith" had come with the gold rush to that wild and wicked boom town of Deadwood. He was young, sturdy, clean, compassionate, courageous —every inch a man and a Christian. He had come not to dig for gold and not to get rich by exploiting the weaknesses of other men. He went to that town for Jesus Christ. He helped the down and out, befriended the lonely and forsaken, cared for the sick, comforted the dying, and was an uncompromising voice for sanity and for righteousness. He preached in saloons and dance halls, the only meeting places in the town. When rowdies tried to break up a meeting, he was man enough to win a respectful hearing or to throw them out. Ere long the name of "Preacher Smith" meant something up and down that gulch. He was feared by some, loved by many, and respected by all.

But he did not limit his work to Deadwood. Over the mountain some twenty miles away was a rough, tough cattle town named Spearfish. He made that place his parish too. One Sunday morning, after preaching in a Deadwood gambling hall, he set out for his preaching appointment in Spearfish.

Friends warned him, saying: "Don't go. It's too dangerous. Indians are on the warpath again." But always he had been warned. He had been warned not to become a minister, especially not a Methodist minister. He had been warned not to go to Deadwood and not to attempt preaching in saloons, gambling halls, and dance halls. He had been warned not to thrash a rowdy and throw him out and never to travel unarmed. But he believed he was upon the King's business, and always he went ahead quiet, serene, indomitable.

So he died, even as did his Lord, a young man going ahead for God. And so the monument represents him striding ahead alone, facing toward Spearfish, and bearing his only weapon, a Bible in his hand.—Everett W. Palmer.

EXPLANATION. Two men, talking about the incarnation, walked along a country path on which one spotted an anthill. "There," he said to his friend, "is an illustration for us. How can we get across our ideas to the ants if we so desired?" The friend suggested that it was impossible because ants and men live in different worlds. The first said it would be like the incarnation. "We could do it if we become as an ant." The message of the incarnation is not difficult to understand when we realize this is just what God did. Christ became a man among men.—Arthur House Stainback.

SUCCESS STORY. Paul Tournier tells us that Darwin was a believer and that in the first edition of *The Origin of Species* he spoke frankly of God as the director of this whole evolution. His book however had such great success and was received with such enthusiasm by the German materialists that Darwin became intoxicated with his success and cut out God in the second edition.— Gerald Kennedy.

THE GREATEST GIFT. When Marco Polo was dying at the age of 70, he was asked to confess his lies since he was about to face his God. On his return from the East he had told stories of wonder and of marvelous cities. The people did not believe him, so he was asked to confess his lies. His last answer was, "I never told the half of it." Well, that was what sent those early disciples out into the world. They knew that the greatest gift the world had ever been given was in the person of Jesus Christ. In him God had given himself, no longer just things which he had created but his own person. They experienced this gift. They knew of this grace. And they went out saying they could not tell the half of it.—C. A. McClain, Jr.

GOD'S HANDS. Alexander Irvine tells the story of an Irish peasant woman who had lost her only son. She came to his mother's cottage for help and comfort. In present grief and past unconcern she felt herself beyond God's love and care. Anna Irvine talked quietly to her for a time. Then she led her to seek God's help in prayer. "Kneel down by the bedside, Liza, and ask him to help you," said Anna. "But I wouldn't know what to say." replied Liza. "Auch weel," said Anna, "just repeat after me." So they prayed for comfort. Then Anna concluded with the words, "Now, God, just reach down your hand and lay it on my head." Even to Liza's dull intellect the thought was startling. "Oh, Anna," she said, "I couldn't do that. He wouldn't do that." Anna persisted. Liza bowed her head and prayed, "Oh, God, just reach down your hand and lay it upon my head." As gently as a maple lays its leaf upon the earth on a clear autumn day, so Anna laid her hand upon Liza's head. She kept it there for a moment, then took it away. Liza was on her feet in an instant. "Oh, glory be," she said, "he's done it. He's done it." "Sit down, Liza," said Anna, "and tell me about it." Liza replied: "A queer wonderful feeling went down through me. And the hand felt just like your hand, Anna." "Ay, Liza," said Anna, "it was my hand. God is always looking for hands to do his work, and sometimes he takes the hand of a poor auld creature like me, Liza, to come and help a poor auld creature like you. He wants to help us all, Liza. His arm is not shortened, just as the Bible says."—Henry David Gray.

PRAYERS BEHIND MOODY. Dwight L. Moody once preached in a North London church. The morning service was characterized by nothing unusual. At the close of the evening service however practically the whole congregation went into the inquiry room. The next day Moody went to Dublin, but an urgent message from the pastor of the North London church brought him back. He preached there for ten days, and four hundred persons were added to the membership of that church as a result. That did not happen by chance, nor was it wholly the effect of Moody's preaching. A shut-in member of that

church had read an account of Moody's work in America. She prayed that he might visit her church. When her sister returned from worship the morning Moody preached and told her about the service, she said, "I know what that means: God has heard my prayers." Beyond all question he had. Moody believed that the prayers of this invalid woman and the revival that resulted from them were responsible for his return to England again the next year. —Sidney W. Powell.

FORGIVENESS. In a book entitled *God in My Unbelief* a church member whose name is John Forsyth was spewing poison on the board of his church of which he was a member. He was creating frictions and quarrels, and then one night the board meeting broke up with the people angry. The pastor went outside in despair. He said this about his experience: "I walked up and down the road afterward, trying to think how peace was to be restored among us, praying that John Forsyth might be forgiven for the hurt he was doing. As I turned in my walking, I came within sight of his window, and I stopped, thinking of the man sitting there behind the drawn blinds. Something cried out in me because I had not been able to mend what was broken. In that cry I knew what I had never known before. I had often been praying for him, but I knew in the flash of that moment that even in my prayer I had been separated from him. I had been looking at his sin and judging it and asking that he might be forgiven. I had not been standing beside him—my sinfulness beside his sinfulness—asking that we both might be forgiven. Christ had been seeking me too in this, and I had not discerned him. This was the cross—his seeking and my blindness and disobedience."—Robert C. Brubaker.

A SHOCKING AFFAIR. They mocked and railed on him and smote him; they scourged and crucified him. Well, they were people very remote from ourselves, and no doubt it was all done in the noblest and most beautiful manner. We should not like to think otherwise.

Unhappily, if we think about it at all, we must think otherwise. God was executed by people painfully like us, in a society very similar to our own— in the overripeness of the most splendid and sophisticated empire the world has ever seen. In a nation famous for its religious genius and under a government renowned for its efficiency, he was executed by a corrupt church, a timid politician, and a fickle proletariat led by professional agitators. His executioners made vulgar jokes about him, called him filthy names, taunted him, smacked him in the face, flogged him with the cat, and hanged him on the common gibbet—a bloody, dust, sweaty, and sordid business.

If you show people that, they are shocked. So they should be. If that does not shock them, nothing can. If the mere representation of it has an air of irreverence, what is to be said about the deed? It is curious that people who are filled with horrified indignation whenever a cat kills a sparrow can hear that story of the killing of God, told Sunday after Sunday, and not experience any shock at all.—Dorothy L. Sayers in *A Matter of Eternity*.

TWO AND ONE-HALF.    Dwight L. Moody is said to have once returned from a meeting with a report of "two and one-half conversions." "I suppose you mean two adults and one child," said the man who was his host. "No," said Mr. Moody, "I mean two children and one adult. You see the children can give their whole lives, but the adult only has half of his left to give." How true this is! Suppose that Paul would have been converted at 70 instead of 25. There would have been no Paul in history. There was a Matthew Henry because he was converted at the age of 11 and not at 70. There was a Jonathan Edwards because he was converted at eight and not at 80. And there was a Richard Baxter because he was converted at six instead of 60.

ON TALENT.    A young minister preached a sermon on the subject of Christian stewardship. Starting with the parable of the talents, he urged his people to place at God's disposal the gifts and abilities with which God endowed them.

After the service a man came up to him and said: "Pastor, I'm not a particularly gifted man. I really don't feel capable of teaching in the Sunday school or canvassing for money or doing any of the other things that you talked about this morning. But I do have one talent that might be of some use to the church."

"And what is that?" asked the minister.

"Well," said the man, "I have the talent of criticism. I can criticize your sermons. I can criticize the choir. I can criticize everything about the church. What should I do with my talent?"

The minister remained silent long enough to pray for wisdom; then he replied: "Do you remember what the man of one talent in the parable did? He buried his talent in the earth. I suggest you would be well advised to do the same."—Eugenia Shepard.

MARCHING OFF THE MAP.    Centuries ago when Alexander the Great was on his rampage to subdue the world, the successes of his campaign brought him and his armies deep into Asia Minor. So far were they from Macedonia and so unacquainted were they with the unknown countries into which they were plunging and pillaging that, despite their victories, Alexander found that his men were loathe to go farther and were becoming afraid. His chief staff officer gave him the reason: "Sir, we have come so far that our maps are useless. Our men are bewildered and fearful because we have marched right off the map."—Francis Dunn.

OFF GUARD.    Maldwyn L. Edwards tells of the time he returned to one of his former parishes for a centennial celebration. No sooner had he appeared than he was cornered by a woman who proceeded to bring him up to date on her family. "And of course you know about my dear husband, Albert," she gushed. "Since you left, Reverend, Albert had died and gone to heaven!"

Dr. Edwards says that he vaguely remembered Albert as a Christmas-and-Easter Christian whose personal moral life left much to be desired. Struggling to make conversation, he responded: "Oh! So Albert died and went to heaven? Well, I must say I'm sorry."

Somehow that response did not seem well received, so Dr. Edwards tried again. "What I meant to say was, I'm glad!"

The expression on the widow's face revealed that the amendment had done little to help the original statement, so Dr. Edwards made one last, heroic attempt. "What I really meant to say was, I'm surprised!"—Raymond W. Gibson, Jr.

BECAUSE OF HIM.    Nineteen centuries after his birth we cannot forget that there once lived in this world a man of the name of Jesus. There is the Christian church to remind us. There is the art of Michelangelo and the music of Bach. There is an "apostolic succession" that is truly a magnificent tradition of unselfish devotion and service. There is a civilization influenced to some extent by Christian beliefs and principles. There is our own individual conscience which to a far greater extent than we realize reflects the teaching and example of Jesus. There is the conviction, now widely held, that the things which Jesus Christ stands for—these and these alone—are the things that make for peace.—Ernest Fremont Tittle.

DRAWN BY A STAR.    For many months during World War II a friend of mine was reported missing in action. He was a lieutenant in the Air Force and had not been heard from since his buddies saw his plane being fired on over France and heard him say over his radio that he was going down. Later he told this story. When he regained consciousness, he found himself in the home of some French peasants. A mother and her daughter had pulled him from his burning plane and carried him to their simple dwelling. They dressed his wounds and cared for him for many days and nights, all the time on the careful watch for the enemy who would have imprisoned them for their act of hospitality. They shared with him their simple fare of bread and barley water. For weeks they nursed him back to health. Then came Christmas Eve. Now the lieutenant learned the reason for their self-sacrificing courage, for out of a bit of cardboard these peasants cut the figure of a star and put it in his crippled hand. Doing this they spoke the universal language, giving the universal sign which said in effect: "We have been drawn by the star."—Homer J. R. Elford.

# INDEX OF CONTRIBUTORS

# SERMON TITLE INDEX

*(Children's stories and sermons are identified CS;*
*sermon suggestions SS)*

# SCRIPTURAL INDEX

# INDEX OF PRAYERS

# INDEX OF MATERIALS USEFUL AS CHILDREN'S STORIES AND SERMONS NOT INCLUDED IN SECTION IX

# INDEX OF MATERIALS USEFUL FOR SMALL GROUPS
## NOT INCLUDED IN SECTION V

# INDEX OF SPECIAL DAYS AND SEASONS

# TOPICAL INDEX